Readings in
PHYSICALLY HANDICAPPED EDUCATION

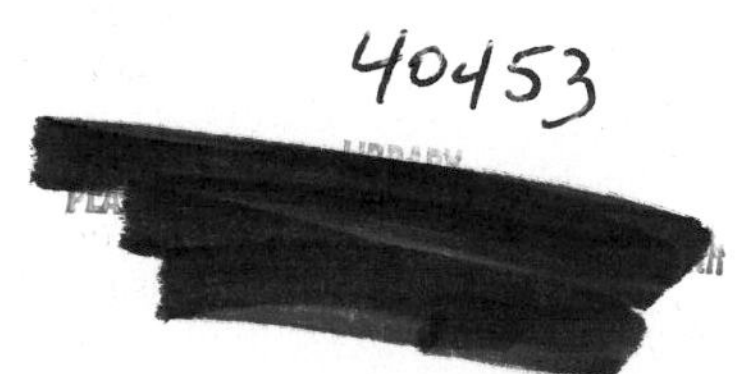

Special Learning Corporation

42 Boston Post Rd. Guilford, Connecticut 06437

SPECIAL LEARNING CORPORATION

Publisher's Message:

The Special Education Series is the first comprehensive series designed for special education courses of study. It is also the first series to offer such a wide variety of high quality books. In addition, the series will be expanded and up-dated each year. No other publications in the area of special education can equal this. We stress high quality content, a superb advisory and consulting group, and special features that help in understanding the course of study. In addition we believe we must also publish in very small enrollment areas in order to establish the credibility and strength of our series. We realize the enrollments in courses of study such as Autism, Visually Handicapped Education, or Diagnosis and Placement are not large. Nevertheless, we believe there is a need for course books in these areas and books that are kept up-to-date on an annual basis! Special Learning Corporation's goal is to publish the highest quality materials for the college and university courses of study. With your comments and support we will continue to do this.

John P. Quirk

ISBN No.   0-89568-012-2

SPECIAL EDUCATION SERIES

- ● Autism
- * ● Behavior Modification
  - Biological Bases of Learning Disabilities
  - Brain Impairments
- ● Career and Vocational Education
  - Child Abuse
  - Child Development
  - Child Psychology
  - Cognitive and Communication Skills
- * ● Counseling Parents of Exceptional Children
  - Creative Arts
  - Curriculum and Materials
- * ● Deaf Education
  - Developmental Disabilities
- * ● Diagnosis and Placement
  - Down's Syndrome
- ● Dyslexia
  - Early Learning
  - Educational Technology
- * ● Emotional and Behavioral Disorders
  - Exceptional Parents
- * ● Gifted and Talented Education
- * ● Human Growth and Development of the Exceptional Individual
  - Hyperactivity
- * ● Individualized Educational Programs
- ● Language & Writing Disorders
- * ● Learning Disabilities
  - Learning Theory
- * ● Mainstreaming
- * ● Mental Retardation
- ● Motor Disorders
  - Multiple Handicapped Education
  - Occupational Therapy
- ● Perception and Memory Disorders
- * ● Physically Handicapped Education
- * ● Pre-School Education for the Handicapped
- * ● Psychology of Exceptional Children
- ● Reading Disorders
  - Reading Skill Development
  - Research and Development
- * ● Severely and Profoundly Handicapped Education
  - Slow Learner Education
  - Social Learning
- * ● Special Education
- * ● Speech and Hearing
  - Testing and Diagnosis
- ● Three Models of Learning Disabilities
- * ● Visually Handicapped Education
- * ● Vocational Training for the Mentally Retarded

●   Published Titles   * Major Course Areas

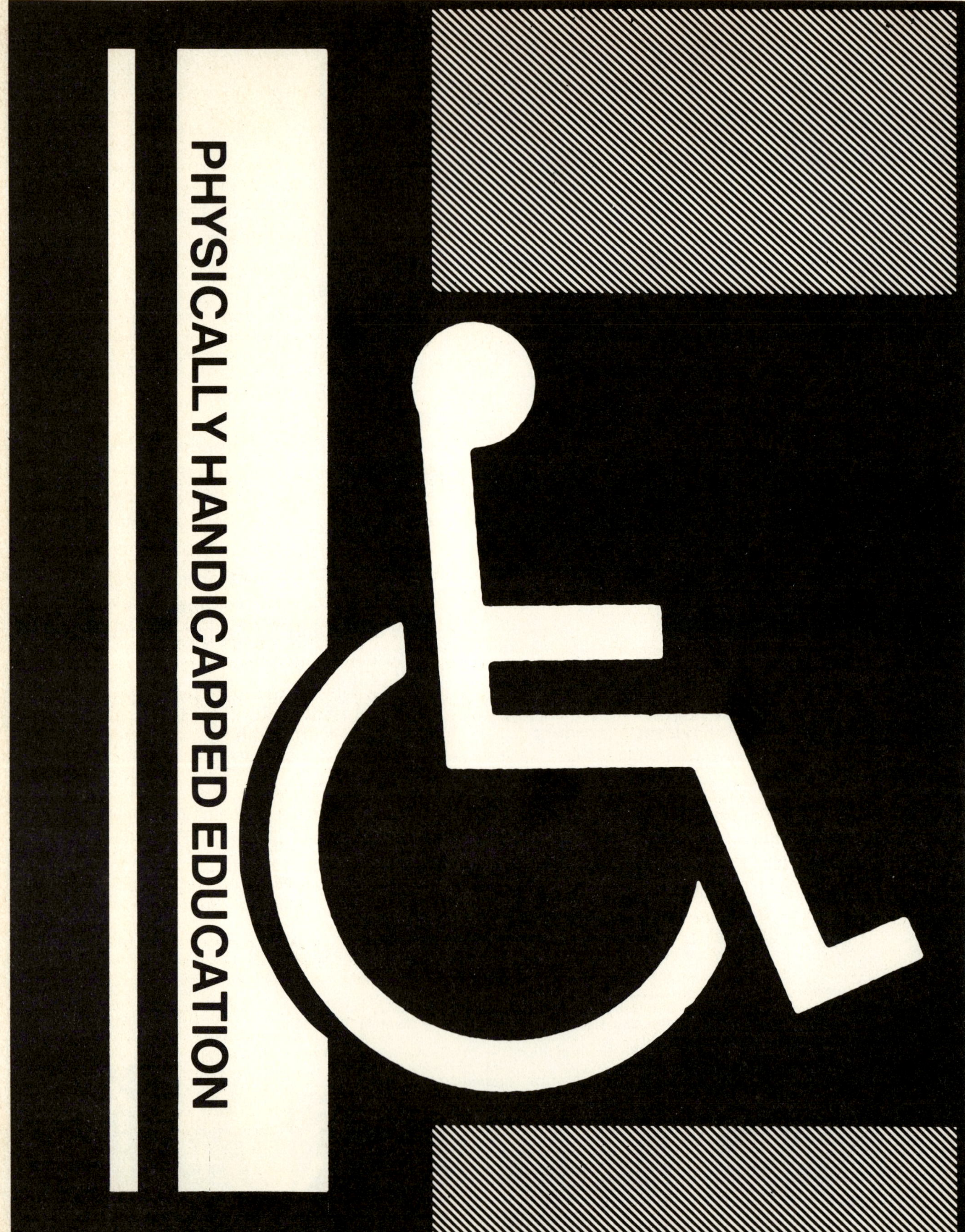
PHYSICALLY HANDICAPPED EDUCATION

CONTENTS

4. Barrier Free Design

GLOSSARY OF TERMS

adductor A muscle used to draw toward or past the median axis of the body, also to bring together similar parts such as the fingers.

angular gyrus A cerebral convolution that forms the back part of the lower parietal region of the brain.

ataxia A form of cerebral palsy marked by incoordination in voluntary muscular movements.

athetosis A form of cerebral palsy maked by slow, recurring, weaving movements of arms and legs, and by facial grimaces.

cerebral palsy Any one of a group of conditions affecting control of the motor system due to lesions in various parts of the brain.

congenital Present in an individual at birth.

cystic fibrosis A hereditary disease due to a generalized dysfunction of the pancreas.

diplegia Bilateral paralysis affecting like parts on both sides of the body.

dysarthria Difficulty in the articulation of words due to involvement of the central nervous system.

dysgraphia Inability to produce motor movements required for handwriting.

hemiplegia Paralysis of one side of the body.

hypertonicity Excessive tension in the condition of a muscle not at work.

kinesthesis The sense whose end organs lie in the muscles, joints and tendons and are stimulated by bodily movements and tensions.

laterality The preferential use of one side of the body, especially in tasks demanding the use of only one hand, one eye, or one foot.

meningitis Inflammation of the meninges (the membrane converting the brain and spinal cord) sometimes affecting vision, hearing, and/or intelligence.

monoplegia Paralysis of one body part.

muscular dystrophy One of the more common primary diseases of muscle. It is characterized by weakness and atrophy of the skeletal muscles with increasing disability and deformity as the disease progresses.

paraplegia Paralysis of the legs and lower part of the body; both motion and sensation being affected.

proprioceptive Pertaining to stimulations from the muscles, tendons, and labyrinth which give information concerning the position and movement of the body and its members.

prosthesis The replacement of an absent part of the body by an artificial one.

response The activity of an organism or an organ, or the inhibition of previous activity resulting from stimulation.

rheumatoid arthritis A systemic disease characterized by inflammation of the joints and a broad spectrum of manifestations often involving destruction of the joints with resultant deformity.

sensorimotor Any act whose nature is primarily dependent upon the combined or integrated functioning of sense organs and motor mechanisms.

spasticity Excessive tension of the muscles and heightened resistance to flexion or extension, as in cerebral palsy.

tonic Characterized by contraction of a muscle sufficient to keep the muscle taut but not sufficient to cause movement.

triplegia Paralysis of three of the body's limbs.

trauma Any experience that inflicts serious damage to the organism. It may refer to psychological as well as to physiological insult.

tuberculosis An infectious disease characterized by formation of tubercules (small, rounded nodules produced by the bacillus of tuberculosis) in the tissue of the lungs.

PREFACE

Some type of handicap is involved in the lives of millions of young people today. In a world of unprecedented medical, technological, and educational advances, it is inconceivable that any group of individuals could be barred from the opportunities important in everyone's life. However, the physically handicapped population, to a large degree, are often forgotten persons. As a result, society is deprived of a vast resource of talents and abilities.

Alloted appropriate educational, occupational, or medical services, the handicapping condition can be overcome or counterbalanced. Earl Schenck Miers, a successful author, husband, and father, and himself physically handicapped emphasized this point when he wrote the following words: "Today if a crippled child possesses normal intelligence, is educated properly, and receives the faith he deserves, it is no longer acceptable for anyone in placing a prop under his body to place a ceiling over his potential achievement."

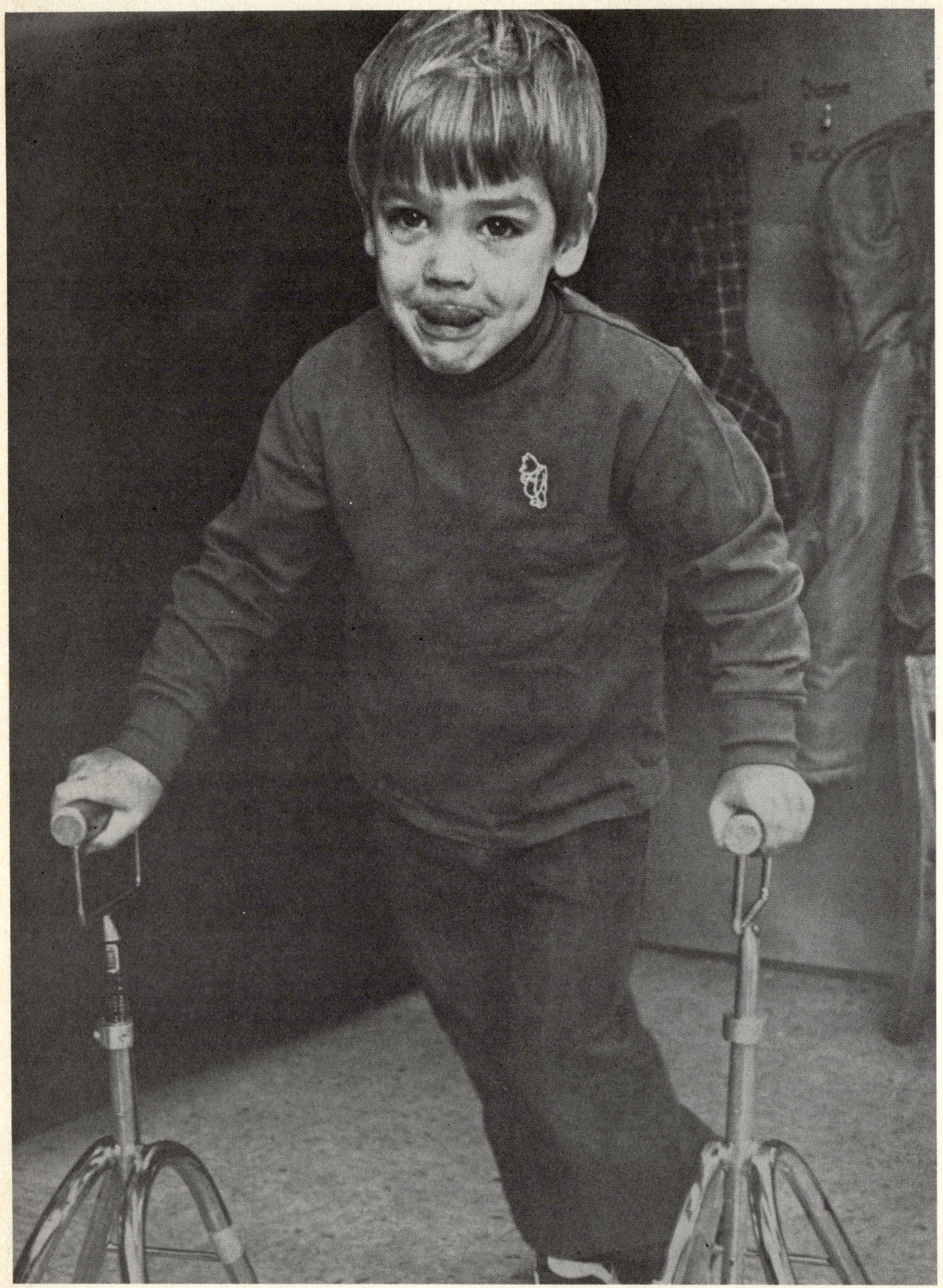

Physical Handicaps: An Overview

Throughout history, the situation of the physically handicapped has been generally unfortunate. That trend is changing now, however, as modern medical and educational advances improve the outlook for this sizeable population. Due to the fact that their handicap is usually obvious to society, centuries ago they were subject to much scorn, contempt, and punishment. Many were even put to death as part of religious rites. Although there are some isolated instances of protection, it was not until the eighteenth century that a more enlightened viewpoint began to develop.

During the nineteenth century the emphasis for serving the physically handicapped was chiefly upon physical care and surgery. The first orthopedic hospital in America was founded in 1854 in Brooklyn, New York by Louis Bauer and Richard Barthelmoss. The first public school class for physically handicapped children was established in 1899 in Chicago, with many other cities soon to follow.

Throughout history, particular individuals stand out as innovators in promoting the advancement of the physically handicapped. One outstanding person in particular, Edgar F. Allen, devoted his life to the well-being of the physically-handicapped, establishing the National Society for Crippled Children and Adults which is now the Easter Seal Society.

The period between 1935, when the Children's Bureau of the Department of Labor allocated appropriations in the existing forty-eight states for physically handicapped children's programs. In 1938, through the efforts of the late President Franklin D. Roosevelt, the National Foundation for Infantile Paralysis was established. Finally, the United Cerebral Palsy Association was established in 1950 to service this sector of the physically handicapped.

Through the efforts of such associations coupled with the medical and educational advances of recent years, the outlook for the physically handicapped has improved drastically. No longer should this population remain isolated from society. New public awareness of the many capabilities of the physically handicapped may now begin to grow. The physically handicapped child of tomorrow will have more doors open to him than was ever dreamed of in past years.

LATEST ON HELPING THE HANDICAPPED
"We Have Come a Long Way"

*INTERVIEW WITH DR. HENRY B. BETTS,
MEDICAL DIRECTOR, REHABILITATION INSTITUTE OF CHICAGO*

Once given up as hopelessly crippled, many victims of illness and injury now can resume a useful life. A leading medical authority came to the magazine's conference room to describe the newest in treatments.

Q Dr. Betts, is the U.S. making much progress in rehabilitating victims of injuries or illness so that they can return to leading active lives?

A Unquestionably yes. We have come a long way in helping people—through therapy, education and new devices—who not very many years ago would have been regarded as incurable or hopelessly crippled. You pass many of these people on the streets every day without even knowing it.

Q How many people in this country today are crippled in one way or another by injury or disease?

A There's no very good estimate, but the total number is enormous. Strokes and heart attacks alone disable millions of people. There are about 120,000 with spinal-cord injury; about 500,000 more with multiple sclerosis.

The important point is that physical handicaps touch literally every family in this country. Everybody is going to be physically handicapped to some extent—unless they undergo sudden death before the handicap occurs.

Q Can you estimate the economic loss from disabilities?

A The thing that's been proven is that when you rehabilitate someone with a physical disability, for every dollar spent the economy gains $10 in return by making a taxpayer out of a potential welfare recipient.

Q What are some of the chief causes of disability?

A Stroke, arthritis, Parkinson's disease, multiple sclerosis, spinal-cord injury, cerebral palsy, amputations, muscular dystrophy and other neuromuscular problems. These are the life-expectancy disabilities we deal with at centers such as the Rehabilitation Institute of Chicago.

Perhaps the major contributor is increasing age. Another is increasing speed and industrialization—and therefore more accidents. And the third is the greater "heroism" on the part of physicians and hospitals in saving lives. For instance, 25 years ago, someone who suffered an amputation, was in an auto accident or had brain damage or spinal-cord injury might die. But now their lives are saved, and when they come out of their comas they have a physical disability.

Q Can anyone with a physical disability benefit from rehabilitation?

A Not all of them, no. In our Chicago Institute we select patients who can benefit. They are referred by physicians and by agencies, and we screen them very carefully.

But, generally speaking, I would say that the great majority of the disabled can benefit from rehabilitation to the extent of achieving a life of some independence—particularly if they get into the system early.

Q How soon should a person start rehabilitation after suffering a disabling injury or illness?

A Right away; the minute the vital signs—pulse, respiration, blood pressure—are normal.

Q Why is that so important?

A Because, first of all, physically it's very important to get going in order to work with whatever residual strength there is. And, secondly, it's extremely important psychologically for the patients to feel that they're not being "dumped."

It used to be that someone who had a stroke or a spinal-cord injury would languish around a hospital until his money ran out, with nothing much being done about him. Then one day someone would say, "Oh, well, maybe we could think about rehabilitation." In that period you could imagine what their feelings are—that he or she is essentially rejected, and will be forever. If you start rehabilitation right away, they'll know that at least people are going to make an *effort* to bring them back into the mainstream.

Q Specifically, how do you go about rehabilitating a disabled person?

A First, we try to understand exactly what kind of persons they are and what their expectations are in life—what their relationship is to their family and their community and their job. We try to understand what the over-all picture of that person is. That's the first thing.

And then you do all kinds of technical things like exercising and training in activities of daily living.

Also we have a bioengineering center in our facility—Northwestern University—and they have invented things there that allow one to run a wheel chair or run almost anything just by sipping and puffing in a little straw. Those are the dramatic things that people like to hear about.

Q How long do you spend rehabilitating someone?

A We make an effort as long as

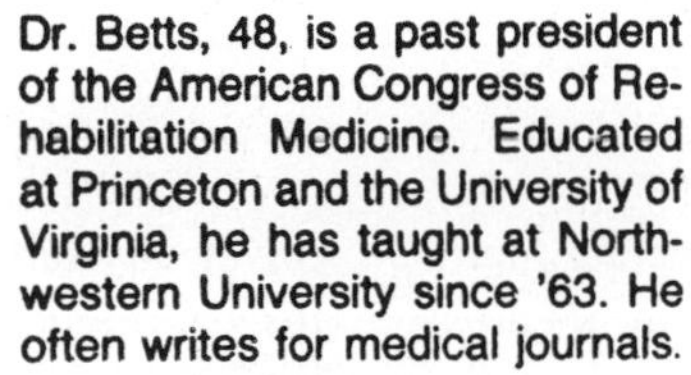

Dr. Betts, 48, is a past president of the American Congress of Rehabilitation Medicine. Educated at Princeton and the University of Virginia, he has taught at Northwestern University since '63. He often writes for medical journals.

"Latest on Helping the Handicapped–We Have Come A Long Way," *U.S. News and World Report*, Vol. LXXXII No. 4, January 31, 1977. ©1977 U.S. News and World Report.

Bioengineering. A severely disabled person can operate this new computer-typewriter by sipping and puffing on a straw.

LATEST ON HELPING THE HANDICAPPED

they're improving, and that's the only rule of thumb. The average length of stay in our Institute is 52 days.

Q What does that cost?

A Two hundred and forty dollars a day. That includes room, board, physicians—everything.

Q Is it usually covered by insurance?

A Yes—by medicare, medicaid, Blue Cross-Blue Shield—most insurance—workers' compensation or vocational rehabilitation.

Q What do you do physically—surgery, prosthetics?

A We have full-time, salaried physicians who are in charge of a team of people. That team involves therapists, rehabilitation nurses, speech pathologists, vocational counselors and others whose job is to help the patients to care for themselves and, hopefully, even to return to their work.

We also can call in plastic surgeons, internists, cardiologists, orthopedic surgeons, general surgeons and so on. And, of course, we use all sorts of prosthetic devices.

Q You mentioned one device by which you can control a wheel chair by blowing on a straw. What other recent inventions have there been in this area?

A The myoelectric arm is one you may have read about. You attach it to the stump of an amputated arm, and whenever you want to move the fingers, you just think about it and they move. When you want to close the fingers, they close by picking up impulses in remaining muscles.

The bioengineers also have developed a typewriter that works with a computer system by this sip-and-puff system through a little straw. It throws letters onto a screen, and the person typing selects out of that.

Q It sounds like a very expensive device. How would a person make use of something like that?

A That is a research device, and I'm sure it will be very expensive at this stage of development. But you've got to remember the return benefits. Let's say an electric wheel chair costs $1,000. This is a lot of money. But that $1,000 wheel chair may make it possible for someone to go to work instead of staying in bed all the time. What is that worth?

Q What sort of emotional or psychological problems do handicapped people face?

A The first problem they face is dependency, and dependency is a terrific psychological burden for anybody, particularly in this society and particularly for men. You think of

what the masculine image is—right or wrong—and for a man to suddenly be left dependent is devastating. It is a very shattering experience. So the first psychological problem they face is that they are dependent in a society where independence, aggressiveness and productivity are put at a premium.

The other thing is what may be least discussed, and that is the matter of sex. The patient may be thinking more about that than any other one thing and talking about it the least. People who have strokes, rheumatoid arthritis, spinal-cord injury and so on are terrified that they are not going to be able to perform sexually.

Q Can they perform?

A Often they can, but they think they aren't going to be able to. And don't think age has anything to do with it. Men of 80 who have strokes and may become impotent—they don't like that at all.

The other thing is economic. They're terrified that they're not going to be able to meet the economic needs of themselves and their families.

Q What is the patient's usual reaction to these worries?

A They get extremely depressed. I consider that normal. Frankly, if I have a patient who doesn't get depressed about being suddenly paralyzed, I think that maybe they're schizophrenic.

The next stage they are likely to go through is hostility and be angry at God or whomever. You know: "Why me? Why did this happen to me? I was a good guy, and I was nice to my family and so on, and why did this happen to me?" And: "Damn God and everybody else who has anything to do with it." A little guilt is thrown in there, too.

Then this hostility overflows to us, to the physicians and nurses, because we don't cure them. They say: "Well, here I've come to this place. It's costing $240 a day. They told me it was a wonderful place, but I'm not getting well. I mean, I'm still paralyzed. Who do these people think they are?" Most patients go through this anger phase, and then it begins to even out.

Q How do families of disabled people react?

A That's the whole "ball game," in a way. The relationship between the patient and the family, or the community, is the final solution. If someone who is terribly paralyzed can go back to a receptive and loving society—be that a family or society as a whole—the paralysis doesn't seem quite so bad.

Q Is it true that families tend to reject severely injured or severely disabled people?

A Yes. Almost everybody rejects them. That may sound too harsh, because a loving wife is not really going to end up rejecting a loving husband. But the immediate impulse—after having been attuned all your life to rejecting people who don't look like everybody else and then you've got one on your hands—well, of course, you start out with at least some little segment of rejection.

Say that as a wife you have built your life on the fact that your husband is a strong, vigorous man, great in society, recognized as a big man by everyone. Then suddenly you have some dependent soul who is crippled—by anybody's standards. That is very distressing, needless to say.

IF THE FAMILY IS "BURDENED WITH GUILT"—

Q What do you tell these patients' families?

A That's almost unanswerable, because they are all so entirely different. All I can tell you is that we get to know the family extremely well, and we work with them through these things. If they do feel an impulse to reject the patient, you have to indicate to them that it doesn't necessarily mean that they're the greatest sinners of all times.

Of course, they don't want their husband to be handicapped. That's normal. They shouldn't feel badly about that and become so burdened with guilt that they are unable to move.

Q. Basically, you teach the patient and family to live with the disability—

A Right—because we're not going to cure very many of them. They don't come in paralyzed and go out all well very often. You're usually going to send them out still with some kind of a disability. Our goal is to bring them to the maximum and then teach them, their families and the community to adjust to whatever residual remains.

Q. The attitude of the community toward the handicapped is important—

A Yes, extremely so. In a large center like ours, we've tried very hard to have an impact on the community relative to their attitude toward the handicapped—to employ them, let them in the museums, let them in the concert halls, let them get through the streets, into the stores, things like that.

Q. Are you talking about ramps for wheel chairs, wide doors and those kinds of conveniences?

A Among other things. It's just an access into the place. It's having a bathroom stall that's accessible to the wheel chair, the drinking fountain that's low, and a telephone that's low, and a few seats where a wheel chair can go. That's all.

Q. That can involve a lot of expense—

A There's a lot of cost to redoing places to make them accessible, but there's no cost to building anew.

In Chicago, for instance, every curb that's being redone is going to be ramped. They're not going all over town tearing curbs out and ramping them, but whenever they do anything to them, they ramp them.

In new buildings, such as the new segment of the Art Institute of Chicago, they're going to be accessible. Here in Washington, they are building a new addition to the National Gallery of Art, and it's going to be accessible to the handicapped—thanks to Nancy Hanks and Carter Brown. My feeling is: Why not? It doesn't cost any more. It looks nice. You do eliminate majestic stairways, but that's about the only thing.

OUT OF PAIN, "EXTRAORDINARY" GIFTS—

Q. Do handicapped people do better when they mix with the rest of society, or is it better for them to associate with people in a similar condition?

A I think it's very rare that it would be the latter. It seems to me that the best thing for themselves and for society is to live together. There are going to be some people who are so tremendously disabled or retarded that you can't realistically expect that. But for most of the handicapped, the best thing is to be a part of society.

First of all, handicapped people prefer being out in the community with other people. And to tell you the truth, I really think that the community benefits from that. In every single instance where we've gotten a handicapped person employed or back into the mainstream, we have heard from people who have said that this person has added considerably to the lives of the people around them.

The reason is that these people have been through the fire. We, who are not handicapped, try to ignore the fact that pain and suffering exist. Well, let me tell you that these people have gone through an extremely hard time. As a result, they are very likely to be extraordinary in what they can contribute to the people around them.

Q. Do you find much job discrimination against handicapped people?

A I can think of no case in our Institute where former patients have had to take legal action after being turned down for a job. I am sure that there are people who have been rejected for work, but you have to remember that we try very hard not to put them into a job where they are not going to be useful, and we make a lot of contacts before they even get there.

Q. What about the expense that may be involved for an employer asked to hire a handicapped person?

A I have had no reluctance on the part of employers at the level of presidents and chairmen of boards to employ handicapped people. However, I've had reluctance on the part of personnel directors who didn't want to go out on a limb.

Keep in mind that we have tried to line up the right person with the right job. We don't try to find an executive position for someone with severe brain damage, or recommend a blind person to be a librarian.

Q. Some of the "hire the handicapped" programs claim that these people are actually more dependable than others in certain jobs—

A In a given job, they *are* more dependable when you find the right person for the right job—because of their motivation and because of the kind of thing that they've had to go through. I seem to oversimplify it and make it sound easy, and I don't really mean that because there's a whole. broad spectrum of problems involved.

MILITANCY "MEANS THERAPY WORKED"—

Q. Are disabled or handicapped people more militant today about jobs, transportation, housing and so on?

A Yes. They have become much more militant in the last five years. They are now much more outspoken and much more critical of the entire "system"—critical of society and critical of all of us who have done this rehabilitative work.

Personally, I think it's a rather healthy attitude. The fact that they are now speaking out more means to me that the therapy has worked. After all, we've tried all these years to make them independent and part of the mainstream of life— and part of the mainstream of life nowadays is that you speak up and be heard from.

Some of my colleagues don't like it because some of the things the handicapped say about us are not totally heart-warming. But personally I think that's very useful.

Q. Even after rehabilitation, don't the handicapped still face a certain public prejudice?

A Absolutely. Historically, we relate an obvious physical disability with evil. In fairy stories, for instance, the guy with a hook for a hand is always a bad guy; the hunchback is a bad guy; the person with one eye is a bad guy. We learn this from early childhood.

Then all you need to do is read the ads, and everybody is bouncy and young and beautiful. Even our Presidents try to be young and beautiful. It makes it very hard on people who don't fit that mold.

The reality is that some of the greatest contributors to society can be people who don't fit that mold—including our ancestors, many of whom came to this country because they were essentially misfits somewhere else.

So at this point, if you don't fit the mold you've very often got a rough deal in this country. You can look at the physically handicapped and see that they don't conform because they don't look like everybody else. And that should not be the way to judge them.

I wouldn't ever go around and say, "All of you must hire all the handicapped." I don't know what jobs you have open, and I don't know what every handicapped person can do.

All I can say is that they should be judged on an individual basis without a preconceived idea—just the way everybody else should be judged. And in that, they have not gotten a fair shake.

Modifying Attitudes toward Physically Disabled Persons

JOY DONALDSON
MELTON C. MARTINSON

Abstract: An attempt was made to modify attitudes toward disabled persons via a panel presentation by individuals with visible physical disabilities. Differential effects of live, video, and audio presentations were assessed, as were sex treatment variables. Results suggested that both the live and video presentations had significant effects on attitudes as measured by the ATDP. No significant differences were found between the responses of male and female subjects. Implications for practical use and for further research are discussed.

EXTENSIVE research has been conducted in the past decade on the existence of negative attitudes toward the physically disabled child and adult in numerous population groups, and the delineation of variables associated with such attitudes. However, there has been little research in the area of modifying or changing attitudes toward disabled persons.

A review of the literature yielded a limited number of experimental studies (Granofsky, 1956; Rusalem, 1967; Rapier, Adelson, Carey, & Croke, 1972; Wallston, Blanton, Robinson, & Pollchink, 1972; Lazar, Gensley, & Orpet, 1971; Wilson & Alcorn, 1969; Clore & Jeffrey, 1972) that focused on the modification of attitudes toward physically disabled children or adults. Only four (Rusalem, 1967; Rapier et al., 1972; Lazar et al., 1971; Clore & Jeffrey, 1972) have shown significant modifications of attitudes toward disabled persons in a positive direction. As Kutner (1971) has pointed out, "It remains for action and experimental research to determine under what conditions stereotypes toward the disabled tend to break down" (p. 155).

The Problem

This study grew out of an awareness of a need for the modification of attitudes toward disabled individuals and an interest in identifying techniques which might influence the perceptions of teachers or teacher trainees enrolled in education courses or short term workshops. Previous experience in inviting a panel of physically disabled young adults to speak to college classes in special education suggested that many nondisabled students had never heard a disabled person express his feelings about his physical condition or his perceptions of the attitudes of the nondisabled majority, even though many of the nondisabled had some experience or contact with children or adults with disabling conditions. Subjective reports of students hearing such a discussion suggested significant changes in perceptions of physical disability, with many students reporting a feeling of greater ease and comfort in teaching or in

JOY DONALDSON is Assistant Professor, Special Education Unit, and MELTON C. MARTINSON is Director, Coordinating Office of Regional Resource Centers, University of Kentucky, Lexington.

1. PHYSICAL HANDICAPS

social interactions with disabled individuals. Such reactions raised the question of whether a panel discussion by a group of physically disabled individuals might produce significant differences on measurable dimensions of attitudes toward disabled persons.

As a result of the inconveniences involved in repeated personal appearances by a group of disabled persons, a need for the assessment of the relative effectiveness of media in transmitting the panel discussion was also perceived. Moreover, it was felt that if presentations via video or audio transmissions could modify attitudes toward disabled persons, a number of implications might exist for the use of educational or public television and radio. Learning experiences in education, psychology, and sociology courses or in business and industry might also be designed.

The purpose of this study, then, was to assess the effectiveness of a panel discussion of views and perceptions of physical disability by a group of individuals with visible disabling conditions on a measure of attitudes toward disabled persons, while assessing the differential effectiveness of live, video, and audio presentations of the discussion. Because a number of previous investigations have suggested that females tend to be more positive in their attitudes toward the disabled than males (Higgs, 1972; Lazar, Orpet, & Fogg, 1971; Conine, 1969; Titley & Viney, 1969), the study also investigated these differential effects.

Method

Subjects

There were 120 nondisabled students from introductory psychology classes randomly assigned to 4 experimental groups, with 15 males and 15 females assigned to either a live, video, audio, or control group. A total of 96 students actually participated in the experiment. Although an attempt was made to obtain a balanced design with equal numbers of males and females in each group, disproportional cell frequencies were obtained. Subjects were predominately Caucasian and were either freshmen or sophomores at a large university.

Instruments

The Attitude Toward Disabled Person Scale (ATDP) Form 0 (Yuker, Block, & Young, 1970) was used as a dependent measure. The ATDP attempts to measure the extent to which respondents perceive the disabled individual as different and to some degree inferior or disadvantaged. A score which is low in relation to others (as scored in the present study) is interpreted to indicate that the respondent sees the disabled person as being relatively similar to nondisabled persons. A high score is interpreted as a negative attitude. Extensive analysis of the validity and reliability of the ATDP has been reported (Yuker et al., 1970).

Procedures

Panel members were 3 male and 3 female young adults with visible physical disabilities. Conditions represented by male panel members were cerebral palsy (congenital, ambulatory), blindness (adventitious, using guide dog), and quadraplegia (adventitious, in wheelchair). Physical conditions represented by female members were cerebral palsy (congenital, in wheelchair), blindness (congenital, using guide dog), and paraplegia (adventitious, in wheelchair). All panel members were perceived to be well adjusted and verbally expressive.

A nondisabled male and female served as panel moderators, raising questions related to panel members' personal views of their physical conditions, their perceptions of the attitudes of the nondisabled toward them, their social lives, and occupational goals. The 50 minute discussion followed an informal and relatively nonstructured format, with moderators raising questions and occasionally summarizing portions of the discussion.

A posttest with randomization design was used (Campbell & Stanley, 1963) with subjects in treatment groups responding to the measurement instrument immediately following the presentation. The control group responded to the assessment instrument only.

Subjects in the live treatment group observed the panel discussion, with no verbal interaction among panel members or subjects being allowed. Two video cameras that were located behind subjects taped the presentation. Because the video cameras were not totally concealed, subjects were told that only panel members would be on camera during the entire session. Assessment instruments were distributed following the presentation, and directions were read by the administrator.

Video group subjects viewed the panel discussion via a closed circuit television monitor in an adjacent building. After the presentation was seen, assessment instruments were distributed and directions given to the live group were read by the administrator.

Audio group procedures were identical to those of the live and video groups, with subjects listening to an audio tape recording of the presentation. Control group subjects were told that they were participating in a study related to physical disability as were all other groups and were asked to respond to assessment instruments.

Data Analysis

A 2 × 4 (sex × treatment) fixed effect factorial design for analysis of variance with disproportional cell frequencies was used. Since cell frequencies were nonorthogonal, an unweighted means analysis was used in all calculations. Hypotheses were tested at the .05 alpha level.

Results

Results of the analysis of data obtained from scores on the ATDP are reported in Table 1. As the table indicates, no significant interaction effects for the sex × treatment variables were found. The main effect of treatment was found to be significant with the F statistic of 7.2359 significant at .0004. The main effect of sex was not significant at the .05 level. To complete presentation of the data, cell and marginal means for the entire design are presented in Table 2.

TABLE 1

Analysis of Variance: Attitude

Source	df	MS	F	P
Treatment	3	966.25	7.24	.0004
Sex	1	281.70	2.11	.1500
Interaction	3	51.87	.39	.7649
Error	88	133.54		

TABLE 2

Cell and Marginal Means: Attitude

	Live	Video	Audio	Control	Mean
Male	43.55	51.60	56.40	61.85	54.58
Female	43.50	50.50	51.58	55.57	50.50
Mean	43.52	51.05	54.26	58.71	

Since a significant main effect was found for treatment on the attitude measure, Scheffe tests were used to compare treatment group means (Guenther, 1967). Results of Scheffe test comparisons are presented in Table 3 in which significant differences are indicated between live and video, live and audio, live and control, and video and control groups but not between the video and audio or between audio and control treatments.

TABLE 3

Scheffe Tests of Treatment Group Means

Group means	Difference between group means
Live, Video	7.5*
Live, Audio	10.7*
Live, Control	15.2*
Video, Audio	3.0
Video, Control	7.66*
Audio, Control	4.5

* $p < .05$

Discussion

In relation to the original research problem, results suggested that both a live and video-taped discussion by a panel of physically disabled individuals were effective in modifying stereotypic attitudes toward the physically disabled. A theory of why a discussion by physically disabled individuals might positively affect attitudes toward disabled persons was not directly tested in the design of the study. It might be postulated, however, that panel members themselves represented nonstereotypic images of disabled persons; it was evident from their responses that they were neither overly sensitive to discussing their disabilities nor indulgent in self pity. For example, stated occupations or occupational goals and responses to questions related to their social lives were not unlike those which might be expected from a group of nondisabled persons. Since the ATDP measures the extent to which respondents view disabled persons as not essentially different from nondisabled individuals, it is not surprising that attitudes were affected by the discussion.

Furthermore, in view of previous research findings of the importance of credibility of the presenter in attitude change (Hovland & Weiss, 1952), it might be assumed that results were in part related to the credibility of statements made by disabled panel members as a function of personal images presented. A number of assertions were made, for example, that disabled individuals are really not different except that they may move about in a wheelchair or use a guide dog. The arguments may have been especially forceful as a function of the congruence of the image represented by the presenters. Thus, not only were physically disabled members highly credible as conveyors of information related to physical disability but credibility of their arguments of the relative normalcy of disabled persons was enhanced by the personal images projected.

The findings of significant differences

between the live and video treatment groups may have been a function of the reduction of available informational cues from the live to the video situation. The nonsignificance of the audio presentation on both dependent variables suggests that the visual information that panel members were physically disabled may have been a significant factor in attitude modification.

The finding of no significant differences between male and female subjects on the post-test measures of attitude toward disabled persons is especially interesting in view of the large number of nonexperimental investigations which have found significant sex differences. Results of the present investigation may be interpreted in relation to the findings of Rapier and others (1972), as well as those of Higgs (1972). Rapier and her associates found that initial significant differences in attitudes toward disabled children between boys and girls disappeared after 1 year of a treatment which consisted of placement of a disabled child in a classroom. Higgs (1972) observed that females were more positive in their attitudes, but they were also more knowledgeable about disabling conditions and tended to have more contact with disabled individuals.

It may be postulated that the relationship is a circular one, with exposure to disabled persons breaking a pattern of less knowledge, less contact, and less positive attitudes for males. Since other researchers have only established the existence of sex differences without focusing on the effects of treatment on such differences, the findings of this study seem important in relation to the sex variable and attitudes toward disabled persons.

Although sex differences as well as interaction effects were found to be nonsignificant, cell and marginal means for the attitude measure, as shown in Table 2, are worth noting. In all treatment conditions, the means of male subjects are higher than those of female subjects, reflecting more negative attitudes. Moreover, while means of male and female subjects are almost equal in the live treatment group, differences become progressively greater from the live to the video to the audio to the control condition. It might also be noted that differences between male and female subjects are minimal in the live and video groups, which were those found to be significantly effective as treatment groups, while sex differences are larger in the relative ineffective audio group and in the control group.

Conclusions cannot be made from the preceding observations as a result of the statistical nonsignificance of the findings. The finding of no significant differences between male and female subjects on the measure of attitudes toward disabled persons, however, supports the postulation that sex differences

may tend to disappear when male subjects are exposed to disabled persons in a controlled or positive situation and are given information relating to disabilities.

Implications and Recommendations

The finding of significant effects on the attitudes of subjects viewing a live or videotaped discussion by a panel of physically disabled individuals suggests that such a discussion may be an effective means of facilitating positive attitudes toward disabled persons within a relatively short period of time. Educational implications include the possible use of such a panel in regular or special education courses, in psychology and sociology classes, or in industrial settings. However, it remains for further research to determine the effectiveness of the design when used with these population groups.

The effectiveness of the videotaped presentation suggests a technique that is relatively simple, short term, and feasible for widespread application in modifying prejudices toward the disabled. Again, it remains for further research to determine whether such a video presentation is effective in modifying the attitudes of populations other than the one used in this study. In addition, factors such as the effects of audience size or presentations via educational and public television should be studied. The discussion design used in the present study suggests a model for initial investigations in these areas.

Nonsignificant differences found between male and female subjects suggest that the existence of more negative and stereotypic attitudes on the part of males as established by a number of previous investigations may be a function of lack of information and contact on the part of males. Further research should attempt to determine whether initial sex differences become nonsignificant as a function of exposure to disabled persons and information related to disability.

Since interaction between subjects and panel members in the live treatment condition was precluded in the design of the present study, the realistic differences that might exist between an in-person appearance by a group of individuals with physical disabilities and a videotaped discussion were not assessed. Further research might assess differences in effects that may occur when subjects are allowed to interact with panel members. Such an assessment would seem important in view of practical implications for classroom application of the technique. Lastly, further research is needed to determine long term behavioral effects of the present design.

Reactions to the Handicapped —Sweaty Palms and Saccharine Words

Jack Horn

Your palms sweat. Your face feels tight. You smile and nod agreeably, trying hard to look interested in the conversation, but you'd really rather be somewhere else. The occasion could be a job interview, a particularly disastrous blind date—or perhaps you're talking to an amputee, a paraplegic or a victim of cerebral palsy.

Dartmouth psychologist Robert Kleck has been studying meetings between handicapped and nonhandicapped individuals for 10 years, uncovering a wide gap between what most people report about the contact and their true feelings. They say, "I liked that person. I enjoyed interacting with him." But their bodies tell a different story. Physiological readings indicate high anxiety, and nonverbal behavior—eye contact, gestures, body movements—suggest avoidance and rejection.

The fact is, most of us feel uncomfortable around hunchbacks, paraplegics and others who are disabled or disfigured in some way. And we feel uncomfortable about feeling uncomfortable. So we smile more than usual, nod approvingly at opinions we don't share and be-have too agreeably. This performance makes us feel better, but it disrupts the normal give-and-take through which all people, handicapped or not, learn to deal with others.

Because some handicapped people get constant feedback that their actions and ideas are being accepted uncritically, Kleck said, they learn to express themselves in ways that seem inconsiderate or overly assertive. This behavior gradually hurts their relationships with the nonhandicapped, who don't see the role they've played in encouraging the behavior they dislike and who ascribe it to overcompensation for the handicap.

Kleck has devoted most of his time recently to problems that physically handicapped children face. At a summer camp attended by equal numbers of handicapped and nonhandicapped boys, he found that contact wasn't enough by itself to overcome the handicapped child's poor acceptance. After the first three weeks of camp, each boy looked at head-and-shoulders pictures of the others and chose the ones he liked most and the ones he liked least. The handicapped boys consistently received the worst ratings.

Kleck is looking for ways to increase social acceptance of handicapped children and adults. More contact with others is a start, but the *nature* of the meetings is most important. "If you contact [handicapped] people in a social context which emphasizes their liabilities," he notes, "your attitudes become more negative. If you contact them in situations which emphasize their advantages and abilities, your attitudes become more positive."

In a summer camp, for instance, arts and crafts centers and biology workshops are obviously better places to meet than the baseball diamond. In everyday life, buildings designed with ramps, doors wide enough to handle wheelchairs easily and other facilities for the handicapped are great equalizers. This is one reason that more and more organizations of handicapped persons are lobbying and demonstrating for such facilities on local, state and National levels.

Kleck also would like to see more work done on social and psychological ways to normalize relations between the handicapped and others. There might be, for example, an ideal point in a developing relationship for a handicapped person to reveal his or her attitudes toward the disability to the nonhandicapped friend. Kleck feels this kind of openness might help their relationship.

Much depends, though, on the handicapped person's ability to handle what Kleck calls "the attribution dilemma." Does he attribute the way people act toward him to his handicap, or to the rest of his person and personality? Some people use their disability as a crutch to explain why others don't like them. But many handle the dilemma so well that others like them and respond to them as persons, independent of their physical problems. Kleck wants to discover how handicapped people accomplish this.

"Reactions to th Handicapped–Sweaty Palms and Saccharine Words," *Psychology Today*, November 1975. ©1975 Ziff-Davis Publishing Company.

Overcoming the Odds

Elisabeth Keiffer

Debbie Phillips was born with a right leg only half as long as the left. But with her family's warm support, she has become a champion skier, a blue-ribbon rider— and a delightful girl for whom the words "I can't" don't exist

Debbie outfitted for three-track skiing, on the slopes in Vermont during her first year of competition. She was so excited to be in the race that she put her number-three tunic on backwards!

Often, after 15-year-old Deborah Phillips of Binghamton, N.Y., has put her mare, Lucite, through her paces at a horse show and—like as not—won a ribbon, the judge's jaw will drop as he watches her dismount. For the pretty, brown-eyed girl who sat her horse so smartly and took the jumps so confidently is not like the other contestants. Her right leg is only half the length of her left, with a small foot where a knee should be. Although the mysterious birth defect is barely noticeable when she is on Lucite's back, it becomes painfully apparent when she straps on the heavy metal leg brace she must wear to walk.

But from babyhood Debbie has made it clear to all that, despite nature's cruel trick, she was not going to grow up handicapped. Today, besides riding, she skis in international competitions, plays a wicked game of tennis, swims like a fish and drives both a Honda motorcycle and a snowmobile. She makes top grades in school, has plenty of friends and plans to wear her mother's wedding dress when she gets married. The words "I can't" simply don't exist in Debbie's vocabulary.

When I met Debbie last spring, she had just returned from a triumphant trip to the French Alps, representing the United States in the junior women's division of the first International Amputee Skiing Championships, held

Debbie with her mare, Lucite; the family dog; a nephew, Jamie Phillips; and her proud parents, Betsy and Philip Phillips.

at Le Grand Bornand, France. She earned the honor of competing in the championships by winning every event in her division in the national three-track finals in Colorado, put on by the National Inconvenienced Sportsmans Association, a 3,000-member organization formed in 1967.

Three-track or tri-track skiing, Debbie explained, is a technique developed for those who cannot compete on two skis. Instead they use one ski plus two short poles equipped with mini-skis on the ends, which act like outriggers. It is the same technique by which Teddy Kennedy, Jr., relearned to ski after his right leg was amputated for bone cancer in late 1973. "The good leg gets to be tremendously strong," Debbie says, "and you maneuver by shifting your shoulders and arms."

"She doesn't ski, she glides—with the grace of a ballerina," a French reporter marveled in a newspaper account of the international competition.

Debbie lost a gold medal by one second to a 30-year-old German competitor, and despite the fact that she was by far the youngest skier on the slopes, had never competed in a downhill event before, and had to cover distances twice as great as she was used to, she came away with three large, shiny silver medals. They hang in the Phillipses' den, in Binghamton, alongside her numerous American trophies and facing a wall of horse-show ribbons.

Debbie does all these things so well not so much to prove what she can accomplish in spite of her handicap but because, like the rest of her family who are all splendid athletes, she has a boundless enthusiasm for sports and their challenge. "If I see something new," she says, "and it looks like fun, I just have to try it."

In her 15 years, Debbie has more than dispelled the worries her brother, Flip, now 27, expressed when the saddening revelation about the new baby's deformity was made to him and his two sisters. "We couldn't bring ourselves to tell them until just before she came home," Mrs. Phillips recalls. "Flippie's big concern was whether she'd be able to play baseball."

Mrs. Phillips is able to smile now at the memory of that question.

It could not have been easy to smile when the doctors broke the news to Philip and Betsy Phillips that their fourth child was tragically different from the others. Inexplicably—for she was not a thalidomide baby—Debbie had been born with only half a femur, or thigh bone, and that was cocked out at a 90-degree angle to her body. Her right hand was also affected. It has only three fingers; the third and fourth are fused with one set of bones and two fingernails. But Debbie has full use of her hand, just as she has full control over her short leg and small foot.

By the time Debbie came home from the hospital, after the usual five days, her parents had reached two important decisions: They were going to make sure Debbie received the best physical rehabilitation modern medicine could offer, and they were going to do everything in their power to help her grow up like their other children —happy, outgoing and independent. They have succeeded in both aims, but insist that much of the credit goes to Debbie herself.

Judging by photographs, she was as beguiling a baby as she is an attractive young girl, with the same huge, dark eyes and wide, slow grin. "She was a total ham," her mother recalls fondly.

Debbie let it be known at an early age that she had a mind of her own. Given confidence by the lack of restrictions her parents imposed, she was walking with a brace at 11 months, learned to swim at two and, by the time she was six, had traded her tricycle for a two-wheeler that she pedaled with her left foot.

"She's never seemed the least self-conscious about being different," Debbie's 23-year-old sister, Pam, says. "In fact, I'd call Debbie a total extrovert."

Philip and Betsy Phillips' determination that their child should grow up just like any other child was tested when they enrolled her in first grade of the school her elder brother and sisters had attended.

"It never occurred to us to do anything else," says Mr. Phillips, a handsome, stocky man who designs and markets home alarm systems. "But the principal called us in and said she felt Debbie should go to a school for the handicapped. We were absolutely astounded! Debbie was not only brighter, probably, than many kids her age, but she was also more active than most of them. She might be different, but she certainly wasn't handicapped, and we were not about to have her progress impeded."

After some lengthy consultations, Mr. Phillips adds, Debbie was allowed to enroll in the grade school and go to class as others did.

An ironic footnote to this story is the letter Debbie received from Binghamton's Superintendent of Schools on her return from Le Grand Bornand last spring.

"Dear Debbie," he wrote. "May I take this opportunity to tell you how proud we are of you and your achievements. You have brought honor to your family, your school but most of all, to yourself." Not many 14-year-olds receive letters like that.

Though Debbie's short leg has not slowed her down, it has undoubtedly cost her more pain and discomfort than most people endure in a lifetime. For several years, starting when she was three months old, she had to sleep head downward on a slanted board with heavy weights attached to her tiny feet to exert balanced traction on her legs. Like the tedious exercises Mrs. Phillips had to put her through every day, the traction was designed to stretch the short leg as much as possible.

At seven, when it became clear that Debbie would need an artificial limb some day, she underwent two painful operations, one to straighten the crooked right femur and the second to stop any further growth of her stunted leg, which was now the right length for a prosthetic device. For four long months the little girl lay imprisoned in a body cast with her legs in a spread-eagle position. Two metal pins went from the outside of her right leg inwards to keep the bones in place; often they pinched her unmercifully.

Mrs. Phillips recalls, perhaps better than Debbie, the misery of those four months. "We moved a hospital bed into the living room and I slept on a mattress beside it every night in case she needed something."

In spite of the constant discomfort, Debbie did her schoolwork with a tutor every day to keep up her studies and, to the amazement of her doctors at Boston's Children's Hospital, even managed to learn to struggle around in the heavy body cast.

1. PHYSICAL HANDICAPS

Shortly after she had recovered from her second operation, Debbie decided that as long as everyone else in her family was so crazy about skiing, she'd like to try it too. The problem was that although all the Phillipses are excellent skiers, they couldn't teach Debbie the tri-track method she would need to use. Fortunately for her, a young instructor at Greek Peak, a ski area near Cortland, N.Y., broke a leg that winter and, forced to master tri-track skiing himself, soon taught it to Debbie. Since then she has been a regular at Greek Peak, which awarded her a lifetime membership—"good till I'm 80!" Debbie says, flashing her impish grin —after her victory in France last spring.

During the last two winters, as a member of the Tri-Track Ski Club, an organization of skiers who have the use of only one leg, she has taken on the volunteer job of teaching other one-leg skiers at Greek Peak.

Much as Debbie loves skiing and enjoys entering competitions, that sport takes second place to her real passion —riding. "I guess I love horses more than anything else in the world," Debbie confides. Her mother, an able horsewoman herself, put Debbie on horseback for the first time when she was only three, and apparently the magic bond that often exists between little girls and horses was forged then. When Debbie was 12, her parents bought a pony named Firecracker for her, and Debbie completely trained her first mount. She won many blue ribbons on Firecracker, and learned to jump.

By the time she was ready to enter jumping competitions at 14, Debbie had outgrown her beloved pony, so the dappled mare Lucite (officially known as *Toute Ma Vie*, French for "my whole life") was bought.

Virtually every day after school, Mrs. Phillips drives Debbie to the riding stable outside of Binghamton where she keeps Lucite, and during summer vacation, Debbie is likely to spend the entire day out there. In the past two years, she has entered so many shows in New York and Connecticut that her father recently bought a camper to make traveling to them simpler.

In spite of all her pursuits, Debbie isn't at all certain how she sees her future. Although she is an excellent student and enjoys school, college is still only a "maybe." Horses are very definitely in the picture, though she isn't exactly sure what sort of career she can build around them. "But whatever I do, it will be something with animals," she says.

Though Debbie admits she's probably more of an athlete than any of her friends—last summer she learned to water ski and she's "dying to try karate"—sports are far from being her only interest. As they do for any girl her age, pretty clothes, fun and boys loom large.

Although she is still not anxious for the operation that would replace her small right foot with an artificial knee and lower leg for fear it would impede her in sports, her parents think eventually Debbie will welcome the chance it will give her to walk on two feet.

Adolescence, Mrs. Phillips confides, was a period they as parents had secretly worried about, since it can be fraught with heartache and confusion for even the most superbly endowed child. Their daughter had coped remarkably in a child's world; they wondered if she could do it as successfully in the crueler adolescent years. Would her difference from others, about which she had always seemed so unselfconscious, become too heavy a burden for her? These questions, Mrs. Phillips says, were part of the reason they encouraged Debbie to enter such competitions as the Amputee Skiing Championships, where she would meet others with a variety of handicaps and know she was not alone.

But their worries, Mrs. Phillips now believes, appear to have been unnecessary. Now in the tenth grade, Debbie seems to be treading the path to adulthood with the same combination of determination, humor and poise that has brought her this far. As her sister, Pam, said about her, "Debbie's got everything going for her—personality, looks, drive. But mostly she has a fantastic love of life. Even though she's my little sister, I think she's an amazing girl."

EDUCATION OF THE HANDICAPPED TODAY

Though much remains to be done, the condition of special education has never been better, says the National Advisory Committee on the Handicapped

About half of the Nation's eight million handicapped children, the United States Congress pointed out in framing the new Education for All Handicapped Children Act of 1975, do not receive an appropriate education, and about a million are excluded from the public school system entirely. It is illustrative of the difficulties which handicapped people have traditionally faced that disturbing though such figures may be, the condition of educa-

> **Handicapped children have a right to education geared to their needs and aspirations**

tion of the handicapped has never been better. Moreover, the climactic juncture of several powerful movements suggests that this Bicentennial year may mark the start of a new era.

In any case, the proportion of handicapped youngsters receiving an education has seen a steady rise. The 45 percent still being neglected (see table) compares with more than 60 percent six years ago and nearly 90 percent only 20 years prior to that. Though a new national commitment to serve every handicapped child by 1980 has greatly expanded the needed number of special education teachers, the gap between supply and demand is at least 100,000 narrower than the 325,000 that prevailed in 1969. Moreover, today's special education personnel receive broader and more intensive training than was the case then, and have the advantage of continuing advances in technology.

By far the most striking change, however, has been the development of a new way of looking at how people with handicaps fit into the education picture. Until very recent times those handicapped children who received any schooling at all did so on sufferance, as an expression of charity. Even then most were barred from regular classrooms, on such grounds as that their presence might be "detrimental to the education of others" or "inadvisable." There was the not uncommon conviction that many handicapped children, especially the more severely handicapped, could not benefit from education and that admitting them into the schools would therefore be a waste of money. In all such instances the decision resided entirely with school authorities. Parents had no choice but to accept what they were offered, even if they were offered nothing.

In law and as national policy, education is today recognized as the handicapped person's right. Moreover, that right cannot be abridged, even on such grounds as that the necessary funds are not available. And handicapped children are seen as having a right not just to whatever kind of education someone else may see fit to provide them but to an education that is geared to their particular needs and aspirations.

This acknowledgement that handicapped persons have rights no less inalienable than those of other American citizens can doubtless be traced in part to the emergence of a more enlightened sense of equity as regards minorities in general. More forcefully to the point, however, has been the specification of these rights in three particular arenas—in the States, as expressed in fundamental revisions of education statutes; in the courts, as expressed in precedent-setting decisions; and by the Federal Government, as express-

1. PHYSICAL HANDICAPS

ed in a succession of laws aimed at strengthening education of the handicapped in all its aspects.

A number of forces have impelled the advances that have been made in recent years, particularly during the past ten, and prominent among them has been a "consumer" movement led by organizations of parents of handicapped children and more recently including groups formed by handicapped persons themselves. Such professional associations as the Council for Exceptional Children and others concerned with discrete areas (e.g., the blind, the deaf, the cerebral palsied) also joined the fray. While a few of the organizations and associations making up this consumer movement were in existence prior to the turn of the century, most came into being during the 1940s and 1950s. Initially they were formed essentially so that parents of handicapped children could discuss their experiences and give each other moral support. In time, however, they became preoccupied with practices—exclusion from public schooling being a prime example—which effectively denied their handicapped children a meaningful role in the society. In seeking redress they turned to two of the most basic of democratic instruments—the State legislatures and the courts.

As the level of government primarily responsible for education, the States have to one degree or another displayed a concern for education of the handicapped since the early days of the Republic. It was not until the 1910-20 decade, however, that the first States enacted statutes making education of the handicapped a requirement (the pioneers being New Jersey, New York, and Massachusetts), and though this step advanced the theory that the State responsibility for education extended to all children rather than only some, in practice the feeling remained that public schooling was a preserve into which the handicapped need be admitted only if other students (and local taxpayers) would not thereby be inconvenienced.

It was this kind of exclusion that parent organizations and other advocacy groups, beginning in the early 1960s, selected as their principal target. Using publicity, mass mailing, public meetings, and other techniques of public information—and making direct contact with influential public and private citizens—they mobilized for action. The result was a surge of activity by State legislatures. The goals were first, to enact laws making educational opportunities for the handicapped not simply permissive but mandatory; and then going beyond that, to break away from the custodial mode that had often characterized schooling for the handicapped and instead provide substantive learning experiences.

Today all but two States—Ohio and Mississippi are the exceptions—have adopted statutes that make education for the handicapped mandatory. In States where the advocacy groups have been most effective, the laws are broad and comprehensive, embracing such matters as the training of special education personnel, the acquisition of needed facilities and materials, advisory councils that include handicapped adults and parents of handicapped children in their membership, cooperative regional arrangements for getting greater resources at less cost, and procedures for the review and evaluation of programs. There are incentives to comply with the law and penalities for failure to do so. It is a measure of the distance that has been traveled in making education available to the handicapped that 20 States now have laws which not only mandate education for handicapped children but include in that mandate children of preschool age.

In some instances the role of advocacy groups in the enactment of these laws has gone beyond the application of pressure, to include developing a model law, facilitating this law's movement through the relevant legislative committees, lobbying for sufficient votes to get the bill passed, and finally writing the implementing regulations. Independently and as members of coalitions—about 25 such coalitions are now active in various parts of the Nation—the consumer groups have played and are still playing a crucial role in building public support for the enactment of State education laws that respect the needs of handicapped individuals.

Even more spectacular has been the exertion of pressure from another direction, the courts. What was to become a national phenomenon began in 1971 when the Pennsylvania Association for Retarded Children filed suit on behalf of 13 retarded children in that State. Citing guarantees in the U.S. Constitution of due process and equal protection of the laws, the suit argued that these children's access to education should be equal to that afforded other children. In a consent agreement the court found in their favor.

One year later the Federal court in the District of Columbia made a similar ruling involving not only mental retardation but the full range of handicapping conditions. All children, said U.S. District Judge Joseph Waddy in the case of *Mills vs. Board of Education,* have a right to "suitable publicly supported education, regardless of the degree of the child's mental, physical, or emotional disability or impairment." Moreover, in response to arguments that this position would impose an intolerable financial burden on the community, Judge Waddy added the following: "If sufficient funds are not available to finance all of the services and programs that are needed and desirable in the system, then the available funds must be expended equitably in such a manner that no child is entirely excluded from a publicly supported education...."

There followed during the next few years an avalanche of suits as other groups in other jurisdictions asked the courts to enforce handicapped children's constitutional

ESTIMATED NUMBER OF HANDICAPPED CHILDREN SERVED AND UNSERVED
BY TYPE OF HANDICAP

	1975-76 SERVED (Projected)	1975-76 UNSERVED	TOTAL HAND. CHILD. SERVED & UNSERVED	PERCENT SERVED	PERCENT UNSERVED
TOTAL: Age 6-19	3.860.000	2.840.000	6.700.000	58	42
TOTAL: Age 0-5	450.000	737.000	1.187.000	38	62
TOTAL: Age 0-19	4.310.000	3.577.000	7.887.000	55	45
SPEECH IMPAIRED	2.020.000	273.000	2.293.000	88	12
MENTALLY RETARDED	1.350.000	157.000	1.507.000	90	10
LEARNING DISABILITIES	260.000	1.706.000	1.966.000	13	87
EMOTIONALLY DISTURBED	255.000	1.055.000	1.310.000	19	81
CRIPPLED & OTHER HEALTH IMPAIRED	255.000	73.000	328.000	78	22
DEAF	45.000	4.000	49.000	92	8
HARD OF HEARING	66.000	262.000	328.000	20	80
VISUALLY HANDICAPPED	43.000	23.000	66.000	65	35
DEAF-BLIND & OTHER MULTI-HANDICAPPED	16.000	24.000	40.000	40	60

rights. By now the number exceeds 40, and in none of the completed cases has the decision gone against the plaintiffs. The impact of these court rulings has been immense, not only in opening up school doors but in stimulating provisions in State laws to improve the quality and comprehensiveness of education offered to the handicapped.

Of parallel importance has been the role of the Federal Government, particularly during the past ten years. Actually Federal support for education of the handicapped goes back a century and more—to 1864 and the establishment in Washington, D.C., of Gallaudet College, serving the deaf; and to 1879 and the creation in Lexington, Kentucky, of the American Printing House for the Blind. Valuable though these actions were, however, they did not betoken a Federal commitment to education of the handicapped. Nor did an action taken in the 1930s when the U.S. Office of Education, by then more than 60 years old, first assigned a member of the staff to monitor the condition and progress of "special education," as education of the handicapped was by then being called.

A significant shift in posture was inconspicuously launched in 1954 when the Congress passed legislation providing for cooperative research in education, a proposition regarded with such minimal enthusiasm that it was not funded until 1957. When a $1 million appropriation was belatedly voted, $675,000 was earmarked for research having to do with the education of the mentally retarded. Subsequently, thanks in large part to the activities of the advocacy groups and particularly to statements made by such national leaders as John F. Kennedy and Hubert H. Humphrey, both of whom had handicapped children in their own families, interest was generated in reaching out a bit further.

In the following few years came legislation covering such matters as captioned films for the deaf and support for training teachers and other education specialists for the mentally retarded, the deaf, and the speech impaired (and later, all other groups of disabled children). A much broader development came in 1965 with the passage of the Elementary and Secondary Education Act, Title I of which included coverage of the handicapped. In that same year and in the year following came two major bills amending ESEA so as to give greater emphasis to its provisions for special education. The first, Public Law 89-313, provided support for the education of handicapped children in State-operated schools and hospitals. Even more noteworthy was the second, Public Law 89-750, which created a new Title VI of the Act. This new "title" or section was the prototype of the basic Office of Education program for the handicapped in existence (in greatly revised form) today. In addition to establishing a grant program aimed at strengthening State programs for all handicapped children, P.L. 89-750 brought into being the Bureau of Education for the Handicapped and the National Advisory Committee on the Handicapped.

In session after session thereafter the Congress continued to strengthen the Federal role. During the next six years about a dozen new bills directly concerned with special education—covering such matters as early childhood education for the handicapped, the establishment of deaf-blind centers and regional resource centers, education for gifted and talented, and many others—were signed into law. In 1970 came Public Law 91-230, known as the Education of the Handicapped Act, which combined previously passed legislation into one codified entity.

Thus was the groundwork laid for Public Law 93-380, the landmark Education Amendments of 1974. Beyond authorizing higher levels of aid to the States, P.L. 93-380 was in particular noteworthy for its specification of due process requirements protecting the rights of handicapped youngsters, for its support of the principle of placing such children in the least restrictive educational environment commensurate with their needs, and for requiring the States not only to establish a goal of providing full educational services to handicapped children but to develop a plan setting forth how and when the State expects to achieve that goal.

In November of 1975 this important law was greatly broadened by the enactment of an even more significant measure, the Education for All Handicapped Children Act, Public Law 94-142. The new bill calls for a massive expansion of the authorized levels of the basic State grants program—to a possible annual total of more than $3 billion by 1982—and although *authorizations* are not to be equated with actual *appropriations*, these funding provisions are in any case an indication of the magnitude of Congress's concern. Of probably greater immediate significance are some of the positions taken in the bill. First, unlike other Federal education laws, P.L. 94-142 has no expiration date; it is regarded as a permanent instrument. Second, the Act does not simply involve another expression of Federal interest in special education programing in general, but rather a specific commitment to all handicapped children. And third, P.L. 94-142 sets forth as national policy the proposition that education must be extended to handicapped persons as their fundamental right.

With the comprehensive provisions of Public Law 94-142 and related Federal legislation, together with the advances mandated by the courts and increasingly being incorporated into State education statutes, the basic machinery would seem to be in place for propelling education of the handicapped into a new era. The handicapped person's right to a good education is now guaranteed, and though lamentably often there has been a serious difference between actual practice and what State and Federal laws supposedly require, there is now at least a firm foundation on which to build.

Thus perhaps the basic challenge in special education today is the conversion of promise into reality. One such promise, for example, requires seeing to it that handicapped children are educated in the least restrictive environment commensurate with their needs, or more loosely (and with much confusion) "mainstreaming." Desirable though this concept may be, there is considerable question as to whether the education system—and indeed the special education sector of that system—knows exactly how to go about putting it into practice.

The crucial central issue goes far beyond optimum pedagogical practices or research or funding or the mechanics of moving youngsters into different settings. The overriding issue in this and all other provisions affecting the handicapped is the matter of attitudes.

The progress of the past 200 years, and the last ten in particular, will in fact remain essentially meaningless until handicapped people win their appropriate place not just in "regular" classrooms but in the "regular society," there to be judged not on the basis of their disabilities but on the basis of their worth as human beings.

FOR MORE INFORMATION
This article is taken from the 1976 annual report of the National Advisory Committee on the Handicapped. The complete report may be obtained by writing to the National Advisory Committee on the Handicapped, Room 2604 ROB No. 3, Washington, DC 20202.

WHAT'S BEING DONE FOR 35 MILLION HANDICAPPED

IN ORLANDO, FLA., a father confined to a wheel chair wanted to see his children in a play. He could not, because he was unable to maneuver down steps into a public auditorium.

Chances are the situation will be remedied. After the man complained to city authorities, plans were discussed to install a lift for wheel chairs.

The case is typical of changes now under way across the country—a massive drive, costing billions of dollars, to make it easier for the nation's 35 million handicapped to carry on as easily and independently as possible.

The efforts are mainly the result of orders issued by the U.S. Department of Health, Education and Welfare to halt discrimination against the physically and mentally impaired. The rules, covering all recipients of HEW funds, have spurred such projects as the modification of buses and buildings to allow easier access by people in wheel chairs.

Less publicized, but equally far-reaching, are efforts at the State and local levels which are now coming to fruition. Examples:

• Los Angeles provided more than 6,500 ramps for handicapped persons at street intersections and around hospitals, sanitariums, public buildings and senior-citizen housing areas. The program, which began five years ago, cost 3.2 million dollars.

• Philadelphia allocated about 1 million dollars toward making every public and cultural center, such as museums and health facilities, accessible to the handicapped. A city official estimates that it probably will take another 2 million dollars to bring other public buildings, including schools, into compliance with the law.

• The District of Columbia has opened a 2.4-million-dollar recreation center for the handicapped. The completely barrier-free building includes a swimming pool especially designed for easy access for those with physical disabilities.

A lot for a little. Some communities have been surprised at how much can be accomplished by relatively small outlays. Boston is spending $80,000 to remove architectural barriers in three nutrition centers for senior citizens, some of whom are handicapped. It means eliminating steps and revamping kitchens and bathrooms.

Private firms have joined the effort. In two new hotels in downtown Los Angeles—the Bonaventure and the New Otani—all rooms can be used by the handicapped. An older hotel in Washington, D.C., the Sheraton-Park, has modified and renovated all of its public areas and one third of the rooms.

Diamond's department store in Phoenix has salespersons trained in sign language to make shopping easier for the deaf. Trans World Airlines offers a new "handicapped lift"—a mobile unit to transport physically impaired people from terminal entrances directly to the planes.

Also coming: projects to teach the handicapped far more effectively than has been done in the past. Indiana University's Center for Innovation in Teaching the Handicapped estimates that the federal rules will require about 250,000 more school personnel to meet special, nationwide needs of those who are physically impaired.

Backers of the programs for the handi-

Passenger in wheel chair moves without help on Washington's subway system.

Helping handicapped to plane. Efforts are increasing to make them more mobile.

capped say that beneficial effects have been far broader than was originally anticipated.

Donald C. Tillman, Los Angeles city engineer, reports that the new ramps also proved to be useful to blind people—especially after a small edge was added at the bottom of the incline to separate the street from the sidewalk.

Many of the handicapped consider the effort far from complete. Lawsuits to force faster compliance are pending in some areas.

In Cleveland, the county commissioners are being sued in an attempt to force changes in a new courthouse. The complaints are that there are no areas in jury boxes for wheelchairs, that ramps are inadequate, that bathroom mirrors are too high and that employe rest rooms are inaccessible to the handicapped.

Another suit is pending in the District of Columbia, to require the addition of two or three more elevators at every stop on the new Metro subway system. At least one elevator at each station already is built for the handicapped, but some physically impaired people insist that the existing lifts are inconvenient.

Metro officials, in response, argue that it will cost 65 million dollars for elevators at each of the 86 projected stations in the system and maintain that costs for more lifts are unwarranted. They say that only about five people a day use the elevators at the 25 stations that have been completed so far.

Some complaints. Here and there, open hostility has greeted some of the new rules. Florida's department of transportation is trying to prevent enforcement of a federal mandate for the installation of low floors and wheel-chair access ramps for handicapped riders on public buses.

Officials claim that the regulations would raise the price of a 35-foot bus from about $70,000 to $130,000. They estimate that the cost of operating public transportation in Florida would increase by about one sixth.

Florida Mass-Transit Operations Director William W. Miller calls the federal decision "very poor" and adds: "I don't think the matter has been truly thought out from an economic and service viewpoint. It's very difficult to get away from the emotions of this issue, but it has to be done."

Yet many officials believe that the changes will benefit their communities.

Observes Genny Waddell, liaison officer with the handicapped for the mayor of Nashville, Tenn.: "The handicapped are feeling that they are not something to be set off on a side street but belong in the main community. They are saying that they have been overlooked, and that they are not second-class citizens."

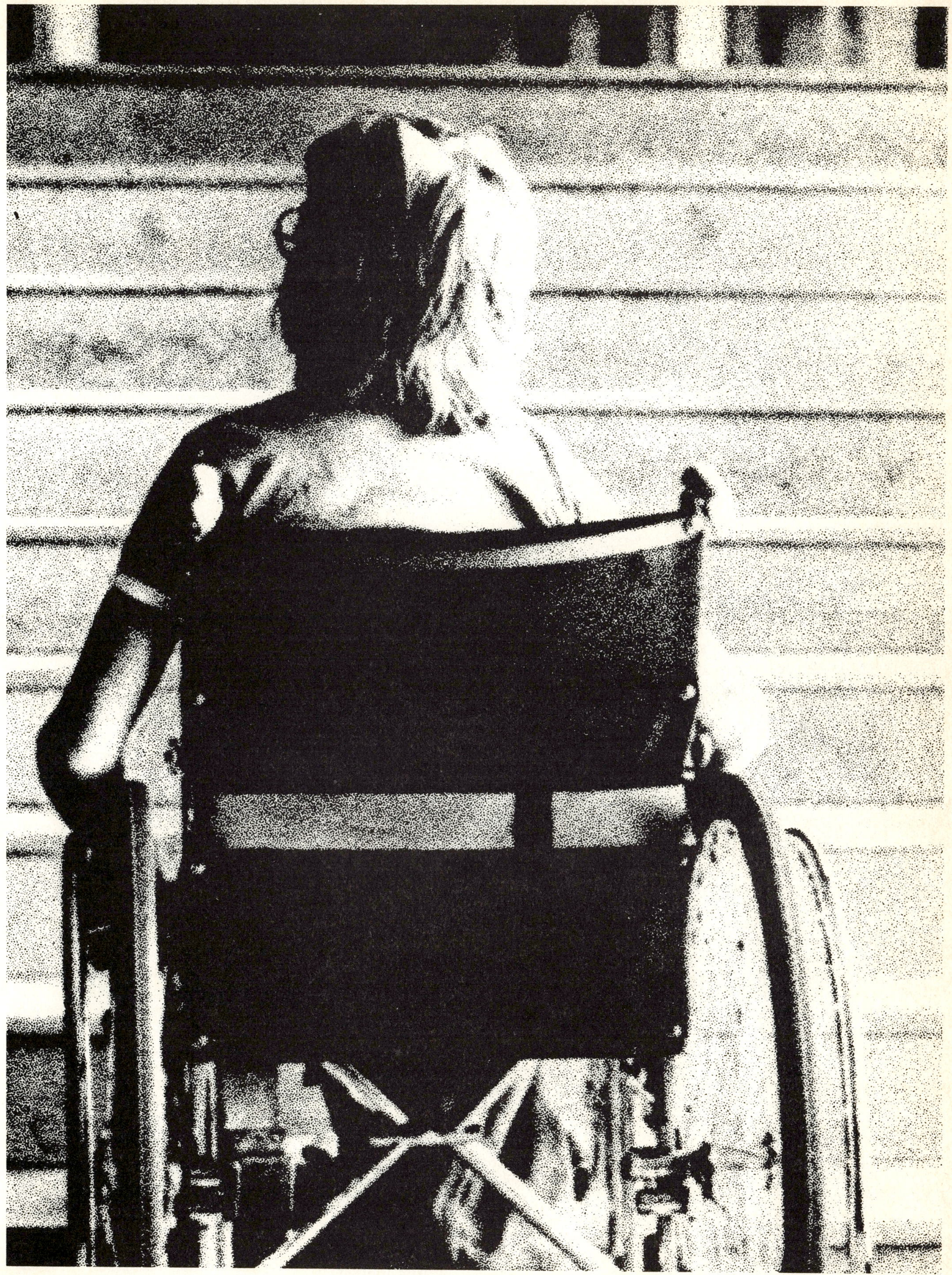

When Children Ask About Handicaps

Judith Wagner

More than likely a woman in a wheelchair, a man with one arm, or a little girl wearing leg braces will touch off questions from a small child. In many instances the answers will be impatient and incomplete or not given at all. The child will be left to wonder How did it happen and what caused it? Did it happen because the person was bad? Can I catch it? Will the person ever get better? What should I say to such a person? Should I try to help?

There are, however, an estimated seven million children with at least one adult friend who does not shush their questions. Fred Rogers, principal character on the award-winning children's television series, "Mister Rogers' Neighborhood," talks to his viewers about handicaps, sometimes openly, sometimes indirectly. The program, which is aired daily over some 250 stations of the Public Broadcasting Service, makes the important point that all children — those who are handicapped and those who are not — may benefit in knowing something about physical disabilities.

For the third consecutive year, Family Communications, Inc. (FCI), which produces the program at WQED in Pittsburgh, is developing handicap-related educational materials under a contract with the Office of Education's Bureau of Education for the Handicapped (BEH). During the first two years of the project, the primary emphasis was placed on integrating handicap-related information into the context of the television series. In the third year, however, there is a shift toward creating nonbroadcast materials specifically for and about handicapped children.

One purpose of the BEH project is to bring about changes in attitudes toward handicaps, according to Paul Ackerman, Chief of Program Development Branch at BEH. The ultimate goal is to have a world that sees the person first, the handicap later — a world that reacts to the needs of the person first, the handicap second. "It may sound like semantics," Dr. Ackerman says, "but I believe it is important to think in terms of a person with a handicap, not a handicapped person."

Toward explaining this viewpoint to young children and getting them to accept it, BEH looks to build on the relationship of trust that Mister Rogers has established with his young viewers. "Fred Rogers' main message to children is, 'You are very special and I like you just as you are.' His forte with children is attitudes and values," Dr. Ackerman says.

Barry Head, Director of Special Projects at FCI, holds this trust to be inviolate and talks about the precautions FCI takes in originating handicap-related materials: "We look at ourselves as communicators. In developing books, cassettes, films, and television programs, we seek guidance from the experts — parents, special educators, classroom teachers, and medical people who live and work with handicapped children day to day." And since FCI also believes an understanding of individual differences is fundamental to understanding the effect of different handicaps upon individuals, a new "Neighborhood" story line was created to present the concept in an entertaining fashion.

"Planet Purple was designed to be a springboard, a starting place for discussing all kinds of differences in people — age, sex, religion, race. From here, we could move toward discussing handicaps, a special kind of difference," Mr. Head explains.

Although many changes have taken place in Planet Purple as its episodes accumulated, it began as a place of almost total sameness, where everyone and everything was purple. All the boys were named Paul, and all the girls, Pauline. When Lady Elaine Fairchilde, a puppet character from the Neighborhood of Make-Believe, visited Planet Purple, she was at first taken with the idea of sameness. Eventually she came to realize the complications of total sameness, and the purple Pauls, Paulines, and pandas — constituting the entire population of the planet — likewise learned the advantages of individual differences. In fact, they even devised a plan to make individuality an important component of life on Planet Purple.

With episodes leading to these conclusions as a background, more specific information about handicaps was incorporated into the series. First Chrissy Thompson, a nine-year-old girl with spina bifida, a congenital birth condition that required her to use braces and crutches in order to walk, became a regular member of the cast. Then Tim Scanlon, an actor with the National Theater of the Deaf, and Eric Kloss, a blind saxophonist, provided other opportunities for Mister Rogers to talk with children about handicaps. The addition of Chrissy to the cast represents a significant departure from the show's format, it being the first time any child has appeared regularly.

"The program is built around the notion that Mister Rogers is sharing in a one-to-one relationship with each child who views the program," Mr. Head explains. "While Chrissy's regular appearance somewhat dissipates this illusion, we felt it was vitally important to have a real person, not a puppet, to help us deal with the issue of being handicapped."

On one occasion, the telephone rang at the home of the McFeelys, Chrissy's grandparents, while Mister Rogers was visiting the family. The point to be made was that Chrissy likes to do things for herself, so off she went to answer the telephone. While Chrissy was out of the room, Mister Rogers asked her television grandparents about her condition, inquiring about her braces and crutches and the prognosis for her future. In a later segment, Mister Rogers talked with Chrissy herself.

"The segment was unscripted," Mr. Head recalls. "It was uncomfortable for Chrissy, I think, but what came out of it is the idea that we can discuss these things with a person with a handicap if we do it with affection and sensitivity. We hope that seeing and hearing exchanges like this will affect the attitudes of children so they will not be caught in the trap so many adults find themselves caught in — the mental trap that makes us so intent upon avoiding the handicap that we never give ourselves the opportunity to know the person."

Mr. Head describes Chrissy as a spunky child with a flair for having fun and a penchant for theatrics that makes her a na-

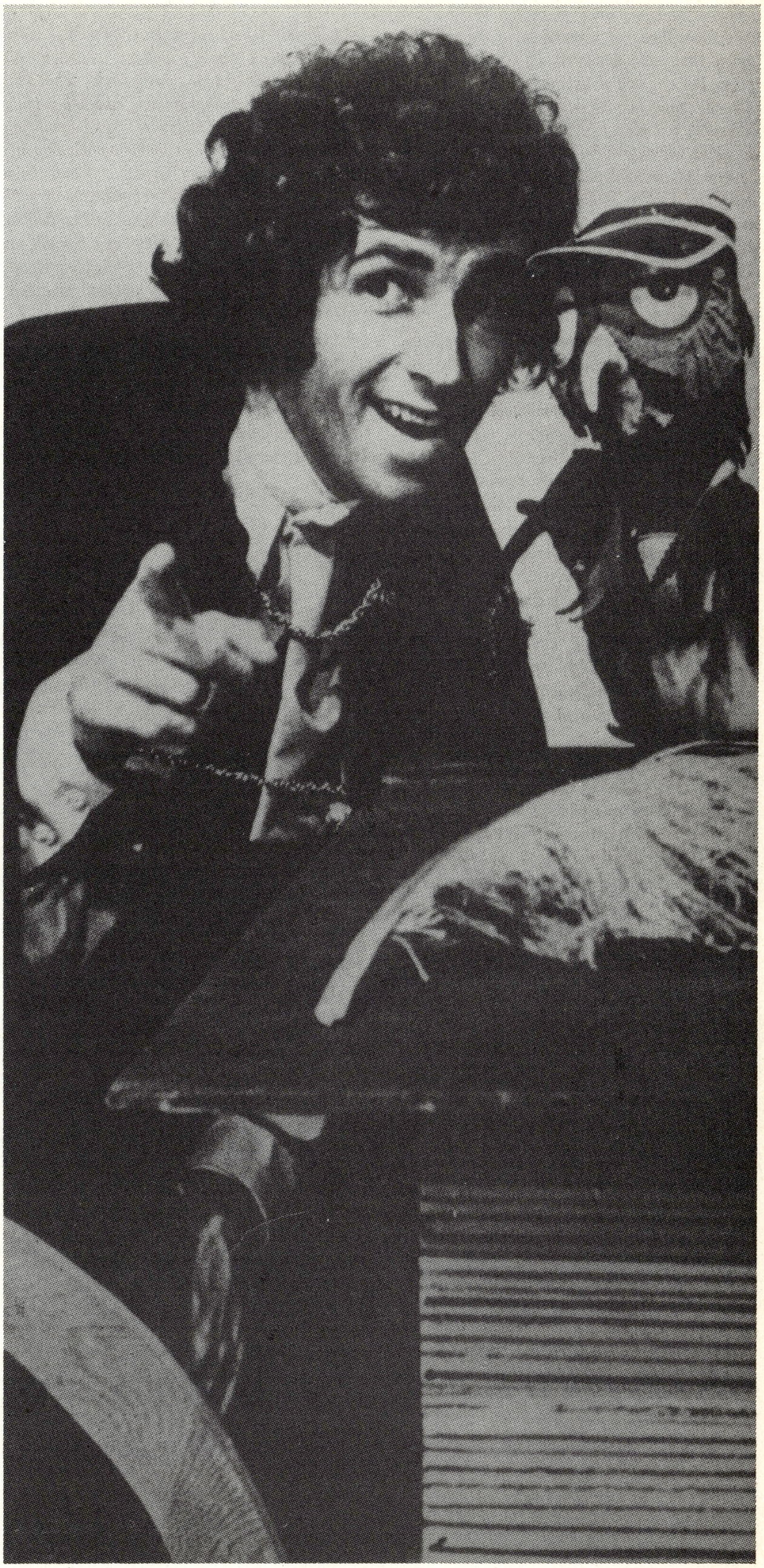

tural for the "Neighborhood" role. However, in the beginning, he and other members of the staff were concerned that FCI might be exploiting Chrissy by using her as a kind of prop for discussions about handicaps. "But we soon realized," Mr. Head says, "that it pleases her to help other children understand. On the show she is not portrayed as the handicapped kid, but rather as a member of a family, a student, a friend, another person in the Neighborhood—a child with feelings and ideas and problems like any other child. Of course, the handicap is not irrelevant or ignored, but neither is it central in most of her appearances."

Chrissy is particularly interested in letters that explain how her appearance on the show has been important to another handicapped youngster. One such letter, from a mother in California, reported that Anne, her five-year-old daughter, had given up trying to walk and had resigned herself to her wheelchair. After seeing Chrissy on television, the child got back into her braces and crutches and told her mother she wanted to "walk for Mister Rogers."

In contrast to Chrissy's handicap, Tim Scanlon's deafness is not immediately apparent. "Tim opened the door for discussions about other kinds of disabilities," Mr. Head says. "Episodes involving him are our most intense and direct so far. We deal head-on with prejudice directed against him because he cannot hear and because his speech is impaired."

Planet Purple, Chrissy, and Tim Scanlon segments have each been repackaged into sets of five half-hour video cassettes, which along with teacher's guides, will be available through FCI in the near future. The sets are appropriate for regular, special, and integrated (handicapped and nonhandicapped) group settings. Their effectiveness may hinge on the expertise and sensitivity of teachers who bring them into the classroom, according to Mr. Head, who says, "We realize that any discussion of handicaps may unduly single out children with disabilities. We rely, therefore, on the teachers who use the cassettes and guides to help make them as instructive as possible for children by following through with activities and discussions that they feel are necessary to satisfy the informational and emotional needs of the group."

Dr. Ackerman notes that new laws in education for the handicapped move toward placing children in the least restrictive environment possible, depending on their difficulty. He favors this idea of "mainstreaming" because he believes that segregating handicapped children into compartments prevents them from learning the skills they need to function successfully in the mainstream of society. He also states that as a conservative estimate, at least ten percent of the American popula-

tion is handicapped, and he maintains that very few children with disabilities would require separate education if schools were better able to meet their individual needs. "As a system learns to respond to and respect differences in all children," he says, "the education of handicapped children within so-called regular classrooms becomes less complicated, but at the same time more relevant to their needs."

Dr. Ackerman and Mr. Head agree that teachers, Scout leaders, recreation directors—any adults who work with groups of children—can make the world a happier place for those with disabilities by increasing their youngsters' sensitivities through good example and teaching them how to respond to the handicapped in ways that do not unnecessarily single out their handicaps.

In the course of the BEH project, FCI has realized that its messages for all children may take on singular significance for children with handicaps. "This is true on both cognitive (academic) and affective (emotional) levels," Mr. Head says. "For instance, when we talk with children about taking care of their bodies—washing, eating, sleeping—or when we deal with how it feels to try something and fail, these subjects may have implicitly more powerful messages or meanings for a child with a handicap."

Concepts involving body integrity are often more difficult for handicapped children than for others, Mr. Head explains. "Most children are very concerned about where they begin and end," he says. "The issue may be particularly confusing for a child who cannot use part of his body or who must wear braces. By showing a handicapped child as a person first, we believe we are getting across the idea that the human being is not synonymous with the braces or the wheelchair or the hearing aid, but rather an individual with some special kinds of differences."

At the end of the current season, FCI will conclude production of new "Neighborhood" programs and look for other ways to communicate with children and families about important subjects. "We

don't think of 'Mister Rogers' Neighborhood' as going into reruns," Mr. Head says. "We have a large library of programs—enough for a generation of youngsters. Then, when the current viewers' little brothers and sisters are ready, the series will be running again for them to see." He notes that segments will be changed whenever necessary to keep them up to date.

The creation of nonbroadcast materials designed specifically for use with handicapped children breaks down into three major themes: self-concept, self-confidence, and motivation or task persistence. Scheduled for completion in the near future is a series of materials tentatively entitled "I Am, I Can, I Will," and consisting of 15 video cassettes, 15 audio cassettes, teacher's guides, and at least five supporting books. It will be directed especially toward the visually impaired, hearing impaired, orthopedically handicapped, emotionally disturbed, and mentally retarded.

Although Mr. Head concedes it is difficult if not impossible to measure the results of the BEH project, he is convinced of its utility. "The television series and other materials are entities in themselves," he says, "but their value will be multiplied manyfold if parents and teachers use them as a catalyst. Enlightened discussions about handicaps in homes and schools will help answer a child's unasked questions and generate sensitivity toward people with disabilities."

Explanations must be simple and direct, he cautions. Wording is most important. For instance, saying, "the woman *lost* her arm in an accident" may lead a child to wonder whether an arm can be lost like a rubber ball. A better explanation might be, "The woman's arm was badly hurt in an accident, and the doctor had to take it off so the rest of her body could get well."

Moreover, adults should try to "listen" for questions children do not articulate. When questions go unanswered, children are likely to make up an answer they can understand from their own experience. One question they frequently do not ask aloud is, "Can it happen to me?"

Responses should be simple and realistic. Sugar-coating does not make the question go away and it may do irreparable damage to an adult's credibility. The trick is to say just enough in just the right way.

"Perhaps we are babysitting more than we would like to know," Mr. Head says of FCI's work. "Certainly we are not changing the mood of the world about handicaps or anything else. But every once in a while, we hear of specific cases and we know we are having an impact—a teacher who thanked us for heightening her sensitivities to the individual differences of her students, for example, and the little girl who walked for Mister Rogers."

The stories are many. Each, in its own way, indicates that in many places the messages are getting through.

The Office for Handicapped Individuals
(OHI) is a federal advocacy agency created to improve the services and information available to all handicapped people through U.S. Department of Health, Education and Welfare programs. OHI does not give grants. It was created by Congress as a staff resource for the Secretary of HEW, to aid in planning, evaluating and coordinating programs for handicapped people and to gather and disseminate information.

Many federal programs for handicapped people existed before the passage of the Rehabilitation Act of 1973 that established OHI. These programs provided services, research, training, technical assistance and information. However, there was no single agency to assess, comprehensively and systematically, the total impact of federal programs on the lives of handicapped people. Through OHI this overall perspective on programs and needs will eventually be possible.

As a means of developing a rational, nonpolitical assessment of just what the needs of handicapped people are, OHI is collecting information and distributing it to appropriate decision-makers. This is its advocacy role.

In its overview role OHI has been dealing with several basic issues. Definitions have been developed to establish the limits of the office; data have been gathered on the scope of federal programs, funding and plans for services; needs of handicapped persons have been queried through consumer surveys; statistics on handicaps have been examined and OHI's Clearinghouse on the Handicapped has been working to improve access to data from all information sources, public and private.

Defining "Handicapped"

An early task was to define who OHI would serve. The legislation that set up the office defined the term "handicapped" in a general sense. Over the years other federal programs carried various other definitions. Clearly, a definition was required that could accommodate previous definitions but still be explicit.

The definition of a handicapped individual, now established in law and used by OHI, is "an individual who, because of a physical or mental condition, or impairment, is at a disadvantage in performing one or more major life activities." (Life activities include communication, ambulation, self-care, socialization, education, vocational training, employment, transportation, adapting to housing, etc.) The term further means "any person who (A) has a physical or mental impairment which significantly limits such person's functioning or one or more of such person's life activities; (B) has a record of such impairment or (C) is regarded as having such impairment." To deal effectively with a range of issues and agencies, OHI tries to analyze the meaning of the word "handicapped" in various programs and contexts. Three or four questions are routinely asked:

1. Handicapped by what (usually a disorder or disease condition)?
2. Handicapped compared to what? (What is the standard that places this person or group outside the norm?)
3. Handicapped for what? (Education? Transportation? Employment?)

In some cases, OHI asks:

4. Considered by whom to be handicapped?

Complexity of Rules and Guidelines

It is not enough to know how particular programs define the term. The degree, or even the presence, of a handicap may be only one of the criteria for determining whether a person is eligible to be served by a particular program. Good examples of this are the Social Security Disability Insurance programs, in which previous covered employment is the overriding eligibility factor, and the Supplemental Security Income program, in which the primary criterion is total income available to the family. The number of eligibility requirements and definitions in use today, and

1. PHYSICAL HANDICAPS

their complexity, render OHI's task of coordinating and evaluating programs for handicapped persons as difficult as it is mandatory.

Moreover, there is no federal service delivery "system." Rather, we have a hodgepodge of programs with different histories, purposes, structures and ways of doing business. OHI surveys show more than 200 federal activities directed toward handicapped people in one way or another and over $22 billion spent annually. Nor is this the total picture. OHI is also aware that what happens locally throughout the U.S. — where handicapped people are being given, or denied, adequate services and assistance in becoming independent — is as important as what happens in Washington, D.C.

The trend in government today is to decentralize decision-making authority away from a few federal programs to the states. To obtain services or to compete effectively for federal block grants to state governments, handicapped people and their advocates have to be knowledgeable about legislation and various agency guidelines. OHI publications are designed to provide and keep current this all-important information.

How Many People Are Handicapped?

Reliable statistics on the numbers of handicapped people in the United States are hard to come by. OHI staff have been working with the Census Bureau, the Urban Institute and the National Center for Health Statistics to improve data collection. Compiling adequate, verified, consistent data for making program and funding decisions is a compelling priority, but a very costly and long-term undertaking. Even with more accurate counts we will know only the magnitude of the problem, not the details of individual needs.

Consumer Involvement

Consumers are important resources for OHI. They are, after all, in the best position to identify needs and evaluate the effectiveness of programs at the local level, where the service is actually delivered. The upcoming White House Conference on Handicapped Individuals is intended to involve handicapped consumers in articulating and recommending ways of dealing with consumer needs. OHI is sponsoring two seminars in conjunction with the White House Conference: one on coordination of federal programs and another on information needs and how to meet them.

OHI is also considering ways to obtain consumer input on a more effective, permanent basis. Internships for handicapped college students within OHI are one idea on the drawing boards; another is a broad-based consumer panel with several working subcommittees.

Needs of Handicapped Persons

OHI has surveyed 1018 local organizations of handicapped consumers. The lack of information about the availability of services is the most frequently cited problem among those polled. As additional findings come in, they will be shared with public and private service agencies and will be used to shape OHI's own programs.

OHI's Clearinghouse on the Handicapped

Yet, in the words of OHI's Acting Director, Dr. William J. Bean, "Information is everywhere and that's a big part of the problem." There is a lot of information, but no systematic means of drawing upon it. In addition the whereabouts of certain information is often known only to a particular, limited "clientele."

The OHI Clearinghouse on the Handicapped is not a storehouse of massive quantities of information and data. Instead, its staff refers inquirers to sources that can help. For example the Clearinghouse puts parents with educational concerns in touch with Closer Look, the National Information Center for the Handicapped. Closer Look, in turn, may refer questions to the OHI Clearinghouse. The Clearinghouse acts as a central referral point for information about federal programs and about various other public and private services.

After two years the OHI Clearinghouse has compiled listings of all information services in the handicapped field that are available without geographic or membership restrictions. Now the Clearinghouse is in a position to make referrals to almost 300 organizations serving the interests of handicapped people across the country.

A first effort to catalog state-level programs is a source book for staff use in state crippled children's services, based on a survey conducted by Clearinghouse staff. Compiling and disseminating comprehensive information about local agencies and services is unrealistic at the federal level. Nor is this necessary. Rather, the Clearinghouse will explore the possibility of forming a cooperative network among national, state and local information services.

At present the Clearinghouse serves handicapped people and their families, organizations and agencies, professionals working with the handicapped, the general public and Congress. Most inquiries are currently handled by referral to appropriate national information sources or state offices. In some instances an appropriate publication is available and sent out by way of response.

As areas of wide concern are identified, the Clearinghouse will put together general information packages and new materials. Soon lists of journals and newsletters on a range of topics will be available, along with information on how to order them from organizations and publishers. A book on federal funding and booklets on legislation are already in print and available from OHI Clearinghouse.

Federal Funding

The funding book, *Federal Assistance for Programs Serving the Handicapped*, is useful as a referral tool for service providers. It also gives an idea of the extent of federal efforts on behalf of the handicapped. It provides summaries of 85 major federal programs providing money, information or technical assistance for the support of service delivery to handicapped people. The largest share of federal funds goes to income maintenance through programs such as Social Security Disability Insurance and Supplemental Security Income; veterans' programs receive a significant share (over

$9 billion of the $22 billion total).

Three programs of grants to the states are funded at $100 million to $600 million. The biggest of these is for vocational rehabilitation; it is followed at quite a distance by maternal and child health services, the main thrust of which is prevention of disabilities, and, third, by handicapped preschool and school programs.

Legislation Affecting Handicapped Individuals

For the past several congressional sessions OHI has produced a booklet describing pertinent new federal legislation. Single copies of "A Summary of Selected Legislation Relating to the Handicapped" are available free of charge from the OHI Clearinghouse. Part I, listing legislation from the first half of the 94th Congress, includes information on federal regulations stemming from the legislation.

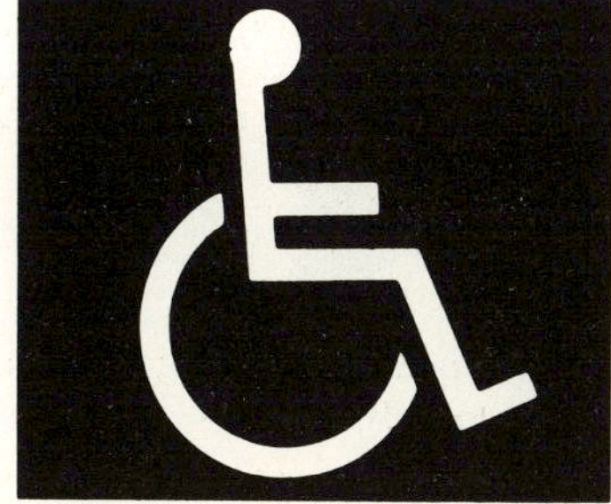

WE WELCOME YOUR COMMENTS

Only through this communication can we produce high quality materials in the Special Education field.

Special Learning Corporation
42 Boston Post Rd. Guilford, Connecticut 06437

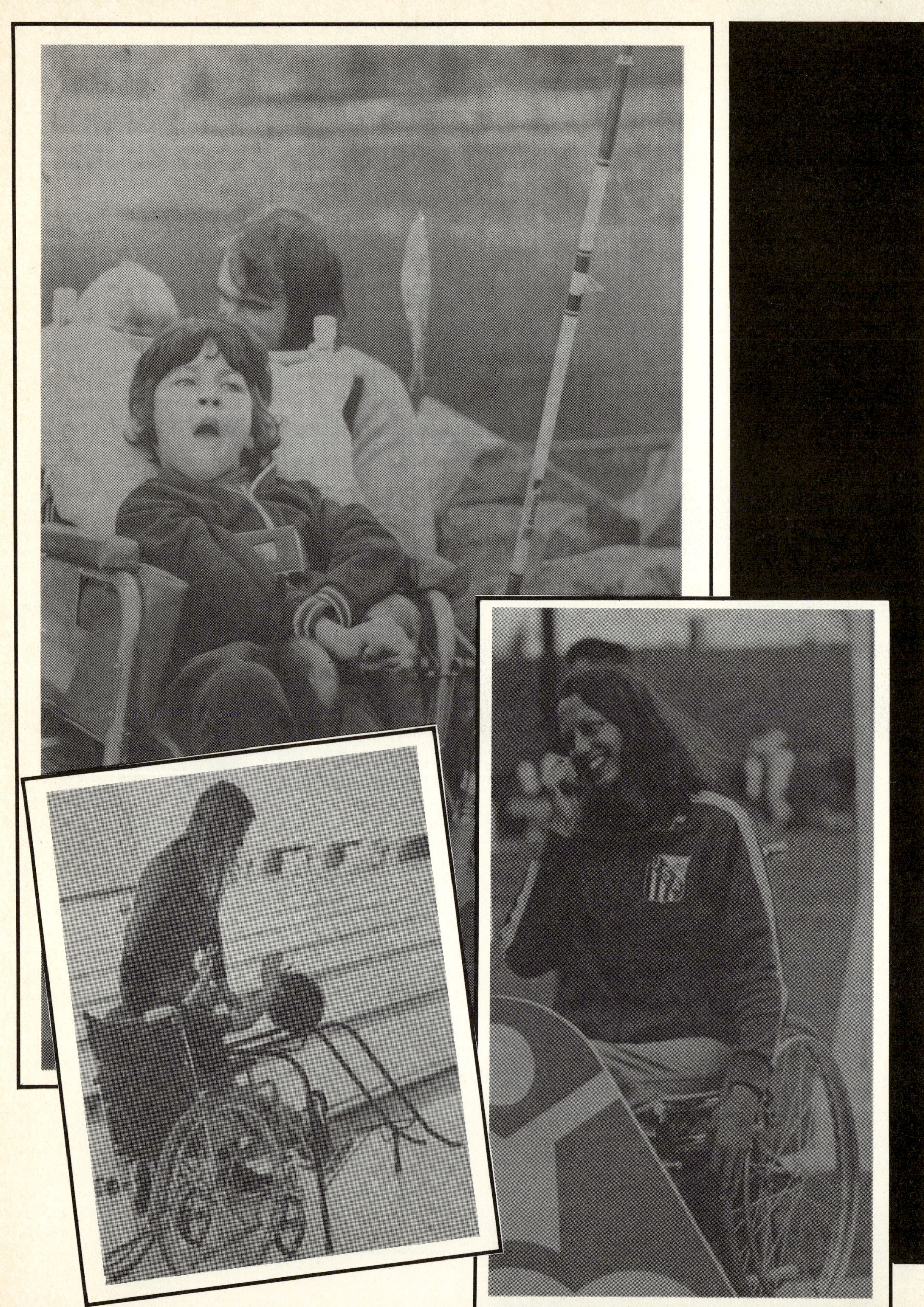

Causes and Prevention

Children who are born with handicaps include defects of the nerves, muscles, or bones as a result of inheritance or of defects in development during the prenatal period. Defects include the absence of an arm or arms, clubbed hands or feet, defects in the neck, legs, hip, and spine.

Smaller proportions of children have various orthopedic conditions which may not incapacitate them, but will warrant special educational arrangements since the child is classified to be orthopedically handicapped. These conditions might be curvature of the spine, hunched back, or wry neck complications.

Post natal crippling conditions which may occur later in life include accidents, a congenital predisposition, infectious disease such as polio, also known as infantile paralysis, which attacks the gray matter of the spinal cord, thus paralyzing the individual. With the advent of the Salk vaccine, medical science has greatly reduced the incidence of this disease. Hemophilia is another crippling source which is of a congenital heredity defect of blood coagulation found almost entirely in males with females as the carriers. There is no cure at present for hemophilia. Juvenile arthritis, a chronic, slowly progressive disease which causes swelling and pain in the joints of the body, is also known as "Stills disease" or rheumatoid arthritis, with no known cause or cure at this time. Another cause of physical handicaps is muscular dystrophy which strikes voluntary muscles of the arm, thigh or calf muscles. Causes are of inherited characteristics coming from either parent, with no definite source known at this time. Children who are afflicted with muscular dystrophy usually do not live to adulthood.

Children who suffer other health impairments are those who might experience special health problems with weakened physical conditions. These include, rheumatic fever which inflames the heart, joints and brain, or in some cases all three. Diabetes is a metabolic disturbance in which the liver fails to utilize and properly store body sugar, and is hereditary in nature. Nephrosis is a condition of the kidney, also known as Bright's disease, which affects kidney function of the renal tubules. Rheumatic fever causes inflammation of the heart, joints, and the brain. Other causes include congenital heart defect, respiratory disorders, cystic fibrosis, asthma and tuberculosis.

Prevention of these crippling diseases of children are chiefly a medical problem. The orthopedically handicapped child is 1) a child who is born with a given handicap or 2) a child who acquires a crippling condition later on in life. Facts point out that over one third of all physically handicapped children have cerebral palsy. With all these factors being taken into consideration, medical researchers continue to strive for new and improved methods of research into prevention possibilities for the future.

Cerebral palsy: "My baby is slow..."

This article was prepared in consultation with:

Billy F. Andrews, M.D., professor and chairman, department of pediatrics, University of Louisville School of Medicine

Henry Banks, M.D., orthopedic surgeon; immediate past president, American Academy for Cerebral Palsy, Boston

Edna M. Blumenthal, R.P.T., physical therapist; former director, Care and Management Program for Cerebral Palsied Infants, North Carolina Cerebral Palsy Hospital, Durham

Roger Freeman, M.D., child psychiatrist, University of British Columbia, Vancouver

Lawrence Taft, M.D., pediatric neurologist; president, American Academy for Cerebral Palsy; professor of pediatrics and rehabilitation medicine, Albert Einstein College of Medicine, New York City

Editor: Mary Alderman

Early recognition: The first clue to C.P. may be a mother's observation. Developmental screening tests may become routine. Suspect it if motor development is slow or unusual, primitive reflexes persist, or muscular tone is abnormal.

The surest aid to diagnosing cerebral palsy during infancy is a prejudiced eye.

For instance, the likelihood of brain damage would be foremost in your thinking if an infant were premature, if there were a history of rubella during the first trimester of gestation, a low Apgar score at 1 and 5 minutes after birth, hyperbilirubinemia, or complications at delivery.

Clinically, you'd look for C.P. if there were evidence of even one of its four cardinal signs:

1. slow motor development;

2. unusual patterns of motor development;

3. persistence of primitive reflexes; or

4. abnormal muscular tone.

Your first clue to cerebral palsy may be a mother's concern:

"My baby has trouble sucking."

"He pushes the nipple and food out of his mouth."

"I can't get his legs apart to change his diapers."

"My baby is so nervous."

"He never moves himself."

"He cries whenever I pick him up or turn him over."

"He's slow."

"He crawls like a bunny."

"He runs with one arm up."

Or, parental boasting may first alert you to C.P.:

"He can already roll over!" There may be something wrong when an infant turns himself from prone to supine position at an unusually early age. If the infant has severe tension in his spinal extensors, ability to roll over may be simply accidental. Opisthotonos, bowing of the back from the tight extensors, can flip the baby over.

"He's definitely right-handed" or "... left-handed." Normal infants are ambidextrous until about 18 months of age or later. A younger baby who seems to prefer one hand should be suspected of having a motor deficit of the opposite extremity.

While parents are usually the first to notice developmental problems, new tests are now available that may lead to developmental screening becoming as routine as height and weight measurements at the appropriate age levels.

Suspect C.P. when a baby is slow to reach the normal milestones of motor development. If the motor milestone delay is greater than the adaptive, social and language development, it suggests cerebral palsy. On the other hand, if the infant is equally laggard in all areas of development—adaptive, social, language and motor —you would suspect overall developmental retardation as well as a gross motor deficit; the infant most likely has both mental retardation and cerebral palsy, a combination found in about half of all cerebral palsied patients.

If a baby is excessively "floppy," your differential diagnosis should include C.P. His hypotonia may reflect loose ligaments or lower motor neuron disease, but it could as well be an early manifestation of an upper motor neuron disease.

An unusually hypertonic infant may also be signaling C.P., especially if the deep tendon reflexes are exaggerated. However, hypertonia can be due to hypocalcemia or other metabolic disturbance, which should be ruled out by appropriate tests.

In newborns, you'll find general observation and functional tests more useful in recognizing cerebral palsy than a formal neurological examination because they test subcortical functions. An infant with hydranencephaly, for example, may test out as neurologically normal as a newborn. A newborn should reveal dominance of the prone flexion posture, his arms flexed beside his chest and his knees drawn up under his abdomen; a preference for the extensor posture would be abnormal. Watch the newborn's spontaneous movements: Are they strong, weak or absent? Tremulousness after four days may be very significant although tremulousness with crying—especially rapid tremor of the chin—is normal during the first four days of life. After four days, however, when crying or sudden movement causes tremor in one or more extremities, it may indicate hypocalcemia or brain damage. On the other hand, asymmetry in movement in a newborn is more indica-

tive of a lower motor neuron or local problem than of brain damage. For instance, if one arm doesn't move as well as the other, you'd look to brachial plexus injury, a fractured clavicle, or a broken arm as likely causes.

Detection in older infants: Suspect C.P. if he clenches his thumb in his palm, kicks legs in unison, hyperextends his neck unless supported or moves his tongue in and out continuously. C.P. and mental retardation can be differentiated by the levels of motor, adaptive, social and language development. Presence of the obligatory tonic neck reflex indicates CNS involvement.

As in the newborn, you can rely upon observation as your best indicator of C.P. in an older infant. As the baby sits in his mother's lap, look for the following signs:

»thumb clenched in palm, if he is older than 4-5 months;

»persistent use of only one hand when playing with a toy;

»failure to transfer objects from one hand to the other by 7 months;

»failure to take his hand to his mouth;

»difficulty in supinating his forearm;

»keeping one hand fisted, if he is older than 4 months;

»kicking legs in unison rather than in bicycle-fashion;

»keeping legs in an extended or crossed position;

»keeping one leg rigid with ankle extended;

»keeping both ankles extended;

»everting one or both ankles;

»inverting one or both ankles;

»holding toes in flexed position;

»hyperextension of neck unless

his head is supported;

»dropping of chin onto chest unless supported;

»rounded back when seated, if over 8 months old;

»paucity of gross body movements;

»falling forward—head to knees —unless supported;

»moving tongue in and out of his mouth continuously—the reverse tongue motion of athetotic cerebral palsy;

»nystagmus;

»unusually bright and beautiful eyes, but lack of response to sounds or other stimuli;

»evidence of lack of vision.

In addition, while the baby lies on his back on the examining table, watch for these clues:

»dropping of head into hyperextension when you pull him by his hands to a sitting position;

»collapses forward when placed in a sitting position if he is over 8 months;

»wormlike involuntary movements, usually not evidenced until the child reaches 18 months of age;

»involuntary rotary movements of the shoulders and/or hips;

»inability to roll from back to face;

»failure to reach for an interesting object with one hand;

»trembling or inaccurate aim when reaching for an object; and

»good use of hands, but lethargy of his lower extremities.

In differentiating C.P. from mental retardation, take special note of intention tremor or athetotic movements of the hand when the baby reaches for an object. Primarily retarded babies without a motor deficit will have immature motor patterns without dyskinesia. For example, a 10-month-old retarded baby will not

C.P. profile: Types of cerebral palsy and their characteristics

Spasticity is characterized by hyperactive reflexes and exaggerated stretch reflexes. A stretch reflex is elicited by a quick pull on the muscle, which causes rebound contraction or kick-back. If, for example, a baby's hip adductors are spastic, his legs rebound into a scissored position after his mother tries to pull his legs apart to change his diapers. If the elbow extensors are spastic, the baby's arms will stiffen as the mother tries to get his arms into sleeves. Spasticity may be present in any muscle of the body in any degree of severity. It may be present in all four extremities, in the lower extremities only, or be unilateral.

A spastic quadriplegic infant is blocked in everything he tries to do—reaching for a toy, rolling over, sitting up, creeping, pulling up on furniture to stand upright. If severely involved, he may not even be able to use his hands to protect his face when he rolls involuntarily from his back to his face. If he topples backward from a sitting position, he may not be able to reach out for the floor to break his fall. Because of such frustrating and painful experiences, the severely involved spastic quadriplegic may hesitate to try anything new. In addition, he startles easily, and his arms and legs may stiffen into extension when he's picked up or cuddled. Typically, the family avoids picking him up as well as cuddling and playing with him. Deprived of normal growing achievements, the severely involved spastic quadriplegic child tends to become withdrawn and fearful.

Athetosis is a condition in which normal movements are thwarted by superimposed involuntary movements. The many different types of athetosis include tension, non-tension, rotary, dystonic, and shudder. When the athetotic infant tries to reach for a toy, his arm may go in a different direction at each attempt. He may achieve his goal accidentally, yet fail in his next 10 tries. In contrast to the spastic child, who is likely to give up trying, the athetoid usually persists because he occasionally succeeds. The athetotic C.P. responds normally to cuddling and is usually picked up often by family members. The athetoid may blow up from frustration, but this emotional release is usually not a temper tantrum.

Ataxia is characterized by a disturbance of balance, incoordination of the upper extremities, hypoactive reflexes, usually a horizontal nystagmus and paucity of movement of the lower extremities in infancy. When lying on his stomach, the infant may pull himself forward by his arms alone, pulling his legs along behind. As he gets older and pulls up on furniture, he stands with an unusually wide stance. If he isn't holding on, he "waves in the breeze" and, if unprotected, will fall. He doesn't realize he is off balance until he is so far off that he can't right himself. The ataxic child also has difficulty with coordination and may blow up from frustration.

Mixed cerebral palsy is another variation. This type presents some characteristics of all three classifications—spasticity, athetosis, and ataxia.

---

apply a pincer grasp when reaching for a small pellet, but may use a raking movement of all four fingers without evidence of partial or involuntary movement.

Finally, while the baby is still on the table, turn him to his stomach to check for these signs:

»catching one or both arms under his body;

»failure to lift head and chest from table if he is over 5 months;

»using only one forearm to support his body while raising head and chest from the table;

»using both forearms for support, but keeping hands fisted;

»failure to place palm or palms flat on the table and straighten his elbows to raise his head and chest;

»using hands well but dragging his legs.

Upon direct examination, there is one primitive reflex which, if abnormal, is a strong indicator that you will be dealing with a motor problem—that is, the tonic neck reflex.

When you turn the baby's head so that the chin is over one shoulder, the baby will assume a fencing position: his arm and leg on the chin side will be extended while his arm and leg on the occiput side will be flexed. This reflex is usually present from birth to 4 months of age, and its persistance beyond 6 months is highly indicative of central nervous system pathology.

An obligatory tonic neck reflex is abnormal in a child of any age. In this case, the baby cannot move his arms and legs out of the classic fencing position while his head is held in position for the tonic neck reflex for more than 30 seconds.

Every baby at 6 months of age should have this simple screening test for C.P.:

»place a cover over the baby's face;

»if normal, the baby will pull the cover off, usually using both hands;

»persistent use of one hand makes it highly likely that the youngster is abnormal.

If you fail to find increased reflexes or increased tone in the

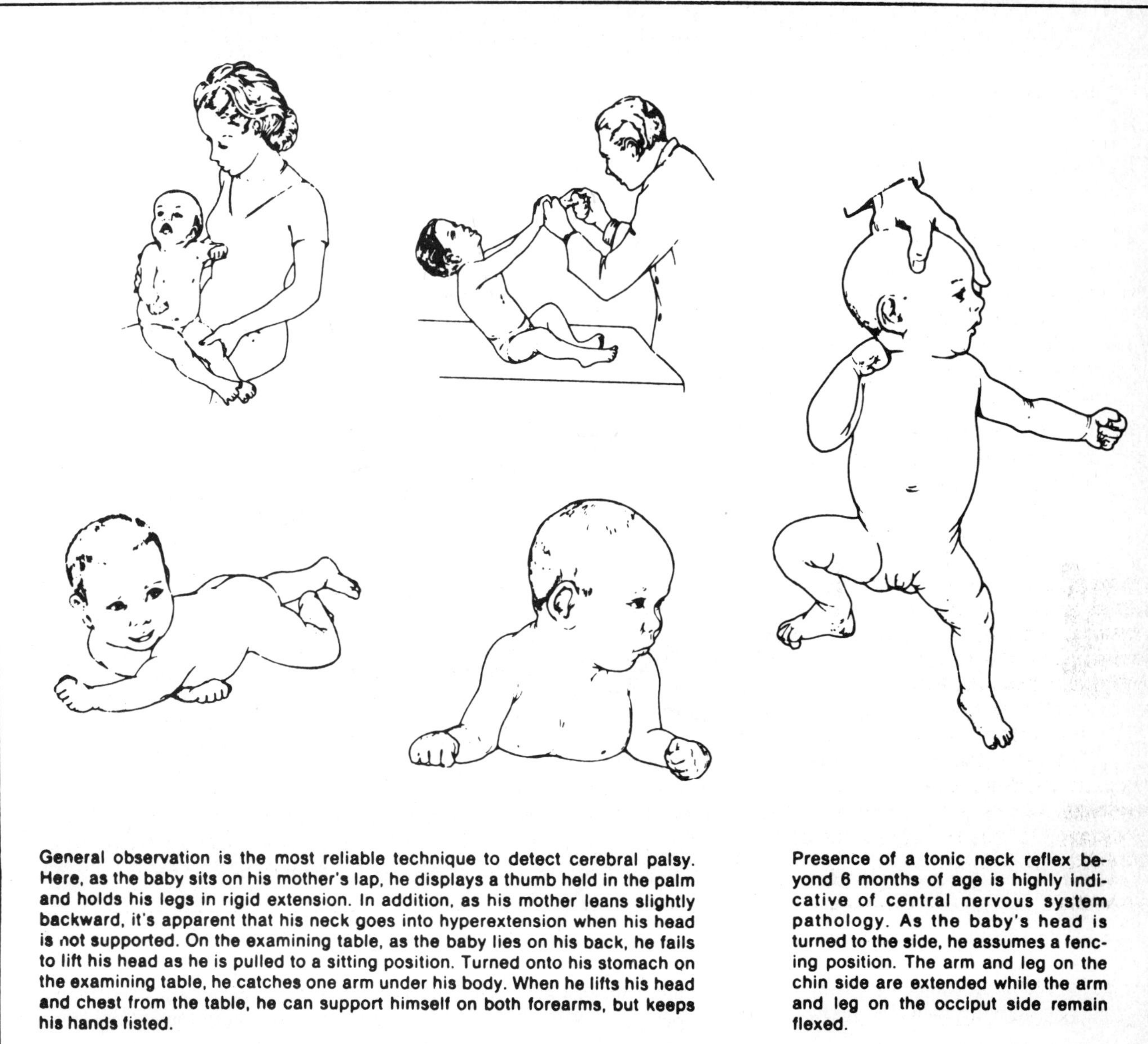

General observation is the most reliable technique to detect cerebral palsy. Here, as the baby sits on his mother's lap, he displays a thumb held in the palm and holds his legs in rigid extension. In addition, as his mother leans slightly backward, it's apparent that his neck goes into hyperextension when his head is not supported. On the examining table, as the baby lies on his back, he fails to lift his head as he is pulled to a sitting position. Turned onto his stomach on the examining table, he catches one arm under his body. When he lifts his head and chest from the table, he can support himself on both forearms, but keeps his hands fisted.

Presence of a tonic neck reflex beyond 6 months of age is highly indicative of central nervous system pathology. As the baby's head is turned to the side, he assumes a fencing position. The arm and leg on the chin side are extended while the arm and leg on the occiput side remain flexed.

sluggish extremity, don't rule out hemiparesis. At this early stage, it's best to base judgment on functional abnormality rather than on formal neurological signs.

Also, when you pick up the baby under his arms, with his back toward you, and hold him out in front of you, a normal baby will draw his legs up or bicycle. In contrast, a spastic baby may go into extensor thrust or scissors, and an ataxic baby may sit in the air, with hips flexed and knees extended.

As the child grows, the clinical picture of brain injury changes, even though the lesion is nonprogressive. For example, a baby with bilirubin encephalopathy presents signs of kernicterus from the third to fifth days of life, and will be hypertonic, opisthotonic with hyperactive reflexes, and have a poor Moro and an obligatory tonic neck reflex.

If the child survives, there will be a gradual change to a state of normal muscle tone and normal reflexes around the second week. The only clue you will have to a nervous system pathology will be an obligatory tonic neck reflex and, possibly, hypertonus during agitation.

Characteristically, the normal

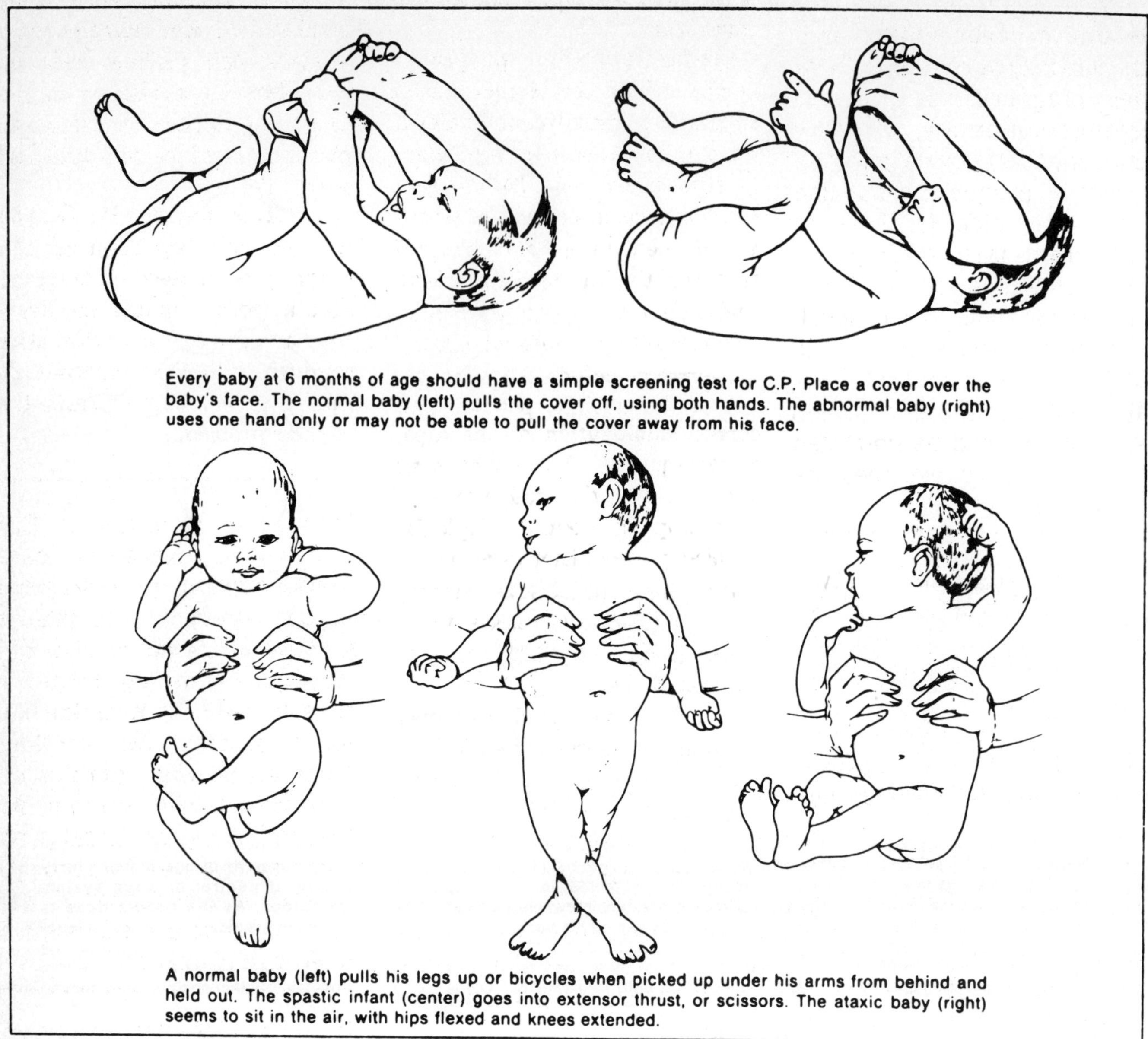

Every baby at 6 months of age should have a simple screening test for C.P. Place a cover over the baby's face. The normal baby (left) pulls the cover off, using both hands. The abnormal baby (right) uses one hand only or may not be able to pull the cover away from his face.

A normal baby (left) pulls his legs up or bicycles when picked up under his arms from behind and held out. The spastic infant (center) goes into extensor thrust, or scissors. The ataxic baby (right) seems to sit in the air, with hips flexed and knees extended.

muscle tone persists until the baby is 2-3 months old, at which time a gradual change to hypotonia takes place. The deep tendon reflexes will remain normal, the only abnormality being the obligatory tonic neck reflex.

At 10 months of age, it is easy to confuse this type of cerebral palsy with mental retardation. A diagnosis of C.P. is based on the history of hyperbilirubinemia and persistence of the tonic neck reflex.

At 12-18 months, the baby shifts gradually from a hypotonic state to rigidity; slowly, the typical involuntary writhing athetoid movements add to the clinical picture. Apparently the normal parts of the nervous system need to mature to a certain degree before the classical athetoid cerebral palsy can manifest itself.

When your observation of an infant detects a combination of the overt signs, a presumptive diagnosis of cerebral palsy is well founded.

The abnormality may be subtle, or as obvious as the thumb clenched in the fist. When the clinical picture points to C.P., you'll want to refer the child and family to a specialized center for specific diagnosis which will differentiate between the types of cerebral palsy such as spasticity and tension athetosis.

Referral for treatment: Wait-and-see care may be obsolete. Treatment programs during infancy prevent deformity, improve function, and provide the family with an avenue of action and contact with other families with C.P. Infant training programs can provide the sensory experiences essential to the development of cognitive functioning. While surgery is ordinarily delayed until age 4-5, subluxation of the hip should be corrected before the child assumes the upright position.

The ability to make this type of differential diagnosis requires varied experience, unusual for anyone without a special interest in cerebral palsy.

The traditional practice of routinely following a cerebral palsied child until he is 4-5 years old may be obsolete.

A recently completed seven-year study of 201 children at the North Carolina Cerebral Palsy Hospital suggests that a treatment program should begin as soon as cerebral palsy is suspected and before the child is 30 months. Generally, the younger the child, the more satisfactory were the results of treatment for both the child and the parents.

Among the advantages of early treatment are these points:

»Range-of-motion exercise may help to prevent contractures and deformity often associated with spasticity.

»A hemiplegic is more likely to learn to use his affected hand as a true helping hand rather than as a club-type prop or to reject it completely. With the proper treatment, it is more likely that the thumb will eventually be used for opposition.

»Infant-training programs performed by the mother under supervision usually emphasize a multi-stimulation approach. Early stimulation provides the sensory experiences considered essential to the development of cognitive functioning—to feel objects and shapes, textures and weights, and relate them to visual clues.

»Surgery before the child assumes the upright position can correct subluxation of the hips, a consequence of overwhelming spasticity of the adductors, in spastic quadriplegia or diplegia.

»Early recognition of a convulsive disorder, which is common with cerebral palsy, makes it easier to control the attacks with anticonvulsants.

»Professional guidance may prevent the secondary emotional complications to which a handicapped child is prone.

»The parents' worries are acted upon. Parents of C.P. children consistently voice resentment toward a physician who says there is nothing to worry about when first asked about a child's delayed development.

»Parents begin working with the child under supervision at the peak of their interest in the physical well-being of the child. Also—and most important—they feel they are helping their child, instead of feeling powerless and defeated.

»If the child is mentally retarded, parents come to their own slow realization through working with him. Awareness of the child's unresponsiveness or lack of progression often prompts the family to ask "Doctor, what will we do when he becomes too heavy to carry? Should he go to a special school?"

»Total evaluation—including biochemical and chromosomal analyses—can perhaps rule out hereditary disease before another pregnancy occurs or before the parents' fears interfere with their sexual life.

»Parents may receive counseling that will help them act consistently with their child rather than at odds with one another.

»Through contact with other families with C.P. children the family gains a better perspective of their problem.

Systematic checkups: A C.P. child needs preventive care. Measure the lower extremities at each visit. A lift is indicated to prevent functional scoliosis if discrepancy in leg length is greater than 1 cm. X-ray the hips for subluxation two or three times a year when there is severe spasticity in the adductors. Visual, hearing or dental problems should be referred promptly. Keep a serial record of head circumference and exact age of milestone attainment.

It's essential to establish a system of periodic checks to help prevent further complications. For instance, subluxation of the hips is a common problem requiring early recognition and surgical correction. X-rays of the hips should be done two or three times a year for any patient who has severe spasticity of the hip adductors. In hemiplegics, functional scoliosis due to a discrepancy in leg length is a frequent complication and requires measurement of the lower extremities from the anterior superior iliac spine to the medial malleolus at the ankle every time the patient visits the office. If the

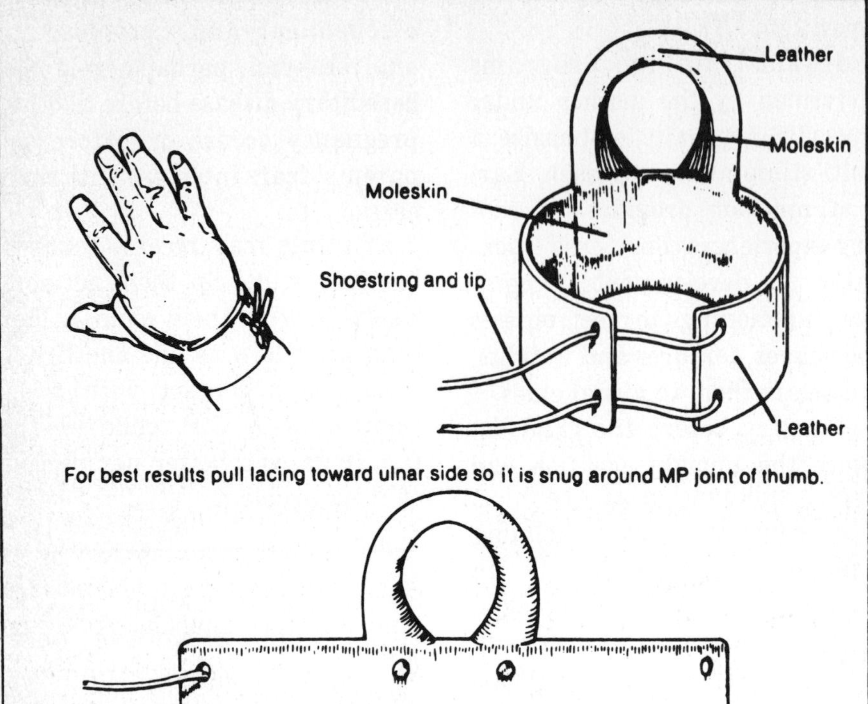

For best results pull lacing toward ulnar side so it is snug around MP joint of thumb.

A thumb splint helps to get the thumb out of the palm. This soft leather band is covered with moleskin. It fits around the wrist with a loop around the thumb; the loop must fit right down into the metacarpophalangeal joint. The band is tied with a shoestring on the ulnar side of the wrist.

shortening exceeds 1 cm., a lift is necessary.

If the child has a visual, hearing or dental problem, prompt referral is indicated.

More than 75 per cent of cerebral palsied children have strabismus, and steps must be taken to prevent the development of amblyopia ex anopsia.

An articulation problem or language delay may indicate a hearing loss, a not unusual finding in a C.P. patient. Dental caries and malocclusion also are frequent problems and are more often due to dental defects than to poor dental hygiene.

Because of the child's lack of mobility, overweight often becomes a problem which adds to the overall distress.

If the child has seizures, check response to anticonvulsants, watching for toxic effects.

While the child is under your care, it is important to keep a careful record of head circumference and exact age of milestone attainment.

This is especially necessary when a child with a maldevelopment is referred for specific diagnosis since it's often difficult to determine if the lesion of the brain is static or progressive.

Home treatment: Instruct parents to expand the child's experiences. Range-of-motion exercises can prevent contractures and deformity in the spastic C.P. Wrist tipping and a special thumb splint may help the hemiplegic to keep his thumb out of his palm. Athetoid C.P.s can gain judgment in direction and balance through exercise.

If it is impossible to include the child in an infant program, the parents can, with your guidance, carry on a treatment program at home. First offer these guidelines which will enable the parents to expand their child's experiences:

1. Tell the parents to allow the child to move about in his own way whether it's creeping, crawling or walking. If he can push something ahead of him, a small walker might be helpful.

2. If the child has one good hand and one bad hand, caution the parents against forcing him to use the bad hand. His bad hand will be the helping hand as he grows older. Advise them to give him large blocks or balls that require both hands. He should be encouraged to use both hands in functional activities, so he doesn't forget that he has two hands.

3. Suggest providing plenty of toys and objects to play with and examine. If he can't explore his world, tell the parents to bring many different objects to him, and to name the objects and help him to feel, taste, and bite them as he would if he could move easily.

4. Recommend placing the child in different positions. Even if he doesn't like to lie on his stomach, he should have that experience. It's not good for him to lie always on his back looking up at the ceiling. If the child can't sit by himself, advise the parents to prop him up with pillows or place him in an infant seat, making sure that he can't topple sideways. Even if he's "floppy," being propped in a seat will not affect his back.

5. Stress the need to expose the child to as many sensory experiences as possible both indoors and out. For example, he should be

permitted to see, feel and smell raw foods, hear their names, and watch them being cooked.

6. Ask the parents to pronounce words slowly and distinctly and to encourage the child to repeat the names of objects. Discourage sign language.

7. Let the parents realize the importance of giving their child a chance to do things for himself. If a toy is impossibly out of reach, tell them to move it close enough so he can move to get it himself. Instruct the parents to provide enough help to preclude constant failure, but to guard against preventing the child from achieving something on his own. Emphasize that they must let him learn how to amuse himself so he can develop self-reliance and a measure of independence and pride.

8. Caution against rushing him or impatience with his slowness in manipulating his body.

If the child is an athetoid, acquaint his parents with these techniques to aid development:

1. guiding their child's wavering hand to grasp a toy;

2. placing both of his hands on a ball and helping him to hold it and later, helping him throw it;

3. guiding his thrashing legs in a slow bicycling movement;

4. placing the child inside two automobile tires in a tailor-sitting position so he can learn to sit without being thrown off balance by involuntary movements;

5. guiding his hand to his mouth as he holds a cookie;

6. holding the child in an upright kneeling position in front of the sofa with a rolled-up towel under his ankles;

7. putting the child on his stomach, on a blanket on the floor, for 10-30 minutes daily. If his head control is poor, a parent should stay with him.

While you would not expect tranquilizers and neuromuscular relaxants to relieve spasticity, a mild tranquilizer may be of benefit. Anxiety seems to exaggerate rigidity and spasticity, and an antianxiety agent may be of value.

The physical problems of cerebral palsy are so severe that it is easy to overlook its grave psychological implications. The families need counseling and should be referred to resource agencies such as the Easter Seal Society or the United Cerebral Palsy Association which can help them through educational and recreational programs. A future article in Patient Care will offer help on counseling the families of these patients.

Seven Cost-Effective Models for Treating Spinal Cord Injuries

J. PAUL THOMAS

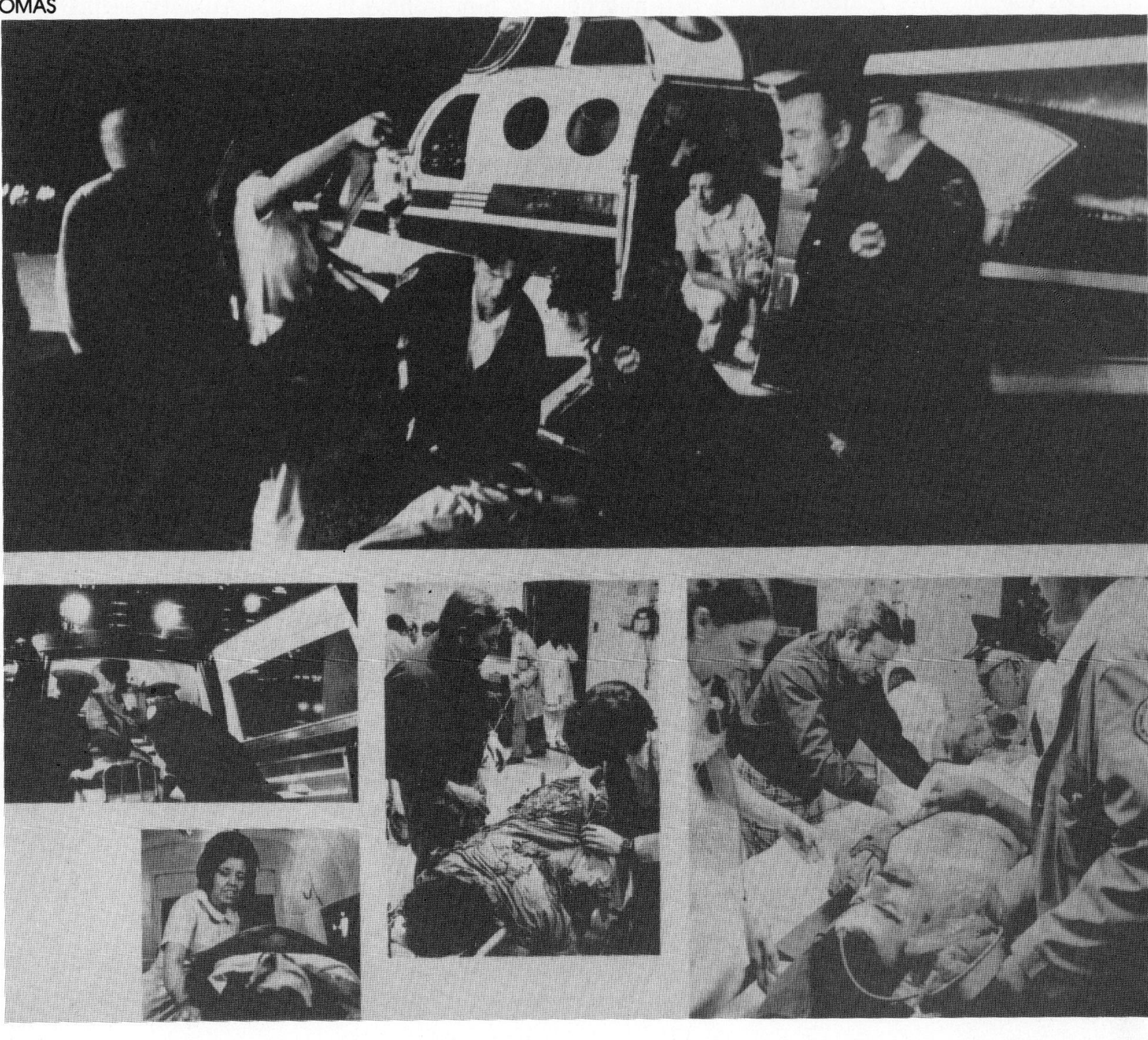

Rehabilitation has long recognized the significant economic and social impact made on society by patients with spinal cord lesions, especially when compared with other types of neurologic conditions. New spinal cord injuries (SCI) occur at an estimated 7,000 to 10,000 cases yearly. Annual mortality is estimated between 1,800 and 3,000 deaths, far below the 200,000 from stroke, but about equal to those of epilepsy, multiple sclerosis, and Parkinson's disease. Estimates of the total number of SCI cases in the U.S. are placed between 100,000 and 125,000. The annual cost of care is estimated at $2.4 billion; cost for all other neurologic conditions is much lower.

Several major reasons account for the apparent discrepancy between the relatively low number of cases and the high estimated cost of care.

Firstly, SCI occurs in a young population. In a survey of over 700 new patients at the Texas Institute for Rehabilitation and Research in Houston, the average age at onset was 25. Excluding industrial accidents, for which the average age was 40, the average is between 21 and 22 years. SRS research indicates 80 percent of SCI occurs in the 15 to 30 age range.

Secondly, patients with traumatic spinal cord lesions now live longer than previously. During WW I, the average life expectancy was 6 to 12 months postinjury. During WW II, the average was approximately 2 to 3 years postinjury. Presently, it is not significantly shortened in most patients who receive adequate care, such as that provided by SRS projects described later in this paper.

Thirdly, a spinal injury, particularly in the upper spine, is a severe catastrophic injury that affects most bodily organ systems, and it requires treatment and rehabilitation by a variety of specialists.

Also, over the last decade, several SCI programs have observed a change in the ratio of new paraplegics and quadriplegics (SCI categories) from 65 percent and 35 percent, respectively, to 50-50, and now many are experiencing 65 percent to 70 percent quadriplegics in their new patients.

Based upon an SRS-supported study conducted at Phoenix's Good Samaritan Hospital and on the expert opinion of insurance industry representatives, the lifetime costs of an average quadriplegic is $325,000 to $400,000. This figure is based upon an average age of 31 with an additional conservative life expectancy of 20 years or 50 percent of the normal additional life expectancy. (See table.) Because of lower costs for initial hospitalization, attendant care, and medical complications, the costs for a paraplegic are estimated to be $180,000 to $225,000.

Estimated Lifetime Costs For A Quadriplegic

Initial Hospitalization (240 days at $120 per day)	$ 28,800
Routine Maintenance ($200 per year for 20 years)	4,000
Hospitalization for Complications (60 days/year x $100 = $6,000 x 20 years)	120,000
Environmental Modifications	1,000
Lifetime Medical Costs	$153,800
Attendant Care ($6,000/year x 20 years)	120,000
Loss of Income ($6,000/year x 20 years)	120,000
Vocational Rehabilitation and Training	3,000
Total Costs	$396,800

SRS research projects have analyzed specific cost data for the various medical SCI complications. As examples, the closing and treatment of a decubitus ulcer (bed sore) averages $7,000; clearing a urinary infection, $4,000 to $6,000; kidney stones, $5,000, plus the possible loss of the kidney; and contracture deformities average $2,000 to correct.

Perhaps more important than the costs of disability is the loss of independence and the quality of living. Rehabilitation workers around the world have long recognized these patients as a special challenge to their professional capabilities, patience, and frustration tolerance. More than any other disability, spinal cord injuries cause catastrophic physical and psychological problems that augur rehabilitation failure. All too often, they spend months in hospitals, followed by the rest of their lives in nursing homes.

Generally, they are not rapidly referred for rehabilitation, many facility staffs are not experienced or equipped to handle them, and continuing medical complications prevent effective rehabilitation planning. Consequently, only a small number achieve the level of self-sufficiency, family participation, and vocational success that they should. As an example, very few cases are rehabilitated each year by the State-Federal rehabilitation program.

The Role of SRS

In 1967 and 1968, several experts testified before Congress for a national effort to improve and expand rehabilitation services to the spinal cord injured. Subsequently Congress directed SRS to study methods and alternatives of delivering the wide range of services needed. Several conferences of nationally recognized specialists were held. SRS research findings were evaluated and gaps were identified in the present service delivery system.

Consequently, SRS proposed a conceptual model to Congress, to other health research agencies, and to the rehabilitation field. It has gained international attention and recognition. The model provides for rapid case finding and referral, early rehabilitation coordinated by a highly sophisticated team, a mechanism to use all the necessary community agencies and services to facilitate rehabilitation success, and a long term community followup program to assure that gains and adjustments are maintained.

In June 1970, the Good Samaritan Hospital in Phoenix was awarded a research grant that brought together the resources of the Spinal Cord Injury Service of Good Samaritan, the Barrow Neurological Institute of St. Joseph's Hospital, the Arizona State University, the Arizona Division of Rehabilitation, and the air evacuation program of the Highway Patrol.

Since then, SRS has supported six additional model regional systems on a demonstration basis. Besides measuring and analyzing the effectiveness and costs of the model system approach, these projects also evaluate regional or local variations and modifications in SCI service delivery.

In addition to project funding, significant gains have been achieved by SRS in coordinating the total national effort of SCI rehabilitation. As examples, SRS and the National Institute for Neurological Diseases and Stroke (NINDS) collaborate in research project review and monitoring, information exchange, and program consultation. The award of four of the seven SRS grants has been to institutions that receive NINDS planning grants for Acute SCI Treatment Research Centers. Also, SRS works closely with the Veterans Administration SCI centers, Regional Medical Programs, and the Emergency Medical Services for HEW and DOT. From the nongovernmental sector, the National Paraplegia Foundation and Paralyzed American Veterans have been consulted.

The model system has the following five objectives:

2. CAUSES AND PREVENTIONS

■ To establish within a catchment area or region of natural patient flow, a multidisciplinary system of providing comprehensive rehabilitation services to meet needs from point of injury (emergency treatment and transportation) through acute care (rehabilitation, including vocational and educational preparation, community and job placement, and long-term followup);

■ To demonstrate and evaluate the benefits to persons served in regional systems and to determine their cost effectiveness;

■ To achieve new knowledge through research in reducing and treating SCI and its complications;

■ To demonstrate and evaluate the development and application of improved methods and equipment essential to the care, management, and rehabilitation of the SCI; and

■ To demonstrate methods of community outreach and education for the SCI in housing, transportation, recreation, employment, and other community activities.

Current Project Activities

The original Model Regional System at Good Samaritan Hospital is in its 4th grant year while the other six have about 18 months experience. All seven of the model regional systems are making excellent progress in meeting project objectives described above.

Of major significance has been the establishment of standardized data base. This joint data gathering allows standardization of nomenclature and definitions; specification of effective measures, patient variables, and cost benefits; and the development of a single computer program for identical statistical treatment and analysis.

Also coordination of all system components assures that areas of service from emergency evacuation through acute medical treatment and rehabilitation care are thoroughly meshed for rapid and efficient rehabilitation. To achieve project objectives, including the collection and analysis of specified data, each component of the system must be fully operational and coordinated with all other components. The existence of the service delivery model is basic to all project activities.

Aside from the basic project evaluation and systems analysis of medical, physical restorative, and psychosocial and vocational services, other activities include research, teaching and public education, prevention, and community advocacy.

Good Samaritan Hospital is a leader in SCI public education and teaching. Each year, many hundreds of hospital administrators, medical school and university officials, community and health service planners, and rehabilitation personnel gain

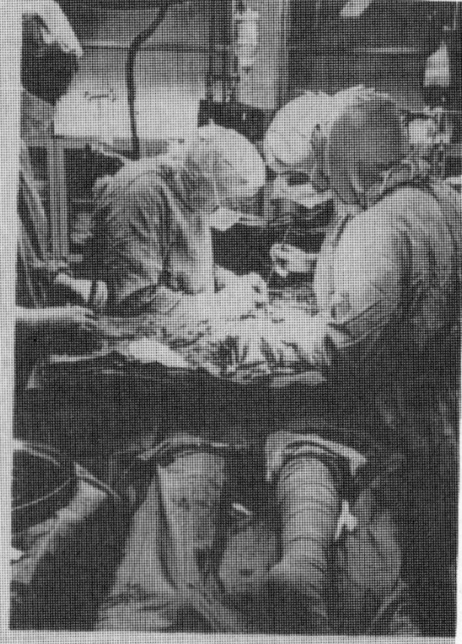

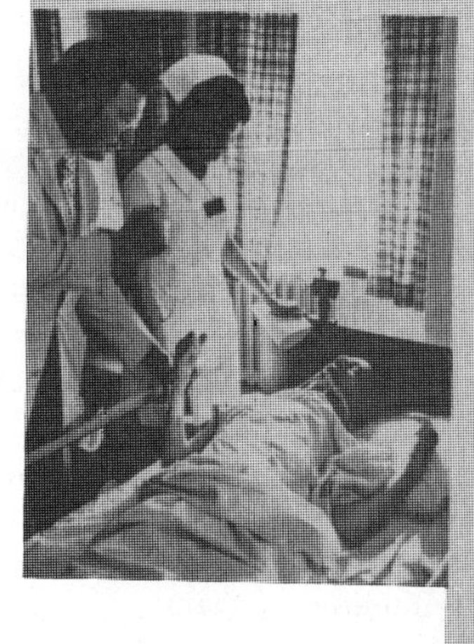

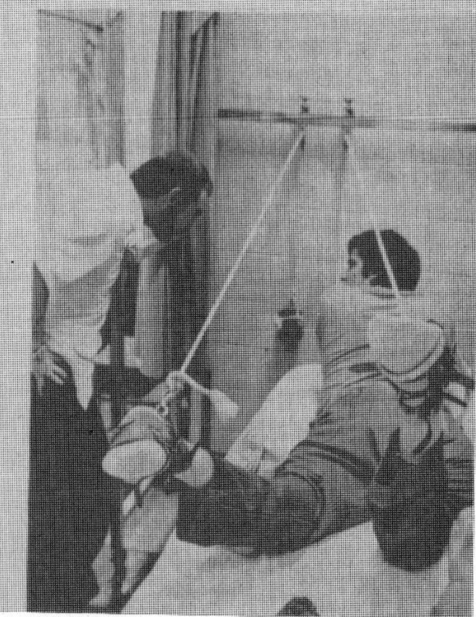

first hand knowledge at the hospital.

In October 1973, the International Conference on the Acute Management of Spinal Cord Injuries was hosted by the Good Samaritan staff and the Veterans Administration. Physicians from 14 countries observed the latest clinical techniques, many of which were developed through the combined research efforts of Good Samaritan and St. Joseph's Hospitals.

Project staff at the *University of Alabama* in Birmingham has developed innovative programs to meet local needs and conditions. A handbook, written by the nursing team, helps the patient learn self-care techniques. It describes and illustrates methods for performing -procedures in the home, utilizing equipment available to the patient and his family in this environment.

The center has conducted 1-day seminars for public health nurses from every county in Alabama. At the conclusion of the fourth and final seminar, 126 public health nurses had attended.

A home-health care team provides innovative followup services, in addition to gathering information on the adjustment and complications of patients. It has successfully placed into employment more than twice the cases previously rehabilitated.

Staff at the *Texas Institute for Rehabilitation and Research* (TIRR) in Houston report an increasing number of high-level spinal cord injuries (cervical vertebra 1, 2, and 3) with involvement of breathing mechanisms. According to Dr. R. E. Carter, Director of the Spinal Cord Center, there is a 2 to 1 admittance ratio of traumatic quadriplegic patients to paraplegic patients.

Because of the many respiratory quadriplegics at TIRR, a special research project is evaluating the use of electrical stimulation for electrophrenic respiration. In a patient with a high spinal cord injury above the third cervical vertebra, the phrenic nerves to the diaphragm which control the majority of respiration may be spared. About 20 years ago a method of stimulating the phrenic

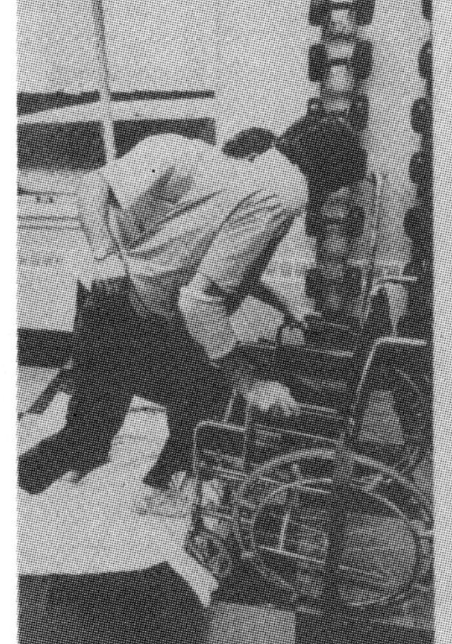
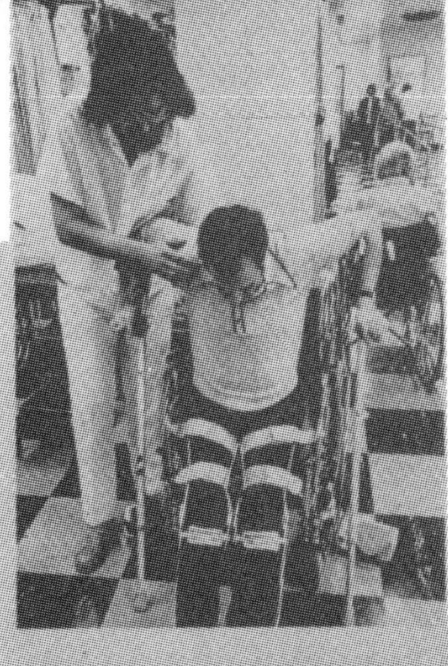
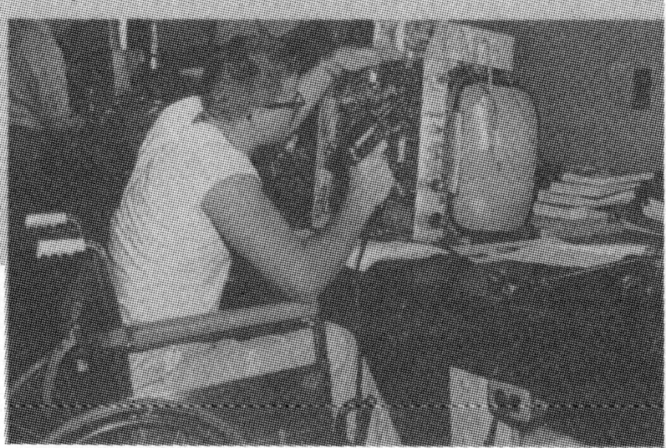

nerve was devised for polio patients. This technique has not always been successful with SCI patients. More recently, implanted electrodes, which are attached to a subcutaneous receiver, have been utilized with a transmitter placed over the skin. This allows the diaphragm to be paced.

Several patients have now received implants. One, a complete lesion injury at C 1-2, is able to breathe by means of an electrophrenic respirator, thus obviating the use of cumbersome breathing equipment. This has improved her mobility, and she has finished her 1st year of college, functioning well in a wheelchair.

Also at TIRR, alternatives to community living are being evaluated.

In New York at the *Institute of Rehabilitation Medicine* neuroelectric diagnosis is being investigated. Once perfected, the method should aid physicians in determining functional neuromuscular potential.

At the Virginia Model Regional System, which incorporates the *Woodrow Wilson Rehabilitation Center* and the *University of Virginia School of Medicine,* several research activities have been initiated. The IBM Corporation is cooperating in one project to train and place severely disabled persons in homebound employment as computer operators and programers. The project is developing improved services to the severely disabled.

First, training services are expanded to include the full range of occupations ranging from computer terminal operator to computer programer. Secondly, technical back-home assistance is provided the trained client to help assure his successful functioning as a homebound employee.

In another research area, the university hospital's Department of Orthopaedic Surgery is evaluating specially designed and implanted springs for spinal column fixation. This technique was introduced by Dr. Marian Weiss of Poland during an SRS-sponsored consultation. By implanting coil springs along both sides of the spinal column, fracture dislocations in the thoracic region appear to be reduced more quickly and effectively than by other surgical intervention. This enables the patient to enter therapy and gait training programs more quickly after injury, with fewer complications and less deconditioning.

In the psychological area, the *University of Washington* Model Regional System in Seattle continues to study behavior modification and operant conditioning techniques to control pain and behavior. To date, this behavioral approach promises to become an effective intervention to prevent dependency and withdrawal.

The *Northwestern University* Model System project staff in Chicago are conducting research similar to that at the University of Virginia. By combining the patient populations, a larger sample for clinical evaluation is possible. Its staff has also developed a special cervical spine fixation unit for application at the accident scene. It immobilizes neck fractures during extraction and transportation. The physicians have trained the ambulance attendants of the Illinois Emergency Medical Services Program in proper methods of evaluating, handling, and transporting spinal cord injury cases. More than 40 fixation units are being evaluated.

Preliminary Effectiveness Data

To date, very preliminary information has been collected by the several projects. Only the original model system in Phoenix has been collecting systems and cost data for 3½ years. Although the data is incomplete and should be considered tentative, there are identifiable trends in system effectiveness and cost benefits.

Data from the 1st year's experience of the six other projects appear to generally confirm the following:

■ Length of initial hospitalization and rehabilitation is averaging 101 days, opposed to 180 to 240 days in a nonsystem.

■ Costs for initial hospitalization and rehabilitation are averaging $11,000 compared to $18,000 to $28,000 for first hospitalization in a nonsystem.

■ More than half of the system patients are being admitted to acute care hospitals within 4 hours after injury.

■ More than half of new spinal cord injuries are of quadriplegic level. Many high level C1, C2, and C3 quadriplegics with total paralysis and respiratory dependence are living because of improved emergency care and transportation. This places new demands on service providers.

■ Forty-two percent of injuries are incomplete lesions with potential for some neurological recovery. Improved medical and surgical techniques are increasing functional recovery, at a saving of $150,000 per case.

■ The incidence is approximately 35 new cases each year per million population. Mortality rate is estimated at 10 percent within 1st 6 weeks postinjury.

■ Proper followup after rehabilitation can reduce annual medical costs of $4,000 to $6,000 to less than $1,000.

■ The VR rate and successful community adjustment can exceed 75 percent of all surviving SCI cases.

Collectively, these projects represent a most important research and demonstration effort by a federal agency in partnership with sophisticated private sector rehabilitation institutions. Their success can lead to the experience and know-how for developing a truly cost effective, beneficial service delivery program.

The baby who refused to die

**At birth she was too tiny, too young, too sick to survive.
Twelve weeks premature, she'd been hemorrhaging for hours
and was showing signs of hyaline membrane disease.
But I wanted to save her more than anything
I'd ever wanted in my life...**

by David M. Bell, M.D.

I am a pediatrician. I came by that title by the usual route: college, four years of medical school, and an internship and residency entirely devoted to the medical problems of children.

A major part of my training was in the intensive-care nursery for newborns in one of America's largest metropolitan hospitals. It prepared me technically for the hour-by-hour crises that are a way of life for any pediatrician, but it could not —and did not—prepare me for the joy and fear, exhaustion and conflicts that I experienced while I struggled to save my tiny patients.

At the time, I could not understand my feelings. It was not until a woman we'll call Mrs. Martin came into our hospital that I finally was able to face them. That was when I truly became a doctor.

Mrs. Martin was seven months into her pregnancy when she and her husband arrived in the emergency room. An examination showed her to be bleeding from the vagina, and she was immediately sent to the delivery floor, where she began having mild contractions. Soon she was in early labor, but still bleeding. Because I was the resident on duty in the nursery that evening, I was called to the delivery floor by the obstetricians. Pam, one of the hospital's best pediatric interns, came with me. We introduced ourselves to Mrs. Martin, telling her that we were the doctors who would be taking care of her baby if the premature labor could not be stopped. After talking with her and listening to the baby's heart, I collected a sample of the leaking blood, explaining that it would be tested to find out whether it was she or the baby who was bleeding.

"I have lost three children already," Mrs. Martin suddenly said as I was about to leave. I wondered why this information had not been on her chart, and asked what had happened. "I have had three miscarriages; only one was even five months along. We have been trying to have children for six years now." Mrs. Martin seemed embarrassed by her revelation. It was as if she were telling me a secret about her body's failure.

"We will do all we can to see that you have a healthy child this time," I said, adding as I left that I would be back after the results of the blood test were in. Pam and I walked slowly back to the nursery.

When I warned Alice, the night nurse, that we might be getting a $6\frac{1}{2}$-month preemie, her reaction was typical. "I forbid it," she said. "Go back upstairs and tell that baby to stop bleeding and to stop getting born." Alice always forbade babies from being born sick and at night, but it never seemed to do any good. She loved children, and knew more pediatrics than most specialists. In fact, Alice can look a day-old preemie right in the eye and say with all seriousness that he will be healthy until he is 18 months old— when he will get the chicken pox. If, heaven forbid, two sets of sick triplets should be born on the same night, I would want Alice to be on duty.

I took the blood to the lab, added some chemicals, and the shade of the blood changed. This was ominous, for it meant that it was the baby who was bleeding, not Mrs. Martin. Even if labor could be stopped, chances were that the baby would die of blood loss in the uterus. The baby could be saved only if he were delivered—but this infant would be 12 weeks premature, and children born this early have little chance of survival. However, unless both bleeding and labor were to stop naturally, there could be no choice. The baby would be arriving tonight.

I went back to the nursery and told Pam the results of the blood test. She moaned—another night of no sleep. (Nature's time clock and that of humans do not always jibe.) We assumed that the placenta had partially pulled off from the side of the womb, and that this was the cause of both the bleeding and labor.

Premature children present unique medical problems. Fetal age is determined by weeks, and a full-term normal baby is about 40 weeks old. Baby Martin would be only 28 weeks, more or less, and at that age his body organs still might be incapable of sustaining life. The child's lungs might not be developed enough to properly exchange air, his liver might be unable to cleanse toxic elements from his blood, and his defense against infection would be very poor. Only about 40 percent of the babies born at 28 weeks survive.

Pam and I spent the next two hours preparing for the birth of Baby Martin. In case the baby were in shock from blood loss and needed a transfusion, we obtained blood from the blood bank. We checked the emergency equipment on the delivery floor, making sure that the oxygen tanks were filled, the necessary drugs and equipment present, the two warmer tables in good condition, and that the EKG heart monitor and blood-pressure machines were working well. It was midnight by the time we finished.

I walked back to Mrs. Martin's room with the memory of her previous pregnancies weighing on my mind. She was in strong labor, but when I came in she sat up, anxious about what I would have to say. I explained as clearly as I could that it was the baby who was losing blood, and since there was no way that we could stop the bleeding, the child would have to be delivered—for both her sake and the baby's.

"Do babies born this early . . . do they live?" she asked.

I did not know how to answer her question. I wanted to say yes, that she would finally have a child after her years of trying, but I couldn't. "It is too early to tell whether your child will live," I said. "Less than half of all babies born this early survive. But we will do all we can."

She was stunned. For 6½ months she had been hoping for this baby, praying for a healthy child. Now she was facing tragedy, the same tragedy she had known three times before. She began to cry and I held her hand gently, saying I was sorry.

The call came about 2 A.M. Pam and I rushed to put on clean scrub suits and scour our hands and arms. In the delivery room, Mrs. Martin recognized us through our caps and masks.

While I waited, holding a sterile blanket for the baby, Pam went into the adjoining room to turn on the warmer and the other machines. Before long, a head appeared, then shoulders and arms, then a tiny female body, covered with amniotic fluid and blood. When the obstetrician sucked the mucus from her mouth, Baby Martin began to cry and move about, weak and a little pale, but alive and breathing. As I carried her to the infant room, I stopped at the head of the delivery table to show Mrs. Martin her newborn daughter.

The baby was breathing normally and was maintaining her body temperature on the warmer table. But her heart rate was too fast and her pressure ominously low because she'd been bleeding for so long. What she needed—and immediately—was a transfusion, so we gave her some packed red blood cells through a catheter placed in her umbilical vein. (To have cross-matched the blood accurately would have taken from one to two hours, and invited a risk of heart failure. We could only go ahead, hoping no severe problems would result.) After the transfusion, Baby Girl Martin seemed to look better. Carefully, we moved her warmer table down the hall toward the elevator and the nursery on the floor below.

When an infant is born at 28 weeks, lung tissue is barely formed. The little air sacs called alveoli, which exchange oxygen for carbon dioxide in the bloodstream, are present, but a chemical called surfactant, which holds these air sacs open, has often not developed. As a result, the alveoli collapse, and a thick membrane starts to grow over them, making the exchange of oxygen and gases treacherously difficult. This condition, called hyaline membrane disease, is the leading cause of death in premature infants. Only rarely will a 28-week preemie have manufactured enough surfactant to escape it. Yet this was our hope for Baby Girl Martin. The next six hours would tell us if it would come true.

By the time she was one-half-hour old, Baby Girl Martin was being welcomed to the nursery. Alice carefully picked her up, supporting her head and back with one hand, letting her tiny legs flop over her wrist, and placed her on the scale: about one pound, 11 ounces. At first, we did not speak while we worked, but as the minutes wore on, we began to look at the baby rather than the blood pressure or the EKG machines. What we saw was a beautiful human being—an almost perfect miniature with shiny pink skin covered with tiny white hairs. She wrinkled her nose and tried crying again.

"Does she have the 'disease'?" Alice asked casually.

"I don't know," I said. Alice's question made me lose count of the respirations, but they were about 40 or 50 a minute.

"She's a nice baby . . . sort of looks like a fish, Freddie the Fish." As Alice spoke, Baby Girl Martin pursed her tiny lips and blinked her eyes—looking remarkably like a fish.

"Okay, Freddie the Fish Martin it is," I said, as I gently felt for her liver and kidneys.

"But I wouldn't spell that with an 'F,'" Alice replied. "With a 'Ph' instead."

"Okay, Phreddie Martin, welcome to our nursery." I laughed. Now that we'd given the baby a name, she was a real person.

When Phreddie Martin was about an hour old, she started showing the first signs of hyaline membrane disease. Her nose flared, and she began to breathe a little more rapidly. This meant her air sacs were beginning to close, and she was struggling to push air in and out. When the disease becomes severe, babies may be forced to breathe at a rate of 120 times a minute, eventually dying of exhaustion or asphyxiation. We took an X-ray, and from the cloudy picture we knew Baby Girl Martin would soon be fighting for her life.

In hyaline membrane disease, there is usually a steady deterioration for the first two days as the lungs struggle to exchange gases. If Phreddie worsened quickly she would die, but if she worsened slowly and survived the first critical stages of the disease, the membranes might recede and she might live. The stage was now set for one of the most dramatic struggles of modern medicine: getting a baby through the early, crucial hours of hyaline membrane disease.

After warming Phreddie's heel with a towel, we drew some blood for a blood-gas test, and I took it to our blood-gas machine—which is known hereabouts as Tillie the Terrible. Tillie may look like a machine to an outsider, but not to us who work with her. We know her for what she is: a Power in the hospital, a high-ranking member of the staff, someone to be treated with respect. Tonight I made an extra effort not to upset her when I woke her up. She would be my most important ally in the fight to save Phreddie Martin.

Tillie went into action. Her lights lit up and she informed me that the blood oxygen was a little low, but not low enough to begin giving a supplement. We still had time to think and prepare. Baby Girl Martin was alive and breathing, and she had the disease, but she was the first living child the Martins' had had. I was determined to keep their beautiful premature infant alive.

At 4 A.M. Baby Girl Martin was still holding her own. She was having some trouble pulling air into her lungs—with every breath you could see the faint outline of her ribs as she strained—but her skin was pink and she had the energy to move and cry and suck on a nipple.

Because our last blood-gas count was

even lower than the first, we decided it was time to place a plastic dome or "hood" with a hole cut in it over Phreddie's head. We could then add extra oxygen to the air she was breathing.

When I'd finished padding the neck hole with towels to prevent oxygen from escaping, I stood back to take a fresh look at Phreddie Martin. Her toes curled in a charming fashion; she was very, very tiny, but she was a little person just the same. Through the hood I saw her opening her eyes, looking anxious. At the end of each breath she gave a barely audible grunt; then she gathered all her strength and pulled in air. Her arms and legs lay still, outstretched on the table—a sure sign the effort of breathing was beginning to tire her.

Using a small syringe, I drew more blood from a catheter in the umbilical artery, and while Pam checked the blood for anemia, I did another blood-gas test. The oxygen in her blood was now up to 55 percent, just where we wanted it. The hood had helped. However, there was a negative sign too: The carbon-dioxide content was also going up, indicating that the hyaline membranes were sealing her air sacs closed.

The odds against Phreddie Martin had now fallen to about ten to one.

Death is part of my job; doctors see people die all the time, it is a fact of life. But it is one that I, at least, cannot yet take in stride. As a measure of self-protection, I tried to keep my distance and to stop hoping for the impossible. I told myself again and again that Phreddie was no more than a fetus, much too small to be human. If she died, she'd be just an anonymous abortion.

Barely one hour later, Baby Girl Martin was having to struggle for breath harder than before. But the changes were still coming slowly and I knew we should be thankful for that. She did look exhausted, though. When she breathed, you could clearly see all her ribs and her straining neck muscles. I knew it would not be long before she would need the help of a respirator. And

a preemie that has to go on the respirator at six hours of age does not have much chance of survival.

While Pam watched over Phreddie, I left the nursery to visit Mrs. Martin. She was asleep when I came in, but awoke as soon as I touched her on the arm.

"Is she alive?" Mrs. Martin asked.

"Yes, she's alive, but she's not doing very well." I went on to explain hyaline membrane disease as best I could, and to tell her that the baby would soon need the help of a machine to breathe. I was too tired, though, to explain things properly, and I could not bring myself to answer the questions Mrs. Martin could not bear to ask. We sat silently for a few moments.

"I will come back soon and we can talk more," I said. "We will do everything possible to save your daughter." At that moment, I wanted Phreddie Martin to live more than I ever wanted anything in the world before.

But things were not going well. Back in the nursery we could see it was time to get our tiny patient ready for the respirator. The machine would force oxygen into her lungs, and then through the hyaline membranes into her bloodstream, keeping her alive until she began healing by herself. The procedure

is a lot riskier than it sounds. Because it calls for high pressure, there is a constant risk of blowing out (called pneumothorax) the infant's lungs, and with a collapsed lung, a preemie as young and sick as Phreddie would surely die. Nonetheless, the respirator was her only hope.

Working slowly and carefully, Pam placed a very small tube in the baby's trachea (the windpipe, which connects to the lungs). The respirator was then attached and the tube taped to Phreddie's mouth. At first, she began to suck on it a little, but it was uncomfortable, and although the machine pushed in a breath every few seconds, the baby did not understand that she could relax and let it breathe for her. Instead, she

fought the tube, trying to breathe by herself. We were worried. If Phreddie were to try breathing out when the machine pushed in, her lungs could burst. To prevent this, we gave her a large shot of morphine, a purposeful overdose which knocked her out completely. Finally, a drugged and motionless Phreddie stopped fighting.

After taking a new blood-gas measurement, we set the respirator's dials to deliver the proper amount of oxygen at the proper amount of pressure. The latter setting was critical, for it determined how much oxygen would pass into the bloodstream. We were now at a pressure of six, with the oxygen content at 40 percent. As the disease worsened, we would have to raise the levels of both pressure and oxygen again and again to keep her alive.

After another blood test, we took an X-ray, administered a small transfusion to replace the blood we had been taking for our tests, and sent a blood sample to the biochemistry lab to check for jaundice. The dawn's light was coming into the nursery and I needed some coffee badly.

By seven in the morning, Baby Girl Martin was no better. She was now five hours old, and as I watched her lying limp on the warmer table, I asked myself why we were working so hard on a baby who was going to die. I really could not answer my own question. Probably if I'd not been so exhausted, I would never have asked it at all.

When Emily and Steve, the resident and intern who would relieve Pam and me later in the day, came in, I introduced them to Phreddie. I had had to raise the pressure to seven, but I reported that so far, there did not seem to be any major complications—aside from the probably fatal disease in her lungs. At that point, I was so sure Phreddie was going to die that I couldn't bear to look at her as I talked.

Brief Reports

Predictive Value of Infant Intelligence Scales with Multiply Handicapped Children

Rebecca F. DuBose
George Peabody College for Teachers

The predictive value of infant intelligence scales with multiply handicapped children was investigated through the administration of a mental measure on two occasions to 28 children, divided into two age groups. A Pearson product-moment correlation coefficient of .69 ($p < .001$) was obtained for the younger group and .83 ($p < .001$) for the older group. When subjects were divided according to IQ level, a nonsignificant correlation coefficient was obtained for the high-IQ group and a significant correlation ($r = .81$, $p < .001$) for the low-IQ group. These results indicated that infant intelligence tests are highly reliable predictors of later intellectual development when given to a population of multiply handicapped children.

While tests of infant development are notoriously poor predictors of later intellectual functioning in nonretarded populations (Bayley, 1970; Goffeney, Henderson, & Butler, 1971), a number of researchers have recognized their value with severely delayed children (Cavanaugh, Cohen, Dunphy, Ringwall, & Goldberg, 1957; Erickson, Johnson, & Campbell, 1970; Illingsworth, 1961; Werner, Honzik, & Smith, 1968). Illingsworth, for example, kept records of 122 infants who were labeled as mentally retarded after rough developmental assessments during well-baby examinations, although they did not possess obvious characteristics associated with mental retardation. One year later, 75 percent of the children performed on a retarded level. Using the Bayley Scales of Infant Development, VanderVeer and Schweid (1974) identified 23 children (ranging in age from 18 to 30 months) as retarded. When tested 1 to 3 years later, 75 percent of the 15 infants initially found to be in the moderately to profoundly retarded range remained in that category. None of the children initially identified as retarded were ''normal'' at the later testing. These results suggest that infant intelligence tests can be useful in predicting later developmental functioning when mental retardation is suspected.

Predicting the course of development in severely retarded children will become increasingly important as mandatory education laws bring these children into the public-education classrooms. Long-term plans are essential if local, state, and federal funds are to be used to cover educational costs. If these youngsters are to be served, then guidelines to plan short-term intervention strategies are needed. Determining where to begin and what objectives to set requires some form of assessment. Assessment should include a battery of tests covering every facet of information needed for planning the youngster's educational program. Some form of a valid and reliable mental measure should be included in the battery.

Additional sensory and physical impairments cause many of these children to be considered untestable (Dodrill, Macfarlane, & Boyd, 1974). Kiernan and DuBose (1974) found that severely and profoundly impaired, including deaf–blind, children can be assessed using infant scales with slight adaptations in the presentation of items. If scales of early mental development are found to be reliable predictors of later development in severely handicapped children, then data can be provided for preparing immediate and long-term goals. The present study was designed to investigate the predictive value of infant intelligence tests when given to deaf–blind–retarded youngsters.

Subjects were 28 (17 males, 11 females) multiply handicapped children evaluated over a 5-year period by members of a diagnostic team from George Peabody College for Teachers. Each subject was evaluated at least twice as a part of a comprehensive psychological–educational assessment. All but 5 subjects had an etiology of rubella syndrome with significant auditory and visual impairments. Of the other 5 subjects, 2 had myleomemingoceles, and 3 had chromosomal abnormalities of unknown origin. All but 2 subjects were nonverbal; however, those two had significant hearing deficits and could not be tested as though they were hearing children. The mean chronological age (CA) at the time of first testing was 72 months (range 32 to 117) and 104 months (range 63 to 135) on the second testing.

Examiners administered the Infant Intelligence Scale (Cattell, 1940), the Mental Scale of the Bayley Scales of Infant Development (Bayley, 1969), or the Merrill–Palmer Scale of Mental Tests (Stutsman, 1948) based on each child's suspected impairments and abilities. These three instruments are heavily loaded with performance tasks and require very little usable vision. When needed, signs and gestures were substituted for oral instructions. Totally blind youngsters were permitted to feel a model before being requested to replicate the model.

The age and estimated ability of each child was the major factor in test selection. The Merrill–Palmer was given to all children estimated to have skills on at least an 18-month level. For subjects below this estimated ability, the Bayley or Cattell was selected. Where possible, mental ages (MAs) and IQs were determined using scaled norms in the manual of each test. In cases where CAs exceeded norms, it was necessary to arrive at an MA score and to then convert this to a ratio IQ, a procedure which unfortunately introduces unknown sources of error.

A mean of 29 months elapsed between first and second testings. During the intervening period, all subjects were enrolled in educational programs. Six were enrolled in full-time residential programs, and the remaining 22 subjects participated in self-contained special-education classes in their home communities.

A total of 28 children were given the same mental measure on two occasions. Table 1 presents the means and standard deviations (SDs) of the test results. Pearson product-moment correlation coefficients were .69 ($p < .001$) for the younger group (mean CA = 51 months) and .83 ($p < .001$) for the older group (mean CA = 101 months). For the group as a whole, the mean MA on initial testing was 29 months; on the second testing, 36 months.

TABLE 1
IQ Means and Standard Deviations (SDs) on Testing Occasions for Younger and Older Groups

Group[a]	First testing		Second testing	
	Mean	SD	Mean	SD
Younger	34	15	30	15
Older	43	23	39	20

[a] $N = 14$ in each group.

Table 2 presents the means and SDs for the two groups when divided according to IQ level. The Pearson product-moment correlation for the high-IQ group was .44 ($p > .05$) and .81 ($p < .001$) for the low-IQ group. This finding suggests considerably greater stability for the low-IQ group.

TABLE 2
Means and Standard Deviations (SDs) on both Testing Occasions for High- and Low-IQ Groups

Group[a]	First testing		Second testing	
	Mean	SD	Mean	SD
High IQ	55	11	46	15
Low IQ	21	10	23	12

[a] $N = 14$ in each group.

The results of this study strongly support the findings of Illingsworth (1961) and VanderVeer and Schweid (1974) concerning the utility of infant intelligence tests in predicting later mental development in severely handicapped children. All children labeled as retarded on the first testing were also found to be retarded on the second testing occasion. Only one child found to be severely or profoundly retarded on the first testing occasion was found to be above that range on the second occasion. Two children thought to be only moderately retarded on the basis of the first test fell in the severely retarded range at the later testing. Of all the children tested, 81 percent remained in the retardation classification range of their first evaluation. With this group, which ranged in age from 2.5 to 9.5 years at first testing, CA was unrelated to predictability of IQs.

The finding that the low-IQ children were more stable than the high-IQ children deserves further attention. A few extreme differences were noted (-25, -28, -23) upon closer examination of individual scores. Several explanations are offered. In testing very young children with known sensory deficits, particularly deaf–blind individuals, examiners are extremely careful to allow the benefit of any doubt. Perhaps this occurred more frequently on the first testing occasion. Certainly the test demands at higher levels became more strenuous, requiring a substantial language base in contrast to the sensory motor schemas dominating tests at earlier levels. The higher scoring abilities were apparently more variable and thus more difficult to assess accurately. These results indicate a need for an expanded study using a larger subject pool so that test predictions for high- and low-IQ groups can be compared under more favorable conditions.

In conclusion, results of this study have shown that infant intelligence tests are highly reliable predictors of later intellectual development when given to a population of older multiply handicapped retarded children. These findings are in no way generalizable to all infant intelligence scales or to other populations; however, the results offer strong support for previous findings of the predictive value of infant developmental tests with severely handicapped children. It is recognized that these youngsters will make only minimal gains even in excellent educational programs; therefore, scores will remain predictably stable and can be reliably included in the planning for their immediate and future needs.

FOCUS...

ETIOLOGY OF VARIOUS

PHYSICAL HANDICAPS

TYPES OF PHYSICAL HANDICAPS	CAUSES	PREVENTION
POLIOMYELITIS (Infantile Paralysis)	Virus infection which attacks gray matter of the spinal cord causing paralysis.	Salk vaccine
HEMOPHILIA (Bleeders Disease)	Congenital hereditary defect of blood coagulation found almost entirely in males with females as carriers.	Currently no cure or prevention.
ARTHRITIS	No demonstrated cause . . . A slowly progressive disease causing pain, and swelling in joints of the body.	Currently no cure or prevention.
MUSCULAR DYSTROPHY	Inherited progressive disease of voluntary muscles, such as the arm, thigh and calf. Muscle fibers are replaced by fatty tissue resulting in weakness of muscles.	Children affected rarely live to adulthood.
(A) CHILDHOOD	Begins around age of 3 . . . with false enlargement of muscles due to fatty tissue accumulation.	
(B) JUVENILE	Begins in childhood with slow wasting of muscles in the shoulder girdle affecting the use of the legs.	
(C) FACIO-SCAPULO-HUMERAL	Weakening begins in childhood or early adult life, with gradual loss of control of facial muscles, the shoulder blade muscles, and the muscles of the upper arm.	In all cases disuse of muscles will speed deterioration.
RHEUMATIC FEVER	Inflammation of the heart, joints, brain, or all of these . . . sometimes followed by streptococcus infection of the throat or scarlet fever.	Complete recovery with little heart damage.
DIABETES	Hereditary metabolic disturbance wherein the liver is unable to utilize and properly store body sugar.	Controlled diet with periodic injections of insulin.
NEPHOSIS (Bright's Disease)	Disturbance of kidney function of renal tubes.	Prolonged medical treatment.

PHYSICAL HANDICAPS

TYPES OF PHYSICAL HANDICAPS	CAUSES	PREVENTION
CYSTIC FIBROSIS	Inherited disorder of the pancreas causing a chronic infection of the lungs.	Few children survive beyond adolescence.
ASTHMA	Disease of the bronchial tubes of the lungs marked by attacks of difficult breathing caused by allergies.	Medical treatment.
TUBERCULOSIS	Exposure to tubercle bacillus. . . affecting the lungs most commonly.	Medical treatment through drugs such as streptomycin, paraaminso-salicylic acid, cycloserine and insoniazid.

NEUROLOGICAL FACTORS . . .	CAUSES	PREVENTION
CEREBRAL PALSY Prenatal conditions:	May be caused by conditions of prenatal anoxia, from premature separation of the placenta, severe anemia in the mother, serious heart condition or shock, also metabolic disturbances. Perinatal conditions: Injury at birth . . . with difficulties with the cord and placenta which reduce oxygen supply causing anoxia. Postnatal conditions: Childhood diseases such as meningitis, encephalitis, influenza, possibly high fever of typhoid, diphtheria, and pertussis. Other causes include injuries from accidents, toxic poisoning from lead, anoxia, carbon monoxide or strangulation.	Medical, educational and therapeutic treatment in varying combinations according to severity of handicapping condition.

ENROLL IN WORK STUDY (Take extra turn.)
SPECIALIZED TRAINING APPROVED
GOOD PERFORMANCE RATING (Pick up salary bonus.)
HANDICAPPED PARKING
EARN 4 COLLEGE CREDITS
GO BACK 2 SPACES
ADVANCE TO BONUS
CHANGE CAREER
ADVANCE 5 SPACES
COMPLETE APPRENTICESHIP (Pick up salary bonus.)
OPPORTUNITY KNOCKS
HANDICAPPED PARKING
PARKING
HANDICAPPED PARKING

Educational and Occupational Services

The education of physically handicapped children is not as "special" as is the education of other exceptional children from the standpoint of academic alterations. The provisions which must be made within the school system are of a physical nature, alloting for the difficulty in modality. The child who is crippled by muscular dystrophy, for example, is not necessarily affected in the way he learns. Although, he may have psychological and emotional problems to deal with, derived from the physical handicap, the learning process involved in academic areas is basically the same as a non-crippled child. This is not to say that all physically handicapped children are not in need of any type of remedial instruction.

Often due to physical limitations, sensory defects, intellectual limitations, and varied psychological disabilities, a number of physically handicapped children are educationally retarded. Special equipment, coupled with appropriate techniques and a specialized staff, are often necessary for effective educational programs to exist.

As todays society begins to recognize the virtually untapped potential of our physically handicapped population, current occupational services will improve. Repeatedly demonstrated as efficient, dedicated employees, the physically handicapped in today's world allowed the chance to take part in employment situations, can contribute much to our society. Open minds and a change in attitudes, can open this door.

ENLARGING THE CIRCLE
The Parent-Infant Program at United Cerebral Palsy

BERTA RAFAEL

Berta Rafael is Director of Early Education and Day Care at United Cerebral Palsy of New York City, Inc.

Carrying an infant for 9 months and then finding the baby develops differently from other infants is a frightening, lonely, and disheartening experience. Many parents report that no one will answer their many questions, because it is not always possible to diagnose atypical development in a young infant.

United Cerebral Palsy of New York City, Inc., in 1971, undertook the responsibility for providing services to parents of infants with atypical development. The Parent Infant Program was originally part of the Early Education Project partially funded by the Bureau of Education for the Handicapped Children's Early Education Assistance Act (Public Law 90–538). The purpose of the program was to provide the earliest possible educational services for those infants who are diagnosed or suspected of atypical development and the families of these infants.

The program was created because it was believed that:

1. The earlier intervention begins the greater the success in developing the child's maximal functioning.
2. Parents can become skilled in the management of their child through guidance and thereby contribute to the child's increased functioning.
3. Parents need to be educated toward a better understanding of the organic, psychological, genetic, and educational factors related to the handicap.
4. Parents need ongoing support toward coping with the shock, pain, and guilt, as well as the "aloneness" when first confronted with the fact that they have an impaired child.
5. The more guidelines parents receive in the education of their impaired child while young, the more accepting they become of the child's and their own needs.
6. Parents experience relief and hope when they are guided toward helping their child.

INFANTS

Infants are selected from those considered high risk or impaired, based on medical information and family history, and are accepted into the program from about 3 months to 2 years of age. Infants are grouped according to ability in groups of not more than four. Between the ages of 2 or 3 years the children are transferred into the nursery classes at United Cerebral Palsy or referred to another agency.

PARENTS

Admission is based on the commitment of one or both parents, or a substitute caregiver (this may be a grandparent, aunt, or guardian), to the philosophy of the program and to working within it. Parents must be willing to attend the program once or twice a week with their infant. At a preliminary screening interview, the social worker explains the program to parents, while other staff members observe and evaluate the infant's functioning. Thereafter, members of the team meet to discuss whether or not parents and child can benefit from the program. Admission is based on this decision.

The delivery system emphasizes the parent as the "learner and doer." This means that, in addition to observation, parents participate directly in all the activities related to their child's development.

STAFF

The staff members are, to a large measure, the special ingredients of the service delivery system. The best planned curriculum is of little value without a highly skilled and harmonious staff. Staff members are selected by the following criteria:

1. Individual expertise in their own discipline.
2. Willingness to work as part of a team.
3. Willingness and ability to share their own skills and knowledge with colleagues from other disciplines.
4. Ability to develop a framework which creates an atmosphere that supports growth.
5. Enthusiasm and ability to motivate parents.
6. Willingness to accept parental feelings even if they are hostile and angry.
7. Willingness to share with parents their knowledge about the learning and functioning of the infant and at the same time to learn from parents the many insights and skills that they have developed in the management of their child.
8. Ability to communicate, to explain, to give reason, to deal in specifics, and to stay away from ambiguities, sweeping generalizations, and stereotypes.
9. Patience and willingness to wait for success.

The staff at the United Cerebral Palsy Parent Infant Program consists of a physical therapist and/or occupational therapist, a speech therapist (who is also an expert in feeding techniques), an early childhood teacher, a psychologist, a social worker, and the director of early education. A medical consultant is available when needed.

ASSESSMENT

In order to develop an organized, appropriate, and yet flexible program for each infant, a careful assessment of the child's strengths and weaknesses is made by team members. This assessment is based on medical referral material and is made in consultation with each child's physician.

The assessment is carried out in the presence of the parents or designated substitute caregiver. Reports of home behavior are important components of the assessment. Based on the developmental status of the infant at the time of assessment, objectives are set and strategies developed to reach these objectives. The strategies form the curriculum for each child.

The objectives and strategies are based on fine task analysis so that success can easily be obtained. The joy and satisfaction of reaching an objective becomes the reinforcement for child, parents, and staff. When a set of objectives has been reached, a new one is developed. If an infant does not reach an objective as planned, a review is made to determine if (a) the objective was set incorrectly; (b) the strategies were at fault; (c) parental cooperation is missing; or (d) other variables, such as illness, interfered with achievement. New modified objectives and strategies are then developed with some of the possible reasons for failure in mind.

THE PROGRAM

The staff works in close harmony with the family to plan appropriate intervention techniques for each infant. They observe the rate and quality of the child's development and work toward normalization. The program is based on principles of child development, which include the belief that children learn through play. To facilitate this learning the environment is adapted to the physical needs of each child.

Physical Therapist's Role

Each staff member has a variety of responsibilities. The role of the physical therapist is to teach and share with staff and parents the physical management of the child. Parents are taught a variety of skills which include:

1. Lifting and carrying the baby.
2. Positioning the baby—prone, side lying, side sitting, and so forth.

3. EDUCATION

3. Achieving correct sitting, if possible (proper seat belts, foot rests, arm rests, special chairs).
4. Positioning for dressing (so the baby can see body parts being dressed and actually participate in the process).
5. Positioning for toileting (if ready).

Speech Therapist's Role

The speech therapist's role is to reach and share with all staff and parents skills such as:

1. *Feeding techniques:* Checks maturity and normalcy of the baby's sucking, biting, chewing, and swallowing functions. If necessary, normalizes oral functioning or recommends the next developmental stage, that is, weaning from nipple to cup or straw; progressing from strained foods to thicker textures, then to finger food, then to utensils.
2. *Vocalization:* Checks to see if baby is vocalizing. Is baby imitating sounds? differentiating sounds? babbling? If not, makes appropriate recommendations, including proper motivation or better positioning.
3. *Language development:* Teaches parents to speak to the baby appropriately (few words repeated often), and sees that the infant learns from himself out. Therefore, emphasis should proceed from body parts to familiar people and objects, action, and then descriptive words. The idea that an object is present and then may disappear and reappear is an important concept in language development, and parents are shown how to incorporate that into play with their child.

Teacher's Role

Teachers share with all staff and parents the concept that educational interventions are based on developmentally appropriate activities, with much care given to the right amount of stimulation. The teacher assists parents in establishing a trust relationship between themselves and their child through adequate cuddling, cooing, and comforting. This may be especially difficult when an infant is seriously impaired and therefore responds to affection in very limited ways. The teacher helps parents and other staff select appropriate toys, with emphasis on one toy or educational material at a time, and stresses focusing the child's attention on this material in order to provide a successful experience.

The most important area around which the teacher builds curriculum is the five senses or modalities. Two purposes are accomplished: first, evaluation of the efficiency of the child's senses; and second, use of all channels for learning. At the infant stage, unless we know for sure that the infant is blind or deaf or that the taste organs are impaired, we do not accept sensory loss as irreversible and therefore stimulate all senses. Such stimulation will lay the foundation for sensory motor, perceptual, and cognitive learning.

Social Worker's Role

Due to the isolation of most parents of young handicapped children, parent discussion groups have been developed under the leadership of a trained psychiatric social worker. In these group meetings parents can help each other by relating their own experiences, or they can turn to staff for education and support. Many parents find that their family and friends rarely recognize the suffering and pain experienced when first confronted with the awareness that they have an impaired infant. Support from the social worker and other parents will help develop the coping behavior necessary to bear such a burden.

The social worker also provides individual counseling as indicated. An important function of the social worker is to provide for interaction and liaison between hospitals, referral sources, other agencies, and all people involved in the child's care. The social worker assists the family members in their relationship to each other and to the handicapped child. He assists in obtaining equipment necessary for easier living, in finding more suitable housing, and many other needs of the family.

Psychologist's Role

The psychologist helps evaluate the infant's level of functioning through observation and the use of various screening inventories, such as the Denver Developmental Screening Test and the Bayley Infant Scale. Depending on the severity of the impairment, one of the many developmental checklists is used. The infants are periodically retested and reevaluated to help measure their progress. Emphasis is placed on the gains the infants make relative to their own rate of development. The psychologist works in cooperation with the teacher and assists in developing ongoing objectives and strategies to enhance the infant's cognitive, sensory, and perceptual-motor development.

Supportive counseling and guidance are also given to the parents to help them understand the expectations and limitations of their child's impairment. For example, many parents of Down's syndrome infants do not expect their children to learn at all and have to be convinced that learning is possible. Many parents progress and feel encouraged when this is pointed out to them.

The psychologist also helps the parents understand the effects of their behavior on the infant's development. Often the emotional interchange between parent and child is colored by the impact of the atypical development. Thus the parents may react with greater intensity, with more protection and less freedom for the infant, or they may react in a negative fashion, making undue demands or neglecting the child. Parents are made aware of the most productive way they can interact with their child and they are guided toward this end.

HOME VISITS

At the United Cerebral Palsy Center parents are guided in the management and education of their infant. They need to carry this learning into their home environment. To facilitate this, home visits are made by one or two of the team members. These staff members help parents with feeding, dressing, bathing, and toileting of the infant. They may make suggestions regarding toys, transportation, or positioning the child for participation in family activities. The home visit is also designed to assist parents in budgeting their time between the care of the handicapped infant and the needs of the rest of the family.

CONCLUDING COMMENTS

Overall, the Parent Infant Program is built on mutual respect among staff members and between staff and parents. Everyone appreciates the uniqueness of each child in all areas of development. An atmosphere of joy in achievement (however small) and focus on each child's success is maintained throughout the program.

Developing Daily Living Skills

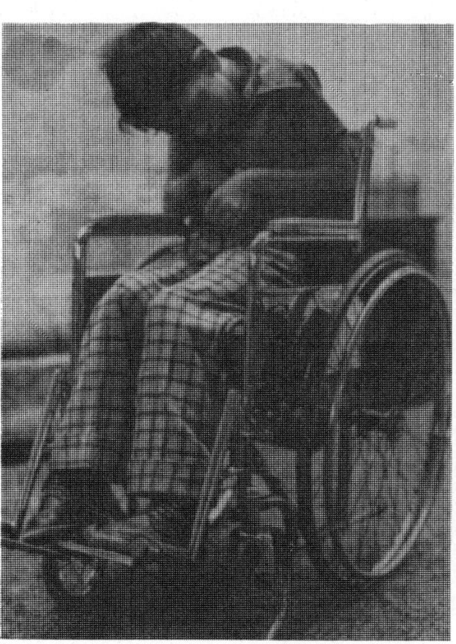

The accomplishment illustrated in these photographs took hard work and patience not only on David's part, but on that of his parents and others working with him.

Youngsters with disabilities, including those with a severe physical disability, like to be independent — as independent as possible in their ability to move about. The disabled child, his parents and his therapist can estimate how much time and effort will be necessary to enable a severely disabled child to accomplish certain objectives and self-help tasks.

Whether a child, his family and his therapist decide to make the necessary investment of hard labor to "develop the daily living skills" demonstrated in this article is an individual matter.

Our purpose here is to illustrate — with photographs by Tam Cherin — how one youngster with a severe physical disability learned to get out of his wheelchair and onto "regular" furniture by himself.

The Struggle of Accomplishment

The accomplishment illustrated in these photographs took hard work and patience not only on David's part, but on that of his parents and others working with him. It was not easy for David's parents to stand aside as he struggled to learn the step-by-step procedure necessary to get out of his wheelchair. It is very difficult to learn this skill.

David's self-esteem went up when he was finally able to do this by himself. In the process, however, he endured a great deal of frustration and some pain as well — he acquired a good many black and blue marks along the way.

Adaptations in Gear

Besides enlisting the patience and restraint of his parents, therapist and teachers helping him, David's effort required adaptations in his wheelchair. The brake had been rather hard to reach and awkwardly shaped so that it was difficult to grasp. This brake was extended with a piece of rigid plastic tubing covered with rubber hose to make it easier for David to reach.

At the beginning of his training David wore gloves with a special material on the palm. The material, dycem, is a non-slip plastic that helps solve problems of grasping. (Other similar materials have different trade names.) Although it was not required later on, dycem provided the increased friction David needed at first to get a hold of the brake handle. Once David mastered this part of the task, he no longer needed the gloves.

The seat belt on David's wheelchair was changed so that he could manage it himself. Velcro was substituted for the buckle-fastening method. Finally, the heel straps that held David's feet to the pedals of the wheelchair were removed.

Step-by-Step Procedure

The following step-by-step procedure was developed for getting in and out of the chair:
1. Lock the wheelchair.
2. Push the foot pedal up out of the way.
3. Undo the seatbelt.
4. Pivot the body. With the chair locked in place it could be used for support, especially on a carpeted floor.
5. Ease the body down to the floor. David at first wore a padded helmet to protect his head when he fell.
6. Crawl to destination.

David can now accomplish the tasks described and illustrated here in a minute and a half. It took almost a year of determined practice on his part, and patience and encouragement on the part of his teacher, therapist and parents.

We have not described all the specific details of David's training program. Individual parents and professionals can cooperate in developing — and revising as necessary — an effective program, taking into consideration the sensitivity, skill and endurance of everyone involved.

TEACHING HANDICAPPED CHILDREN —AND THEIR PARENTS

By ANDREW HAMILTON

When Belle Dubnoff taught junior high school in Pasadena, California, during the early 1940s, her attention was inevitably drawn to a dozen or so boys who plainly didn't fit in. Though their I.Q.'s were found to range from 90 to 135, they disrupted classes, casually took off from school with no explanation, and of course made poor grades.

"Let me put them all in one class and see what I can do with them," suggested Mrs. Dubnoff, a former San Francisco social worker with a degree in child psychology from the University of California, Berkeley.

"O.K.," said the principal wearily. "I'll be glad to have someone take them off *my* hands."

This special class of boys, ranging from 12 to 17 years of age, was assigned to a barren workshop. Mrs. Dubnoff decided that she first had to build a sense of mutual trust and acceptance, and toward that end she launched a series of free-wheeling open discussions. One of the by-products of these sessions was the revelation that in tune with those World War II days, all of these boys seemed to share a comsuming interest in aviation. So she promptly devised a curriculum centered around man in flight: progressing from the myth of Daedalus to the Wright brothers to Charles A. Lindbergh to the air armadas of World War II.

The effect, she recalls, was electric. Slow readers pored over sky adventures; haphazard spellers proved able to handle even the most complicated aviation terminology; those poor at math began to sharpen such skills so they could work from blueprints of model planes. Soon the class was even publishing its own newspaper.

"What we did," Mrs. Dubnoff says, "was to improve their self-image, in this case by capitalizing on their interests, and they responded magnificently."

In later years she heard from some of these so-called delinquents. One was on the staff of the Internal Revenue Service. Another had graduated from Princeton. A third was a member of the California State Department of Education.

Meanwhile Mrs. Dubnoff had gone further in her thinking about children who didn't fit the standard pattern. She became particularly interested in disoriented and handicapped children, and convinced that work with them should be launched at an early age. So in 1948 she started her own school, with three pupils. The first classroom was a spare bedroom in her home. As her "school" grew she found other space, for a time occupying an unused room in a nearby church.

And again she proved to herself that the "different" youngster need not be a failure: An eight-year-old mongoloid boy could not read or write, but was a whiz at recognizing every make and model of car on the street. Another was a seven-year-old brain-injured boy who couldn't make out street signs but always knew where he was "by the telephone wires—Did you ever notice they're all different?" A third was a five-year-old handicapped girl, so dehydrated at birth doctors did not expect her to live. With Mrs. Dubnoff's sympathetic understanding and teaching skills, all three graduated from high school.

Today, the nonprofit, nonsectarian Dubnoff Center for Child Development and Educational Therapy (located since 1962 in North Hollywood) has won a national reputation for aiding severely disturbed children and others with exceptional needs.

Support for its work has come from the U.S. Office of Education, the State of California, tuition fees, private donations, and a fund-raising foundation called Therapeutic Education and Child Health (TEACH).

"At times over the past quarter of a century, it was touch and go," says Mrs. Dubnoff, as slim and clear-eyed as when she was trying out for the U.S. Olympic swimming team four decades ago. "But now in our 25th year we're firmly established, though the tragic fact remains that we must turn away hundreds of children each year because there are not enough classrooms or scholarships available."

She takes both comfort and pride, however, in the proposition that the Dubnoff Center and others like it have enabled many children, who might otherwise have been institutionalized to be rehabilitated through specialized education in a day school setting. They have proved, she says, this basic point: "We can no longer put these children away. There are no more excuses. They are not impossible to teach   only *difficult* to teach."

Born Belle Wax in New York City, she came to Los Angeles at the age of eight, attended UCLA and later the University of California at Berkeley, and received her Master's degree from Whittier College in California. Then came a brief period of social work in San Francisco, two years in Russia doing psychological research on infants, followed by teaching in the public schools of Pasadena and Los Angeles.

During her lifetime, Mrs. Dubnoff points out, a virtual revolution has taken place in the handling of handicapped and disturbed children. Some methods have relied principally upon psychological and psychiatric approaches, some on chemotherapy techniques, some even on electric shock treatment. For her own part, she stresses two basic elements as essential to any effective program:

"First, the handicapped child should be identified as early as possible. We used to think of reaching the child by the age of six; now we are convinced that the first two or three years are the most important.

"Second, education is in many ways perhaps the most effective

"Teaching Handicapped Children and Their Parents," Andrew Hamilton, *American Education*, October, 1973. ©1973 U.S. Department of Health, Education and Welfare.

Mrs. Dubnoff (standing) finds that the enhancement of handicapped children's self images is vital to their educational development

therapeutic tool in the treatment of the handicapped. It teaches self-esteem and self-reliance like nothing else can."

Putting these points into practice, she says, requires close cooperation between school and parents. The first two years a child is enrolled in any Dubnoff program consist of classes for parents as well as for the children themselves—group meetings, films, discussions, observation periods.

"Teachers can do much for a child," she points out, "but the understanding and cooperation of both the father and mother is essential."

Recent research indicates that about one child in every ten suffers from learning disabilities. As defined in the Federal Education of the Handicapped Act, learning-disabled youngsters are those with "disorders in one or more of the basic psychological processes involved in understanding or in using language spoken or written," and they are characterized by "imperfect ability to listen, think, speak, read, write, spell, or do mathematical calculations."

Such are the children that the Dubnoff Center, licensed by the State of California, seeks to deal with. It enrolls 150 students (aged six months to 12 years) who are unable to function in a normal school environment—boys outnumbering girls five to

FOR HANDICAPPED CHILDREN AND THE LEARNING DISABLED, SAYS MRS. DUBNOFF, "THE FIRST THREE YEARS OF LIFE ARE EVEN MORE CRUCIAL IN ESTABLISHING MOTIVATION THAN THE FOURTH, FIFTH, OR SIXTH."

three and 90 percent of all students possessing speech difficulties. The teacher-pupil ratio is one to three, and the staff includes medical, psychological, and speech specialists. Children begin to learn by playing and enjoying themselves—and through such experiences acquiring the motivation to develop educational skills.

The basic unit of the Dubnoff Center operation is its Elementary Day School, where teachers and specialists provide programs for dysfunctioning children ranging in age from four to 12 years and heretofore considered "unteachable." One example: Debbie, a three-year-old with an I.Q. of 93 who had been dropped from Head Start and a private nursery school because of violently destructive behavior. For almost a year Dubnoff teachers worked with her before she began to blossom. But at age five she had stopped screaming and hitting, began to express herself, and increased her I.Q., Mrs. Dubnoff says, to 117.

Then there is a tutoring program for children at all grade levels in public or private schools who need special help during and outside regular class hours, which run from 9 a.m. to 2 p.m. Those with extremely difficult learning problems are taught in one-to-one or small group situations.

"As the saying goes, we win a lot, but we also lose a few," says Mrs. Dubnoff. "For example, there is 14-year-old Tony, one of the brightest, who simply can't learn to read in spite of our most heroic efforts."

A compensatory education nursery program begun in 1966 offers special education to 30 typically developing children from poverty areas. Supported by a grant from the State of California, it operates for two groups of 15 children, each on 3 1/2-hour-per-day sessions. In addition, it provides family assistance.

An experimental program launched in 1969 focuses on children diagnosed at birth or shortly thereafter as "high risk" infants. One child was so sensitive to being touched that she would try to "rub

off" a friendly pat on the cheek or an arm about her shoulder. Funded by a number of sources, including the U.S. Office of Education, the program "enrolls" 32 children ranging from newly born to five years of age. Its objective is to help parents understand this particular form of handicapping and successfully deal with it.

Another 1969 grant from the U.S. Office of Education provided funds to evaluate and create instructional materials for handicapped children in the three-to-five age bracket.

Out of this endeavor came what is called the "Learning Wall," a large acrylic fiber screen which, by means of rear projection, shows life-sized motion pictures or slides of scenes that provide a special kind of spark to the child's interests and imagination. Many shy, withdrawn youngsters have been coaxed out of their shells by the images they see on the Learning Wall. Hyperactive children have grown so interested they have learned to sit still instead of fidgeting and wiggling. One autistic youngster ran up and hit the Learning Wall. His teacher was delighted. "It's the first time he's reacted to *anything*," she said.

In all these various undertakings the staff seeks to maintain close relationships with other schools, health centers, welfare organizations, and other community groups. It offers teacher training to qualified college students who need experience in the classroom.

A visitor to the center quickly discovers that its programs are marked by considerable order and structure. "It is important that these children get a sense of stability," points out Mrs. Dubnoff. "They should know they will go to school every weekday morning, that the same teacher will be there, and that what they were working on yesterday can be finished today. Permanence gives them a sense of security."

The school also encourages its pupils to achieve a sense of identity. Upon entering the school some of them do not even know their names. Staff members thus make it a point to identify "Joe" or "Betty" or "Mark" repeatedly in conversation and games; their names and pictures are placed beside their "cubbies" where they hang their jackets; there are mirrors in the classrooms and the children are encouraged to inspect themselves from time to time. Since most of the children have perceptual-motor problems, they receive training in muscle coordination; and toward teaching them to get along with others, they play together, study together, and eat together. In these and other aspects of the program, however, the dominant theme is one of instilling in the children an appreciation of their own individual worth—of improving their self-images.

In addition to its teaching function, the Dubnoff Center serves as a research facility. It is associated with the Mental Retardation Clinic of Los Angeles' Childrens Hospital; the San Fernando Valley Community Health Center; the Center for Speech and Hearing and the Schools of Education and Social Work of the University of Southern California; Pacific Oaks College; Antioch West; and the California State Universities at Northridge and Los Angeles.

"Until recent years," Mrs. Dubnoff says, "the field of early learning has been neglected by many educators and psychologists because the child from birth to three years seemed too inaccessible. We now know this is not so, and that the first three years of life are even more crucial in establishing motivation than the fourth, fifth, or sixth."

She concedes that deprivation of stimulation in the early years can be compensated for and is not altogether irreversible. On the other hand, she says, experience has convinced her that *attitudes* on the part of children toward themselves and the learning experience are established early in life and probably cannot be reversed.

"What is most needed in families and schools," she says, "is not Band Aid remediation for disadvantaged children but a

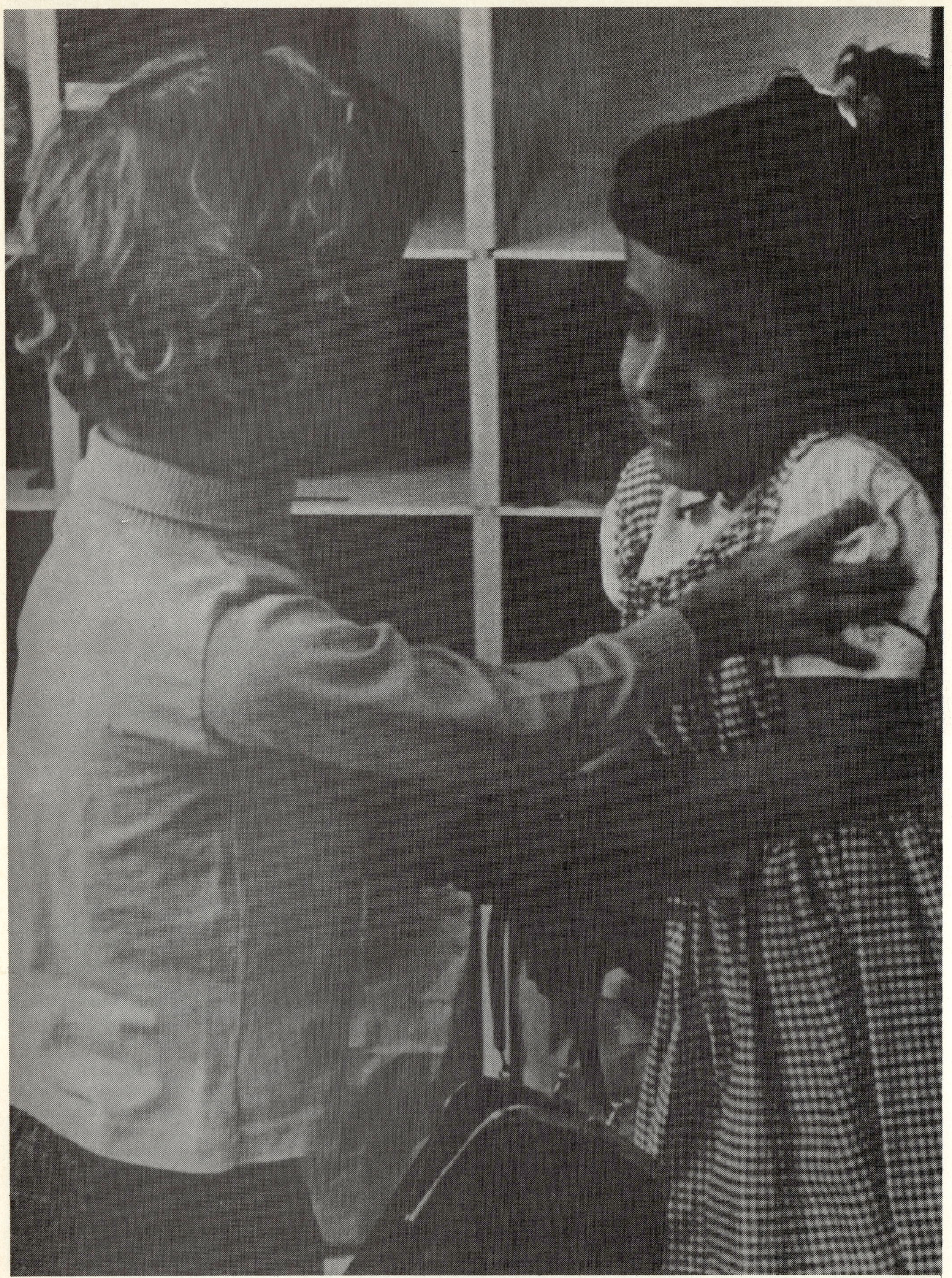

From learning how to enjoy themselves and play without aggression the children acquire motivation to develop educational skills

Perceptual motor coordination as well as considerable merriment is derived from participation in various playground activities

fundamental understanding of the problems and challenges and opportunities involved. Mothers can frequently become as effective, or even more effective, than professional educators in their interaction with children.

"Bringing up a so-called 'normal' child is difficult enough. But if a child has a handicap of any kind, many parents may get the feeling that the situation is beyond their control. The problem then may evolve a distressed child/perplexed mother syndrome. On top of the original handicap, emotional overlays may develop that may take years to strip away."

That this kind of thing need not happen is demonstrated, Mrs. Dubnoff says, by statistics showing that 60 percent of the 2,000 emotionally and physically handicapped alumni of the Dubnoff Elementary School have returned to public schools and are leading useful rewarding lives.

On the basis of justice and equity alone, she says, no child should be deprived of an education because of a handicap. But the issue, Belle Dubnoff insists, goes further than that:

"Helping these children realize their inherent potential is also important to society as a whole. They have much to contribute, if we in turn contribute patience and understanding and the particular kinds of educational opportunities that fit their particular needs."

Mr. Hamilton is a freelance writer in Los Angeles.

FOR MORE INFORMATION

More information on the work described in the foregoing article may be obtained by writing to Mrs. Belle Dubnoff, The Dubnoff Center for Child Development and Educational Therapy, 1526 Victory Place, North Hollywood, CA 91606.

r I Was Lost
eath my belt
omach was a stone
was the
hollow a lone.
Define
as they
poem:

What Every Child Needs to Know

By Susan Bookbinder

When meeting a disabled person, ordinary children can be so taken with the aids and appliances that they become insensitive to the person using the equipment.

Mainstreaming disabled children into the public school system will be successful only if all school personnel are fully committed to trying to meet the special needs of these special children. Federal and state regulations spell out the support systems that must be available to these children. We often overlook that understanding and commitment are required from the other children as well as from teachers and staff. Too often the children's questions, fears and concerns about disabilities are dismissed or ignored.

No educational plan for a disabled child can be effective if it takes place in an environment where he or she is separated from the other children by an invisible barrier of curiosity and fear. The right to learn in the "least restrictive environment" means more than simply the right to a formal education; it implies the right to participate in ordinary school life, to have friends and activities as nearly typical as possible.

A tremendous burden of responsibility is placed on ordinary school children to welcome and understand their disabled classmates, to make the

social aspect of mainstreaming work. However, rarely is a systematic program offered to help children handle such a responsibility. As a result disabled children often experience school as an unfriendly, lonely place or, worse, a place where they are teased or ignored by the other children.

Realizing this problem, Meeting Street School in East Providence, Rhode Island, has developed a curriculum for ordinary elementary school children that deals directly with their questions and concerns. This curriculum is based on the idea that when ordinary children understand the reasons, visible effects and consequences of disabilities, they will try to treat disabled children as they would anyone else.

Curriculum

The curriculum consists of eight two-hour sessions spread over a four-month period. Two sessions each are devoted to blindness, deafness, mental retardation and physical disabilities. For each of these disabilities the curriculum includes:
- simulation activities
- work with aids and appliances
- discussions with disabled adults
- movies, videotapes, slides, printed material
- group discussion

Simulation Activities

In the simulation activities the children, under guidance, pretend that they are disabled in one way or another. They are restricted in various ways so that they can feel the effects of having particular disabilities. For example, a child is blindfolded. She goes with her sighted guide to wash her hands. She comes back to her desk, unwraps a cupcake, pours herself a glass of juice, eats this snack and throws away the garbage. After all the children have participated in this experiment, they discuss how it felt to be blind and how it felt to be a helper.

In other sessions they try to understand a movie with the sound turned off — simulating deafness. They wear thick socks on their hands and try to tie their shoelaces and button up a shirt — simulating fine motor difficulties. They try to say nursery rhymes without moving their lips or tongues — simulating one effect of some forms of cerebral palsy. They walk around the room trying to hold up heavy sandbags — simulating the feeling of wearing braces or prosthetic devices.

After going through the 20 experiments in the curriculum, the children can understand why various disabled people walk, move, behave or communicate as they do. They appreciate that a person with a disability may feel just the way they do despite these differences.

Work with Aids and Appliances

The second aspect of the program is exposure to aids and appliances that people with disabilities might use. When meeting a disabled person, ordinary children can be so taken with the aids and appliances that they become insensitive to the person using the equipment. In this part of the curriculum the children are allowed to examine and use the equipment. They are encouraged to ask questions about why and how it is used. It is hoped that the children will become so familiar and comfortable with the special gear people with disabilities often depend on that when they meet a disabled person they will not be distracted from the person by the equipment.

In classroom demonstrations, the children learn to write in Braille, to use finger spelling and some sign language and to take care of hearing aids. They travel with a white cane; use wheelchairs, walkers and crutches; examine braces and artificial limbs; and work with physical therapy equipment. These and many other materials, all of which are borrowed from local agencies, are left in the classroom for the children to explore and use with their teachers over a period of several weeks.

Children who are exposed to aids and appliances in this way find them challenging and fascinating rather than strange. Instead of reacting to a person who uses such equipment with silent stares or derision, they are more likely to respond with acceptance and friendliness. They know that the equipment is not the person.

Discussion with Disabled Adults

Perhaps the most important part of the program is the opportunity for the children to meet and talk with disabled people. The curriculum includes four discussion sessions. In each session the principal speaker is a disabled adult who is comfortable with young children and their uninhibited questions. Disabled adults who can lead the discussion can be recruited through local chapters of such organizations as Easter Seals, United Cerebral Palsy, National Foundation for the Blind, Alexander Graham Bell Association for the Deaf and the National Association for Retarded Citizens. The speakers talk about their childhoods, families, interests, jobs, school experiences and other aspects of their lives.

We let the children know that it is permissible to ask questions. And children want to know everything: How did you realize you were blind? Why are your arms so skinny? Do you get lonely being deaf? Do you get mad that you're handicapped? Can you play ball? How do you take a bath? The questions are endless.

This is the first time that most of the children have talked freely with someone who has a disability. It is hoped that the quality of the experience as well as the substantive answers to their questions will influence their attitude toward other disabled people they may meet at school or in the community. The children in our programs, without exception, have been excited to meet the speakers and have responded to them with warmth and sensitivity.

Movies, Videotapes, Slides, Printed Material

Books, movies, slides, videotapes and pamphlets are made available so that the children can learn as much as possible about the nature of various disabilities during the course of the project. Many parents report that their children bring books and pamphlets home to share with their families and friends. National organizations can help locate and borrow materials that will help answer the children's questions about people with disabilities.

Group Discussion

Throughout the program, ample time is available for children to voice their questions and feelings to each other and to us. By making the workshops as warm, personal and accepting as possible, we hope to affect the whole feeling and emotional tone that the children will carry with them throughout their lives when they think about or actually deal with disabilities.

Staff

The success of the program depends upon the quality of the staff who run the sessions. At Meeting Street School we trained both teachers and volunteers, including parents, from the community. Staff training involved most of the techniques used with the children in the curriculum itself: simulation activities, the study of written and audiovisual material, discussions with disabled people and group discussion.

For more detailed information about staff selection and training or curriculum, write: Susan Bookbinder, Project Coordinator, Meeting Street School, 667 Waterman Avenue, East Providence, RI 02194.

Too often the children's questions, fears and concerns about disabilities are dismissed or ignored.

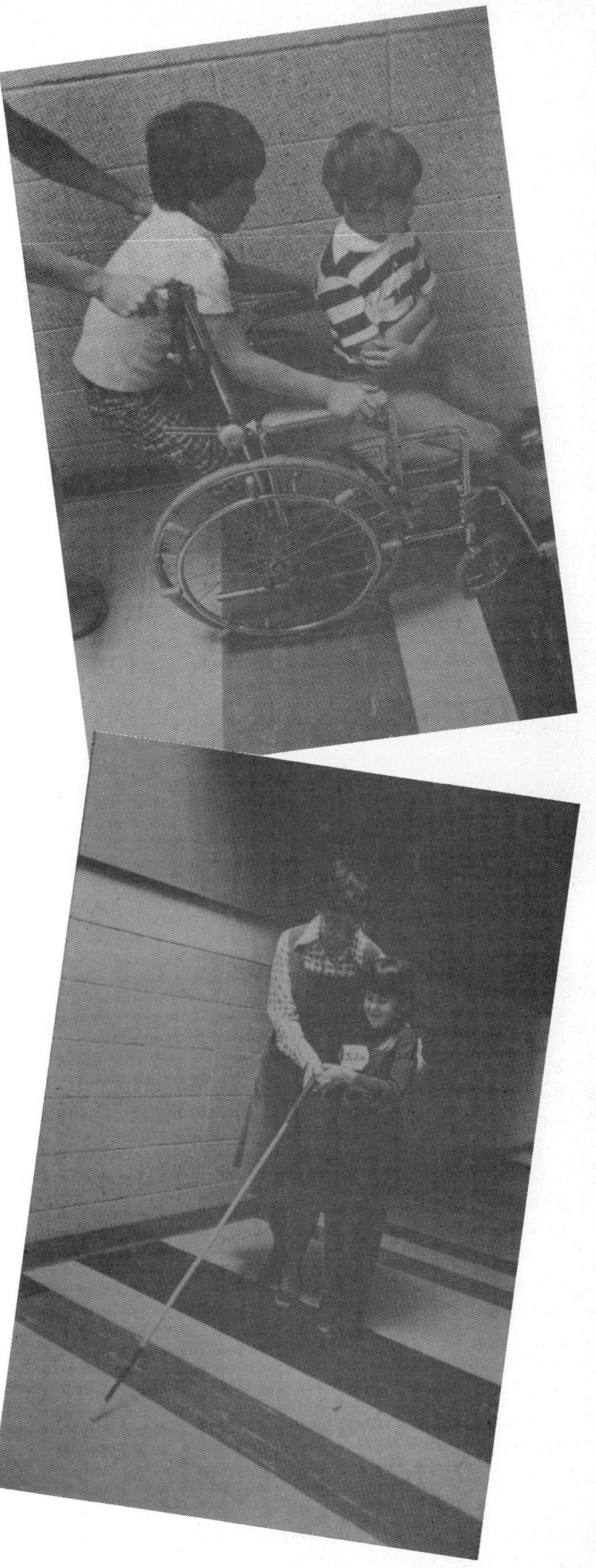

THELMA BOSTON Miracle Worker

Mrs. Boston had two dreams. One was to care for the children nobody else wanted, the other was to have a proper home for them. How she made her dreams come true is nothing short of magic.
By Mary G. Crawford

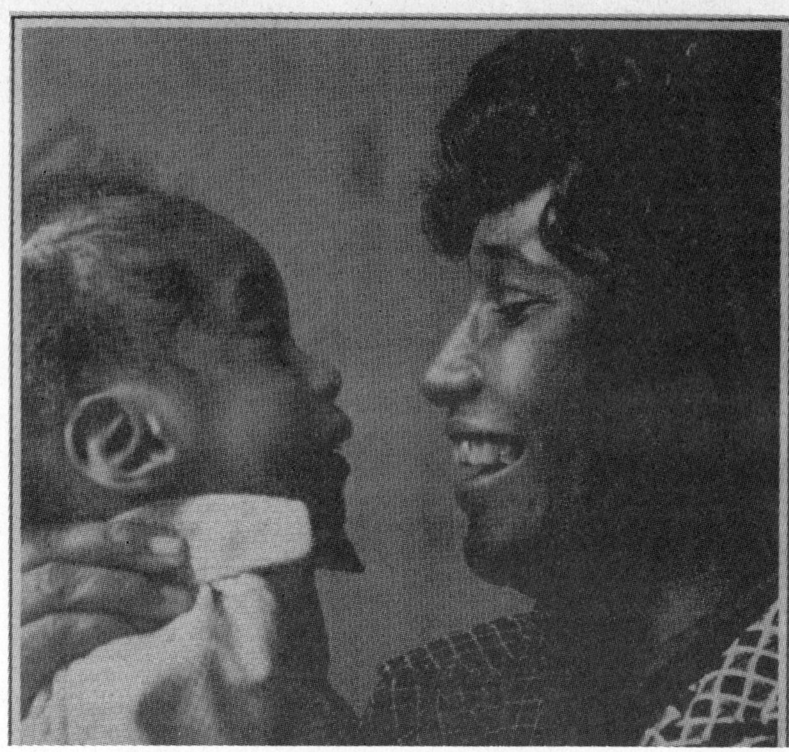

Prosperity Street is an unlikely place for a miracle. Ironically named, it wanders bleakly for three or four blocks through a shabby area in the Oak Cliff section of Dallas, Texas.

But at 2826 Prosperity, a miracle has indeed taken shape. It is a gleaming, 12-room, 3½-bath, one-story, red-brick home for handicapped foster children. It is, as far as anyone connected with the project can determine, the only such home in the nation which has been totally conceived, designed, constructed and equipped with privately donated materials, labor and money. No government funding whatsoever was used in the project.

The inspiration for this miracle is Thelma Boston, a 51-year-old black foster mother. Her foster children, numbering 13 at present, are the "throwaways"—the ones no one else wants. They are victims of child abuse, cerebral palsy, muscular dystrophy, mental retardation —the list is endless and tragic. They are all severely handicapped in mind or body or both. In the 11 years that Mrs. Boston has been a foster mother, she has cared for 85 children of all races and sizes, most of them handicapped. The present group (there are always children arriving and leaving) ranges in age and disability from Mike, an 18-year-old victim of muscular dystrophy who paints and plays the piano from his wheelchair, to two-year-old Kelly, a tiny girl whose brain damage is so severe that she is, virtually, a vegetable. Mrs. Boston showers them all with love, and most of them blossom under her care.

Before the new home was built, Mrs. Boston and her brood lived in a crumbling frame house, and existed on little more than the county's foster-child allowance.

The Dallas County allowance for handicapped foster children ranges from $172 to $195 a month per child, depending on the severity of each child's disability. This allowance is supposed to pay for everything except medical checkups and treatments and other expenses directly related to the children's handicaps—but the money is never quite enough. Mrs. Boston used to receive occasional donations of money and supplies from churches and individuals, but not on an organized or regular basis. As a result, Mrs. Boston often had to dig into her personal income from property rentals to pay for her children.

Mrs. Boston has had remarkable success with her multihandicapped group. For instance, when Kelly came home from a hospital stay in early 1973, the doctor told Thelma Boston that the baby probably would

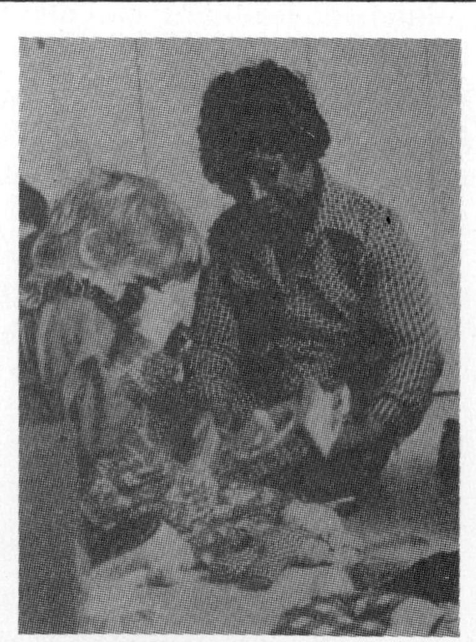

In the past 11 years, Mrs. Boston has taken care of more than 85 foster children.

not live more than two weeks. Two years later Kelly is still clinging to life. Although she cannot respond, she receives the same love and care as the others, and Mrs. Boston talks to her as though Kelly could hear and understand it all.

Then there's Billy, a ten-year-old boy. His mother had German measles when she was pregnant with him and as a result, he's retarded. He has a severe hearing loss, is blind in one eye and has only partial sight in the other. When Billy was brought to Mrs. Boston two and a half years ago, he could do little else but flop around on the floor, banging his head and screaming. At the time, the caseworkers told Mrs. Boston that he would have to be force-fed. "I just said, 'Yes, yes,' " she says. "Then when suppertime came, I made some gelatin dessert and then whipped it light and fluffy and put it in front of him. He picked up a spoon and ate it by himself." There is a note of quiet triumph in her voice.

Billy now scampers around the house with only a slight unsteadiness, and he is slowly learning the sign language of the deaf. He doesn't scream any more.

Eddie was discovered beaten and abandoned in a ditch in 1967. Blind and retarded, he is thought to be about 13 years old. When Eddie arrived at Mrs. Boston's home in early 1972, he would curl up in a ball in a corner and rock back and forth. When anyone tried to touch him, he would scream and bite. Eddie has changed from the frail, withdrawn, wild creature he was to a reasonably robust boy who feeds himself and finds his own way around the house.

Mrs. Boston's success is especially remarkable because she has had no formal training for her job. In fact, she has only a tenth-grade education. But her unique combination of instinct, love, common sense and optimism, to which the children respond, couldn't be taught in any school. She has taken several short training courses in physical therapy and care of handicapped children that are offered to foster parents. And a spokesman for the Dallas County Child Welfare Unit says she is one of their best, most conscientious foster mothers. One of Mrs. Boston's friends says proudly, "When Child Welfare has an impossible case, they send him to Thelma."

Thelma Boston did not plan to care for handicapped children when she entered the foster-parent program. In fact, she became part of the organization almost by accident. About 11 years ago, while visiting one of her daughters in a nearby neighborhood, she noticed a large number of children in the yard next door. "I asked my daughter where all those cute little kids came from," she says. "She told me it was a foster home. Then she asked me, 'You want some of those little kids, Mom?' " Mrs. Boston laughs heartily. "So I asked her how to join up." The Bostons' own eight children—five boys and three girls—were all grown.

The Bostons applied to the Child Welfare Unit and were accepted as foster parents in 1965. She had just resigned from 13 years of working as head cook in several large Dallas high schools, and her husband, Roosevelt, called "R.B.," operated a gas station.

Foster parenthood for the Bostons was fairly uneventful for the first couple of years. Then, in 1967, a child arrived who needed special help. Seven-month-old Shirley came to the couple with a clean bill of health from medical personnel. But she never cried, and that worried Mrs. Boston.

"She just lay there. Some days she was better, livelier, and some days she was worse. I knew something was wrong, so I started keeping a record of everything she ate and drank each day."

By trial and error Mrs. Boston gradually eliminated the foods from Shirley's diet which seemed to be causing the trouble. At the end of three weeks, she presented the doctor with a detailed analysis of Shirley's many food allergies and a much perkier Shirley.

After that, Child Welfare began sending Thelma Boston other children with handicaps, as well as normal children. "I had to spend so much time with the handicapped kids, it wasn't fair to the others," she recalls. "So I called up Welfare and told them they'd have to make a choice—to send me either *all* normal kids or *all* handicapped. They asked me which I wanted. I told them I wanted the ones no one else wanted." With that phone call, the Bostons' home became a warm haven for some of the most hopeless children in Dallas County.

In 1969, Mrs. Boston's husband, R.B., was shot to death by two gunmen during a holdup of his gas station. Alone, she immersed herself in caring for the children in her deteriorating little house.

Several weeks before Christmas, 1972, a Dallas television station broadcast a brief appeal for help in making Christmas brighter for Mrs. Boston's children. C.G. Barham, a 51-year-old painting contractor who is called "Slim" by friends, heard the appeal. "I figured they'd be getting a lot of stuff," he says in his Texas drawl, "so I didn't do anything about it right then. But a couple of days before Christmas I called Thelma Boston and asked if she had been offered enough to go around to all the kids. She said no one had offered anything."

Mr. Barham and his vivacious wife, Marilyn, called several friends. Together they collected enough new and almost-new clothes and toys to fill two large barrels. "Then we got a turkey, and we picked up some fruit, candy and nuts. I probably overdid it on the candy and stuff," he confesses, "but I kept thinking about those little kids."

On Christmas morning, the Barhams took their goodies to Mrs. Boston's house and spent the morning playing Santa Claus.

The Barhams appreciated Mrs. Boston's ability and devotion more than most parents because their own daughter, Judith Ann, had cerebral palsy for 12 agonizing years until her death six years ago. In a way their involvement in the project has become a kind of memorial to Judy.

Impressed by Mrs. Boston's sincerity, and appalled by the run-down condition of her surroundings, Mr. Barham resolved that Christmas Day to help her the best way he knew how. "Well, thunder," he exclaims, "I know a bunch of people in the construction business. I figured we ought to be able to fix her place up for her." So he set about rounding up help.

Before he had gotten very far along, he discovered that Mrs. Boston had been dreaming of a new, modern house for her children. Undaunted, he raised his sights and resolved to build that new home with the help of "a bunch of guys I know in the unions," and anyone else in the construction industry who would agree to help.

Beginning in April 1973, Mr. Barham went from office to office talking to contractors, distributors, suppliers, installers—anyone who had anything that could be used in the new house. When he wasn't out "asking," he was on the phone telling the story of Mrs. Boston and her children to anyone who'd listen.

Architectural and interior design plans, geared to the special needs of handicapped children, were donated through professional organizations. Bit by bit, concrete, electrical equipment, air conditioning and plumbing were given. Money also began to trickle in from businessmen, housewives, schoolchildren and clubs throughout the North Texas region. One woman who wished to remain anonymous sent $2,000 through her church.

As the donations continued to mount slowly, Mrs. Boston asked that a foundation be set up to handle donations, oversee the construction and operate the home. In the fall of 1973, the Thelma Boston Foundation for Handicapped Children came into being, chartered by the State of Texas and granted non-profit, tax-exempt status by the Internal Revenue Service. The site was prepared in February 1974; the home was completed and occupied Thanksgiving week, 1975.

The new home is worth about $200,000, according to Mr. Barham, not counting the special equipment. The air-conditioned building can house up to 16 children—with emergency space for four more.

For years, Mrs. Boston's only staff consisted of three relatives who offered regular, part-time assistance. There was also drop-in help from friends and other family members. Today, the staff consists of a cook, a secretary, and six child-care attendants working in shifts, so that Mrs. Boston has help 24 hours a day.

Operating the home is expected to cost $40,000 a year above the county allowance. As of this writing, the Dallas County Mental Health and Mental Retardation office and a few other organizations and individuals have pledged part of this amount for the first year of operation. The rest is expected to come in by way of small contributions throughout the year.

Watching Thelma Boston with her children is a real treat. She is constantly loving, encouraging, teaching—helping her children develop. Of medium height and build, she has an ageless, unlined face that glows from within. She seems tireless, although she hasn't had a vacation in six years.

Her day usually begins at 6 A.M. First, she looks in on the babies as the cook prepares breakfast. After waking the older children, she helps them dress, and serves them breakfast so that they will be ready for the school bus that takes them to classes at special schools. Then the children who don't attend classes are fed and dressed. The ones who can dress themselves are encouraged to do so.

She uses every opportunity to reinforce what the children are taught in school. For instance, Billy is learning sign language so Mrs. Boston pauses several times during the day to "talk" to him with her hands, urging him to repeat her "words" or to answer. Billy's school sends a sheet of instructions home with him, illustrating the words he has been learning.

Thelma Boston takes the children to their frequent medical-clinic visits herself and on the cook's day off, Mrs. Boston is back at a familiar job, preparing meals in the big, shiny kitchen.

With food prices skyrocketing, Mrs. Boston has had to pinch pennies in many ways: she makes "baby" food from the same foods everyone else eats by putting it in a blender; she buys surplus bread at a bakery, fresh fruits and vegetables at the city-run Farmers' Market, and canned goods in case lots from a wholesale grocery warehouse.

When "Slim" Barham visits, he is treated as a favorite uncle. He follows the progress of each child and checks the results of all tests and checkups. If a child must go into the the hospital, as they often do, he drops by to see him or her whenever possible.

Perhaps the two most outstanding characteristics shared by everyone involved in this project are humility and total lack of selfishness—everyone is always eager to point out someone else's generosity, while taking little personal credit.

To Mrs. Boston, the home is a dream come true. "It's just gorgeous," she says with a happy smile. "It's just about like I dreamed it would be." But her delight in the new home and her staff of helpers stems mainly from the fact that they enable her to spend more time with her children—these children that no one else wants.

Working with severely handicapped children would depress most people—not Thelma Boston. "This is something that really has to be done," she says thoughtfully. "I feel like I'm doing a *real* job. Sometimes I work with a child four or five months before they even realize they're supposed to smile. And when they smile at me, it makes it all worth it." That's Thelma Boston's own miracle on Prosperity Street.

All of the children's names used in the story have been changed for their protection. For further information about the Thelma Boston Foundation for Handicapped Children, write to: 2826 Prosperity Street, Dallas, Texas 75216.

YOU CAN GET...
•THERE——FROM——HERE •

Signing car to a deaf student at a street crossing.

Travel and Community Experience for Multiply Handicapped Students

LAUREL J. MacWILLIAM

Laurel J. MacWilliam is a mobility instructor in the Waltham (Massachusetts) Public School System and a consultant in the Boston area.

■ Any agency preparing special needs students for maximally independent living and employment must provide instruction in independent travel and use of community resources. Yet curricula for the instruction of sighted special needs students in independent travel skills have received little systematic development and evaluation. Even curricula for teaching independent travel to visually handicapped students frequently leave the student standing at the door of community resources.

Acquisition of travel skills should be coupled with acquisition of social, communication, monetary, temporal, and self care skills that will be needed once *inside* the restaurant, post office, or other community resource. This coupling provides better motivation for the learning of independent travel skills and facilitates the implementation of appropriate reinforcement and repetition. It also provides a structure for transferring the learning of independence from an instructional setting to a total life style for special needs persons.

The Protestant Guild for the Blind's Learning Center for the Multiply Handicapped has developed a mobility/community experience program which has fostered independence in travel skills and use of community resources by the multiply handicapped, both those who are visually handicapped and those who are sighted. The goal of this program is for students to travel and use their community resources as independently as possible.

Travel and use of community resources provide opportunities to integrate and apply skills in a variety of areas. The student on a restaurant trip, for example, is required to be dressed and groomed appropriately, to be responsible in use of time and money skills, to be accurate in reading maps and menus, and to be effective in dealing with the public. Similarly, each student receives a weekly paycheck for vocational productivity and has a savings account at the local bank. Weekly bank readiness classes and bank trips provide the student with an opportunity to apply skills in budgeting, signing a check, completing a deposit slip, traveling to the bank, interacting with the teller, and shopping.

THE TRAVELERS

The students participating in this program are adolescents showing visual, auditory, mental, physical, and emotional impairments. In most cases, the student's primary handicap is compounded by a secondary and sometimes tertiary handicap. Of the 120 students enrolled at the agency, approximately 90% are enrolled in the mobility/community experience program. Students participating in the program have demonstrated necessary prerequisites, which include knowledge of basic spatial concepts such as in-out and up-down; minimal reliability as demonstrated by independently attending most classes and showing adequate impulse control; and adequate physical condition.

The program means status, attention, and independence, so student motivation is usually high. A majority of the students have had some prior formal or informal travel and community experience instruction before entering this program. Entry behaviors range from no experience to habitually inappropriate travel habits to solid appropriate basic skills.

CHARTING THE COURSE

Some sample behavioral objectives might serve to demonstrate specific areas of instruction. These objectives have been categorized into travel skills and community experience sections, with both disability-specific and multidimensional intended outcomes included.

The travel skills section of the curriculum focuses primarily on the psychomotor and cognitive domains. Sequenced objectives in this major area include:

- To travel to and from all scheduled classes within the school using the most direct routes and walking on the right side of corridors and stairs.
- To solicit aid when crossing streets from strangers in a polite and effective manner.
- To travel independently from school to the bank on two successive trips.

While these are examples of objectives for all students in the program, disability-specific objectives are also included. For example, visually impaired students should demonstrate understanding of driveways by self recovering when disoriented in driveways; hearing impaired students should systematically visually scan at each driveway, parking lot, and intersection.

The community experience section of the program focuses primarily on the cognitive and affective domains. Units cover use of the postal system, telephones, banks, restaurants, stores, fire and police facilities, hospitals, and public transportation. Sample sequenced objectives in this major area include:

- To carry out a two step errand in a familiar building.

3. EDUCATION

- To locate and use a pay telephone and a mailbox in a familiar small business area.
- To execute three restaurant trips with a student partner, safely and with socially appropriate behavior.

Disability-specific objectives are also included in this section of the program. For example, students who are unable to read phonetically should be able to recognize a printed sight word vocabulary of at least 15 community words and phrases such as *men, women, exit, telephone,* and *do not enter.*

Multidimensional intended outcomes are an integral part of the program, for example:

- To be properly dressed and groomed while in the community.
- To demonstrate a positive attitude toward the class by arriving within 5 minutes of starting time.
- To complain about the weather not more than twice during an hour lesson.

Specific goals are individualized for each student. For example, the program objective "to execute three restaurant trips with a student partner" might be individualized for a particular student to read, "Ray will execute three restaurant trips with Steve, talking politely to the waitress, tipping appropriately, and returning within 90 minutes."

A SAMPLE ITINERARY

The travel skills content and sequencing are extrapolated from the orientation and mobility curriculum for the visually handicapped. This part of the program stresses understanding of travel concepts, spatial orientation, and maximal use of sensory input. Instruction in independent travel progresses sequentially, beginning inside the building and then branching out to include the campus, residential areas, and small, medium, and large business areas.

First, in traveling inside buildings, the student learns such concepts as self familiarization to the area, the functional components of a building (such as various rooms, stairways, and exits), indoor pedestrian traffic patterns such as walking on the right, and spatial orientation through reference systems of landmarks, laterality, and compass directions. The student is required to follow multiple step directions relayed vocally, manually, in printed or tactual maps, and/or in written phrases, depending on his disabilities.

As the student progresses to traveling in residential and business areas, he learns about self familiarization to these areas, related structural components (such as the block system, public transportation systems, and functions of various public buildings), and pedestrian traffic patterns at street crossings, in congested areas, and on public transportation. He learns how to plan and travel routes in residential and business areas safely, efficiently, and reliably. He also learns to solicit aid at difficult street crossings or when traveling to an unfamiliar destination and to follow the directions given.

The community experience content stresses appropriate monetary, social, and verbal behavior when the student arrives at his destination. This part of the program involves application of classroom skills such as budgeting time, ordering from a menu, shopping from a list, paying the exact amount for purchases or anticipating change, and interacting with the public.

The travel skills instruction is primarily on a one to one basis to ensure safety. Community experience instruction is given in groups of from two to seven students to facilitate socialization goals. Instruction occurs both in the classroom and at the community sites. There is, of course, some overlap between course content and staffing. It has been found most efficient for instructors to specialize in terms of students' primary disabilities (e.g., visual, auditory, or mental impairments). With this structure, those who teach travel and community experience skills to visually impaired students are qualified in the areas of orientation and mobility for the visually handicapped; those who teach hearing impaired students are qualified in deaf education and sign language.

Required materials are easily provided. Most helpful have been visual and tactual maps; photographs of school staff, classrooms, and local community sites; menus; bank deposit and withdrawal slips; and telephone books.

TRAVELING IN STYLE

In learning to cross streets, the student begins at quiet residential intersections, progresses to more heavily trafficked intersections, and then to traffic light controlled intersections. The student learns to judge when traffic is distant enough to allow time for a safe crossing. Systematic visual and/or auditory scanning to both left and right on the perpendicular street and forward and backward on the parallel street must be mastered. The student analyzes traffic patterns, considering the shape of the intersection (e.g., "plus sign," "T," or "offset") and the way in which traffic is controlled (e.g., stop sign, one way street, police officer, traffic light). The student learns to apply pedestrian traffic rules such as crossing only at corners, crossing from corner to corner rather than diagonally, and standing on the curb while waiting. In crossing at traffic light controlled intersections, the safest strategy is to start to cross immediately at the onset of traffic movement in the parallel lane, checking to confirm that traffic in the perpendicular lane has stopped.

The affective domain should be directly considered. Some students show little fear of traffic and need to conceptualize that "cars can indeed hurt you"; others are overly cautious and need evidence that a pedestrian is safe if he travels properly. While criteria for mastery of educational objectives typically do not require perfection, in this case 100% accuracy is extremely necessary.

An important skill for travel is the ability to solicit aid from the public, usually for assistance in crossing streets and in locating unfamiliar destinations. In learning to solicit aid, the student begins by role playing in the classroom and then in the community with the instructor simulating the public. Instruction should stress that the student must ask questions intelligibly, succinctly, and courteously, and that he must attend to the responses. The simplest situation involves accepting assistance in crossing streets: "Would you help me across Trapelo Road, please . . . . Thank you." More difficult situations are those in which the student must locate a person from whom to ask

Unit on restaurants.

It has been found beneficial to incorporate an interim period of independent travel after each stage of instruction. For example, a student completing instruction in a residential area might be asked to deliver letters to the mailbox each Wednesday after school. Similarly, after mastery of skills required to use a small business area, a twice weekly assignment might be to purchase a newspaper at the drug store. This interim period of independent travel not only serves as an evaluative measure, but it also ensures the student's confidence and overlearning before he moves on to higher level tasks.

Students given permission to travel alone to destinations during free time are issued authorizing "licenses." Any restrictions are detailed (e.g., that the student may travel only during daylight), and a validity date is established to ensure followup (see Figure 1). This tangible indication of mastery of a task affords efficient interstaff communication and is usually a source of pride to the student, who sees all too few concrete signs of progress.

FIGURE 1

STUDENT LICENSE

Student's name: _Ray_

Student's address: _7 Main St., Newton, Mass._

Student's telephone number(s): _555-0100_

Is cleared to travel to: _Brigham's_
(list of destinations) _the bank_
Eddie's Deli

Laurie MacWilliam
(Instructor's signature)

Side 1

Any restrictions to travel:

Ray should not travel alone after dark. He should not travel when he is upset.

Issued (date): _May 5, 1976_

Valid until (date): _October 16, 1976_

Side 2

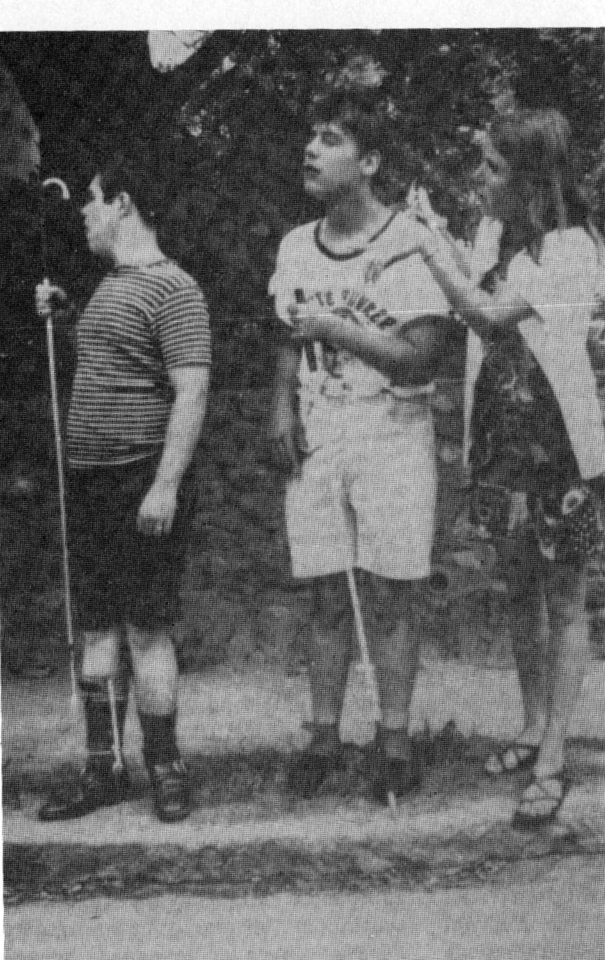

Visually impaired students looking at traffic.

directions to a destination, gain his attention, ask the directions, attend and ask again if uncertain of the response, and then follow the directions.

The student learns whom to ask (e.g., it is often more effective to ask clerks in stores rather than small children), when to ask (after he has reached the general vicinity), and how to ask (e.g., "Excuse me, could you please tell me how to reach Payson's Pharmacy?"). Students lacking oral communication skills learn either to present previously written requests for assistance at appropriate times and places, to mime, or to carry writing materials to communicate specific requests and receive answers. Both in role playing and in real experiences, the student needs to learn to deal with incorrect directions from the public and to decline unwanted aid.

A COMPREHENSIVE TOUR

The interrelationship between travel and community experience instruction is close; in fact, normally no distinction is made. As the student learns residential area travel skills, he is simultaneously learning about the community resources of the postal system (mailboxes) and the fire department (hydrants). As the student learns the business area travel skills of crossing at traffic lights and using maps, he is simultaneously being introduced to such community resources as pay telephones, banks, police officers, and restaurants.

"WALKING TALL"

A program that combines travel training with parallel community experiences assures that students with a variety of multiply handicapping conditions are given the opportunity to "walk tall" as functional citizens of their community.

Mel Evans

Dr. Evans is chairman, Department of Health, Physical Education and Recreation, Jackson State University, Jackson, Mississippi.

IN THIS ERA of great political, social, and economic change, rehabilitation is not a static process. Its pattern of services and programs will continue to change with the thinking and the practices of future years. No simple blueprint of future development can be readily sketched at this time, yet there are certain obvious challenges presented to all who believe in and are concerned with the many aspects of rehabilitation. In recent years, considerable attention and support have been given to the therapeutic recreation profession. In particular, emphasis has been placed on the inherent value of therapeutic recreation to the rehabilitation of handicapped people. Therapeutic recreation has given the rehabilitation process an added dimension; it encompasses the programming of recreation activities for the mental, physical, social, emotional, and educational betterment of handicapped people.

Therapeutic recreation in inner-city recreation programs is almost nonexistent. In many large cities a majority of the inner-city inhabitants are minorities; this presents a tremendous challenge to those of us who are in the mainstream of reform activities with regard to social changes.

Handicapped youngsters have the same need to express themselves freely in a wholesome, nonthreatening recreation environment as do "normal" boys and girls. The desire to run, jump, swim, throw and bat a ball, paint, play musical instruments, or fashion an object from clay is no less intense in the handicapped than in other groups of people.

Although some cities in the United States have provided more than adequate recreation services for special populations, the vast majority of our municipalities have been woefully derelict in this area. Stracke (1969) found in a survey in California that public recreation and parks provided services for less than 1 percent of the handicapped children in that state. A study by Jackson State University in 1971 revealed that only about 10 percent of the handicapped children in the state of Mississippi were being provided with general services. In view of the absence of recreation for the handicapped in county and municipal programs, it seems reasonable to conclude that the number of children receiving recreation services is no greater than those receiving general services.

County and municipal recreators appear to be wearing the same blinders as those worn by the early Greeks. Although the handicapped are not killed outright, they are left to die from the lack of recreative experiences. Even the humanitarians of the age of enlightenment were no match for the power structure that believed the handicapped were less than human and had no rights that deserved to be respected. Where would special populations be today if it were not for people like Helen Keller, Franklin D. Roosevelt, John F. Kennedy, and Maurice Stokes.

This is not to say that those who do not promulgate programs for the handicapped within county and municipal recreation programs are insensitive to the needs of the handicapped. Many directors are confused, some do not know how to handle the problem, and many just have not taken the time to investigate the possibilities that exist within their present programs to provide for special populations.

Those administrators who have the authority and the means need only the will to assign at least one staff member trained in therapeutic recreation to develop programming for the handicapped.

Many will say that funds are not available—the same excuse that society has used to deny minority groups' requests for certain types of programs. Others will claim they cannot find personnel trained in therapeutic recreation. This problem can be remedied by consulting state therapeutic recreation societies, by arranging for a present staff member to be trained in the therapeutic field, or by getting in touch with the Black Universities Consortium on therapeutic recreation at Jackson State University, Jackson, Mississippi.

Being black in the American inner city is a burden in itself; being black and handicapped in an inner city where program directors are insensitive to the needs of the handicapped is an even greater burden. We must begin now to provide our special populations with the recreation opportunities that are theirs by right.

Communication Without Speech

Eugene Wendt is an occupational therapist at the Lapham Orthopedic School, Madison, Wisconsin; Mary Jane Sprague is a speech and language therapist in the Madison Public Schools; Jeanne Marquis is a teacher of the orthopedically handicapped at Gompers Middle School in Madison.

EUGENE WENDT
MARY JANE SPRAGUE
JEANNE MARQUIS

■ In the fall of 1969, Lydell, a 10½ year old boy with cerebral palsy, was enrolled at Lapham Orthopedic School in Madison, Wisconsin. Lydell was severely physically handicapped in all four extremities. He could not walk, he had no oral speech or understandable gestures, and his hand skills were so limited that he was totally dependent on others for feeding, dressing, and ambulation. During an initial visit to the school he was pushed around the building in a baby stroller by his mother. Lydell had not previously been enrolled in any formal school educational program, although he had received homebound instruction and limited outpatient therapy. Since his family did not live in Madison, Lydell was placed with a boarding home family during the school week.

"Communication Without Speech," Eugene Wendt, Mary Jane Sprague, Jeanne Marquis, *Teaching Exceptional Children*, Vol. 8 No. 1, Fall 1975. ©1975 The Council for Exceptional Children.

3. EDUCATION

A PERIOD OF ADJUSTMENT

The first year was a difficult adjustment period. It was Lydell's first separation from his home and family and he was homesick and tearful much of the time. The school program necessarily focused first on his emotional adjustment before more extensive educational and therapeutic procedures could be implemented. He was exposed to play and work situations with other children and to the routine, structure, and stimulation of the school setting. His responses began to fluctuate from excessive outbursts of crying to periods of quiet, attentive behaviors. This period was an equally difficult and trying time for his parents. Their support and close association with their child, along with a strong and loving boarding home family, contributed greatly to Lydell's eventual adjustment.

Classroom and therapy programs during the first year could be described as ongoing diagnostic procedures. Evaluations of baseline behaviors revealed that in the classroom Lydell was able to identify numbers to 10 by pounding on an adapted desk or by squeezing the teacher's arm, and identify colors, written words, and primary reading vocabulary words by pointing with a gross motor arm movement or by vocalizing a gutteral sound. In physical therapy he needed alteration of range of motion, coordination exercises, and body positioning for best trunk and head control.

Lydell's speech therapy session would be held in conjunction with physical therapy. The therapists experimented with different body positions in an attempt to find which was most appropriate for eliciting phonation. A normal erect sitting posture with support was found to be best. A wheelchair would therefore be a future recommendation.

The factors contributing to Lydell's inability to vocalize were poor oral musculature, poor feeding patterns, and poor head control. The occupational therapy program was designed to alleviate these problems. Such techniques as Rood facilitation, desensitization, and proper positioning were initiated. In addition, the occupational therapist decided that continued motor evaluation and training were necessary to decide which arm and hand were most functional.

STEADY IMPROVEMENT

Performance levels at the end of the first school year found Lydell using a wheelchair all day; improving his head control, mouth closure, and swallowing patterns; and beginning a more structured feeding program. Motor development levels had been identified, and his receptive language age was found to be within normal limits. A satisfactory *yes* or *no* response could usually be determined from Lydell's head movement and could be checked when necessary by having him look to the far right at a *yes* card and to the far left at a *no* card. Limited phonation had been attained. Program direction for the coming year was established. Since Lydell had good receptive language, he was placed in a classroom with higher achieving children where he could absorb more as a listener. Special programing would be necessary.

In the fall of his second year at the school Lydell began an intensive academic and therapy program. The feeding program previously initiated was intensified to a daily basis. He was learning to eat all solid foods, chew and swallow independently, and suck from a straw—evidence of general improvement of oral musculature. He was able to produce sound on command, to vary and to prolong the phonation, and to say "hi." However, with a chronological age of 11 years, 6 months, the prospect of his achieving functional speech seemed remote. The speech therapist therefore decided to seek an alternative means of expressive communication.

COMMUNICATION WITHOUT SPEECH

The occupational therapist noted that Lydell's hand skills were still at such a low level that any communication device requiring hand skills was not practical at that time. Because he had achieved better head control, the speech therapist attempted placing a tongue depressor between Lydell's teeth and having him point to letters on a felt board directly in front of his wheelchair. Despite some awkwardness and difficulty with this communication device, Lydell demonstrated that he could learn to spell. The staff was encouraged by his enthusiasm and excitement and the speed with which he acquired a basic spelling vocabulary.

Continuing on the basis that this would be the best mode of communication, the therapists attempted to find a better mouth device for pointing. Numerous devices were tried and, with the assistance of a dentist, a more permanent mouth pointer was designed. The use of the mouth device was impractical in the classroom, but Lydell's new interest in letters and words and his improved spelling ability tended to reinforce and further develop this mode of expression.

Lydell's learning rate was developing faster than his ability to use the mouth stick to express his thoughts. His realization that he could communicate with people in a way that he had not experienced before stimulated all areas of his development, both physical and mental. He worked hard and, after several months, it became evident both in the classroom and in therapy that his left arm and hand were becoming more functional. He was able to control his arm motions in midranges, grasp a pencil or dowel to make a mark on paper, and point to a picture or printed word. He was also appropriately positioned in his own wheelchair. It became apparent that he could use the second and third digits of his left hand by sliding the fingertips to specific symbols or letters. However, he still could not use conventional writing devices or an adapted electric typewriter.

THE LETTER BOARD

The speech therapist suggested the possibility of a letter board that could be used with hand and finger spelling. The occupational therapist designed a board appropriate to Lydell's level of hand skills, which contained letter and number arrangements agreed on by the classroom teacher and speech therapist.

Lydell became skilled in using the board and its use greatly changed his life. Communication became exciting and increasingly important for Lydell and he carried his board with him everywhere. He was able to express his feelings, ask questions, and interact in classroom activities. A sense of humor was fast developing as he learned and used the idioms of spoken language. As his language skill improved, his communication board was altered to contain digraphs, endings, question words, and other whole words important to him in quick communication. The staff realized, however, that the board's usefulness was limited to situations where a second party was present to interpret his message. The next step seemed to be the development of a communication device that Lydell could use more independently.

AN ENGINEERING CHALLENGE

The school psychologist contacted the Department of Electrical Engineering at the University of Wisconsin and explained Lydell's needs. Two students and a professor were interested and responded enthusiastically. They came

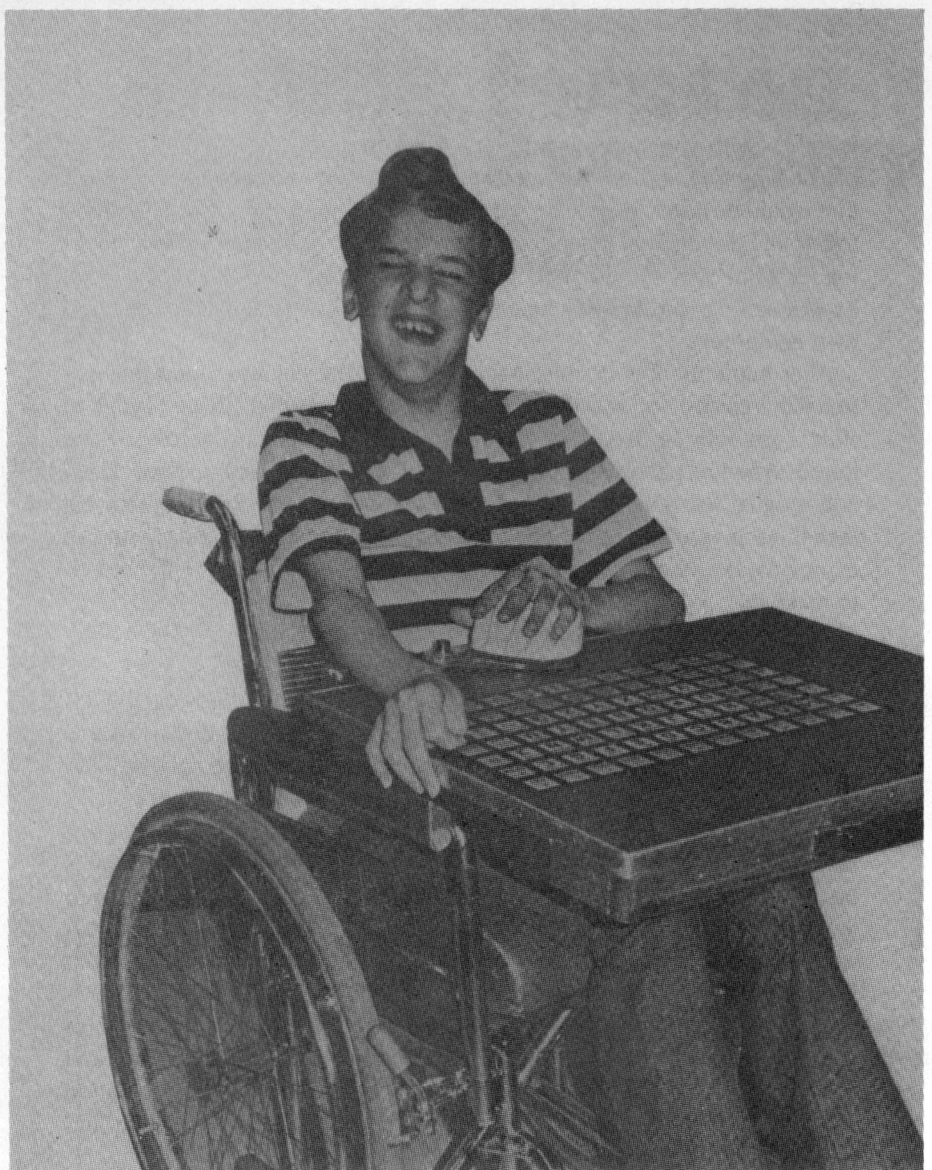

to the school to familiarize themselves with the situation and decided it would be a challenge. A group of engineering students was organized and, together with the multidisciplinary team from Lydell's school, began painstaking trial and error procedures to develop a communication device that would be faster, more efficient, and allow for more independence. They found that the original letter board worked best and the group started looking for some way to automate it. The initial research was done at school, experimenting with Lydell's functional abilities. The students brought their own equipment.

After many months of consultation between the engineers and occupational therapist, a unit was developed in the laboratory that allowed Lydell to slide a specially devised hand unit equipped with a magnet across a letter board. When he paused at a particular letter, a switch under the letter closed and a signal was sent to an electric typewriter to type a printed symbol. As Lydell pointed to letters, he could record them on paper as his method of expressive language. The device was a fantastic breakthrough in the search to make this child more independent.

THE AUTO-COM

Continued research by the engineering group perfected this device and led to the development of the Auto-Com (see Figure 1). This device uses a magnetic letter board and records messages on a typewriter, a television screen, or a tape printout. The television unit is located on a table in Lydell's classroom. Once he is positioned, he can work on an assignment independently, take spelling tests with his class, or talk to friends. The Auto-Com is now portable. It can be attached to his wheelchair and used both as a lap tray and as a communication board. For quick, unrecorded personal conversation, Lydell still prefers to use the communication board manually (with his two fingers and with the machine turned off).

The Auto-Com has opened up a new area for persons who lack expressive language skills, although it cannot be used by everyone. Its effectiveness and ultimate functional use will depend on the individual's unique combination of physical and intellectual abilities in conjunction with the training and support of those involved in the habilitation process.

PROGRESS TOWARD INDEPENDENCE

The Auto-Com facilitates communication for the child who can understand the symbol system and has the motor skill to use and operate the device. Lydell's receptive language processes were intact—he needed only an expressive outlet. Therapy and educational experience were able to build on his capacity and eagerness to learn. The Auto-Com has given Lydell independence in expressive language. It has made it possible for him to compete and participate more easily in classroom group activities; it has increased his speed of acquiring a reading and writing vocabulary by providing immediate visual feedback; it has provided an additional incentive for learning; and it has increased his self image.

Lydell is still severely handicapped. He may always need a protective environment, but progress toward independence has been made. New advances in the Auto-Com enable him to print out whole words and phrases and have increased his rate of communication. He is now enrolled in a middle school (6th, 7th, and 8th grades) and spends part of his day in a special class for orthopedically handicapped and is mainstreamed part time in a regular 6th grade class. His life has been enriched by his experiences in public school education and, because of the combined efforts of many people, he can now communicate, socialize, and appreciate life more fully.

EVERYONE'S A STAR

Deanna Dillon Thursby

For some, music is the complex creation and exploration of a thought or inspiration, while for others it is a simple, relaxing means of escape from complicated everyday life. For musicians music presents security in repetition and structure; yet, for those not musically inclined, it is a frustrating battle of black dots and lines. These differing views demonstrate that music is a unique personal experience that has its own meaning for each individual.

This freedom of personal expression and interpretation is the basic principle behind music therapy. Practiced in a classroom or therapeutic situation, music therapy is the application of music to produce a condition of well being for many handicapped children. Music creates an atmosphere of trust and comfort where one child's opinion is just as valuable and "correct" as that of the next. This is the kind of environment that handicapped children need to achieve their best. They are free to express themselves, orally or in movement, without fear of failure or criticism. And, children are often more willing to try something new in arithmetic or reading if they have had success in another field, such as music.

MOVEMENT SKILLS

Music therapy and music activities, carefully planned and coordinated in the curriculum, are especially helpful in developing movement skills and spatial awareness. Today we seldom find music classes where children only sit in neat rows and sing songs with the piano. Children are encouraged to move to the music and express what they think the music says. What better way is there to learn the parts of the body than with songs and games? Roly Poly, a musical game by Mary Helen Richards (1970), finds children on the ground rolling and stretching to the music. In other singing games, children learn to hop, skip, run, walk, and balance. They use their eyes, hands, fingers, and arms to develop fine motor coordination. Left and right orientation is much easier in a musical game. Children practice concepts like *around, under, above, beside,* and *through.* Tana Hoban's book *Over, Under, and Through* (1973), set to music, provides firsthand experiences with these concepts.

LANGUAGE DEVELOPMENT

Music can also help in language development and communication skills. The language of music uses a system of symbols and notes. It has form, rhythm, and tonal sequences of melody that produce a response. Many music therapists believe that once children discover the language of music, they will use it in organizing their own spoken language and communication.

Language vocabulary is an area where musical activities are very effective. In game form, concrete examples of action words like *jump, hop, skip, run,* and *walk* are presented. Children tap out rhythms, using contrasting words: *soft* or *loud, fast* or *slow, rough* or *smooth.* When children have direct and concrete experiences with these concepts and others like them, they are more apt to master them and use them in their vocabulary.

The most common forms of expressive activities found in a classroom involve writing, speech and language, movement, and music. Yet, spontaneous and natural expression is often difficult for handicapped children. Music creates a climate in which expression can be free and nonthreatening. If children are comfortable and at ease in a situation, they are more apt to relax and become totally involved in what they are doing. They must sense that they are important and that their contribution is valuable.

MAPPING

Listening activities play a major role in developing language expression. A beginning activity involves simple, personal feelings about a piece of music expressed in a picture form, which is called mapping. Mapping is a visual motor response to the rhythm, beat, or melody of a musical selection. The same line of music may be felt and mapped completely differently by two children, and neither child is right or wrong. Each picture is a personal expression of what each child finds most important in a particular piece of music. Music therapists believe that this free personal expression, found in responses to music, can be generalized to an oral spoken language with the same comfort. Eventually, children are encouraged to use words, in the same way they use pictures, to describe a piece of music.

CREATIVE WRITING AND STORY TELLING

A well rounded variety of music can set the mood for creative writing or expression in story telling. If the children have just returned from a field trip to the circus, appropriate music will help revive their excitement and set the mood for writing about their experiences. Stories and experiences can be dramatized, giving children the opportunity to interpret what they read and to express their feelings orally. Music can also improve expression. Participation in a musical activity is a way to release pent-up energy or emotional stress.

The teacher can provide children with many contrasts—musical sounds that seem angry and sad compared to others that seem light and happy. Discussion with the children about their use of music to express their feelings will allow them, in a noncritical and accepting atmosphere, to experiment and discover sounds for themselves.

TEACHERS CAN DO IT, TOO

Teachers should not be afraid to express themselves in front of their students, because they are valuable models. Often, the teacher sees the children for 6 hours a day and is held responsible for the interaction and experiences that take place during that time. If the class is listening to a bright, happy rhythmic piece of music, the teacher should tap his foot to the beat. If the class is instructed to walk like an elephant, with a slow moving, heavy gait, the teacher should join the children to model the expression.

AUDITORY AND VISUAL DISCRIMINATION

Music involves both auditory and visual stimuli, with abundant contrasts: quantity (soft and loud), rate (fast and slow), pitch (high and low), and quality (sharp and flat). Listening activities, with simple variations of musical tones, can develop auditory discrimination skills.

Printed music can provide an opportunity for visual discrimination. Children need not be skilled in reading complex note values and patterns. Simple songs, like "Mary Had a Little Lamb," center around five notes and do not have difficult words to learn. It is usually better to omit the musical staff and clef sign to avoid distraction and confusion at first. Teachers can vary the size, shape, or color of notes, one at a time, to strengthen visual discrimination skills.

SOCIAL GRACE

Social skills are an important part of the curriculum for handicapped children. A teacher or therapist should be concerned about how each child will adapt and fit into the environment. Social awareness of others is important for this adjustment. Simple social graces, often learned incidentally by many children, must be taught to many handicapped children.

Music helps develop social skills. For example, through music children become actively involved in circle games that require group cooperation and teamwork. The children participate in the give and take necessary for cooperation in everyday life. They discover that they are individuals and have something to offer others. They also begin to depend on someone else for help. Musical activities develop accepted social skills for the present and provide a source of future free time enjoyment. The music therapist's goal is to extend the social ability gained in a classroom or therapy session to everyday situations.

ATTENTION!

Attention span and the amount of constructive effort put forth are important in the learning situation. Children must be attracted to and held by the material presented. Attention must be full time, and not a haphazard switch that can be turned off and on. Children learn at an early age to "tune out" the boring or uninteresting. Handicapped children often have numerous problems with attention span. Simple things, like a sudden movement, easily distract them. Music and musical activities present a fun learning atmosphere; children feel comfortable and relaxed. They associate learning with fun and attend more consistently to a musical learning activity. Music, used wisely and judiciously, can help keep attention alive.

SETTING THE MOOD

It is the responsibility of the teacher or therapist to create an environment where distractions are minimal, presentations are appealing and relevant, and children feel successful and important. Rather than worn out worksheets, a musical game that will get the children moving and actively involved may be used. As a substitute for reading from a basal text every morning a musical reading activity may be tried. Children may role play or manipulate puppets, with authentic music to set the proper mood. For example, *Elementary Science Study* (1968), an instructional program, enlivened their unit on dinosaurs with the song "Dry Bones." History lessons may be accompanied by authentic music of the culture or period. For instance, the music of Beethoven captures the stormy mood of Europe during the late 18th century. These activities give a purpose to learning and keep most children interested and involved.

MUSIC + ACADEMICS = SUCCESS

Music therapy and music carefully integrated into the special classroom are not magic, fail-safe cures for all teachers and students. Some critics and teachers believe music has a separate place, set apart from academic subjects. Some feel their ability in music is too weak to use it extensively as a basic part of their curriculum. The major criticism of the program is that a musically oriented special classroom creates an idealistic environment, which is in conflict with the life the children will experience outside the school walls.

Music, used wisely and discreetly, has valuable potential in numerous areas of development. It is a tool and a teaching device that may be used to create an environment that is as valuable as the teacher who uses it. The teacher is responsible for establishing goals and plans for each activity in clear cut, thoroughly organized objectives. A teacher must be sensitive to the needs of the individual children in the classroom and pick and choose the methods of teaching that fit specific problems.

It is up to the teacher to provide a variety of experiences and develop a well balanced environment. Music should not be used all the time or it will lose some of its reinforcing value. There are some skills, like finding a word in the dictionary, that are difficult to combine with music. Yet, with a little time and careful thought, many of the subject areas stressed in the classroom become interesting and relevant with the addition of musical activities.

Classroom teachers need not be highly skilled musicians with a broad background of music theory and technique. Music therapy is not an attempt to produce artists and virtuosos; it is a resource that teachers can draw from to provide additional concrete experiences for their children. Equipped with a book of musical games and ideas, like Mary Helen Richard's *Language Arts Through Music—A Trilogy* (1971) or the *Hap Palmer Record Series* (1969), even the most "unmusical" teacher has a chance. Teachers should not be afraid to include a musical activity because they lack a college degree in music. Teachers know their children best—what they like and dislike and how they react in the classroom setting. A teacher who feels the need for some knowledge of music in order to use it in class should take a college course or comparable independent study in music education or participate in a workshop or inservice training session on how to implement music activities.

After a new activity has been used, it, as well as its objectives, should be evaluated for future use. Teachers should also evaluate their own performance on the activity. Teachers should dedicate their time and talents to creating the best learning environment possible for children. Music and musical activities are very important resources to fill this responsibility.

Education Where It Is Needed

Early Education should also be available for disabled children.

Anne McKenna

Anne McKenna is Lecturer in the Department of Psychology, University College, Dublin. She is also Editor of the International Journal of Early Childhood.

Most children are cared for almost totally by their mothers until they reach school age. However, the number of children under school age in "group care" outside their homes is increasing. It is a matter of opinion what to include in the term "pre-school education." Some writers exclude ages under three, while the upper limit of the term will vary from country to country depending on the legal age for starting school.

Provision of early education also varies widely between countries, but whatever the variation in terminology, time span or provision, the *process* of early education represents a cohesive and widely accepted set of principles and concepts. These originated in humanistic and radical reform movements of the last century, which had among their aims the provision of nursery education for poorer children of the community. Today early education has come to mean the provision of education for all children at the earliest possible moment at which the child can benefit — in other words, it has evolved *from education for the needy to education where it is needed.* And early education is most particularly needed by children who are handicapped socially, culturally, physically, intellectually or emotionally.

Early Detection

Biological readiness for acquiring the foundations of all human skills begins at birth, and if there is a structural or functional defect, maladaptive processes will set in as soon as the organism begins to interact with the environment. To compensate for sensory or intellectual deficiencies, children may therefore acquire a number of undesirable traits such as apparent detachment, disinterest or inactivity. Specialists in early education often are able to assess a child's interactions and quickly detect abnormalities when parents, for many reasons, are not.

When the preschool center is a part of community services, as ideally it should be, these children can be referred to the appropriate specialists for diagnosis and, if necessary, prolonged observation in which teachers can be of inestimable help by reporting on the child's day-to-day adaptions.

It is now recognized that the largest single group of school failures and otherwise troubled school children are from lower socio-economic groups. Children from these groups begin to diverge from their middle class counterparts, in language and conceptual ability, around the age of two years. From this point on, the relative disadvantage increases in a process which primary education has so far done little to avert. It is also known that if compensatory education is initiated at or near the point of divergence, the chances of staving off this disadvantage are much improved.

The pioneering and idealistic move for such education, which started in the United States in the mid-1960's, made many extravagant claims — some of which have not been borne out. Improvements did take place, however, most notably in the more rigorously planned programs. In answer to the objection that these improvements were not maintained, it should be said that early education will not guard against a lifetime of domestic poverty, neglect, and disinterest. It is strange logic which condemns compensatory school programs because the primary school is unable to maintain earlier improvements. And the educational policy of allocating scarce resources for preschool children of low income families is one which no civilized community can any longer ignore.

The Physically Disabled

The concept of early childhood education for children with defects of vision or hearing is not a new one and many schools for the visually impaired or deaf provide pre-school programs for both children and their parents.

Education of the cerebral palsied child is not a totally different process from education of the deaf or mildly handicapped child. And for the majority of crippled children, there is little difference between their cognitive and learning abilities and those of able-bodied children, provided the opportunities and facilities are made available to them.

That all children can benefit from educational intervention before the statutory age for beginning school was a direct application of the experimental work in early learning of the 1950's. Investigations in the late 1960's and on into this decade concerning the rates of competence of skilled movement, language behavior and personality development have driven us even further back, into infancy itself. When Burton White demonstrated in 1973 that the onset of visually guided reading could be brought forward from five to three months, the notion of mechanical unfolding of sensori-motor patterns finally yielded to that of interactionism and quality of exchange with the environment. For the physically disabled, the implications are of far-reaching importance. Coupled with the possibility of "plugging in" the infant to response-contingent stimulation which has been shown to hasten both Piagetian-type secondary circular reactions and social emotional responses (Watson and Ramey), they now offer a detailed description of a learning environment for the physically handicapped from the moment of birth or as soon thereafter as possible.

We now also have a knowledge of the prelinguistic basis for language acquisition, an explicit knowledge of a process which takes place semi-automatically between parent and non-handicapped child between birth and two years and which we can build into the curriculum of deaf and mentally handicapped children from the moment of diagnosis and can continue after the advent of speech. Thus learning *how to mean* is seen as a prerequisite of learning *how to speak*. So too is the process of setting up a common ground of inter-subjectivity or "we-ness" between adult and child, where the adult looks at what the infant regards and comments. In the case of a deaf child, the infant is trained to look at the adult's line of vision before lip-reading his or her comments; in the case of the mentally handicapped child,

while listening to the commentary.

For those children generally termed mildly mentally handicapped and who are generally seen to be affected by a mixture of cultural and familial factors not yet fully understood, early intervention through preschool education is likely to prove the most important source of intellectual advance and, on occasion, if supplied at a sufficiently early age, a preventative measure (Heber). For the moderately handicapped, traditional training procedures, incorporating the learning processes outlined by psychologists, have shown how far performance may exceed previously held expectations.

For the profoundly handicapped, behavior modification routines can instigate the principle of choice whereby, for example, by turning in his cot the child may decide to light the room or by moving a toe muscle to hear the sound of music.

All these principles carry within them the axiom, "the earlier the better," and contain the guidelines for a preschool curriculum for the handicapped.

One might sum up the past decade's research in education of the handi-

capped as a shift of perception, a shift which now views physical and mental handicaps, as well as behavioral problems, as defects of learning or learning disabilities. UNESCO's publication, *Recent Trends in Research of Special Education* (1974), summarizes this view and notes that "because of (it), practice is easily translated into operations familiar to teachers," since "while learning disabilities may be an organic problem in their original cause, their major treatment — as of now — rests within the educational sphere." Moreover, it rests even more firmly within the sphere of early education since, as the report continues, "errors of behavioral development approach irreversibility at a rapid rate and . . . the aberrance they introduce is magnified as development proceeds."

Basic Principles of Early Education

EARLY EXPERIENCE AND ITS EFFECT ON LATER PERFORMANCE. There is now a sound theoretical basis for the developmental theory that learning may be regarded as one continuous

process, from the simple repetitive motor habits of the infant to the accomplished and abstract productions of the adult. But all points on this continuum are not equally important from the educational viewpoint. The earliest years are the years of most rapid development of the intellect, and defects at this time are the most far-reaching. This means that deprivation during the early years is most damaging and, conversely, enrichment most effective.

KNOWING THE NORM AND RESPECTING INDIVIDUAL DIFFERENCES. The norms of development in the first five years of life — as regards motor tasks, perceptual and intellectual problems, relations with peers and self-help tasks — are probably more accurately known than for any other period of child development. This knowledge, plus a training in the naturalistic observation of children in groups, characterize the best in early education training and in diagnostic and evaluative procedures. Also, the historical tradition of the nursery educator as filling a role halfway between a parent and a teacher results in a respect in the pre-school situation for the unique growth pattern of each child.

MATURATION AND READINESS. In previous times, early educators were imbued with the idea that children should not be forced to perform an activity before they are ready. Maturation was seen as an unfolding process from within the child, with the teacher playing a passive and patient role in guiding this emerging behavior. The teacher must now anticipate the next stage of a child's development and present materials and experience appropriate to it. This has become possible because much continuum theory has become embodied in pre-school curricula. It is now possible, for example, to furnish activities for mental ages one to four which will be, in effect, remote preparations for reading readiness.

PERSONALITY OF THE TEACHER. There now exists a clear and operational curriculum which puts early education, properly understood, as far away from baby sitting as primary education is from child minding. This has not, however, displaced the traditional importance accorded the personality of the teacher. Lip service is paid to the quality of personal relations in teaching, but only in early education is it considered the pivotal aspect.

This is not only because the teacher, like a mother, is training the child to relate to adults, but also because the curriculum contains many more affective and social dimensions than can be included in a regular school program. Their success depends upon the personality of the teacher.

For example, the early educator must oversee the separation, usually the first, of child and parent. On this process will depend the early and successful integration of the child to his or her peer group. This is both more important and more difficult for the handicapped child and demands sensitive yet firm handling on the part of the teacher: a warm and sympathetic acceptance of the child's handicap as well as a refusal to accept that little can be expected of this child.

Probably the most important single prerequisite of the early educator working with the handicapped pre-schooler is a clear awareness of unique competence as an educator as well as of the key role of education for the handicapped. Only then will the educator resist being overwhelmed and overawed by what can sometimes look like "real" treatment from medi-

cal and paramedical authorities. But hand in hand with this should go an ability to know and respect the competence of the other resource teachers and medical personnel, as well as the ability to work amicably and cooperatively with them in the interests of the child.

When we hear that the next large group of handicapped children to claim the attention of the educator is likely to be the emotionally disturbed, whose difficulties lie in inadequate relations with others and an inability to manage their own feelings, we can foresee an even more important role for the preschool teacher. Emotional disorder and disruptive behavior are learned patterns which can be unlearned ahd replaced with healthy patterns of adjustment.

SPECIAL EDUCATION FOR PARENTS. A child learns the most from the person with whom he or she interacts most frequently. This is usually the mother. Some mothers are better teachers than others, but even the best of them are often ill-equipped when it comes to interaction with their handicapped child. Thus a mother who might supply a stimulating sound environment for her child — by constant talking and reading — may stop all language activities with a deaf child when she fails to get the expected responses. An appreciation that such a child needs more talking to, not less, can be learned along with other techniques from an early educator. Such a liaison can ensure that the mother herself becomes an effective early educator for her child and can reduce the physical and emotional burdens imposed by handicapped children.

Parents are likely to remain the adults with whom a child will make the most important relationships of a lifetime. They are the first and their effects the most persevering. Their cooperation and partnership are needed at all levels of education, but only in early education has their role been formalized and incorporated into the teacher training process itself. Early educators know that they must be equal partners with parents if gains made in school are to be maintained out of school and sustained after school.

I have tried to show that early education is needed for young handicapped children. I would also suggest that the benefits of early education are not restricted to intelligent middle class parents, who can afford to purchase this commodity for their children in the open market of private education. What we are actually witnessing in many countries of the world is early education for those who least need it, for those who are already in advantageous circumstances. If educators do not face up to the responsibility of seeing that the benefits of early education are supplied where they are most needed, we are in danger of having the education gap between children with social, cultural, physical, intellectual or emotional handicaps and their more privileged counterparts widen even further.

Media and Disability from Sympathy to Education at U.C.P

George V. McNally

For many ordinary citizens the media campaigns of private charitable organizations serving disabled people have been the principal source of information about people with disabilities. In recent years many people – including disabled adults – have suggested that techniques such as telethons and poster children have a negative impact on the lives of disabled people.

A series of provocative articles in THE EXCEPTIONAL PARENT *magazine have voiced this concern. In* What Price Charity? *(January/February 1975) Elizabeth Pieper asked, "How can we expect our children to value independence and productivity given our example of allowing them and ourselves to be used in this endless business of alms begging?"*

In a February 1976 response to Mrs. Pieper, Raymond Cheever said, "So often in the past the emphasis has been on the poor, little, crippled kid – this approach has strengthened, if not actually created in the general public's mind the idea that all disabled people are helpless, little people . . ."

Recently we saw a short TV spot created by United Cerebral Palsy. It was striking because it clearly presented a young man with cerebral palsy as a real person leading a real life. This spot was a far cry from the media presentations that were criticized by Mrs. Pieper and others. We asked United Cerebral Palsy to describe how they came to produce this spot because we thought it would be valuable for everyone to know how this change came about.

The young man staggers toward the parked car, grasps the door handle and jerks it open. Before he can pull himself into the automobile, he looks up and discovers a man staring at him, aghast at the uncontrolled movements he has been witnessing. The young man stares back boldly, then breaks into an engaging grin. "I know what you're thinking," he seems to be saying, "and I understand . . . but I really *can* drive this car as well as you."

The young man's name is Joe Elko, and the scene just described is part of a public service television spot for United Cerebral Palsy in which Joe appears as himself. The narrator of the spot is actor Theodore Bikel, who tells the audience that Joe not only drives his own car but also goes to college and dates a special girl. Does this sound like a handicapped or disabled individual? Yes and no. Yes, he *is* handicapped, and no, his disability does not stop him from enjoying a life that is full and rewarding.

Poster Child

United Cerebral Palsy has been trying to convey this kind of message for some years now. But this attitude did not come about suddenly. At one time the television spots UCP turned out invariably involved a beautiful poster child in a delightful setting — an amusement park or an idealistic beach scene — with a voice-over narration along the lines of "Happiness is helping. . . . How about you?" by someone like Gene Kelly or Henry Fonda.

Of course, the style of the spots in no way took away from their appeal. In fact, glowing letters from network public service personnel attested to how well they were received. A typical appraisal went something like this:

> So often, the day-to-day seriousness of the work of public-service organizations seems to evidence itself in depressing film spots. Therefore we want to congratulate you on overcoming this very natural tendency and creating materials that can be inserted into any program.

Such praise was received gratefully but with definite misgivings. The people who created these spots at United Cerebral Palsy were beginning to feel a gnawing sense, not of guilt, but perhaps of incompleteness or insincerity.

Certainly the children chosen to appear in living color amidst glorious settings with glamorous stars exhibited pronounced handicaps. They usually wore braces or crutches and were struggling to walk on their own one day. But, the UCP staff asked themselves, was this truly a picture of cerebral palsy? Could not these children just as well have been afflicted with polio or muscular dystrophy? And why always children? Should not adults with cerebral palsy appear in the images being shown to the public?

What had once been strictly a fund-raising appeal had become an educational tool as well.

Change

Then, at about the same time, something occurred that gave impetus to what had been taking shape in the minds of the public relations director and staff writer-producer at UCP's national office. One of the participants at a conference in Denver in 1971, a 21-year-old woman with cerebral palsy named Diana Kenderian, propelled her wheelchair into the press room and asked the UCP's public relations people exactly the same question they had been asking themselves: "When are you going to feature adults with cerebral palsy in the national television spots?" It did not take them long to come up with an answer. "How about next year? And how about you starring in them?" Diana's agreement led to two days of shooting on her college campus a few weeks later. She was shown going to classes (sometimes being carried up staircases), socializing with other students and wheeling herself around the campus.

UCP had a new image on film, but an image was all it was. Scripts had not been yet written to tie the pictures together. Since the spots represented a breakthrough for the handicapped adult, the public relations staff reasoned, why not let the handicapped adult tell her own story? Diana was invited to a recording studio in New York where, during a 30-minute taped interview, she was encouraged to express herself freely on such diverse subjects as her own childhood, architectural barriers, public attitudes toward the handicapped and what she most enjoyed in life. These observations were then edited down to serve as voice-over narrations for 60-, 30- and 20-second television film spots, which were aired on the major networks and over local stations throughout the country. In effect, Diana Kenderian had "written" the scripts, for it was her voice that was heard.

A beginning had been made. United Cerebral Palsy, encouraged by the way in which the messages had been accepted by broadcasters, went further the following year. Its new appeals featured disabled people who had achieved a great deal in spite of their handicaps: a college professor, a lawyer, a rehabilitation counselor. All were shown going about their day-to-day activities enjoying equal status with nondisabled professionals.

What had once been strictly a fund-raising appeal had become an educational tool as well. The public was being made aware of the role of the handicapped in society; it was hoped that understanding would follow from that awareness. But part of getting across the idea of understanding involved the thought that children born with cerebral palsy do grow up to become adults with cerebral palsy. Accordingly, UCP produced a set of spots that emphasized just that idea. Youngsters were shown with braces and crutches. The narrator reminded the viewer that although this was most people's image of cerebral palsy, children with cerebral palsy did grow up; when they did, they needed just as much understanding as they had enjoyed when they were small.

This last point was accompanied by scenes of young adults in various circumstances, some with minor disabilities, others with more serious problems, but all depicted as mature, functioning members of society. UCP was building up to what was to become known as the "Joe Elko spot." It went on the air as early as December 1975 and continued to be shown on the networks through January 1976. As far as anyone can determine, it is still seen on local stations throughout the country.

Response

Joe Elko has, in some ways, become a folk hero (he receives a lot of fan mail). He comes across to most of the public as someone easier to accept than they had imagined. Viewers see a young man exhibiting a strange gait and uncontrolled motions that they regard as alien and perhaps a little frightening, but in Joe they also see an engaging young man with the same enthusiasms, drives and interests as anyone else.

If that kind of response can be multiplied a few thousand times, UCP feels it may be getting through to the public the message that handicapped people may look different on the outside but are no different on the inside.

This year's television effort highlights the work of a young doctor who was born with cerebral palsy. He is Tom Strax of Philadelphia, who practices rehabilitative medicine and whose special rapport with patients, from children to the aging, exemplifies the message about the humanness of the handicapped that UCP is endeavoring to get across.

UCP's intention is to tell the truth about cerebral palsy, not to glamorize it. Television is only one medium the agency uses in this effort. Radio spots deal with the same themes, and printed materials feature disabled people of all ages at work, at play and enjoying the ordinary pursuits of daily life.

Such messages seem a far cry from the poster child and other images arousing pity that were once the stock in trade of agencies serving the handicapped. UCP believes that depicting the real nature of disability is one of its responsibilities. This conviction also led UCP to drop its selection of a national poster child seven years ago; it was the first agency in the field, and still one of the few, to eliminate this practice.

If these changes have affected UCP's fund-raising efforts at all, it is for the better. Contributions from the public continue to increase each year. Public education and appeals for contributions are mutually supportive public relations objectives. UCP feels that in melding these aims it is also helping its clients and others who are disabled to live in a climate of greater understanding and acceptance.

Where Handicaps are Forgotten

JEANETTE INGOLD

Miss Ingold is a reporter for the Missoula *Missoulian*.

Bob was a husky, vigorous youngster who early in high school gave up football for a hot rod. He settled into the vocational curriculum, became something of a standout in the shop and mechanics courses, and landed a job two weeks after receiving his diploma. By the time he was 30 he was a highly respected mechanic in an automobile agency and was supporting a wife and three children. Then a transmission fell on him.

The resulting back injury ended his career as a mechanic, but that was the least of it. Bob came out of the hospital bent not just in body but in spirit as well. Unprepared for any other kind of work, he felt unprepared also to re-enter school, particularly as a cripple. Nonetheless, he is once again pursuing a successful career —this time as a project manager for a construction company—thanks to a community junior college training experience that seems to have something to say about the education of handicapped people everywhere.

So does the story of Tom. Tom had been blind in one eye since birth and he walked with a limp. Physically these difficulties added up to more of a nuisance than a barrier, so far as school was concerned. He found himself the object of such relentless pity, however, that life in the classroom became unbearable. He dropped out before completing his first year of high school, thus acquiring the additional handicap of being completely untrained to fill a job. Despite that bleak beginning, Tom is now doing very well in his job with a data processing company and a short time ago received a promotion.

Several social welfare agencies and many individuals played a part in getting Tom and Bob going again, but more essential were their own courage and their determination to function as equals among equals. They were called upon to display those qualities when—after some prodding —they agreed to enroll in an unusual pro-

Is he handicapped? Few notice at Missoula, where he is seen mainly as a solid worker

"Where Handicaps Are Forgotten," Jeanette Ingold, *American Education*, March 1972. ©1972 U.S. Department of Health, Education and Welfare.

gram at the Missoula Technical Center, one of the more unusual of Montana's five vocational-technical schools.

At Missoula Tech, Tom and Bob found no special classes set aside for handicapped persons. The staff studiously avoided categorizing anyone. Privately the school did seek ways (particularly in physical arrangements) to compensate for the problems that handicapped students inevitably face. But in general, Tom and Bob and the other handicapped students were called upon to compete with "normal" students on common ground.

"People mean to be kind when they go out of their way to give the handicapped special treatment," says John Giese, the school's director of adult and continuing education. "More often than not, however, the result is to rob these people of their confidence, thus creating a psychological roadblock to achievement. We are trying to clear the path. We want them to be able to deal with their challenges on their own terms and not have restrictions, no matter how well meant, imposed upon them by others."

That proposition is extended to cover those confined to wheelchairs, and it is made practical by the nature of the school plant. A ramp covers the slight difference in elevation between the school grounds and the entrance to the building. The building contains no classroom doors (noise, which might otherwise be a problem, is muffled by carpeting and acoustical ceiling). Angled tile walls screen the lavatories. There are no thresholds for wheelchairs to cross—just level carpet.

The concept of melding handicapped students into the regular curriculum, treating them as regular members of the student body, is the essence of a program launched by Missoula Tech a year and a half ago. The concept was of course easier to fasten onto than carry out, but the evidence so far indicates that it is working.

Missoula Technical Center opened in 1967 as a conventional postsecondary vocational-technical institution with a large adult evening program.

"It was a good school," says Giese, "but still, basically it was just another school." The student body included the customary number of students with special problems, and the staff made the customary efforts to help them—with the customary lack of success, as indicated by the high dropout rates of the handicapped.

"We could see that we weren't really getting to the heart of these students' needs," Giese says, "and we came to see also that we weren't set up to do so. Moreover, we were simply ignoring the handicapped people who needed training but who for one reason or another were hesi-

Handicapped and "regular" students share the welding bench without distinction

Learning to be an instructional aide, she has overcome diffidence about hearing loss

tant about being in a school. We were dealing only with those handicapped people who summoned up enough nerve to come to Tech on their own, and even with them we were hardly scratching the surface."

As a first step toward improving their batting average, members of the staff, encouraged by school director Gene Downey, began to consider some of the facts of the handicapped student's life. It seemed evident to them, for example, that many such students had become so accustomed to being protected that they were at a loss to deal with situations in which they had to function on their own. For many of them, physical disabilities were accompanied by at least equally

troublesome emotional disabilities. Also, students who had spent many years in special schools where physical therapy tended to take precedence over academic training were often severely deficient in basic reading, writing, and mathematics skills.

Like Tom, many had become so self-conscious about their handicaps and their earlier failure that they were reluctant to reveal them before the faculty and their fellow students. Others shared Bob's apprehension about returning to school after having been away for so many years.

Nearly all were pulled in two ways: They wanted the career training that Missoula Tech could offer, but they were tempted to regard themselves as misfits and were in any case dubious about their ability to make it.

In the search for a resolution of this conflict, members of the staff talked with anyone who might be presumed to have some useful ideas—handicapped people themselves, officials from the State's vocational rehabilitation program, medical doctors, faculty members of the University of Montana, physical therapists, psychologists, workers in Missoula's various public agencies, and many others. Out of these conversations came some basic convictions.

One of these convictions was that there would not be much point in preparing a handicapped person for a job unless he was also prepared to function in the real world. A second conviction was that a program aimed at helping the handicapped would not be worth its salt unless it could reach into the community and make career training available to anyone who could benefit from it. These basic themes were spelled out in a plan calling for the establishment of a novel program for handicapped students within Missoula Tech's regular operations. The goal, Giese said, was to set the stage so that handicapped students could help themselves and take pride in the fact that they were doing so. This concept was refined in some give-and-take between the school and the Montana Department of Public Instruction. Then early in 1970 a proposal was submitted to the department for financial support under the Vocational Education Act of 1968, and after further refinements suggested by department experts, an initial grant of $24,121 was authorized. (Additional sums of $38,158 for 1971 and

---

At Missoula Tech, no special classes are set aside for handicapped persons and no one is categorized.

$37,604 for 1972 were approved.)

With the start of the 1970 fall quarter, 21 students were enrolled in Missoula Tech's special new program—all of them recruited by Mona Frangos, the newly appointed coordinator of the project, and Jon Pozega, who was named project guidance counselor and center admissions officer. Another 30 students with relatively minor handicaps were not officially a part of the undertaking but were informally taken under its wing.

The core 21 had been rounded up with the help of people from a number of State and local social welfare agencies who had been asked to identify likely candidates. Then the University of Montana's Department of Psychology entered

the picture. Associate professors Herman A. Walters and John R. Means made psychological and vocational evaluations of nominees who agreed to become a part of the program.

"What we wanted from the psychological clinic was not a probe into the entering student's particular psychological hang-ups," Mrs. Frangos says, "but rather an indication of possible psychological blocks to learning, career aptitudes and interests, and a general picture of what kind of special assistance and guidance we should be prepared to offer. We wanted to be able to steer the individual into the kind of job that was right for him, and we wanted to be able to help him help himself." Such evaluations are now a routine element in the Missoula Tech program.

The 21 people officially enrolled during the first session of the project ranged in age from 18 to 54. One had taken some college training and 11 had completed high school, leaving nine who needed to catch up on basic learning skills in addition to preparing for a job. As it happened, each of the students signed up for one or more of the programs Missoula Tech offers: electromechanical technology, heavy equipment mechanics, small engine repair, welding, forestry, bookkeeping, clerical and secretarial preparation, mid-management, data processing, preparation to become an instructional aide, and training as a medical secretary. Several entered adult basic education classes at the same time, so they could complete their high school work.

Members of the project staff and the University of Montana and State agency people who were lending a hand with the program saw themselves as having two basic assignments. One was to make themselves always available to work with students on an individual basis. The second was to put into practice the concepts developed in the program's planning phase. The initial plan went into considerable detail, and most of the approaches set forth in it are still being followed. But some of the more effective aspects of the present program evolved from the experience of day-to-day operations.

The original plan, for example, called for backing each handicapped student with a support team specifically composed of a teacher, a counselor, a graduate student in psychology, and a representative of one of the participating State agencies. The team was to meet regularly, evaluate the student's progress and needs, and determine a course of action to help him solve his problems. In practice, however, this arrangement proved to be so formal and inflexible that it wasn't getting the job done. Members of the staff soon observed that the needs of the students varied so much from individual to individual that the rigid team structure more often than not missed the boat. They also saw that the more relaxed the setting, the more useful the flow of conversation, and so they abandoned scheduled meetings and took to gathering in the program's

---

Many of the handicapped students seem more troubled by their educational handicaps than their physical handicaps.

---

combination office and workroom to exchange observations and ideas on a more informal basis.

Equally informal is a learning center that also grew out of the experiences of the program's first year. Offering what appears to be a casually organized combination of learning equipment and individual help, the center is located in a partitioned-off corner of the school library. Among its most popular offerings are informal remedial sessions available to anyone who cares to drop by. Many of the students are frankly having a very tough time.

"People who have been in special classes most of their lives or people who have been injured after being out of school for several years are often far more troubled by their educational handicaps than their physical handicaps," Mrs. Frangos says. "On any given day we'll have students come in who are driven to despair because they feel they just can't keep up. We give them at least enough 'first aid' to get them through the next day's classes."

Often that kind of help is relatively simple to come by, as in the case of John, who is enrolled in the mid-management program. John's hands are so crippled that he can't take adequate notes in class. Solution: His notebook has been replaced by a tape recorder. Similarly, members of the staff make tape recordings of lectures for blind and only partially sighted students, and with the help of community volunteers the center provides such students with tape-recorded versions of textbooks.

In addition to these special arrangements made to suit special situations, each of the handicapped students is paired with a "regular" Missoula Tech student for tutoring. The tutors are selected from among people taking the same courses as the handicapped students and usually from among those attending school under the College Work-Study Program of the Higher Education Act. Missoula Tech's handicapped students benefit also from the interest in the program that has been generated at the University of Montana. "The people there," Giese says, "see this project not only as being an opportunity to perform an important public service but as an opportunity also to provide valuable training for university students who are headed for careers that will call for dealing in one way or another with the handicapped." Several of the Missoula Tech students arrange their schedules in such a way that they can also be in regular attendance at speech therapy classes at the university or receive help at the university's hearing clinic. Graduate students and faculty in the university's psychology department work with students having emotional problems, and three graduate assistants are specifically assigned to the Missoula Tech program as guidance counselors to supplement the services provided by the school's own guidance people.

Of the 21 students in the original cadre at Tech, one dropped out, 11 are working, and nine are continuing their training.

Tech's counselors and the graduate assistants got a sort of backhanded compliment for their work from the younger brother of a 22-year-old student now in his second year in the program. Handicapped all his life, he had been submissive and easy to manipulate, but his experience at Missoula Tech evidently gave a large boost to his confidence and independence. The brother complained to one of the staff members that the young man had become somewhat argumentive and "now he thinks he's somebody."

The make-up of the Missoula Tech staff provides a particularly helpful character to the program that had not figured in the original design. Several of the vocational-technical teachers are themselves handicapped and thus have a special perception of the needs of the handicapped students. All of these instructors had worked in the areas they teach—electronics, forestry, mechanics, or whatever—before injuries led them into the classroom. Thus in addition to offering instruction, they serve as confidants and as clear examples of what handicapped people can accomplish.

The nonhandicapped members of the staff also seem to have an especially easy manner with handicapped students. "Most of them had been in industry or business for many years," Mrs. Frangos says, "and evidently that background has the effect of making them less hesitant about working with handicapped students than are some professional teachers, who tend to feel they need special training."

Learning independence along with algebra—no easy task when you are in a wheelchair

As for how the program is working out, the story is best told in terms of what has happened to the 21 students who formed the original cadre. One of the 21 dropped out. One was graduated as a mechanic and now operates his own automobile repair shop. Nine have full-time jobs and one is employed part-time. The remaining nine are continuing their training.

Mrs. Frangos and the other members of the staff are deliberately vague about how many new handicapped students are participating in the program. Help is provided to any student who needs it, she says—handicapped and nonhandicapped alike—and the goal is to eliminate distinctions between them. It would nevertheless appear that about 50 of the daytime Missoula Tech students are receiving special help of one kind or another under the federally funded program.

"However," Mrs. Frangos insists, "there is no list of handicapped students as such, and they are not grouped together. We think of them as simply being part of the overall student body, and we want them to think of themselves that way, too."

And apparently that's the way it is. The standard registration form used by the school contains a space labelled "Handicaps." This year most of the handicapped students resolutely wrote in "None."

A Traditional Sheltered Environment

Editor's note: Today the dominant trend in rehabilitation is toward integration of the disabled into the able-bodied community. The campaigns for barrier-free design and vocational opportunities for the severely disabled are important components of this integration effort. The Thistle Foundation, reported on here, is an example from Britain of an older approach: the sheltered environment.

Sir Francis Tudsbery launched the Thistle Foundation in 1944 with the aim of providing a small housing estate where disabled veterans could live with their families and receive regular on-the-spot medical treatment. From these beginnings the Thistle Foundation has developed into an advanced housing settlement for the disabled.

In this article the Chairman of the Foundation's Executive Committee discusses the advantages, and some of the problems, of this sheltered environment. Mr. Brown raises some interesting points for comparison of the sheltered environment with the social integration models now being formulated by rehabilitation specialists.

R. G. A. Brown

The Thistle Foundation is a village of 103 houses and a hostel in Craigmillar, Scotland, outside Edinburgh. Catering to the severely disabled and their families, it was launched with the idea of providing medical treatment and specially designed housing for disabled persons which would allow them to live with their families, rather than having to stay in institutions.

The family houses are designed so that the disabled person's bedroom is on the ground floor, with double doors connecting it to the sitting room so that, if confined to bed, he or she can have these doors open and be part of the family circle. On the ground floor there is also a bathroom, kitchen and utility room. Upstairs, for the family, there are either two or three bedrooms and a toilet.

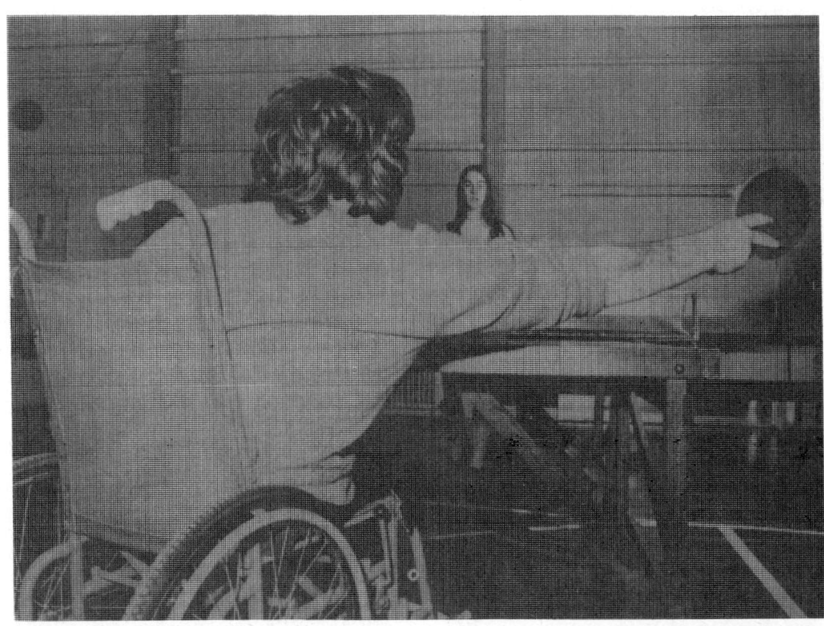

For senior citizens whose families have grown up and left home, there are six bungalows consisting of a sitting room, dining room, two bedrooms, bathroom and kitchen.

Although the Foundation is responsible for the upkeep of the houses, residents are responsible for their living expenses and those of their families. Each resident also pays a weekly contribution of £1.50 to the Foundation, designed to cover part of the cost of medical treatment.

Only Two Rules

There are only two rules for residents: no cycling by children in the covered pathways (for obvious reasons) and no four-legged pets. Otherwise, the home of each resident is considered his or her castle, and families are free to live their own lives with a minimum of regulation and interference by the Foundation. The same rules apply to the hostel, with the additional requirement that the residents have reasonable regard for the working hours of the staff, such as punctuality at meals and notification if they will be out late at night. The residents are free to come and go and do exactly as they wish.

The hostel is a recent addition. It represents something of a departure from the Foundation's traditional role since it is for the single disabled. Designed so that its present capacity of 16 men and women can be doubled, it provides a comfortable home with privacy in the bed-sitting rooms, which have their own basin, toilet and shower. Companionship is available in the common room, quiet room and dining room. Since all bedrooms have their own toilet facilities, segregation of the sexes is not necessary. Residents of the hostel may invite friends in for a meal, or have relatives to stay.

The decision to build the hostel arose from realization of the great need in Scotland for homelike accommodations for the single disabled, who have no families or whose families are no longer able to care for them. In taking on this additional role the Foundation seeks to give the opportunity for a fuller life to some single disabled people who would otherwise remain long-term hospital patients.

Covered pathways connect all the houses to the clinic, where are located the Superintendent and administrative staff, the nursing staff, medical consulting rooms, treatment rooms, physiotherapy department and swimming pool. The occupational therapy department is attached to the clinic.

The main responsibility for looking after a disabled resident rests with his or her family. The nursing staff is there to give the families such assistance as they need in the problems of everyday living, not to take over for the wife or husband. Extra assistance is of course given in cases of illness or emergency. Although nurses are employed on a non-residential basis, 24-hour, seven-day-a-week service is still provided. A doctor visits the clinic each morning, makes any necessary residential visits, and writes out any prescriptions required. A medical specialist and an orthopedic specialist attend once a week.

The physiotherapy department is staffed by two fulltime physiotherapists who carry out any treatment prescribed by the specialists. Arrangements for evening treatment can be made if the resident has regular daytime employment outside the Foundation.

Craftsmanship

Those unable to undertake regular outside employment can find work in the occupational therapy department. Four therapists give instruction in a variety of crafts, and the articles produced are sold for the benefit of those who made them. The standard of workmanship is high, so the demand for soft toys and furnishings, basketry, leather goods and other products outstrips the capacity to make them.

Sports and recreational activities are encouraged. In addition to the swimming pool, there is a bowling green and games courts, as well as open space for archery and field events. During the winter there is a regular program of billiards, snooker, draughts and chess competitions, and the gymnasium accommodates such indoor sports as table tennis and dartchery. The recreation hall is in use nearly every night of the week with programs arranged to suit families of the disabled as well as the disabled themselves.

The Foundation has acquired its own small bus which carries up to six passengers in wheelchairs. The bus is used by the bowling club for away matches, the hostel residents for going to concerts or the occasional evening out, and by the other residents who have no transport of their own for shopping and social outings.

The criteria for admission to the Foundation are that it must be possible to improve or at least maintain the applicant's physical condition, or that the applicant will derive real benefit from the facilities provided by the Foundation. Into the latter category, for example, would come people confined to wheelchairs who live in an apartment at the top of a building and who are never able to get out of doors because there is nobody to carry them up or down.

Originally the Foundation was for disabled former servicemen only, but now disabled males and females without service connections are admitted. Once accepted and admitted, the resident is normally in the Foundation for his or her lifetime. They may, of course, leave at their own request at any time, and there have been a number of occasions when residents have felt that their condition had so improved that they were able to leave the Foundation and set up their own businesses in various parts of Scotland.

Selective Admissions

Nearly every type of physical disability is represented in the Foundation. The Council has a quota, strictly adhered to, for those suffering from progressive diseases. Every effort is made to keep the age range of the residents as wide as possible, so that there will always be an element of young life about. The Foundation is selective in dealing with applications to make sure that the expensive medical facilities available will be used to the full, and that applicants will fit into the social life of the Foundation.

The Thistle Foundation has to rely on the generosity of the public for its continued existence. The only state aid received is a small sum each year from the Regional Health

Authority towards the cost of the medical treatment given by the Foundation to war pensioners who would otherwise have to receive their regular treatment in hospital.

Will there be a continuing need for the facilities and services provided by the Foundation? It is now the duty of the local Authorities to provide suitable accommodation for disabled persons in their areas. The greatest need at the present time in Scotland is undoubtedly the provision of accommodation for single disabled people whose parents have either grown too old to look after them or have died. But because of the economic climate, it is not anticipated that the local Authorities will be able to make any appreciable contribution to the problem of housing unmarried disabled people during the next 10 years.

As far as married disabled persons are concerned, it is of course the aim of the rehabilitation services that such persons should return to their communities as contributing members and as taxpayers. However, there will always be a considerable number of persons newly disabled by motor accidents or disease who will never achieve the degree of rehabilitation which will permit a full life within the community. They will require the sheltered housing conditions and constant nursing care which the Foundation provides.

We recognize that the correct place for disabled persons to live is in the community. From this point of view, places such as the Thistle Foundation should not exist, consisting as they do of a concentration of disabled persons living close together — perhaps, some might say, in a ghetto. Against this there has to be set the economics of providing the daily care and attention which so many severely disabled persons require. If efficient use is to be made of professional staff, expensive medical equipment and such facilities as a swimming pool, one way of achieving this is by user concentration. The funds of a voluntary organization are not unlimited and have to be used to the best advantage.

This situation is not ideal, and therefore every effort is made to encourage the local community to take part in the life of the residents of the Foundation and for our residents to participate in the life of the local community.

FITTING THE HANDICAPPED FOR JOBS

By VELMA KRAUCH

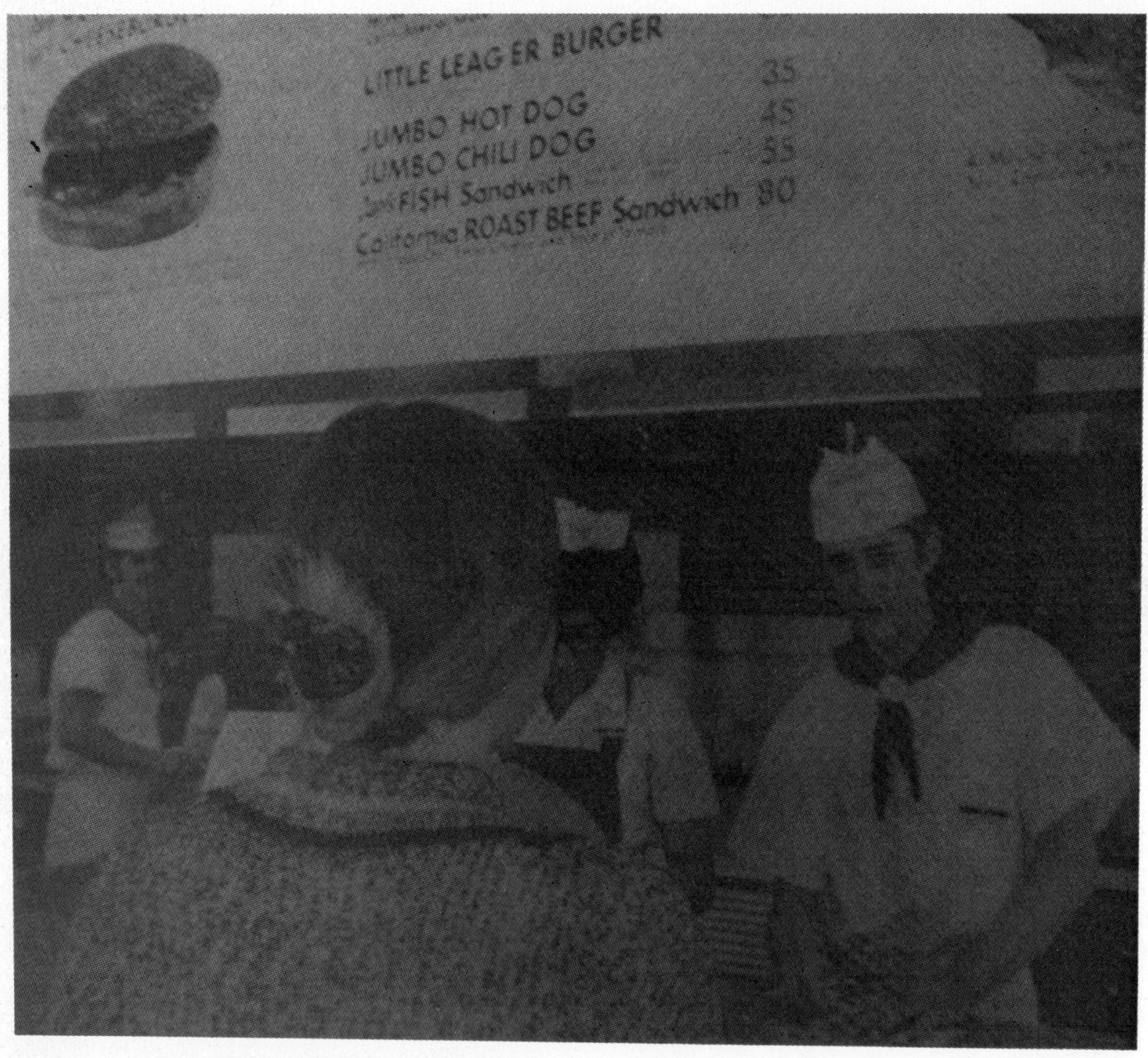

The noontime rush was just beginning. Customers hurried into the small hamburger shop and headed for vacant stools along the counter. As they seated themselves, Bruce, a 16-year-old part-time student worker who had been setting out silverware and napkins, picked up his order pad. This was the cue for a cameraman waiting nearby to adjust his equipment and focus on Bruce.

"One burger, with onion—and hold the mayonnaise," Bruce called out as he carefully translated the words onto his writing pad in newly learned restaurant code. He hung the order slip on a metal rack above the cook's counter, prepared a plate with lettuce and a slice of tomato, then went back to the counter and his next customer.

Most of the office workers and businessmen who flocked into the restaurant for their quick-order lunch were in a hurry; a few were downright impatient. Bruce, trying to conceal his shyness and nervousness, smiled pleasantly as he took orders. Off to one side, removed from the crush and confusion of the lunch crowd, the cameraman continued with the filming, catching the attention of a few customers who paused to stare. Was a movie scene being shot? A TV documentary perhaps, or maybe something to catch on the six o'clock news?

The fact is that this little episode was none of these things. It was instead a part of a job training program. The cameraman was a television producer-director from the Fullerton Union High School District in the Los Angeles area. He was filming Bruce as part of Project Worker, a special Fullerton High career education program launched in 1968 and designed for handicapped students. The program is more particularly aimed at training and finding jobs for three groups: the educably mentally retarded (those with IQ's that fall below the "normal" range according to standard testing and who have learning difficulties and, more often than not, accompanying emotional problems); the educationally handicapped (those with average and above average IQ's but who are afflicted with learning disabilities in one or more clearly defined areas); and the orthopedically handicapped (those with physical disabilities and, in some cases, learning and emotional difficulties).

Says Nolan Noble, administrator of instructional services, "The handicapped student obviously will be competing at a distinct disadvantage because of his limited learning or physical capabilities. We feel it is our responsibility not only to develop programs that will train these high school students but also to graduate them with skills for which there is a specific demand."

Adds Walter Retzlaff, director of Exceptional Pupil Services and overseer of the project, "We're not 'babysitting' anymore. These students are learning marketable new skills or upgrading those they already possess."

Of approximately 700 students in various special education classes throughout the Fullerton district, some 250 are in Project Worker. Within the district there are three centers for the educable mentally retarded, 12 educationally handicapped sections, and one orthopedically handicapped facility. Classes are small, and any one of them will have students of different abilities working at different grade levels. This variegation succeeds because the emphasis is on the individual—the guiding principle being that each individual is unique and of value, that each has the potential for growth, and that each should have the opportunity to develop that potential.

When a student comes into Project Worker, the staff attempts to find out everything it can about his abilities, aptitudes, and difficulties. Staff members consult his school records, administer psychological and vocational tests, discuss his condition with teachers, parents, and others who know him well. Priority is placed on searching out the student's own

On his first in-school job, he's supervised by a teacher

individual needs and special abilities, and his potential for particular kinds of work. Then an attempt is made to match his interests with a suitable job. The emphasis on job training does not mean, however, that academics are left behind.

"If a student's weakness in a certain academic area would prevent him from being hired, then we work on strengthening that weakness in terms of the job he has specifically selected," says John Dewey, a staff vocation specialist. "In some cases, the handicapped person may end up being better trained in that one area than a regular student."

In his beginning year the handicapped student is asked to plot out his personal objectives and goals and start a work-study schedule that calls for classroom-supervised training in such areas as simple office work, washing windows, hosing down patio areas, helping clean laboratories, or setting up for food service in the cafeteria. During this time the teachers closely observe the student's attitudes and performance. Is he able to follow directions well? Is he consistently on time? Does he get along with other people?

"When he demonstrates he's job-ready," says Carol Michael, a department head for the educable mentally retarded, "we

them to spend two hours on the job, another two hours in regular classrooms, and two hours in special education.

To ready himself for on-the-job training, the student begins an individual study plan. He selects three jobs in which he has an interest and then studies the various requirements that go with these jobs and the situations in which he will be expected to perform. His work counselor arranges for him to visit, under supervision, actual work sites in those fields which he has chosen. At these sites he is given an opportunity to talk with workers and potential employers. On the relatively rare occasions when a firsthand visit is not feasible, the staff uses a collection of tapes, slides, pamphlets, and films focused on various job categories.

Students also go through classroom simulations of jobs. If a particular job normally calls upon the employee to work standing up, then the trainee is expected to stand. For one student, a "mockup" station could mean learning to make change from a cash drawer, as was the case for Bruce. For a mechanic trainee, it might mean following directions in repairing automotive equipment, or for a potential nurse's aide, practicing bed-changing techniques with sick patients. Dur-

When the change you've counted out doesn't match the correct answer on the TV screen, you need help from a teacher

place him in an on-campus job situation—the cafeteria, the library, the autoshop, an office, or any number of other available spots. Sometimes with pay, sometimes not. Either way, in most cases the student sets up a pattern of reporting as a regular employee and working for a boss for an established amount of time—usually an hour—each day."

Generally, students hold on-campus jobs during their second year of high school, and most move to an off-campus job during their last two years. Their daily schedule calls upon

ing the tape showings and simulation sessions a teacher or teacher aide is in the classroom to guide the student and reinforce his progress.

To illustrate: Bruce chose to work as a waiter in a hamburger drive-in. With his "minimal brain dysfunction" giving him a memory bank on the level of a seven-year-old, Bruce obviously needed special help. His reading was at a third-grade level. Thus remembering instructions and being able to sift out what applied to him was a continual challenge.

Seated at a table with a cash drawer and real money, Bruce drilled on problems of making change as they were flashed on the small TV screen in front of him. The narrator on the screen posed a specific situation, then paused a number of seconds to afford Bruce time to do the necessary computation and then physically to make the proper change. When the correct answer was revealed, Bruce compared the change he had made with the coins and bills shown on the screen.

In addition to working this exercise, Bruce drilled singly or with a teacher memorizing food prices and restaurant order abbreviations. This drill was done in a corner of the classroom using a Carousel slide projector synchronized with tape-recorded narration. The small screen was darkened by folding out hinged wooden sides and top, thereby eliminating the need to darken the entire classroom. Thus by drilling himself daily, Bruce was able to develop the skills he needed to fill the requirements for his chosen job.

Later in the classroom training, when his job choice has been narrowed to a single selection, a student begins learning from videotapes that have been prepared by the district's full-time television technical adviser in cooperation with a work-study coordinator. A videotape library is maintained at the instructional materials center which distributes tapes to all high schools where the project operates. In some cases, training tapes are provided by an individual company or a particular industry.

When a student's performance is seen to be about on a par with that of the worker in the training film, the teacher records the student's actions on videotape for purposes of comparison and evaluation. When the program first began, tapes that displayed students at their maximum proficiency were shown to prospective employers, but this practice proved to be so time-consuming for the employers that it was dropped. Now, interested employers are briefed on a student's competence by a counselor and given a one-page written report on the student's qualifications.

Once a student attains a degree of proficiency in his classroom drills, arrangements are made to place him with an employer participating in the project for on-job training. The employer evaluates him on a quarterly basis. When needed, one of the student's teachers or his counselor is available to consult with the employer.

To insure a steady availability of jobs for the trainees, counselors regularly visit local business firms to solicit their participation in Project Worker. Says one counselor, Carson Hall, "We do a selling job on the advantages of hiring the handicapped. With the help of a three-minute tape we show an employer how we can save him time in recruiting eligible people for jobs that are hard to fill because, for example, of the unusual hours involved. We have a large number of students available at odd hours for full-time or part-time work. And we assure the employer that if one student doesn't work out, we can replace him with another at no cost in time or money to him." To the extent possible, Project Worker attempts to line up jobs that are within walking or bicycling distance of the student's classroom.

When an employer signs up to participate in the program, the counselor provides the students with a written report describing the various conditions and qualifications called for in the job or jobs this employer can offer—whether the student will work inside or outside, whether he will be in cramped quarters, the moving objects he will need to be aware of and what hazards he might encounter, whether the job requires the students to work alone, what special instructions he will be asked to follow. Accompanying this report is a detailed job description and task analysis. The student thus knows in advance what is expected of him before he opts for a particular job.

During his rush-hour filming scene, Bruce was working a daily two-hour, on-the-job shift which is a component part of his special high school curriculum. Subsequent to this "post-employment followup" staged by a counselor, Bruce had an opportunity to view his on-the-job performance and to hear the comments and suggestions of his classmates and his teacher. Actually, the film was designed not only to indicate to Bruce

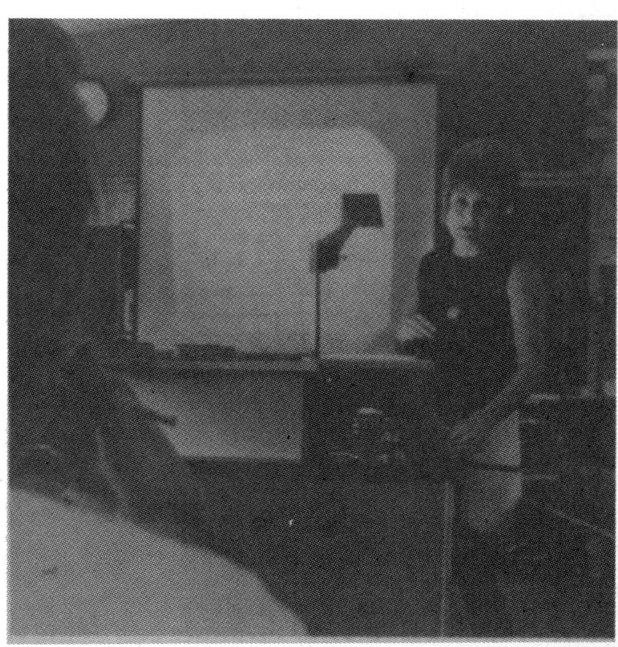

Students receive rundown on their earnings and deductions

those particular aspects of the job in which he needed to improve but, in showing his accomplishment, to inspire in his classmates a determination to do as well.

Teachers frequently serve as cameramen in the videotaping process. For the more tightly focused evaluative work in a classroom, a teacher can use a small, portable taping unit, powered by batteries. When larger areas are involved—service stations, warehouses, or manufacturing plants—the television producer transports regular camera equipment in the district's mobile van.

"Our program is more than just another vocational class for the handicapped,'" says one of the teachers in the project. "These kids have hope now. Many of them have been unable to cope with regular classes and could think of themselves only in terms of failing. In Project Worker, one of our first aims is to help them feel better about themselves, to appreciate what they have, and to know that they have a job potential."

Because his job situation is integrated with his school curriculum, Bruce receives work credit for his hours of employment. Also while on the job he is paid $1.65 per hour, the going wage for his job classification. "We don't allow our students to be exploited," says Retzlaff. "If they are capable of performing in their chosen job, we expect them to be paid accordingly and see to it that they are."

Records to date indicate that close to three-fourths of the students in Project Worker are satisfactorily employed, with the number growing as the semester progresses. The program has attracted the participation of 31 companies, some locally owned, some chain-operated. Among them are restaurants, service stations, motels, a supermarket, a department store, manufacturing plants, and an automotive repair shop. Students prepare for such job classifications as assembler, waitress, food preparer, moldmaker, nurse's aide, service station attendant, secretary, office worker, cook, counterman, and sewing machine operator.

And about hiring the handicapped, what do employers say? "Our problems are no greater with them than with other students," says one restaurant manager. "We recognize that the educationally handicapped perform best in set procedures, and if the procedures vary, they may have a tendency to become confused. So we keep an eye on them. Regular students will look for shortcuts, but handicapped students are rigid in hewing to the line."

Then he adds: "But by the same token, they're usually gung-ho because they're holding a paying job, and a certain amount of prestige goes with that. And for us, it's extremely difficult getting consistent, part-time help. These kids can come when we need them. In the case of Bruce, he's one of my best workers—serious, ambitious, and he's learning to think things out on his own."

Says a local manufacturing-plant owner, "Our mentally retarded worker was so well trained when he first came to us that our regular employees took it for granted he could handle more than he really could or should. As a result, he got into a situation where he made the mistake of slipping up on a crucial ingredient in a plastic mixture, which meant some dollars lost for us. But after that, we just made sure someone checked him at this point of the operation. Now he's one of our best workers—reliable, extremely cooperative, and he takes pride in his work. Last summer we hired him full time as a 'regular.' I wish I had more like him."

Project Worker evolved from a concept of Howard Levine, a teacher on one of the eight Fullerton High School district campuses. Levine had already adapted tape-recordings to his approach to teaching the educable mentally retarded and planned to apply for Federal money to support a program that would train such people in job skills. He was thinking of limiting the program to one school. But the idea generated so much enthusiasm that Nolan Noble and Walter Retzlaff proposed an expanded program to be attempted on a districtwide basis. With Superintendent Leonard Murdy lending assistance and support, Project Worker was launched.

Funds came from a Federal grant under title VI-B of the Elementary and Secondary Education Act and also the Vocational Education Amendments. "We ran up our share of wrong-way streets and dead-end alleys until we finally came up with what we believe is a realistic approach," says Retzlaff. "Now we feel that anyone launching a project of this nature could duplicate it at almost half our original cost."

Understandably, one of the persistent problems is in obtaining personnel who can handle both special education teaching and the technological know-how of videotaping and general television mechanics. Project Worker teachers hold credentials in the field of special education and are required to attend regular inservice workshops during the semester.

Recalls Retzlaff, "We lost a couple of teachers with this new program, but most are very supportive. A few still have reservations, but then there are some so enthusiastic they push us to try new things."

In accenting the positive, one of the satisfying effects of the program has been that the school board and the Fullerton staff have helped make the community think first of the abilities of these young people rather than their disabilities. And in the judgment of Superintendent Murdy:

"Project Worker demonstrates that the educable mentally retarded, the educationally handicapped, and other handicapped students can learn many different tasks, both manipulative and intellectual, when a program of learning is carefully prescribed for each individual. It demonstrates that young people, even those with limited intellectual functioning, can learn when the student is the center of the instructional program. It demonstrates that equality of education is not the same program for all, but the best for each."

Sweeping Rules on Employing the Handicapped

JAMES J. KILPATRICK

BACK IN the fall of 1973, Congress finally got around to approving a comprehensive Rehabilitation Act. It had been a long struggle, involving two presidential vetoes and endless legislative hassles. The act was thought of primarily in terms of vocational rehabilitation of the handicapped, and virtually all the debate turned upon programs of direct aid to handicapped persons through various public agencies.

On April 28, 1977, more than three and a half years later, the Department of Health, Education, and Welfare finally got around to issuing regulations intended to implement the act. More precisely, the new regulations are intended to implement Section 504 of the act. These are sweeping regulations. They will have a profound effect upon every public and private agency receiving federal financial assistance. By extension, the HEW regulations will affect all but the smallest employers everywhere. Yet curiously, the regulations have attracted little public comment. They deserve your sober and concerned attention.

Let me insert a personal word at the outset. Last month I wrote a newspaper column reporting the HEW regulations and commenting upon some of the prospective problems and consequences. To my dismay, the column attracted a deluge of letters—reproachful, angry, and in some cases venomous letters —charging that I lacked compassion, or sympathy, or sensitivity toward the plight of handicapped persons. This I deny absolutely. Not to put too fine a point upon it, I have known at first hand, in my own family and in families very dear to me, the cruel impact of physical and mental handicaps. But it surely denotes no lack of compassion to observe that the implementation of these regulations will impose heavy costs. HEW's own estimate is $2.4 billion over the next three years. Other estimates put the costs at up to $10 billion. These costs have to be discussed, planned for, and somehow met. Nothing is to be gained by ignoring them.

VERY WELL. As HEW Secretary Joseph A. Califano, Jr., pointed out in April, Section 504 of the act was adopted "without legislative hearings and with virtually no floor debate in either house." This is astonishing, for Section 504 is as clear and unmistakable as a clap of summer thunder. It says:

"No otherwise qualified handicapped individual . . . shall, solely by reason of his handicap, be excluded from the participation in, be denied the benefits of, or be subjected to discrimination under any program or activity receiving federal financial assistance."

Pick up the last three words. Under an interpretation by the Attorney General, federal financial assistance means any grant, loan, contract (other than a procurement contract or a contract of insurance or guaranty) or other arrangement by which a federal agency makes available assistance in the form of funds, property, or services of federal personnel. The HEW regulations issued on April 28 apply, of course, only to such assistance through HEW, but the limitation has little meaning. As Secretary Califano said, his rules "will be the basis for other similar regulations that will be issued by all other federal departments and agencies and that will affect all recipients of federal funds."

The Section 504 regulations, quoting Mr. Califano, became a part of the "supreme law of the land" as of June 1, 1977. They have an entirely laudable purpose. The idea is "to open a new world of equal opportunity for more than 35 million handicapped Americans—the blind, the deaf, persons confined to wheelchairs, the mentally ill or retarded, and those with other handicaps." Among the other handicaps specifically included in the Section 504 regulations are alcoholism and drug addiction.

THE NEW regulations, Mr. Califano added, "will work fundamental changes in many facets of American life." In many cases, they will call for dramatic changes in the attitudes and actions of institutions and individuals who receive federal funds or assistance. The rules will open "a new era of civil rights in America."

For such recipients, by way of example, the regulations will have this impact:

• All new facilities must be readily accessible to and usable by handicapped individuals.

• Programs or activities in existing facilities must be made accessible to the handicapped within 60 days, and if no alternatives such as home visits or reassignment of classes will achieve program accessibility, structural changes in the facilities must be made within three years. "No exceptions to the program accessibility requirement will be allowed."

These are among the guidelines for affected employers:

"Employers may not refuse to hire handicapped persons if reasonable accommodations can be made by them to an individual's handicap and if the handicap does not impair the ability of the applicant or employer to do the specific job."

The regulations define handicapped persons in three ways. Most broadly, the definition takes in "any person who has a physical or mental impairment that substantially limits one or more major life activities." Such impairments include "orthopedic, visual, speech, and hearing impairments; cerebral palsy, epilepsy, muscular dystrophy, multiple sclerosis, cancer, heart disease, diabetes, mental retardation, emotional illness, drug addiction, and alcoholism."

In a second group are persons who have "a record of physical or mental impairment," including those with histories of mental or emotional illness. The third group embraces persons who are "regarded as" having a physical or mental impairment, "such as persons with a limp and persons with disfiguring scars."

THE OFFICIAL analysis of the regulations, issued by HEW in April, has this to say to affected employers:

"The Secretary has concluded that a general prohibition of preemployment inquiries is appropriate. However, an employer may inquire into an applicant's ability to perform job-related tasks but may not ask if the person has a handicap. For example, an employer may not ask on an employment form if an applicant is visually impaired but may ask if the person has a current driver's license."

In every applicable instance, public institutions and private employers must begin immediately to make "reasonable accommodation" for handicapped persons. Except where undue hardships can be clearly proven, no waivers or exemptions will be granted. By way of example, "reasonable accommodation includes modification of work schedules, including part-time employment, and job restructuring." In addition, the term may include "physical modifications or relocation of particular offices or jobs."

The regulations, it is emphasized, do not demand the unreasonable. "Thus, a small day-care center might not be required to expend more than a nominal sum, such as that necessary to equip a telephone for use by a secretary with impaired hearing, but a large school district might be required to make available a teacher's aide to a blind applicant for a teaching job."

Manifestly, HEW's rules will have the most immediate impact upon such public institutions as public schools, libraries, hospitals, nursing homes, day-care facilities, and institutions of higher learning that receive federal assistance. Handicapped children, who earlier might have been relegated to segregated institutions or ignored altogether, will be brought into the mainstream of ordinary life. Under the regulations, "every handicapped child will be entitled to a free public education, appropriate to his or her individual need, regardless of the nature or severity of the handicap." Such children cannot be segregated in public schools; they must be educated "with the nonhandicapped in regular classrooms to the maximum extent possible."

AS SECRETARY Califano acknowledged, so extensive a requirement cannot be implemented overnight. "Admitting a deaf child to a class, for example, is a meaningless gesture unless an interpreter is also avail-

able to communicate the teacher's words." For a time, the supply of specially trained teachers and interpreters may be insufficient to meet the demand. Nevertheless, a good-faith effort at compliance is required. Failure to comply may result in a cutoff of federal funds.

In colleges and universities, especially the older institutions, the Section 504 regulations will demand compassionate, imaginative, and perplexing endeavors. "A university does not have to make all of its existing classroom buildings accessible to handicapped students if some of its buildings are already accessible and if it is possible to reschedule or relocate enough classes so as to offer all required courses and a reasonable selection of elective courses in accessible facilities. If sufficient relocation of classes is not possible using existing facilities, enough alterations to ensure program accessibility are required. A university may not exclude a handicapped student from a specifically requested course offering because it is not offered in an accessible location, but [the university] need not make every section of that course accessible."

The foregoing quotations, taken directly from HEW's press briefing of April 28, provide a fair sampling of the new requirements. It perhaps goes without saying that the rules also require affected institutions and employers to "keep such records and submit such timely, complete, and accurate compliance reports" as may be required, including "racial and ethnic data showing the extent to which minority groups are beneficiaries." Plainly, Section 504—the section that was adopted "without legislative hearings and with virtually no floor debate in either house"—eventually will have precisely the dramatic impact Mr. Califano envisions.

LET ME return to the point of beginning. My purpose here is not to be editorial, but to be reportorial. Beyond question, countless handicapped persons have suffered cruel and heartless discrimination in the past. While many employers have gone out of their way to afford the handicapped a fair chance, other employers have thoughtlessly excluded the deaf, the crippled, and the disfigured from jobs they were entirely capable of performing. Now such discrimination becomes unlawful.

With goodwill all around, with careful architectural planning, and with substantial appropriations of public funds, the Section 504 requirements can be met in time. But as HEW's sweeping regulations are extended, it is imperative that public officials and private employers become familiar with these rules. We will be hearing about them, and coping with them, for a long time to come.

James J. Kilpatrick

Arde Bulova's Success in Aiding the Disabled

A study in concentration as students learn the exacting skill of watchmaking. They're at a school conceived by Arde Bulova as a way of helping disabled veterans of World War II. In 30 years, the Bulova school has trained over 1,200 handicapped men and women so they could find useful jobs, not only in watchmaking, but in other fields where precision work is necessary.

President Franklin Roosevelt summoned a group of prominent Americans to the White House during World War II and urged them to start thinking about the day millions of young men and women would be returning to civilian life.

The President was concerned especially about countless thousands who would not return as they had left —those wounded in battle.

Among the people at that meeting was the late Arde Bulova, board chairman of the Bulova Watch Co. He decided almost on the spot to establish a tuition-free school to teach disabled veterans a useful trade.

On May 15, 1944, while the war still raged, ground was broken in New York for the Joseph Bulova School of Watchmaking, named for Arde Bulova's father, who founded the Bulova Co. in 1875.

Today, some 1,250 men and women have graduated from the institution. Over the years, despite two more wars, the number of veterans enrolled in the school has dwindled. But it continues to train the disabled —amputees, paraplegics, and victims of tuberculosis, heart ailments, arthritis and other diseases.

Over $5.5 million has been contributed by the Bulova Watch Co. Foundation and the Bulova Fund for operation of the school. Only in recent years did it begin charging tuition, and then largely because of governmental funds being made available for rehabilitation of the physically handicapped. And even so, the two funds put up about $180 of the current $270 monthly tuition.

Three courses are offered: watchmaking (18 months), watch repair (12 months) and precision technician (nine months). Virtually every student gets a job on graduation—generally starting at $140 to $150 a week—in shops, watchmaking plants or other manufacturing operations where precision is at a premium.

Almost 20 per cent of the alumni own their businesses today.

The school promotes wheelchair sports nationally and internationally and its students compete in basketball, track, bowling, swimming, archery, weightlifting and table tennis.

In its 31 years, the Joseph Bulova School of Watchmaking has faithfully lived up to its dual motto: "To Serve Those Who Served Us" and "To Serve Those Who Need a Chance."

Or, as Benjamin H. Lipton, director since 1955, puts it:

"We are committed to the concept that 'ability, not disability, counts'."

THE ADMINISTRATION:
Hire the Handicapped

SUSAN FRAKER

with HENRY McGEE in Washington

Wally McNamee—Newsweek

Disabled demonstrators in Washington: 'A new era of civil rights in America'

Dozens of the handicapped, some in wheelchairs, gathered for a protest demonstration outside the new offices of Joseph Califano, Secretary of Health, Education and Welfare. Later, some of the crowd followed Califano to his home, and then to a number of his public appearances. Other disabled people, all protesting Califano's delay in implementing a law that would ban discrimination against them, staged demonstrations in Atlanta, Boston, Chicago, Dallas and other cities. In San Francisco, 80 people brought mattresses, food and battery chargers for their motorized wheelchairs and began occupying the regional HEW office on April 5, staying until last week. Said Barry Ryan, who has muscular dystrophy: "We are like the audience in 'Network' that shouts, 'We're mad as hell and we're not going to take it any more'."

Soon they won't have to. Last week, four years after Congress passed the Rehabilitation Act of 1973, which prohibits discrimination against the handicapped, Califano finally signed the regulation required to make the costly and controversial law effective. It seems certain to force sweeping modifications in the employment, education and treatment of more than 35 million handicapped people. Said Califano last week: "It opens up a new era of civil rights in America" and will "work fundamental changes in many facets of American life."

Braille Books: The regulation, which goes into effect June 1, applies to any school, college, hospital or other institution receiving HEW funds. It prohibits employers from refusing to hire the disabled—including victims of cancer and heart disease—if their handicaps don't interfere with their ability to do the job. It also requires employers to make "reasonable accommodation" to their handicapped workers. It mandates that all new buildings be made accessible to the handicapped with ramps, elevators or other conveniences; many existing buildings would have to be modified as well. It also instructs universities to make their programs available to the handicapped (by providing books in Braille, for example) and orders hospitals to establish special techniques for treating the disabled, such as ways of communicating with the deaf in emergency rooms.

The public schools will be affected the most. They must provide free education to 1 million disabled children now denied access to school. And rather than segregating the handicapped in separate classrooms, they must educate them in regular classes with the non-handicapped to the "maximum extent appropriate."

The regulation has been controversial from the beginning. Critics say it is vague, tangled in red tape and expensive. HEW officials estimate it will cost more than $2 billion to implement, but they say the costs will be substantially offset by the productivity of the newly employed handicapped. One of the most contentious issues was whether 10 million alcoholics and 1.5 million drug addicts should be classified as handicapped and thus protected by the regulation. Attorney General Griffin Bell ruled last month that they should be, but Califano indicated that employers could refuse jobs to alcoholics or addicts if they have records of unsatisfactory work performance. "The regulation clearly contemplates [making] decisions on the basis of an individual's behavior caused by such disease," he said.

HEW officials expect protracted litigation over sections of the regulation, partly because employers can be excused from full compliance if it would mean "undue hardship." But the American Coalition of Citizens with Disabilities said it was "90 per cent" happy with the new rule, which, it hoped, would bring the handicapped into the mainstream of American life. And after taking a day and a half to clean up, the handicapped protesters in San Francisco finally ended their 25-day sleep-in.

Help for Entrepreneurs From an Entrepreneur

By VERNON LOUVIERE
Senior Editor

Jeno Paulucci: "There are too many individuals with entrepreneurial spirit, drive, and a good idea who need working capital and guidance, and who are not getting them."

When Jeno Paulucci borrowed $2,500 from a friend to grow bean sprouts in Minnesota, he learned how valuable a small amount of capital can turn out to be.

Mr. Paulucci, son of poor Italian immigrant parents, used the loan to launch one of the great American business successes.

Jeno Paulucci's bean sprouts led him to riches. He created the Chun King Corp., producing Chinese dishes, and sold the firm to the R.J. Reynolds Tobacco Co. for $63 million cash in 1966. He has since gone into numerous other enterprises, including Jeno's, Inc., producer of pizza products, and The Cornelius Co., an international manufacturer of food and beverage dispensing equipment. Most of his enterprises are immensely successful.

Mr. Paulucci is convinced the same kind of entrepreneurial opportunity exists today. But he says one element is missing—equity capital. He wants to help provide that ingredient.

The Small Business Administration recently approved a license for the Paulucci Venture Capital Corp., of Duluth, Minn., to help disadvantaged and minority businessmen get started in business or expand. The new firm, formed under SBA's minority enterprise small business invest-

ment company program, will make available about $10 million in capital investment money with the aid of banks and SBA.

Such MESBICs, as they are known, are profit-making companies in which the government and private stockholders share risks. They make long-term loans and provide management assistance to small firms, and sometimes they make equity investments in firms they aid. SBA has licensed 77 MESBICs in addition to Mr. Paulucci's. The 77 have private capital of $38.2 million and government funding of $40.6 million.

"I started on a risk basis with various companies and turned them into multimillion-dollar operations," Mr. Paulucci says. "Since I, as an Italian-American by the name of Luigino Francisco Paulucci, could go into the Chinese food business in the Scandinavian country of northeastern Minnesota with a $2,500 loan 30 years ago and then sell the business to a tobacco firm for millions of dollars cash, I want to extend the same opportunity of enterprise to others—except today it will take a lot more capital to start.

"There are too many individuals with entrepreneurial spirit, drive, and a good idea who need working capital and guidance, and who are not

getting them.

"Maybe, with this program, we can make individuals and families more self-reliant again."

Mr. Paulucci, who has donated millions to philanthropies, emphasizes that his new firm won't engage in "charities, grants, or giveaways." Instead, he says, the firm will focus on giving the small entrepreneur who has limited capital a fair crack at the American economic system.

While that system has given much to Mr. Paulucci, his rewards did not come without struggle and hard work.

When his first major business achievement, selling Chinese food, captured national attention, the press hailed his "overnight" success. He later told *Nation's Business* ["Dynamic Growth Companies: J.F.P. Enterprises," March, 1970] that "this overnight success had been getting up at 4 or 4:30 every morning for 15 years and fighting competitors, financiers, government agencies, some railroads and airlines, a union or two, and the TV networks, among others."

Slogans are displayed prominently at all of the varied Paulucci enterprises. Some examples: "I Cannot Give You the Formula for Success, but I Can Give You the Formula for Failure—Try to Please Everybody." "Do What You Think Best—Not What You Think I'll Think."

Mr. Paulucci was born in 1918 in northeastern Minnesota iron mining country, where his parents had immigrated six years earlier. As a boy, he pulled a home-made wagon along railroad tracks, gathering stray coals for the family stove. Later, he unloaded boxcars for $1 a car.

"Once, I stood in a long, slow-moving relief line to get a handout," Mr. Paulucci recalled in the 1970 *Nation's Business* article. "I couldn't stomach it, so I just stepped out of the line and never returned. Today, I'm still adamantly against any type of dole or relief except for the helpless indigent. The able-bodied man or even boy can always find a way to earn a living."

A Wheelchair Doesn't Slow This Businessman

As far as M. Connolly Lunsford is concerned, practically everybody has a handicap of some sort. So he doesn't give much thought to his own.

"Actually, people like myself don't see themselves as handicapped," says the 27-year-old Mr. Lunsford, who runs two businesses from a wheelchair—a printing company and a firm that sells and installs automobile hand controls and other such aids for disabled people.

Connolly Lunsford was crippled by polio when he was two years old. But he sought out competition as a way of life, determined not to let his handicap stand in the way of achievement.

Mr. Lunsford holds a black belt, first degree, in karate; a brown belt in judo; and a state championship in weight lifting. He was captain of his high school chess team and a member of a high school debating team that won second place in national competition, and he played on a national championship wheelchair basketball team.

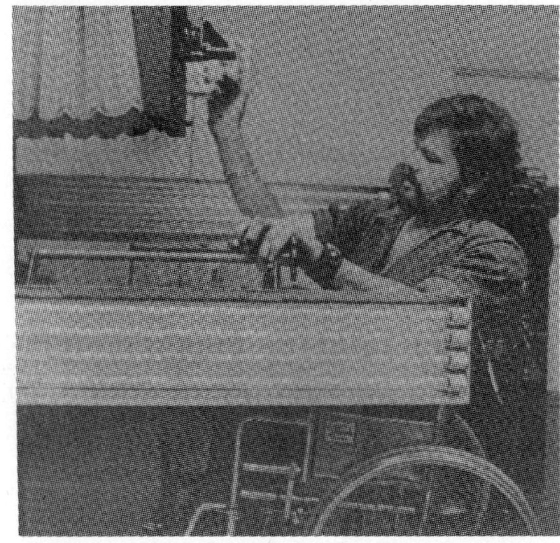

Being handicapped, says Connolly Lunsford, made him competitive as a weight lifter, a karate expert, a chess player, a basketball player, and, today, as a businessman. Here, he works in his instant print shop in Slidell, La.

"Competition is what this world's all about, whether you're physically handicapped or not," he says.

Mr. Lunsford majored in business administration at Florida's University of Miami and attended law school for two years there. While he was in college, he served as a licensed representative of the Manhattan Life Insurance Co.

After completing his education, he formed the Conn Equipment Co., in Lacombe, La., to market devices for disabled persons. Last year, he decided to spread his business wings after leafing through a Commerce Department directory on franchising establishments. He noted that instant printing topped the list of fast-growing franchises. Within a few weeks, he was attending a training school operated by Kopy Kat, Inc., a Ft. Washington, Pa., instant printing franchisor. Several months ago, Mr. Lunsford opened a Kopy Kat instant printing center in Slidell, La.

Connolly Lunsford will have no hangups about hiring handicapped workers, if his new business develops as he expects it will.

"Every handicapped person I know compensates for his handicap in one way or another," he says. "He sets goals for himself and pushes to achieve those goals. Handicapped people take great pride in productivity, and that's a missing element in much of our society today. It really is good business to hire the handicapped."

Who Are The Handicapped Scientists?

Janet Welsh Brown

Who are the handicapped scientists? They include the head of a worldwide allergy research division of a large pharmaceutical company who is deaf, the professor of psychology who is blind, and the manager of a department in a computer firm who is quadriplegic. The AAAS Office of Opportunities in Science will undertake a systematic survey of this group later this year in order to produce a profile of the handicapped scientist. This profile will be instructive in developing programs and resources to help overcome the problems such scientists face.

The Office has already heard from more than a hundred scientists who are deaf, blind, or orthopedically or neurologically handicapped—in most cases as the result of an accident or illness. Some generalizations about these scientists are possible. They are to be found in all fields of science, working in research, teaching, and administration. Most of them were handicapped after their education was begun, assuring the acquisition of basic communication skills and recognition of their intellectual prowess. Most have supportive families, but had to struggle through educational institutions that were anything but supportive.

These successful handicapped scientists have required extraordinary, almost unbelievable, perseverence to acquire an education. The obstacles placed in their way by educational institutions were both physical and attitudinal. In a 1974 survey of ACE-accredited 4-year colleges and universities, 22 percent of the respondents reported that they would reject deaf applicants (*1*). Although there are now some happy exceptions, such as the University of Texas and the University of Illinois, most campuses are unnegotiable for the severely orthopedically handicapped. Nor do most offer any of the counseling and other services necessary to assure the handicapped an equal chance of success.

The psychological hurdles are also great; these people have had to prove themselves over and over again. All of them can tell stories of the professor who, having no experience with the handicapped, routinely dismissed their abilities on the assumption that these students "would not be able to keep up with the reading" because they were blind, or "would not be safe in the laboratory" because a limb did not function. One deaf woman chemist was required to undergo an additional examination to get her Ph.D.—*after* she had completed with honors all the requirements demanded of her "normal" colleagues.

Landing that first job is another problem mentioned frequently by our respondents (*2*). One deaf physicist with a Ph.D. from Yale was told teaching was impossible and he should stick to research, while other deaf scientists have been told by employers that they would not be safe in a laboratory, or that they should stick to teaching the deaf "where they could really make a contribution. . . ." Although the myth that handicapped workers present additional safety hazards has been disproven in practice (*3*), this concern is still widely used by employers to reject handicapped applicants.

Advancement on the job is frequently not open to the handicapped on the basis of merit. They may be deprived of professional give-and-take in the laboratory or full participation in professional associations by colleagues who will not take the time and trouble to include them. Advancement to supervisory responsibilities is often especially difficult for those whose capacity to communicate is impaired. It is somehow assumed that the handicapped will not be able to administer, travel, and communicate with foreigners, although the AAAS file is full of examples of people who do all of these things.

The appeal that many handicapped scientists make is that the able handicapped persons of our society, who are often considered to be an added cost, should be valued as a human resource to be developed. They seek recognition that the patience, incentive, and self-discipline developed by the handicapped are of positive value to the employers of scientists. They hope that changing attitudes will make it possible for all bright, able, scientifically inclined youngsters to choose science without having to be super-achievers in order to reach their goals.—JANET WELSH BROWN

"Who Are the Nation's Handicapped Scientists?" Janet Welsh Brown, *Science*, Vol. 190 No. 4212, November 1975. ©1975 The American Association for the Advancement of Science.

in my opinion

We should open up
jobs to the handicapped

Barbara Pellowski, 17, Grand Forks, N. Dak.

Barbara's article is a prizewinning entry in the 1975 writing competition sponsored by the President's Committee on Em-

Arla S. has traveled to five different states, always searching for the same thing—a job. She'd like to be independent and self-supporting but has had no success in reaching her goal. Arla is handicapped. "Employers don't think of our *abilities*," she explained, "but of our *disabilities*. They won't find out what we can do or let us compete on a fair and equitable basis for jobs. They won't recognize us as individuals."

People are beginning to rethink their ideas about the handicapped. But many still do not realize that the handicapped are neither shut-ins nor individuals who should be content with busywork to help reduce their cost to taxpayers. The physically handicapped can be useful citizens and should be given a chance to perform meaningful work and follow careers in keeping with their desires and abilities. Yet they receive little support in finding suitable employment. Only three percent of disabled adults report that they received any assistance in returning to work after their disablement.

Looking into the problem I found that in my city of fifty thousand people, only two establishments currently employ handicapped individuals on a regular basis. I discovered that the attitudes and hiring practices of employers was one major barrier to employment. Employers are not only discouraging but often have inflexible standards such as rigid physical, educational or pretraining requirements not always relevant to the specific job. All too many disabled people have taken the long, hard road to rehabilitation only to be rejected because of such unfair hiring practices.

I'm also concerned about the architectural barriers to employment of the disabled. Wider doors, larger rest rooms and ramps in public buildings would help. We must focus our efforts on solving the mobility difficulties of these people. Unless we do, how can we ever hope to conquer their employment problems?

Once employed, how do the handicapped perform on the job? Government studies show that they suffer fewer serious on-the-job injuries than the average worker. Absenteeism is not greater and, in fact, is often less among the handicapped. And the length of time at one job is the same as for any other worker. In suitable jobs, their productivity is rated above average.

Employers have not yet realized that by hiring the handicapped everyone benefits. Job-prepared handicapped workers can be an important addition to our nation's work force. And the community has the satisfaction of seeing the disabled help themselves, become self-supporting taxpayers and assume their place in community and family life.

Curtis Brewer Can Do Nothing For Himself . . .

But he's accomplishing quite a bit for others.

By Winthrop Rockwell

Curtis Brewer's arrival in the Washington office of U.S. Senator Jacob Javits (R-N.Y.) was not expected. Brewer, a quadriplegic, had been given $1,000 by a friend who flew with him to the Capitol, then, at Brewer's request, abandoned him in the lobby of the Senate office building. A stranger wheeled the handicapped visitor up to Javits's office.

Brewer was badly in need of physical therapy, but due to bureaucratic obstacles, he had been unable to receive the treatment he felt he deserved. The visit to Washington was a gamble; its purpose, to get attention. So he waited calmly until the senator appeared. Indeed, the presence of the physically helpless black man created an uproar. According to Brewer, when he asked Javits to take some papers documenting his medical condition out of his inside coat pocket (Brewer couldn't do it himself), Javits became uneasy and left the office. The visit ended abruptly when the Capitol police removed Curtis Brewer and kept him in a mental ward for observation that night.

Today, despite the fact that Curtis Brewer is totally paralyzed from the neck down, he frequently confronts men in positions of clout when he is settling a dispute for himself or for others. And few find it possible to ignore him when he installs himself, Job-like, in their offices and settles down to wait.

Brewer would be the first to reject the idea that he has accomplished anything unusual, but the fact remains: Twenty years ago he became a quadriplegic with partial, then total loss of all voluntary movement in both arms, both legs, and torso. Since then, he has married, reared a son, finished his undergraduate degree, completed work toward a masters degree in public administration, held a full-time job as administrator of a hospital laboratory, served as a private ombudsman, gone to law school, and been admitted to practice before the New York state bar last fall—at the age of 48. In fact, since becoming a lawyer, Brewer's most important objective has been to turn a nonprofit corporation called Untapped Resources, which he founded in 1964, into a legal services agency for the physically handicapped.

"Because I've been paralyzed for 20 years, I'm an expert in the problems that handicapped people face. As a lawyer, with my training in public administration, I can serve as a catalytic agent to help disabled people bring their problems to the experts who can solve them," says Brewer.

A husky, handsome man with a completely shaved head (to eliminate itching because he cannot scratch), Brewer has been described by friends as fastidious, hardheaded, brilliant, aggressive, astute, and impeccable in appearance.

When he chooses, Brewer can dominate a room or a group of people with his presence and force of personality, even though, as one of his doctors says, "If you walked away from Curt, he would die since he can do *nothing* for himself without some form of mechanical or human assistance."

Almost the only voluntary movement Brewer has is in his head where he has complete control. His expressions alternate from broad smiles to sober thoughtfulness. Brewer often demonstrates that he has *not* lost all voluntary movement below his neck: With careful concentration he can move the hand resting in his lap a quarter of an inch. "Voluntary," he says looking at his visitor. "That motion was voluntary."

The first signs of Curt Brewer's paralysis came on suddenly in the winter of 1955. At the time, he was working for the U.S. Postal Service in New York City.

"It was absolutely frightening. I didn't know what was happening," recalls Brewer, who was 29 at the time. "My left forearm began stiffening, then the fingers. Then came pressure on my chest and tingling in my toes. I lost sensation in my hand so that it became difficult to get the subway tokens out of my pocket."

For six weeks the paralysis steadily advanced until he was forced to enter a hospital where he remained for five months.

"One day I tried to transfer myself from one wheelchair to another and fell flat on my face," says Brewer. "I cried like a baby. Because it was like doomsday. You know, boom."

None of the physicians at the hospital were able to determine why Brewer was becoming paralyzed. Speculation ranged from hemorrhaging of the spine to multi-

3. EDUCATION

ple sclerosis. It was even conjectured that he may have contracted a virus while working in the overseas mail department at the post office. And today, 20 years later, Lawrence W. Friedmann, M.D., medical director of the Institute for the Crippled and Disabled, in New York, says, "Nobody on God's earth knows what caused Curtis Brewer's paralysis. Except for an utter miracle, there is no hope that he will recover. Medicine is nowhere near a breakthrough in this area."

Brewer's paralytic condition is known as transverse myelitis, which is an inflammation across the spinal cord. At first, his physicians believed that there might be hope for recovery if he could get physical therapy. At Montefiore Hospital in the Bronx, where he was originally admitted, the nurses in physical

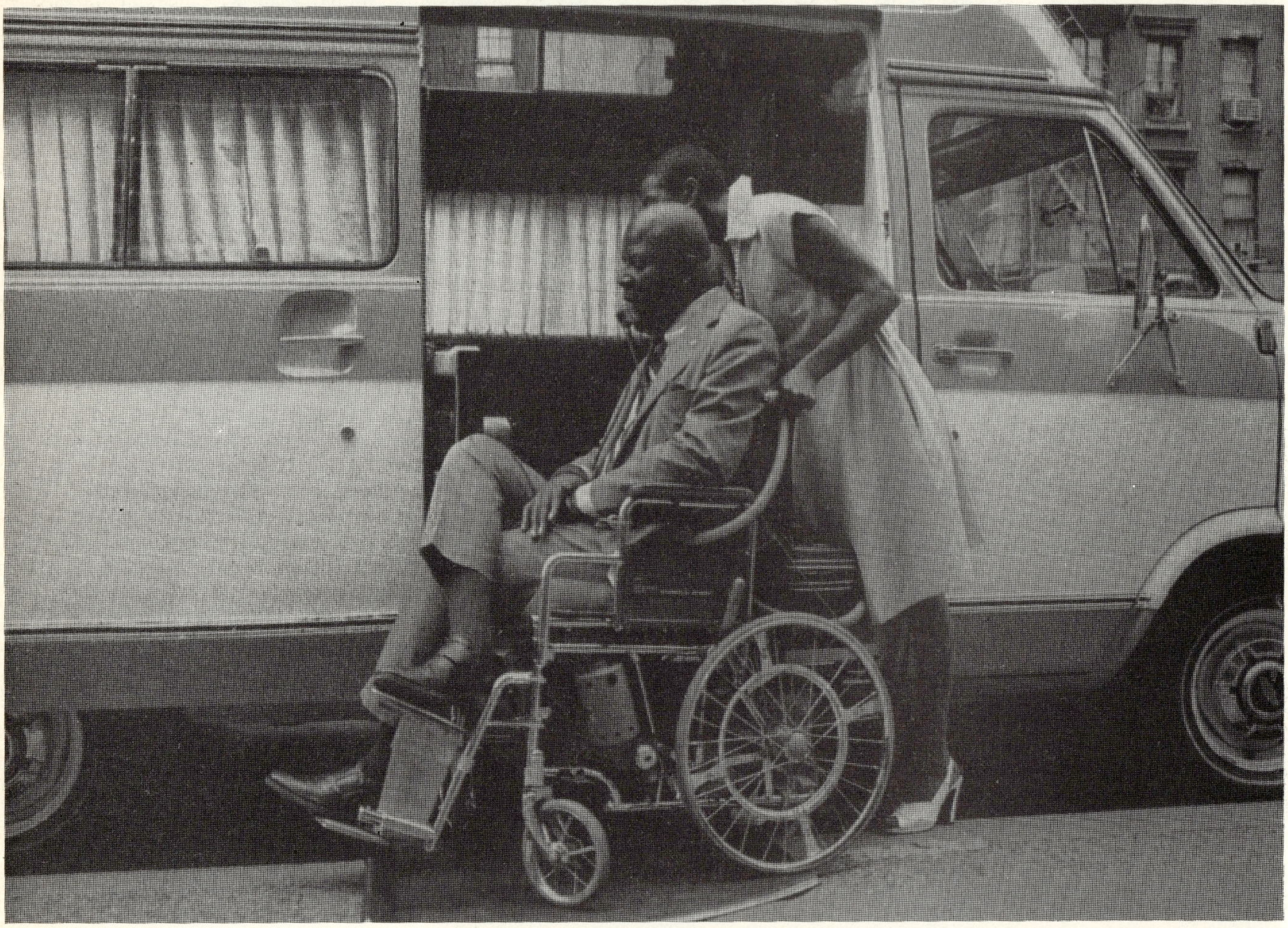

Curt Brewer's paralysis set in more than 20 years ago. At first, "it was like doomsday," he says. Before long, however, he had not only accepted his condition as a quadriplegic but he began to think of it as "a powerful motivating force for achievement." Perhaps it's a combination of gall and astuteness that has enabled him to become the aggressive, dedicated attorney he is today, serving the handicapped.

Clearly, one of the most valuable aids to Brewer's law practice is the van (above) donated by a Michigan furniture research company. It is specially outfitted for Curt as a mobile law office.

therapy told him that, at nearly 200 pounds, he was too heavy for them. In frustration, and against medical advice, Brewer finally signed out of the hospital and went home.

Although he was severely paralyzed, he still had some control in his arms and legs. "For five months I hadn't done any real climbing, but the night I went home from the hospital I climbed three flights of steep steps. The motivation was very, very strong. My wife was on one side and an attendant on the other, and I just pushed up those steps one at a time.

"From that day I began steadily to improve. I began to get up and pull myself around the apartment. My wife took a leave of absence from her job as secretary to the general counsel of RKO Radio Pictures, Inc., and each day I would work to improve my physical strength."

For a while Brewer thought that his private physical therapy program would be successful. Within a few months after getting out of the hospital, he returned to the New School for Social Research, in Manhattan, to finish his undergraduate degree, which he received in 1956. He and his wife Bettie were then living in the Bronx, a long distance from the school. Each day that winter he would climb the icy steps to the elevated train for the trip downtown. It took him two and a half hours each way and sometimes he would fall in the snow, and then laboriously pull himself to his feet and continue on his crutches.

Before long, however, Brewer began to lose ground physically, until he was once again confined to a wheelchair. For the next 12 years he pursued a succession of odd jobs, from selling magazines over the phone, to selling insurance (for which he studied and passed the licensing exam).

Then he decided to continue on to graduate school in public administration at New York University. Though he never completed his degree, for three years Bettie would put him into his wheelchair, put their son Scott on his lap, and push him through the long city blocks from their apartment, then in the East Village, to school.

But by 1968 he had lost virtually all movement below his neck. And shortly thereafter his doctors became aware of a severe respiratory problem. Because none of his voluntary muscles function, the rise and fall of his diaphragm (which helps to draw air into the lungs and then expel it) is entirely dependent on involuntary muscles.

What this means is that Brewer has only about 23 percent of the breathing capacity of a normal person. Whenever he overexerts and increases his body's conversion of oxygen to carbon dioxide (CO_2), his lungs do not have the capacity to remove all of the CO_2 and it builds up in his body and acts like a sedative, making him weary and slowing the functioning of his brain.

In order to offset the CO_2 buildup, at least partially, Brewer wears a respirator most of the time. The respirator resembles an air-filled doughnut around his lower chest; it rhythmically puffs up with air, then collapses, providing a mechanical assist to the breathing action of his diaphragm. This respirator operates from electrical current or the batteries mounted on Brewer's wheelchair.

Curtis Brewer's life is immaculately organized. At his present home in New York's East Village, four attendants work full- or part-time in the apartment. In the morning one of them must literally pull back the covers on his special hospital bed and then bathe him, shave him, dress him, shave his head (twice a week), adjust a special urinary device that he wears almost constantly, move him into the wheelchair, and get him ready to meet the day. This process alone takes two or three hours.

Then he must be fed, one spoonful at a time. When he drinks, the glass must be lifted to his mouth. When he smokes (he knows he shouldn't, but it's apparently his one nervous habit), the cigarette must be placed between his lips for each puff. Even when he is sitting working in the office next to his bedroom, he must ask to have his foot moved to a more comfortable position, for his shoulders to be straightened, for the page of a book to be turned, as well as dozens of other little tasks that most people do for themselves spontaneously.

The Brewers' apartment has been laid out with attention to a normal family environment as well as to Curt's special needs. The living room is homey and comfortable, but down a narrow winding hallway the apartment opens up into a two-room suite which is a combination bedroom and office designed specially for Curt.

When Brewer is not in his wheelchair, he is in bed, and he can do his office work equally well from either spot. The office is fitted with several hundred legal volumes and filing cabinets, as well as a desk for his secretary.

His environment must be kept exceptionally clean since he is particularly vulnerable to bladder infection. Because he is unusually sensitive to temperature changes, the thermostat in the apartment must also be carefully controlled.

Other than his respirator, there is no special treatment for Brewer's condition of paralysis. He takes no medication. He does not even take aspirin because it has a negative effect on his ability to breathe.

Bettie Brewer has been Curt's tireless supporter ever since they were married in 1955—the same year his paralysis began. For years she had to do everything for Curt, carrying all of the responsibilities that are now borne by attendants. In spite of the strains, Mrs. Brewer is a warm and outgoing person, seemingly unhurried in the face of the never-ending needs of her husband.

For their son, Scott, a sturdy and articulate young man of 17, it has not been easy to reconcile his own needs with the demands of his father. Scott says his father is authoritarian, and Brewer agrees that he is. Brewer says, "A child like Scott has got to pull his oar. He's got to contribute. So that means do your chores, and if you don't and you're not pulling your oar, then you're a drag on the family and that's a burden that *we* cannot afford emotionally, financially, or intellectually."

Bettie disagrees. "I feel you teach a child love and security through example. I don't believe in Curt's philosophy."

Scott has great respect for his father, but he recognizes the conflict in his parents' philosophy. He is just as strong-willed as Curt, sometimes daring his father to discipline him, knowing that his father cannot exercise physical authority. Scott knows that he has wanted more than his father could give, not in a material sense but in companionship.

The home tensions have eased considerably, though, since Scott took an apartment last year with a friend, a few blocks away from his parents' home.

But despite those and other inevitable strains of the past years, Curt Brewer has always remained the stalwart, holding the family together. Says Bettie, who is now employed as an assistant in the Department of Clinical Psychology at New York University, "We never went without. Curt has always borne the financial brunt, taken the worry, and seen that we had what we needed."

Replying to a woman who wrote him

not long ago about her own son's paralysis (coincidentally his name was Scott), Brewer wrote:

"Perhaps more than most, you know something about the meaning of disability. While it can be a searing experience for each and every person who confronts it, it can also be one of life's events that calls for that nobility of spirit and imagination which transcends ordinary human perception.

"Do not attempt to sugarcoat the difficulties. Rather, meet them, if you can. No matter what our physical condition is, despair is ever in the shadow and can be a powerful motivating force for achievement."

Curtis Brewer's determined stance has not always endeared him to those who try to help him. Dr. Friedmann recalls that when Curt first came to him in 1964, he was frequently shocked and insulted by the things Brewer said—particularly when Brewer would interrupt to tell the doctor, "You're wrong."

"Here was a man who was so intelligent that you constantly had to tell him why. You had to listen to him and give him medical alternatives," says Friedmann.

"His aggression is terribly important. He would have been dead long ago without his aggression and self-rehabilitation. But that isn't always easy for a doctor to take."

Brewer says that one of the ways he now deals with his disability is not to know too much about it. "I don't want to know all the gory details. I let Bettie keep track of them. The psychiatrists call it selective repression."

But Curt does not repress his ambition or his talents, and others recognize their presence. In 1968 Dr. Sydney Weinstein hired Brewer to be the administrator of his neuropsychological research laboratory on upper Fifth Avenue in New York. In the $12,000-a-year position, he was supervising 50 employees, purchasing, hiring, and doing some fund raising. But before long, the lab became involved in designing equipment that would assist quadriplegics like Brewer.

Under Weinstein's direction and with a $20,000 grant from an interested corporation, a pioneering system was developed to enable Brewer to operate his wheelchair and certain electrical appliances from a switch mounted in front of his chin and operated by pressure from his tongue. The system, which was the first of its kind, worked moderately well but

there were problems.

Then Richard Douherty, chief engineer at a Manhattan electronic design and manufacturing company, appeared on the scene to redesign and improve the entire system.

Douherty combined a radio receiver of an automatic garage door opener with a small computer that then was wired to electric terminals. The terminals could be connected to any device run by electricity such as a light, a radio, a tape recorder, or even the latch on the front door of Brewer's apartment.

Several years later, the New York Telephone Company also took an interest in Brewer and his needs. Said a telephone company executive, "We realized that here was an aggressive person who wanted to move himself and move others. The telephone would be one of his most important tools—one he would be using day in and day out."

The phone company equipped him with a tiny microphone and ear plug fitted to a pair of glasses and hooked to the telephone by a long springy cord that reaches any spot in his office or bedroom. With a touch of his tongue switch, Brewer can reach a special operator who dials all his calls at no extra charge.

Perhaps the most invaluable equipment to Brewer's law practice is a van that is set up as a mobile law office. Brewer can be hoisted into the van on a special lift without leaving his wheelchair. The interior of the van is furnished with a couch and chair for visitors, a small round conference table, a special air conditioning unit to hold the temperature within Brewer's comfort range, a special taping system so that he can dictate notes, a flip-down bulletin board for displaying materials, and a portable respirator unit that operates off the van's battery. Donated by a Michigan furniture research company, the van is driven by one of Brewer's attendants. In it, Brewer can comfortably travel almost anywhere he needs to go to represent his clients.

The cost of the four attendants, the van, and all the equipment in his home has not been small. Brewer receives a disability pension and he has often earned a good income from his various jobs. He estimates that in the last seven years—from over a dozen forms of public assistance—he has received a quarter of a million dollars in support.

Brewer got the idea of going to law school in the late 1960s when he was working as what he called a "private

ombudsman"—a problem solver for handicapped and nonhandicapped clients.

In one case his client had leased a car that failed to work properly, and the client wanted to terminate the lease. One afternoon, Howard Dryer, the lawyer for the car leasing company, answered his phone; Curtis Brewer was on the other end. A long argument ensued over whether Brewer's client would be released from the contract.

After much wrangling they ended up in court, and Brewer, doggedly protecting his client, insisted on arguing the case before the judge. Dryer protested that Brewer had no right to represent a client in court since he wasn't a lawyer.

As Dryer told it later, "I was really angry at him. He pulled every stunt in the book. He had complete guile and he was obviously smarter than 90 percent of the lawyers I knew."

Dryer filed a complaint against Brewer for practicing law without a license. But Brewer saw to it that the complaint got very short shrift.

Eventually, however, the former adversaries became fast friends and Dryer urged Brewer to go to law school. "I could see he was a man who didn't understand the word 'no'," said Dryer. "Here was someone who was using his disability as a stepping stone, rather than an obstacle."

Brewer had two main concerns when he was looking for a law school: doorways and steps. As it turned out, Brooklyn Law School had no architectural barriers, so it was there that he attended classes and received a full tuition scholarship.

For most people, law school is demanding. For Brewer, it demanded every ounce of energy he had. In class he had a special prop on which his books and papers were spread out so that he could follow the lecture. A classmate, Nancy Erickson (who has since become an assistant professor of law at New York Law School), sat next to him each day and turned the pages in his books during the class period. She was paid $50 a week by the New York State Department of Education, Office of Vocational Rehabilitation, to tape every lecture, take extensive notes in class, and summarize every case studied. Each night she would go home and correct her notes, copy them, and give them to Brewer so that he could study them the following evening.

But for a man who could not raise his

hand to turn a page, the process of reading hundreds upon hundreds of pages from legal casebooks became a major obstacle. At first Brewer used a crude instrument consisting of a mouthpiece, attached to a wooden stick with a rubber tip on the end. By clamping the mouthpiece between his teeth and swiveling his head back and forth, he could manage to turn pages.

But most of his books contained more than 1,000 pages, and legal study often requires flipping back and forth from one page to another. Before long, the physical strain of flipping the pages began to take its toll on Brewer's fragile constitution. Unless he could find a different way of reading his books, it looked as if Brewer might have to give up law school.

Then, by word of mouth, two men, John Robertson and John Milward, heard about Brewer's problem. Both were members of the National Microfilm Association and commited themselves to finding a solution. The result was the loan of a sophisticated $10,000 Eastman Kodak microfilm reader and the microfilming of some 35,000 pages of textbooks and legal materials.

Another man, Milton Mandel, then head of the National Microfilm Corporation of America, paid for much of the processing out of his own personal funds because of his admiration for Brewer.

"Curt is too busy to be stopped by his disability," said Mandel. "No one ever forgets Curtis Brewer if they have met him. That's just not possible."

In addition to everything else, Brewer had to petition the highest New York state court for special permission to take four years instead of the normal three to complete his legal education. He also had to arrange to take his exams at home so that he could take part of the exam, rest, take another part, rest, and so on until he finished.

With his law degree, with the long involvement in his pet project, Untapped Resources, with his efforts to reduce architectural barriers and with his network of contacts built up carefully over the years, Curtis Brewer is a man on the move.

As he wrote a few years ago, "Looking back, I can see that ever since I was a scrawny able-bodied kid growing up with seven brothers and sisters in the Roxbury district of Boston, one of my mainstays has been the conviction that there's something special I yet have to do—some contribution I'm going to make that awaits like unfinished business."

Though he's only been a lawyer for a year, Curtis Brewer's contributions have been impressive by any standard. Last year, two weeks before Christmas, he received a personal note from President Ford commending his "extraordinary courage" and "determination." This year he was named Rehabilitant-of-the-Year by the metropolitan New York chapter of the National Rehabilitation Association. Recently, he has also been named to the board of directors of the National Center for Law and the Handicapped. Further, he has been recognized with the Thurgood Marshall Award of the New York Trial Lawyer's Association, a life membership in the NAACP, and the unanimous admiration of all who know him.

Said Mildred Ward, M.D., a blunt drawling southerner who was Brewer's physician a few years ago, "Curtis Brewer is one of my loves. I once told him that he had to be at least a quadriplegic to make him even with the rest of the world. If he could ambulate, nobody else would have a chance."

While working at a neuropsychological research laboratory in New York, Curtis Brewer helped develop an electronic system for himself and other quadriplegics. A tongue-operated apparatus (above) mounted on his wheelchair, allows him to move—forward, backward, left, and right—as well as to operate a microfilm reader and numerous other electrical appliances.

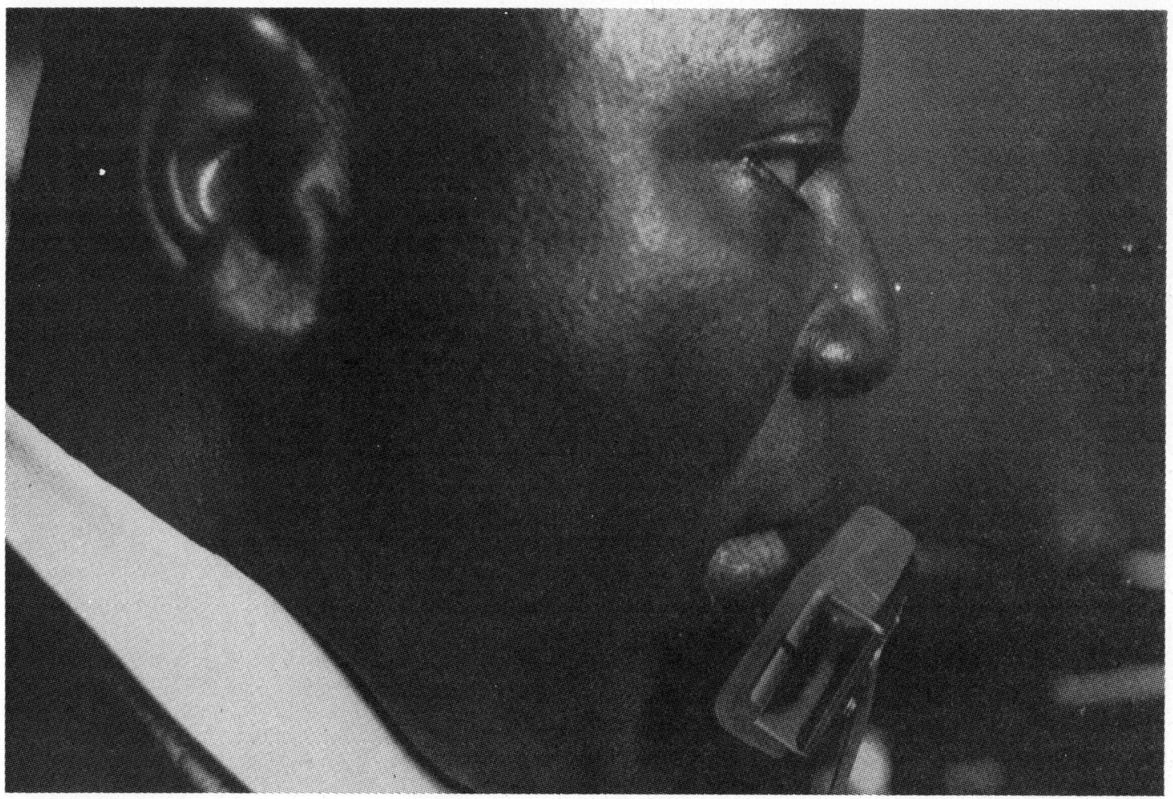

BREAKING DOWN THE BARRIERS

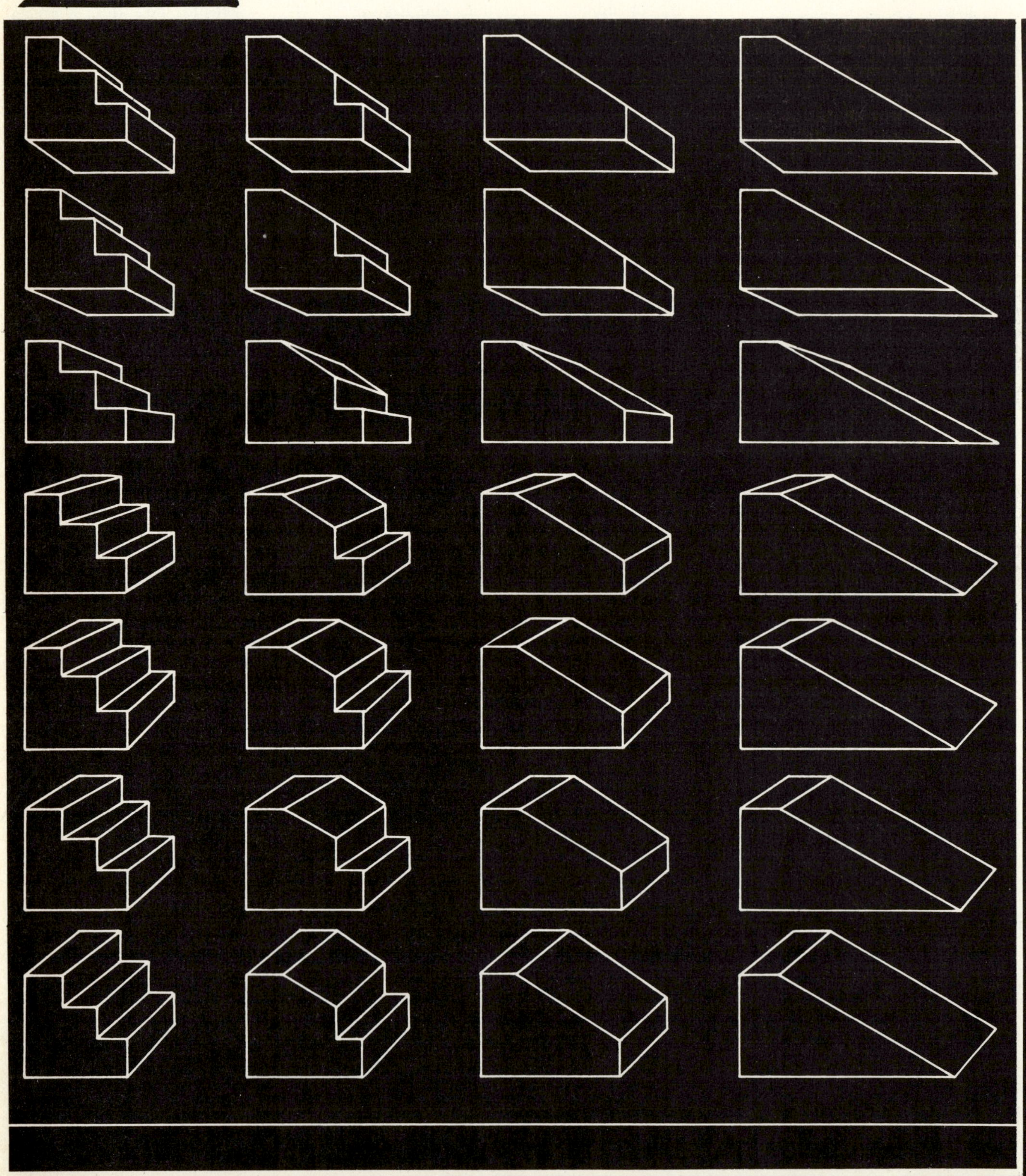

Barrier Free Design

A white stick figure on a blue background representing a man in a wheelchair . . . the symbol which designates accessibility to buildings which have previously been off-limits to the nation's handicapped population. This is just the beginning of the growing number of buildings across the United States which display the symbol that signifies a structure has been specially built or remodeled, adding ramps in place of stairs and curbs, wide doors, knobs of doors and drinking fountains, and toilets at convenient heights for the wheelchair-bound.

These freedoms have not always been so readily available to the million Americans in wheelchairs or to those numbers who experience other handicaps. Each day, over one in ten Americans experiences architectural barriers which keep them from the mainstream of life's activity.

If you will place yourself in the position of a person confined to a wheelchair or crutches, think about the frustration of daily life, when situations are taken for granted by those who function in uninhibited ways . . . consider revolving doors, steps, telephone booths, door handles, bathroom facilities, thick carpeting . . . all

oversights on our part, but this exclusion makes the handicapped population further "hidden" in our society.

However, progress is being made in significant strides in barrier-free design in America. The year 1968 brought passage of the Architectural Barriers Act which covered federal financing of public buildings to be constructed so that the physically handicapped would experience access to them. In 1973, the Architectural and Transportation Barriers and Compliance Board was set up by congress to encompass elimination of barriers which might hinder mobility, recreation, employment and education for our handicapped population.

With the 1970's has come practical application of essential planning in residential, educational, and public architectural planning. Architects include handrails, curving walls, sliding doors. Tactile maps of interior spaces guide blind persons toward interior destinations. This particular section highlights the accomplishments gained thus far in providing a barrier-free world for the handicapped. New public awareness can only move us more quickly in the right direction.

Breaking Down
Architectural Barriers

When Curtis Brewer's son, Scott, graduated from high school last June, the ceremonies were held at Carnegie Hall in New York City. Knowing that the auditorium, like so many public buildings, has steps at every entrance and is *not* accessible to the handicapped, Brewer called ahead to make arrangements for his wheelchair to be carried into the hall. When he arrived at the 57th Street entrance, he was directed to the entrance on 56th, where he sat for 45 minutes in 80° heat while the greasy kitchen fumes from the Carnegie Tavern next door spewed out 10 feet above his head. Meanwhile, inside, unions and management wrangled over the responsibility for getting the quadriplegic into the hall. By the time he was finally brought in, Brewer was visibly gasping for air and the ceremony had been in progress for half an hour.

Brewer was used to such hassles; in fact, he had not only anticipated this one, but had the foresight to alert a reporter at WCBS-TV, who came equipped with a camera crew. The story was carried that night on the local news.

For Brewer, who has no control of the voluntary muscles below his neck, the problems of getting around are a good deal more onerous than for the larger percentage of those confined to wheelchairs. And the fact that he has overcome his handicap is nothing short of remarkable. Now that he's a practicing lawyer, one cause that is consuming a great deal of his time and passion is the fight to eliminate architectural barriers for all handicapped people.

For the past year Brewer has been working with John Cooke, deputy director for Buildings Inspections of the New York State Urban Development Corporation. The two men are studying economic ways of modifying existing buildings to accommodate the disabled. But sometimes bureaucratic roads are slow and ineffective, and Brewer often finds the best method of action is to physically "confront" architectural barriers as he did at Carnegie Hall.

Ironically, the one place Brewer has met a stone wall of resistance is in getting a ramp installed on the front steps of his apartment house. As a result, every time he leaves his apartment, special ramps must be carried out to cover the stairs.

* * *

Every day, architectural barriers keep as many as 1 in 10 Americans from functioning as useful and contributing citizens. At every turn the physically handicapped are frustrated in the activities most of us take for granted. Barriers range from the obvious—steps, revolving doors, phone booths—to the less obvious—thick pile carpeting, certain kinds of door handles, and ramps that are too steep.

According to Jack Catlin, director of Access Chicago, a program dedicated to achieving a barrier-free environment for Chicago's 600,000 mobility-limited persons, architectural barriers are "generally a matter of oversight." Because other people harbor a wealth of myths about the physically handicapped, Catlin believes we exclude them in subtle ways. Those who cannot walk are often part of a "hidden population." Since they are not in the mainstream, they are easily ignored, and few efforts are made to insure their access to our public and private buildings and transit systems.

In recent years, however, more and more handicapped people are not only becoming vocal about their problems, they are also becoming instrumental in effecting change. In 1973, several hundred persons—a great many in wheelchairs—kept an all-night vigil at the Lincoln Memorial in Washington, D.C. to protest a presidential veto (later overridden) of a rehabilitation bill passed by Congress.

Catlin, who suffered a spinal cord injury in an accident less than two years ago, believes the handicapped don't have to be "different." "My life isn't changed," says the robust young man who knows he will live out his years paralyzed from the waist down. Catlin believes that attitudinal intransigence of others is one of the greatest barriers to the disabled. As a result, they too often carry a psychological burden, as well, that would be lifted if they could simply get around, he explains.

Though progress has been described as "spotty" and "inconsequential," there have been significant advances toward a barrier-free America in the past decade. A major legislative effort in 1968 gained passage of the Architectural Barriers Act, designed to insure that federally financed public buildings be constructed so they are accessible to the physically handicapped.

In 1973, Congress created the Architectural and Transportation Barriers Compliance Board. The Board, charged with enforcement of the 1968 Act, is the major national force providing leadership in eliminating environmental barriers that severely impede the mobility, employment, education, and recreation of handicapped individuals. The Board's director of public information, Larry Allison, explains it this way: "An environment designed to accommodate handicapped people will in most cases be a better environment for the able-bodied as well."

The construction of the Bay Area Rapid Transit System (BART) in California, completed in 1973, marked the first modern mass system to accommodate the handicapped—with ramps, elevators, specially structured restrooms, and even braille directional symbols for the blind. Though BART has been severely criticized for a wide variety of reasons, it remains a model for other systems in terms of accessibility to the disabled.

Perhaps the most exciting evidence of weakening architectural barriers is the fact that mobility-limited persons have recently been able literally to broaden their horizons. Thanks to people like Dorothy S. Axsom of Indianapolis, Indiana, who is the president and founder of Handy-Cap Horizons, disabled people are able to take worldwide tours that are offered annually. This year she will accompany dozens of wheelchair-bound adults and children to Morocco; the Costa Del Sol; Phoenix, Arizona; the Grand Canyon; Las Vegas, Nevada; Kalamazoo, Michigan; Scandanavia; and Mexico. Handy-Cap Horizons is a nonprofit volunteer organization, not a travel agency. However, many travel agencies too are now turning dreams of faraway places into reality for the handicapped.

According to the Presidential Committee for Employment of the Handicapped, approximately 52 percent of disabled persons are living below the poverty level. Thus, for most, the luxury of world travel is out of the question. For them, the architectural barriers that daily keep them from obtaining a good education, from working, from realizing their potential, *must* come down.

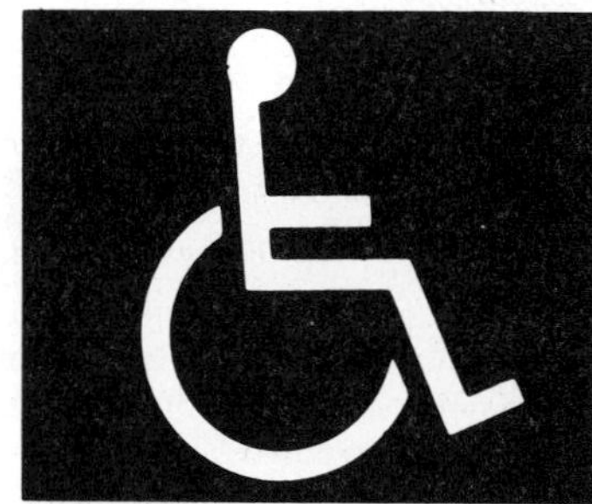

WE WELCOME
YOUR COMMENTS

Only through this communication can we produce high quality materials in the Special Education field.

Special Learning Corporation
42 Boston Post Rd. Guilford, Connecticut 06437

Barrier Free

Construction has begun in Alabama on a library to serve exclusively the more than 52,000 blind and physically handicapped citizens of the state.

Financed fully by a $1,213,040 grant from the U.S. Economic Development Administration's Local Public Works Capital Development and Investment Program, the Alabama Regional Library for the Blind and Physically Handicapped will utilize highly specialized media, equipment, facilities, and staff to serve its clientele.

"This building will be a prototype," said Gov. George Wallace on receiving the grant. "As the first library building designed and built especially for the blind and physically handicapped, it will be a model for the rest of the nation."

The designers—Moss, Garikes & Associates, Architects, Inc., of Birmingham, Ala.—have planned a two-story, 50,000-sq.-ft. structure that will be totally barrier free in conformity with American National Standards Institute guidelines.

"The library will have every feasible innovation designed for the convenience of the blind and physically handicapped. As a result, we will be able to employ handicapped staff and train librarians and others in the techniques of providing library service to the physically less fortunate," said Anthony W. Miele, director of the Alabama Public Library Service.

The basic structure of steel frame and masonry bearing walls will echo the adjacent state library complex. The upper level of the new building, primarily for additional shelving space, will connect with the state library, which will serve as the support facility for the regional operation.

Conceptually, the planners divided the interior into four basic sectors: patron reading and meeting areas; administrative and computer areas; audio-book recording and production areas; and stack and materials handling areas.

Handrails will guide patrons to automatic sliding doors which retract into the walls. In the reception area, vibrant colors and curving walls will provide visual excitement for the handicapped and eliminate certain hazards for the blind. A raised tactile map of the interior will help orient blind patrons. Teletypewriter service and the use of sign language will benefit the deaf and non-speaking patrons. An idea under consideration is to alternate floor and wall textures to further orient the blind.

The patron reading and meeting areas will contain equipment and accessories for loan and in-house use. Blind persons will find on display such items as braille typewriters and computers, laser-beam readers, tools, toys, games, and kitchen equipment. For the handicapped, the main emphasis will be on display and experimental units involving coping skills. These units will be housed in a meeting room whose window wall overlooks an atrium with a waterfall effect. The meeting room accommodates 25 wheelchair patrons, with stored seating for 35 patrons.

Adjacent to patron areas will be the administrative offices. Circulation and inventory operations will be computerized to free staff time for individualized service.

In the audiobook area are four sound-proof booths, recording equipment, and duplicating machines. Through the work of staff and volunteers, books and text-books will be recorded for statewide use and for the eight subregional libraries.

The stack and materials handling areas will provide for the storage of braille books, cassette books, open reel tapes, and other materials. A major function of the library will be to distribute these materials throughout the state.

A special workroom has been designed for the Telephone Pioneers, a volunteer group from the Bell Telephone System, who will repair the machines and equipment necessary for the program. This assistance will greatly help to keep operating costs down.

The library is scheduled for completion in early 1978. The state will continue to serve the handicapped primarily by mail and telephone, but this new building will be a central focus of the program to display, explain, and make available these services.

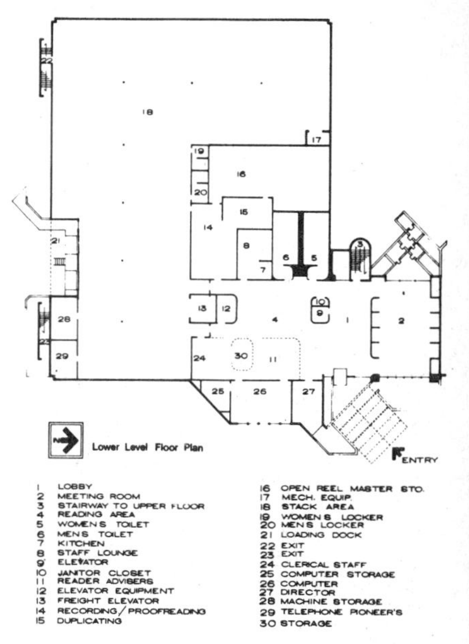

VISUALLY HANDICAPPED EDUCATION

Readings in Visually Handicapped Education is designed to follow the general course of study for students, teachers, researchers and other professionals who work with the visually impaired and the blind. Its in-depth look at the various phases of visual handicaps is excellent. The most significant feature of this book is that it will serve to explain and clarify various differences and theories of instruction.

Special Learning Corporation

42 Boston Post Rd. Guilford, Connecticut 06437   (203) 453-6525

ARCHITECTURAL BARRIERS TO A FULL AND USEFUL LIFE

Wallace J. Lynch

Mr. Lynch is student activities director, Woodrow Wilson Rehabilitation Center, Fishersville, Virginia.

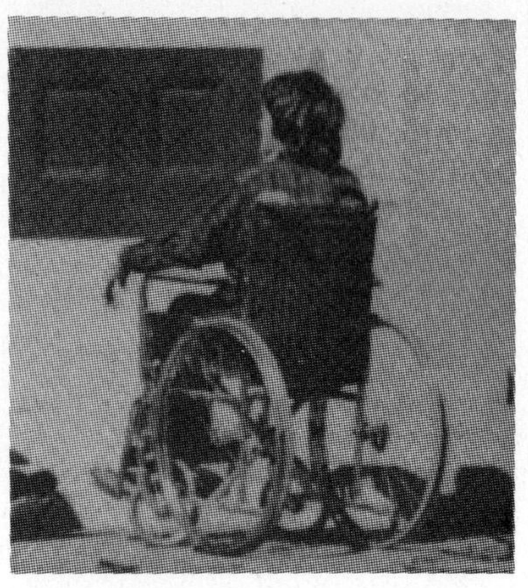

A SCREECH, a crash, a sudden stop. Result—a smashed vehicle containing a crumpled human body which has undergone drastic change. Another spinal-cord injury has occurred. As the ambulance leaves and the shadows fall upon the scene, the victim of this accident becomes another highway statistic.

Treatment by the medical doctor and the physical, occupational, and recreational therapists will assist in restoring this accident victim to function as a member of society. But once the individual has been rehabilitated, how well will he or she get along in the community? Can he or she find a place to live? Function on a job? Share in community projects? Attend church? Eat in a restaurant? Go to a movie? In other words, can this person participate in the normal activities of daily life? Unfortunately, the answer is frequently no.

The basic necessity of shelter is the first problem. Most dwellings are built without thought for the wheelchair citizen. Front steps outside, circular stairways inside, split levels—all combine to prohibit the wheelchair tenant's occupancy.

Consider making a living. Here is an individual who through great effort has regained the capability of working and earning a good wage. He or she wants to live a normal, independent life. But is industry ready for the wheelchair worker? Many employers are unaware of the capabilities of the wheelchair bound; others feel they would have more accidents and absences. (Actually, statistics show better attendance and safety records for the impaired than the unimpaired worker.) Often a person in a wheelchair is barred from employment because of architectural barriers or because he or she can no longer operate the equipment. If industry were willing to make adjustments or adaptations to structures, machinery, and, attitudes, these individuals could have equal opportunity for a full work life.

How about sharing in community projects or attending church? The necessary, often simple, provisions for wheelchair mobility usually have not been made. Curbs, steps, steep inclines, and narrow doors are all impediments to the progress of a wheelchair.

Recreation activities are so varied and numerous that a person should have no problems finding entertainment, even if he or she is in a wheelchair. Right? Not necessarily. How about dinner and a movie? Is there a place to park with enough room to open the door of the car, push the wheelchair out, and unfold it? Is there a ramp cut into the curb? What about those revolving doors? Is there room to get the wheelchair to the restaurant table without disturbing everyone and attracting unwanted attention? Is the table high enough for the wheelchair and its occupant to sit comfortably close?

At the movies, the person in a wheelchair is warned, "Don't park in the aisle. That's a fire hazard." Besides, the incline of the floor tilts the chair forward. So where does the wheelchair-bound person sit? In the back, out of the way, near the noise, and far away from the screen.

Dinner theaters, art museums, concerts, and sports events are popular attractions in every community. But are they accessible to the wheelchair bound? Sure, people are usually willing to help get a wheelchair up a couple of steps, over a threshold, and through a succession of swinging doors; but the person in the chair thereby becomes dependent on others and feels he or she is imposing.

Is your community ready for our wheelchair citizens? If you are not sure, why not discuss this with a vocational rehabilitation counselor, the local committee for employment of the handicapped, or your recreation and park personnel. And by all means give it a personal test. Try living in a wheelchair for a day.

"Architecural barriers to a Full and Useful Life," Wallace J. Lynch, *Parks and Recreation*, Vol. X No. 10, October 1975. ©1975 The National Recreation and Park Association.

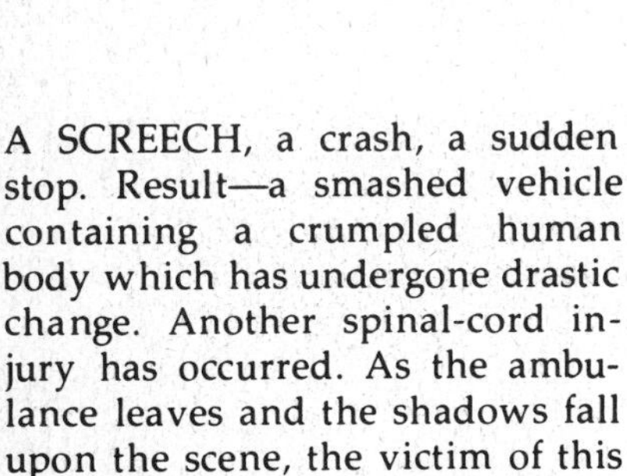

Selwyn Goldsmith

Mr. Goldsmith, a civil servant in the British Department of the Environment, is an authority on housing for the disabled. The third edition of his book, Designing for the Disabled, *is to be published this summer by the Royal Institute of British Architects.*

Increased public awareness of the obstacles which face the physically disabled as they strive to take their place in the everyday life of the community is observable in Britain, as it is elsewhere in the world.

A major element in this effort is in the area of physical access to buildings and transit facilities. While access to buildings is not a matter of argument in Britain, egress in case of emergency such as fire is a cause of increasing concern and controversy.

Before beginning a survey of progress and problems in these areas, it is necessary to outline the structure of governmental assistance to the disabled in Britain. Two governmental departments have primary responsibility: the Department of Health and Social Security (health and welfare); and the Department of the Environment (planning and design of public buildings, transport and housing). Also concerned in their particular spheres of responsibility are the Departments of Education and Science and the Department of Employment.

It is generally up to the local government agencies to effect the legislation passed by Parliament, and to determine how best to use their resources — although of course within the parameters of financial control and the priorities established by the central government.

Minister for the Disabled

Governmental responsibility for aid to the disabled was confirmed by Parliamentary passage of the Chronically Sick and Disabled Persons Act in 1970. Four years later, the sponsor of that bill, Alf Morris, M.P., was appointed the first Minister for the Disabled. Although there were misgivings among the disabled when this post was created — some felt it might be counterproductive to the concept of integration to have a minister concerned solely with these problems, while it might also allow ministers with more general responsibilities to henceforth ignore the disabled — these fears were soon allayed.

Mr. Morris, as Minister for the Disabled, has specific departmental responsibilities within the Department of Health, and beyond that has the job of coordinating the work of a variety of governmental departments, local authorities, and voluntary agencies active on behalf of disabled persons. A positive result of the appointment has been close cooperation between the Departments of Health and Environment on housing services for the disabled poor.

The Chronically Sick and Disabled Persons Act is the only piece of legislation on the British statute books devoted exclusively to services for handicapped people. It includes sections on the duties of local social services authorities to identify the needs of handicapped people in their area, the provision of welfare services (including, for example, help with holidays and the provision of a telephone) and the duties of housing authorities to ensure that disabled people are suitably housed. Most important for architects, it also includes sections on access to public buildings. The crucial section of the Act is Section 4, which requires that when new buildings for public use are planned or existing buildings are adapted, access arrangements are made for disabled people.

Access and the Law

The legal effectiveness of Section 4 is compromised, however, by the words "in so far as it is in the circumstances both practicable and reasonable." When the statute was drafted the qualifying clause was inserted because problems of legal definition were anticipated if access provision had been made mandatory. These difficulties in definition have to do with formulating effective prescriptions which would be sensible, realistic, and universally applicable. There are also problems which are a function of the character of our legislation, whereby Government intervention of the kind that might have been proposed would have been difficult to implement. Understandably, the presence of the escape clause has provoked criticism from agencies working for the handicapped that the Act "lacks teeth."

The matter is debatable, but it is possible that Section 4 is more effective as it stands than it would have been had penal sanctions been more easily enforceable under it. The working of the Act is constantly monitored by individual disabled people and their voluntary organizations, and it is now considered unthinkable that a new theater, library,

swimming pool, or other public facility could be constructed without suitable access arrangements for disabled people. An expression of the government's commitment to the access cause has been the recent launching by the Department of the Environment, in association with the Royal Institute of British Architects and the Central Council for the Disabled, of an awards program designed to encourage the planning of buildings conveniently usable by disabled people. The awards are to be announced in October, and there is to be a national exhibition.

The British Standard Code of Practice CP-96, Access for the Disabled to Buildings, is the principal reference used in connection with the implementation of access provision. The Code, originally published in 1967, is now being revised in line with metric dimensional practice. The basic mechanics of access provision are well known: suitable parking arrangements, adequate ramped or level access to the building, doors and passageways which allow for wheelchair maneuver, elevators big enough for wheelchair use, and the inclusion of toilet facilities usable by chairbound people. These are the simple rules of access, first formulated as a result of the pioneering work of Tim Nugent at the University of Illinois and issued as American Standard (now U.S. National Standard) A117.1.

The British Standard Access code (CP-96) does not of itself have any statutory authority and is not incorporated into legislation or regulations. It has been suggested that it might be incorporated into national requirements for new building construction, but it is doubtful that this would be possible, for the same reason Section 4 of the Chronically Sick Persons Act could not be made mandatory. Until recently, legislation prescribing building regulations gave authority only for regulations having to do with health and safety. But a recently introduced piece of legislation (the Health and Safety at Work Act 1974) gives authority for regulations to be made in respect to "welfare and convenience" as well as health and safety. The Building Regulations division of the Department of the Environment is examining possibilities for the incorporation of access regulations, either directly or by reference to a revised code of practice.

Egress

While access provision is not a matter for argument, the issue causing increasing concern to disabled people is the question of egress, particularly means of escape by disabled people from multi-storied buildings in the event of fire.

The issue is of crucial concern with respect to employment buildings, where there is a threat that disabled people will not have the same opportunities for vocational advancement as their able-bodied peers. The one case that has been legally disputed through the courts concerned a cinema building in Liverpool. The developers' intention was to replace a large auditorium with a ground floor supermarket and a small cinema on the upper floor. The local planning authority, anxious to implement the intentions of Section 4, asked that an elevator be included for disabled patrons. The developers were sympathetic, until it was pointed out that the fire authority would not permit the elevator to be used as a means of escape. As a consequence, disabled people in wheelchairs would not be permitted to use

> *Emergency egress:*
>
> *"Also a*
>
> *moral conflict"*

the cinema. It was decided by the court that fire protection requirements could not be subordinate to disabled access requirements, and the outcome was that the building went ahead without an elevator.

The conflict here is a moral as well as technical or economic one. On the one hand, society says that disabled people ought to be able to use buildings freely. On the other hand, it says that, for the benefit of "public safety and security," they ought not to. Until recently, the conflict was widely ignored in Britain, with the managers of buildings such as cinemas and restaurants taking it upon

themselves to disregard the possibility of hazard. In the last few years, however, partly because of the publicity given to fire tragedies that have occurred, controls on the use of buildings have become increasingly severe. This raises the fear that disabled people might not be permitted to work in multi-storied buildings.

Attitudes to Mortality

At issue is the public attitude towards mortality. For all people in the world there is the possibility that death is imminent, but that possibility is largely ignored. Among many disabled people, however, either because of poor prognosis or proneness to injury, it is a possibility which cannot be ignored. The response should not be to become neurotic about it, but to insist on making the most of the days that remain. It is important to be able to carry on doing the things that are fulfilling, to go to work, to carry on studying, to see shows at the theater, to hear music at the concert hall, and to keep up with the latest films at the cinema.

Given this philosophy of living, the possibility that the local cinema may one day burn down, leaving one stranded in a fixed seat, is not a threat to worry about unduly. The disabled person is entitled to ask of the fire protection officer, "What moral right have you to say 'you cannot come in here because you might die'?" He or she is also entitled to ask of the able-bodied world: "What right have you to impose your norms of security, affected as they are by your neurosis about mortality, on we who are disabled?"

There can be no sensible basis for quantifying the hazards to which it is reasonable that disabled people should expose themselves. Nor can there be any simple technical answers; the issue would not be resolved by the development of an elevator which could be used safely as a means of escape in the event of fire. In the end, judgments have to be individual ones.

Special Small Cars

Elsewhere, the administration of services for the handicapped reflects a more relaxed attitude toward human survival.

4. BARRIER FREE DESIGN

For many years, the Health Service has issued special three-wheeled small cars, known as invalid tricycles, to severely disabled people. There has been extensive criticism of these vehicles as being both stigmatizing and dangerous, but campaigns for their withdrawal have provoked counter-protests from many handicapped who use them. There is evidence that these vehicles are more hazardous than comparable small cars with four wheels, but whether the danger is attributable to the character and performance of the vehicle, or the performance of the driver, is not something easily amenable to investigation.

In January the government introduced a new mobility allowance program for disabled people of working age and children age five and over. The allowance is £5 (10 dollars) per week, available for disabled people unable or virtually unable to walk. Those who are severely disabled but with the capacity to drive may elect to have an invalid tricycle instead.

Disabled drivers or passengers can obtain an official orange badge to display on their cars, which allows them to park at meter bays for an unlimited period, or for up to two hours where parking is not permitted for others. The official circular describing the program also suggests that local authorities consider providing special parking spaces for badge holders close to restaurants, shops, theaters, churches, etc. Such places are to be identified by a sign showing the international access symbol, which is now authorized for use on public highway signs.

Public Transport

The Department of the Environment has issued a booklet, *The Disabled Traveller on Public Transport*, which suggests practical ways to alleviate mobility problems. These suggestions include asking bus operators to draw up close to curbs at bus stops, designing bus steps so that they are as low as possible, placing grab rails and bells within easy reach, and allocating selected seats for disabled and elderly people in buses where few seats are provided.

For train travel, the latest intercity coaches developed by British Rail are to have places left clear for wheelchair users. These places will be in first class coaches only, but disabled travellers will be permitted to travel at second class rates.

The London Transport authority is investigating the possibility of facilitating use of underground trains by the disabled. It is clearly out of the question to rebuild the entire system to cater to all disabled people. On this subject, it is questionable whether the massive amounts of money being spent in such places as San Francisco and Washington to make new rapid transit systems manageable for people using wheelchairs are an effective use of resources. It might be more economical and advantageous to disabled people to provide a taxi service subsidized by public funds.

In recent years, the access department of the Central Council for the Disabled (CCD) in London has been promoting the preparation of access guides for all major towns. The CCD has also published a guide to accessible public toilet facilities, and another of facilities for disabled travellers at British Rail stations. The Automobile Association has issued a guide on the suitability of hotels for guests who are disabled, and one of the principal restaurant guides, *The Good Food Guide,* notes which premises are accessible and which are not.

Housing

New house building in Britain is divided between the public and private sectors, and in between there is what is known as the third arm:

Accessible mass transit facilities:

An effective use of scarce resources?

Artist's rendering of an inclined elevator at the District of Columbia's Rhode Island Avenue METRO station. Estimated to cost almost $5 billion, the still largely unfinished rapid rail system will be accessible to the disabled.

housing associations, which are private agencies building low-cost rental housing, with government aid on the capital expenditure.

House building by public authorities and housing associations is governed by the controls of mandatory space and amenity standards. These standards, known as Parker Morris standards, prescribe minimum overall space standards according to the size of the household accommodated. The minimum is commonly the maximum. While disability organizations advocate the enlarging of circulation spaces in ordinary housing to allow for wheelchair users, in reality there is little or no latitude. The alternative is to see how far, with minor modifications involving no additional expenditure, ordinary housing can be made suitable for handicapped people. This is known as Mobility Housing, the principal conditions of which

are that the entrance is accessible without steps, and that rooms are reached through standard metric

doors giving a clearance of 775 mm (2 ft. 7 in.) from passageways 900 mm (2 ft. 11½ in.) wide. These spaces are not sufficient for people who are chairbound and need comfortable room for maneuver, but they mean that Mobility Housing can cater to the majority of wheelchair users (most of whom use their chairs only when they go outside). It is estimated that ordinary housing of this kind can be used by at least 96 percent of people who are described as handicapped.

For people who are chairbound, local authorities and housing associations are encouraged to build wheelchair housing, which has enhanced space standards and amenities, and which attracts additional government subsidies. Minister of Housing Reg Freeson has launched a special drive on housing for disabled people, with the aim of assuring that each local housing authority has suitable accommodations in its stock of dwellings.

In the private sector, these controls do not apply. A British Standard has been drafted, provisionally called "House Design: Convenience for Disabled People," which is meant to encourage private housing builders to incorporate features making dwellings more manageable by handicapped people.

Finally, the Department of the Environment and the Department of Health are planning new guidance for local authorities on the adaptation of existing housing, to ensure that in all sectors adaptation work is coordinated with new building.

On Campus in a Wheelchair

MARY SINCLAIR

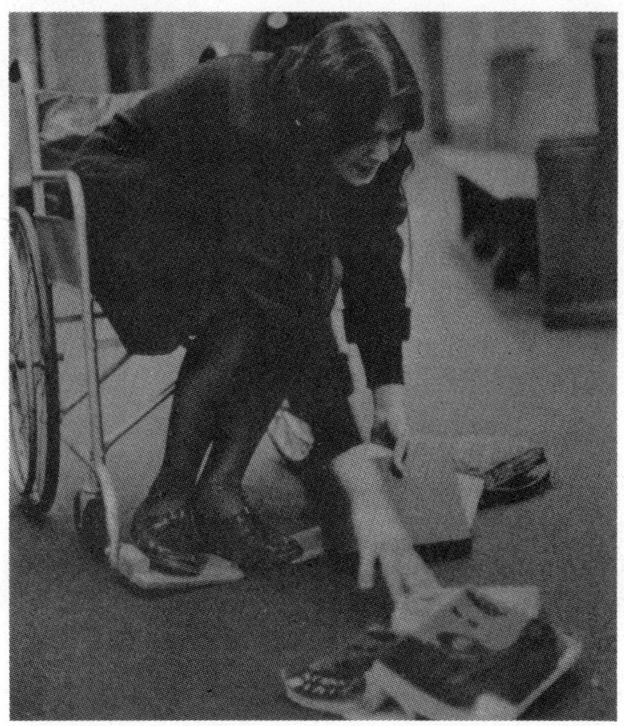

You are standing at a street crossing waiting for the light to change when a young man in a wheelchair rolls up beside you. Are you: (a) unconcerned about his next move? (b) embarrassed by his presence? (c) quick to offer help? (d) uneasy that an offer of help might embarrass him?

You might experience any of these reactions, depending on your attitude toward disabled people. But what if you yourself had recently had a brief stint in a wheelchair. Might your reaction to that young man have been different?

Intrigued by the question, Katherine M. Jeffery and Gerald L. Clore of the Department of Psychology at the University of Illinois set up an experiment in an attempt to determine the effects, if any, a wheelchair experience has in changing or developing attitudes toward the disabled.

The investigators divided students randomly into three groups: role players, vicarious role players, and control. Role players were instructed to take a short trip around campus via wheelchair, stopping off at the student union for a snack. Each vicarious role player was told to follow 20 feet behind a role player and to observe his experiences. Students in the control group, knowing nothing of the others' activities, took a short walk around campus and returned to the test site.

Results indicated that the hour or so spent in—or even near—a wheelchair made some strong impressions. On questionnaires designed to measure attitudes toward the disabled, both role players and vicarious role players responded more positively than did the control group. When asked, for instance, whether the Introductory Psychology course should include lectures on the disabled, students from the first two groups responded "yes" much more frequently than did those in the third group.

Even more important, the effects of both role playing and vicarious role playing appeared to be long lasting. One month after the experiment, participants were called by telephone and asked if they would volunteer to show a disabled student around campus for one hour. Many more role players and vicarious role players volunteered their time than did students from the control group.

Four months later participants were again called and asked, under the guise of a random sampling of student opinion, whether they thought excess money from the student association should be spent to improve intramural sports facilities, increase scholarships for black students, build additional parking lots, or increase campus facilities for disabled students. Once again it was the students in the role-playing groups who consistently voted that the money should be spent on facilities for the disabled.

Ball Is Rolling For Handicapped

Persons confined to wheelchairs will have an easier time getting around campus, and sight-impaired students will have more opportunity to read for themselves and spend less time listening to records, as the result of a new program at Ball State University in Muncie, Ind.

Ball State students with severe visual problems will benefit from a new read-write system which has been installed in a media center, temporarily housed with the Division of Educational Resources in Bracken Library.

Other new devices at the media center are "speech compressor" which plays tapes faster than they customarily would be played, and a braille writing machine to aid students in note-taking.

Funds for the new equipment were provided by a private grant of $25,000 given to the University in 1974.

Accessible

Handicapped students now will have no difficulty in getting into the library or going from one floor to another. Students in wheelchairs can enter by means of a ramp and, once inside, a librarian presses a button and a gate swings open. An elevator with controls reachable from a wheelchair and floor

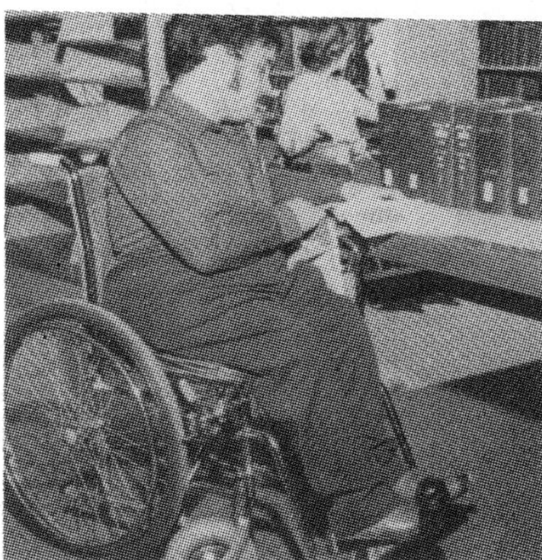

New Bracken Library at Ball State University was designed with consideration for the needs of handicapped. All floors are accessible with low elevator controls and braille floor numbers. Sophomore Erick Dolch here uses library for research project.

numbers in braille carries students to other floors.

Other architectural modifications include curb cuts, a permanent ramp to the student center, and a lift in the English building to carry students in wheelchairs.

'Whittling them down'

"Ball State doesn't pretend to have swept away all of the barriers which block the handicapped," says Richard Harris, director of orientation and coordinator of services for handicapped students. "Barriers can take the form not only of curbs, steps, and narrow doors," he adds, "but also of turnstiles, out-of-reach elevator controls, telephones and drinking fountains, and many other things so much a part of routine living that most people don't give a second thought. We are working on the problems year by year and are whittling them down."

Harris says the number of severely disabled students attending classes at Ball State has increased 50 per cent

New lift at Ball State University, Muncie, Ind., enables sophomore Ric Edwards to by-pass steps on second floor of English buildings. Students in wheelchairs formerly had to be carried up and down steps. Using stairs are students Don Rogers and Karen Reichel.

during the last two years. Twenty-two students are confined to wheelchairs, five have serious hearing impairments, 25 use walking aids, seven are blind, and ten have severely impaired sight.

Future efforts at the University will be aimed toward fire ramps for rear exit doors, consideration of the needs of the handicapped in remodeling campus buildings, and improving the accessibility of more telephones, restrooms and drinking fountains throughout the campus.

Teachers College building forms background as two of 22 Ball State University students who attend classes in wheelchairs return to their residence halls on campus.

"Ball Is Rolling for the Handicapped," *America, Inc.*, Vol. XXV No. 330, March 1977. ©1977 Paralyzed Veterans of America, Inc.

Mobilizing for a Barrier-Free Zoo

A PROFESSOR in Tennessee is helping the handicapped get around the world.

William Campbell, professor of biomedical engineering at the University of Tennessee, counsels designers on identifying and deleting architectural barriers at the burgeoning Knoxville Zoological Park, where 1,000 animals roam in simulated habitats ranging from the Australian Outback to Africa's plains.

"Our goal is to make the zoo fully accessible to handicapped people," Campbell said. "We'll either be a raving success or a roaring failure."

Campbell volunteered his services in 1973 shortly after zoo officials launched a massive program to transform this city's one-time conglomeration of animal cages into an attractive 130-acre zoological park. He persuaded them to commit one percent of the $3.5 million expansion budget to eliminate or renovate physical barriers.

Campbell, armed with gate counts showing at least 28 percent of the zoo's visitors were handicapped, easily won influential disciples to his cause. Among them were Guy L. Smith III, director of the Knoxville Zoological Park, and then-Mayor Leonard Rogers.

"This community wanted us to convert its substandard menagerie of 47 animals into a first-class regional zoo," Smith remembers. "But we'd have failed before turning the first shovel without Campbell's input. A first-class zoo must be accessible to everyone."

Smith, who engineered the zoo's meteoric rise from obscurity, landed a $480,000 federal grant from the Bureau of Outdoor Recreation. It enabled Campbell and design architects to address the barrier problem by incorporating modifications into the zoo's capital improvement plan.

No physical obstacle—whether on the original 11-acre zoo grounds or confined to the drawing board—escaped Campbell's scrutiny. Toilet stalls wide enough to accommodate the handicapped were provided along with lowered pay telephone stations and drinking fountains. Steps were replaced by railed ramps with seven percent gradients so wheelchairs can negotiate them.

"A couple of gradients aren't exactly what we wanted," Campbell said, "because the lengths necessary to attain them would have been obtrusive. We don't want modifications that convey the notion they're for handicapped people."

Campbell, who chairs the Kerbela Shrine Temple hospital endowment committee, knows how to glean crucial grassroots support from Rotarians, Jaycees, and other similar fraternal groups. When double-digit inflation forced zoo administrators to delete braille signs from this year's budget, he salvaged the project with $5,000 donated by Knoxville Lions clubs.

A braille map at the zoo entrance, guidebooks, and tape recorded messages at strategic posts throughout the complex will be operative late this year. Six locator stations will be constructed next season with volunteer labor.

Gary Barrett, curator of education, is extending Campbell's work to the educational level by working with the Development Center for Children and Adolescents. He is using the zoo as an educational medium to help blind and deaf children overcome learning problems.

Deaf children, for example, tour Knoxville's zoo with therapists to learn concepts before words. Then reading materials are tailored to their experiences.

"We're just beginning to scratch the surface," Barrett said. "Zoos are a

Handicapped persons and senior citizens get around the 130-acre Knoxville Zoological Park aboard specially equipped electric vehicles.

"Mobilizing For a Barrier-Free Zoo," *The Social and Rehabilitation Record*, Vol. 1 No. 4, April 1974. ©1974 Social and Rehabilitation Service, Health, Education and Welfare Department.

matchless educational tool, particularly when it comes to working with handicapped children."

The zoo is tucked into the thicketed hills of eastern Tennessee. So even with ramps, Campbell admits, the rugged terrain can provide an Everest challenge to children, elderly persons, and the physically handicapped. Long-range plans include installation of a monorail transportation network to whisk visitors to stations dotted throughout the sprawling complex.

"A monorail system is pretty expensive so we've had to put it on the back burner," Campbell said.

In the interim, Campbell has enlisted support from Knoxville-based state highway patrolmen, who donated two modified Cushman vehicles to transport handicapped persons. The vehicles each seat eight passengers and complement six mid-floor entrances, stymied disabled persons.

Even ancient Egyptian buildings contained fewer physical barriers, since ramps were needed to erect pyramids or other massive stone structures, Campbell observed.

"Historically, we've turned our backs on the handicapped in this country," Campbell said, noting that today "the situation is improving.

"Now, whether an architect is designing a zoo or a high-rise office building, he's more apt to tune into handicapped people," he said.

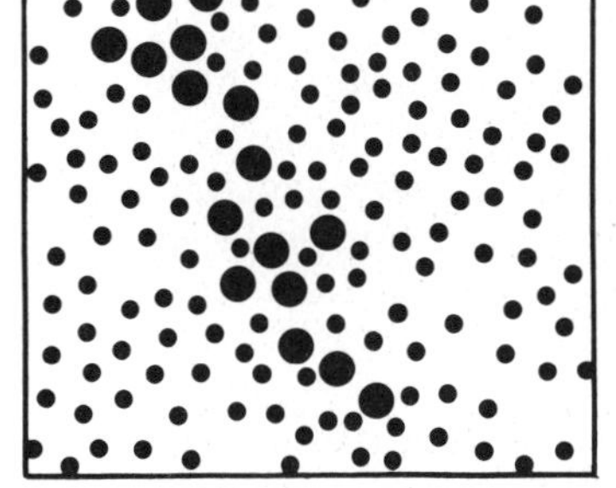

Mainstreaming

Taking an in depth look at the controversy of mainstreaming versus special education classes for the exceptional child, this book presents an overview of the problems and methods involved. The history of mainstreaming, along with future trends are discussed.

For further information concerning this book and other special education materials, contact:

Special Learning Corporation

Special Learning Corporation
42 Boston Post Rd. Guilford, Connecticut 06437

Bringing the Arts to the Handicapped

Jack Horn

We've designed our world largely for the physically mobile and mentally unimpaired, although many people are permanently handicapped and most of the rest suffer from handicaps one time or another. Few buildings are freely available to a girl on crutches, a mentally retarded young adult or a father wheeling a baby carriage.

Usually the barriers are architectural—steps, curbs, narrow walkways or doors, inaccessible toilet facilities. Often they are also attitudinal—discriminatory admission policies, unnecessary safety requirements, or preconceived notions about the undesirability of handicapped people.

The National Endowment for the Arts and the Educational Facilities Laboratory combined forces to create cultural facilities and programs for the handicapped. EFL has issued a report, *Arts and the Handicapped: An Issue of Access*, on what 131 communities and institutions across the country are doing to make their facilities more available.

EFL found that matters are slowly improving, under prodding from organizations and legislation pushing the rights of the handicapped. In education, for example, courts have ruled that institutions and special schools don't give handicapped children an equal education. A major effort has followed to move handicapped children into homes, day services and regular classrooms.

The Architectural Barriers Act of 1968 required that new and extensively renovated public facilities financed by Federal funds must be accessible to handicapped individuals. Enforcement has been spotty, but the Architectural and Transportation Barriers Compliance Board was established in 1973 to see that the law is obeyed.

For information, write: Stanley Thomas, Chairman, ATBCB, Washington, D.C. 20201.

Most states have passed similar laws of their own, usually adopting the American National Standards Institute's "Standards for Making Buildings and Facilities Accessible to and Usable by the Physically Handicapped."

A survey of this state legislation is available free from the President's Committee on Employment of the Handicapped, Committee on Barrier-Free Design, Washington, D.C. 20210.

A number of museums have set up tactile exhibits for the blind. The New Orleans Museum of Art, for instance, hires guides specially trained to express sizes and composition to blind visitors, help them feel and understand sculpture, try on African masks and explore the textures and acoustics of different galleries.

Information: Bonnie Pitman, Curator of Education, NOMA, P.O. Box 19123, New Orleans, La. 70179.

Community centers such as the Riverbend Arts Center in Dayton, Ohio, bring art to the handicapped at the neighborhood level. Riverbend offers studio courses in drawing, enameling, ceramics, silk-screening, woodcarving and a dozen other skills to both the handicapped and the general public.

Information: Patricia Shoop, Director, RAC, 142 Riverhead Drive, Dayton, Ohio 45405.

Access to any type of higher education is difficult for handicapped students, and few colleges or counselors see the arts as a career for the handicapped individual. St. Andrews Presbyterian College in Laurinburg, N.C., is an exception. Planned 15 years ago as a barrier-free campus, St. Andrews has enrolled physically handicapped students who are majoring in music, painting, fine arts, literature, drama and theater.

Information: Director of Communications, SAPC, Laurinburg, N.C. 28352.

The Recreation Center for the Handicapped in San Francisco is a private, nonprofit operation for children and adults. In addition to offering music, dance, crafts and other arts at the Center, staff members and volunteers (some of whom are handicapped) bring material and instruction to people who can't come to the Center themselves. RCH also acts as a clearinghouse for information on similar programs elsewhere in California and other states.

Information: Roberta Schnitzer, Program Director, RCH, 207 Skyline Blvd., San Francisco, Ca. 94132.

Handicapped Resource Group Members Work for Barrier Elimination

Making the environment more accessible to the disabled, promoting the image of the handicapped person as one who is able to function successfully in a professional career, encouraging disabled students to follow the career of their choice—these are some of the goals of the AAAS Project on the Handicapped in Science. Two members of the project's resource group have demonstrated how the handicapped themselves can play a significant role in the accomplishment of these goals.

The two, Robert Larsen and Phyllis Stearner, are scientists employed at Argonne National Laboratory in Illinois, where they have been active for the past 18 months in a campaign to eliminate obstacles that have hindered or prevented the employment of physically disabled workers at Argonne. The effort began when Stearner, who has cerebral palsy and uses a wheelchair, was appointed head of an affirmative action committee at the laboratory. She submitted the committee's final report by mail to lab director Robert Sachs, explaining that she would have preferred to deliver it in person, but she could not get into his office. Stairs made it inaccessible.

Since then, according to lab engineer Henry Hoffnung, a number of changes have been made in the environment at the lab: an intercom was installed to enable visitors to secure passes without leaving their cars; a van equipped with a lift was put into operation to transport wheelchair users from building to building; some 20 ramps were built to provide access to buildings; several dozen washrooms were modified to accommodate wheelchairs; elevators were equipped with braille markings on the control panels; and reserved parking spaces were provided at many buildings for the use of handicapped employees and visitors.

According to Richard Adams, assistant laboratory director for public affairs, contributions to the project have been provided by each of the several handicapped workers at Argonne. "The moving force," he says, "was the handicapped people themselves. . . . There was a complete lack of understanding of barriers. Somebody aware had to point them out." He is particularly enthusiastic about the AAAS project's recent publication of *Barrier-Free Meetings: A Guide for Professional Associations*, which he says will aid Argonne in eliminating barriers to attendance at professional meetings by handicapped employees.

Arthur Vervack, director of the personnel division at Argonne, reports that the lab's affirmative action program now has been broadened to include handicapped individuals. Weekly lists of job openings are circulated to more than 35 agencies and organizations concerned with the physically disabled, and more handicapped people are being interviewed.

Stearner and other laboratory employees also have been active in exposing local graduate and undergraduate students to opportunities in research through Argonne's Center for Educational Affairs. Both she and Sachs met with students from Southern Illinois University recently to discuss career options. It was an event that Stearner had been anxiously awaiting. "I wanted handicapped students to see handicapped scientists working in their chosen careers in a barrier-free environment. Often, counselors steer handicapped people away from careers in science because of either real or imagined barriers."

Larsen, Stearner, and the other handicapped people at Argonne are enthusiastic about the role of the handicapped in initiating the type of changes they have witnessed. In their words, "It is important to recognize that such changes are occurring at just this time, when the regulations of the Rehabilitation Act have . . . been enacted into law. The handicapped themselves can do a great deal to help bring about more accessible working conditions and can effect great changes in attitudinal barriers that have

Phyllis Stearner (left) and Robert Larsen (right) are two Argonne National Laboratory scientists who were instrumental in implementation of a barrier-elimination effort at the lab. Larsen, an analytical chemist, is shown on a specially adapted bench he designed himself; Stearner, a biologist, boards a van equipped with a lift provided for handicapped employees at the lab. Both are members of the AAAS Project on the Handicapped in Science resource group.

"Handicapped Resource Group Members Work for Barrier Elimination," *Science*, Vol. 195 No. 4277, February 4, 1977. ©1977 The American Association for the Advancement of Science.

so long served to retard their entry into professional fields.''

Adams is quick to point out that there are benefits to be derived by the employer, too. A barrier-free environment for handicapped workers is theirs by right, he says, but, in addition, such a project "opens up . . . the mental skills available of those who have a physical disability."

The AAAS Project on the Handicapped in Science resource group, which numbers some 500 people who are blind, deaf, use a wheelchair, or are otherwise physically disabled, encourages all handicapped persons who have had experiences in effecting barrier elimination or other relevant activities to contact Martha Redden, Project Director, AAAS, 1776 Massachusetts Avenue, NW, Washington, D.C. 20036 (202-467-4497).

Movable Pool Floors

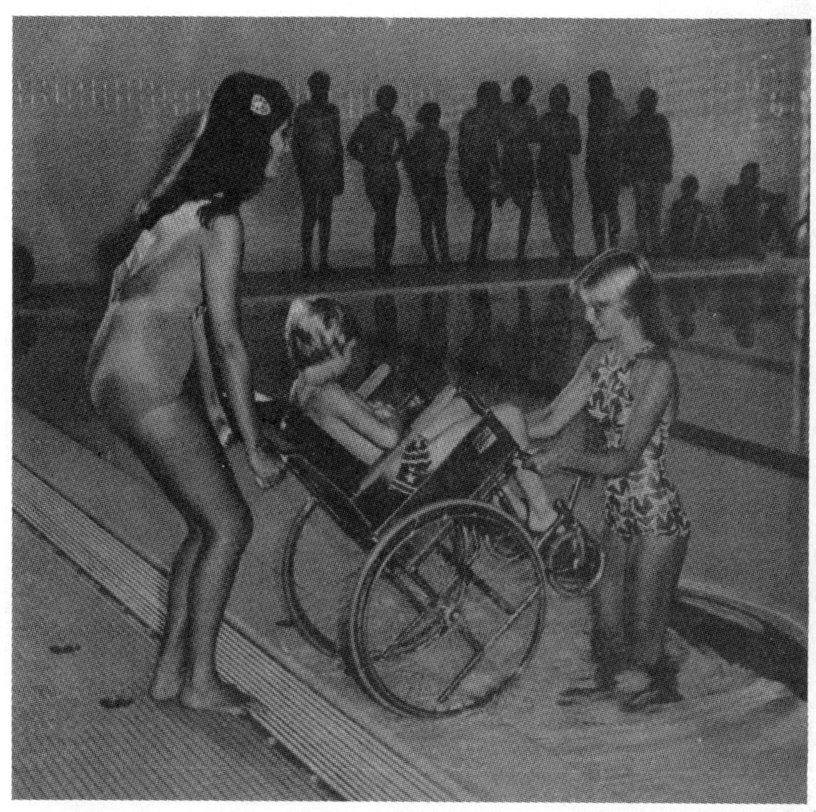

The YMCA swimming pool in Olean, New York, accommodates the handicapped.

SWIMMING POOLS with adjustable floors have for some time been popular in European countries—West Germany, for example, will not subsidize a pool to be built at a school unless the facility has such a floor.

But in North America, the idea is just catching on.

Pools with adjustable floors are a concession to the fact that different swimmers need water of different depths: very young children (and therefore very small) need shallow water; wheelchair-bound people need to be able to roll their chairs onto the pool floor at the surrounding deck level.

A YMCA in Olean, New York, was the first institution in North America to recognize the advantages of adjustable pool floors and put them into practice.

The special floor of the Olean pool is raised or lowered at the push of a button by hydraulic lifts underneath the floor.

The pool is used to teach swimming to school children from 26 schools on a contract basis. Some 80 percent of the children are nonswimmers.

Under another program, children as young as six months are taught to swim.

But perhaps more than anyone else, the pool has benefitted the handicapped in the community.

For wheelchair-bound swimmers, the floor is raised to deck level. The wheelchair is rolled onto the pool floor and the floor is lowered to an appropriate level. The handicapped person simply floats off the wheelchair in the process.

The YMCA purchased the adjustable pool facility from the AFW of North America company, which is based in Olean.

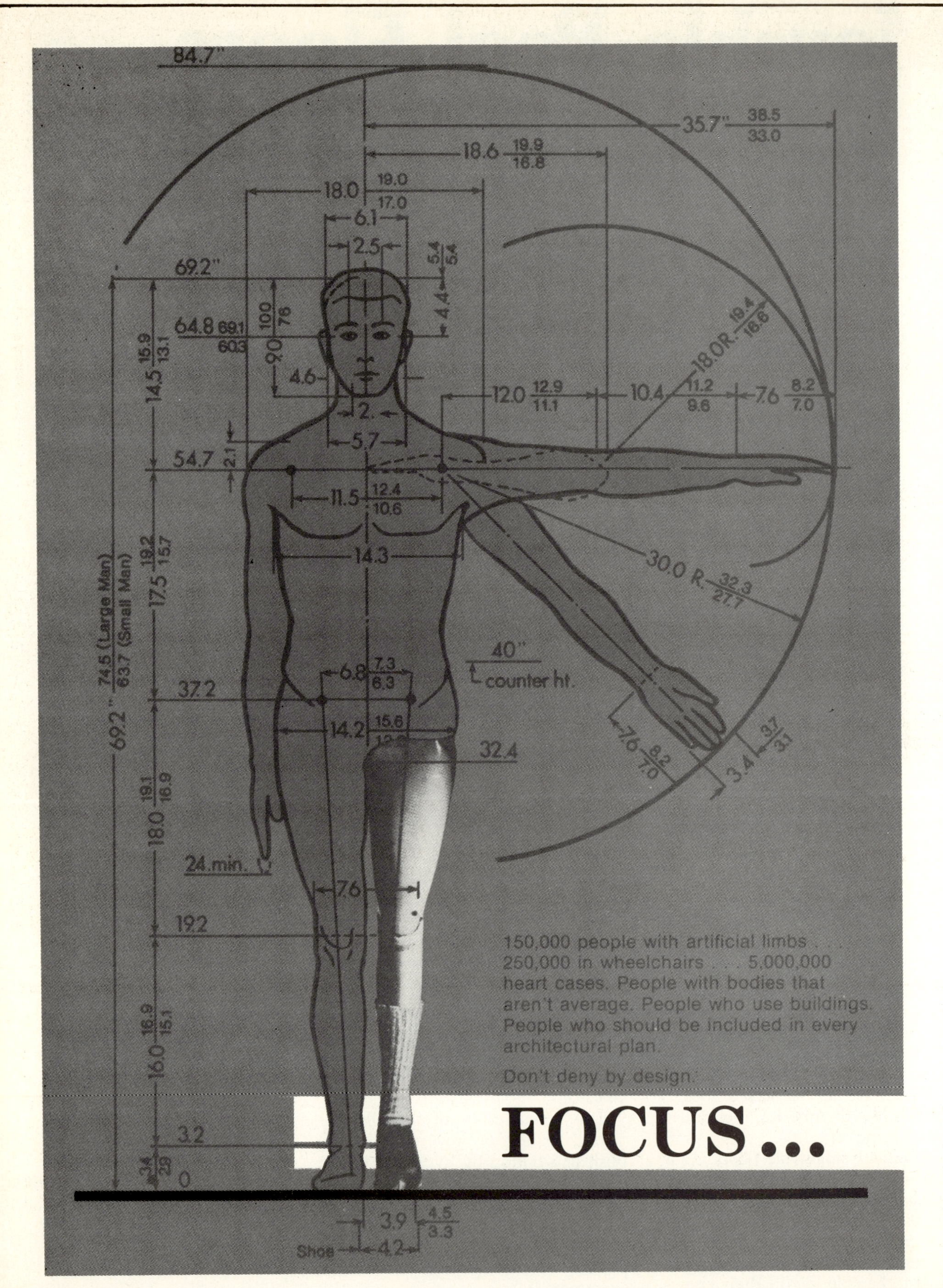

84.7"
35.7"
38.5
33.0
18.6
19.9
16.8
18.0
19.0
17.0
6.1
2.5
5.4
5.4
69.2"
4.4
64.8 69.1
10.0
7.6
19.4
16.6
60.3
18.0 R.
14.5
15.9
13.1
9.0
4.6
12.0
12.9
11.1
10.4
11.2
9.6
7.6
8.2
7.0
2.
5.7
54.7
2.1
11.5
12.4
10.6
17.5
18.2
15.7
14.3
30.0 R.
32.3
27.7
40"
counter ht.
37.2
6.8
7.3
6.3
74.5 (Large Man)
63.7 (Small Man)
69.2"
14.2
15.6
32.4
7.6
8.2
7.0
3.7
3.1
3.4
18.0
19.1
16.9
24. min.
7.6
19.2
16.9
16.0
15.1
3.2
.34
.29
0
3.9
4.5
3.3
Shoe
4.2

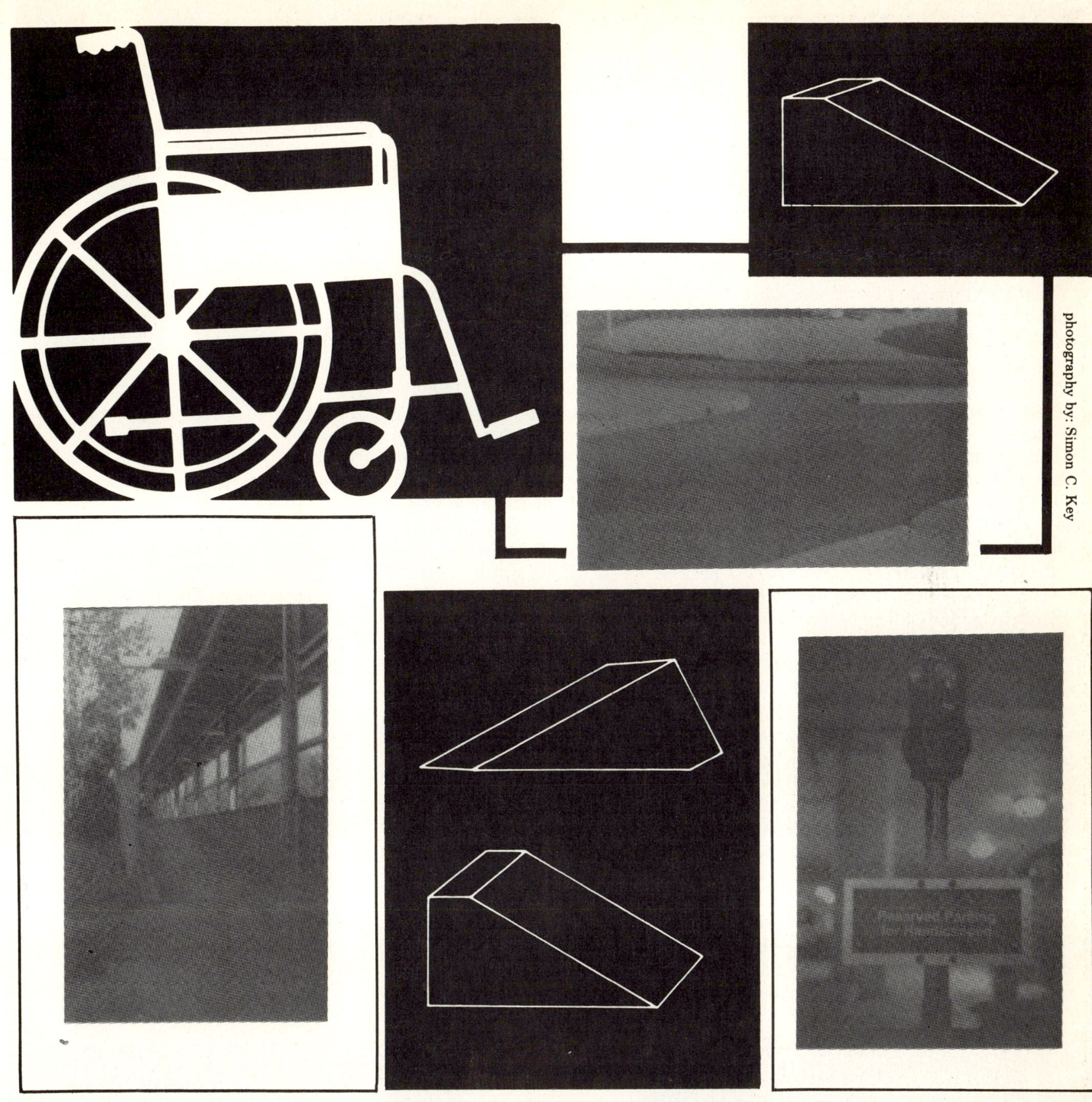

Barrier-Free Design Making Way for the Handicapped

A barrier-free environment for mobility-limited persons is now fast becoming reality through the concentrated efforts of architects the world over. Architectural barriers have been a matter of oversight in the past . . . Now with the physically handicapped coming into the mainstream of life, we can include them in providing access to our public and private buildings and mass transit as these pictures illustrate.

AAAS Initiates Barrier-Free Meetings

Martha Ross Readen

This year in Boston the AAAS rolled out the welcome carpet for the physically disabled in the scientific community. More than 200 persons walked or wheeled over that carpet to attend the annual meeting with their colleagues. For many of this group, full participation in a professional meeting had previously been impossible. At this year's AAAS meeting the housing and meeting facilities selected were highly accessible to wheelchairs, interpreters were available to the deaf, and volunteers were on hand to help as requested. In addition, a resource center and 24-hour-a-day hot line offered on-the-spot assistance.

The AAAS Office of Opportunities in Science, with the cooperation of the Meetings Office, coordinated the activities. The university student volunteers and members of the Massachusetts Council of Organizations of the Handicapped served as the backbone of the accessibility effort. Also, the Boston Advisory Committee, hotel and convention bureau staff, and tour directors eagerly participated by adjusting their plans to accommodate the special needs of the disabled. The tour director, with the help of the Advisory Committee, even managed to have a ramp built at Symphony Hall and provided a van with hydraulic lift to transport people to the Boston Pop's Concert.

Close association with their disabled peers seemed to have had a profound effect on the able-bodied scientists who attended the Boston meeting. Many expressed regret that their colleagues had been unthinkingly excluded in the past. Plans are currently underway to ensure that the Denver meeting and others in the future will be made as barrier-free as possible. Also, efforts will be made to provide whatever assistance is necessary to encourage and ensure the full meeting participation of all members of the scientific community.

Surprisingly, the AAAS staff responsible for the accessibility effort found that the tasks involved were much easier than they had expected. And they confirmed that the benefits received from tapping these valuable human resources far outweighed the efforts in their behalf.

In order to assist AAAS affiliates and other professional organizations to provide barrier-free meetings, the Office of Opportunities in Science is preparing a guide to making professional meetings accessible. The guide, based on the experiences in making the Boston meeting accessible and written with the guidance of a large number of the disabled scientists who attended, will be ready for distribution this summer. The Office also has offered its help to several scientific societies in planning for their future meetings. The American Physical Society at its recent meeting in Washington provided special information and assistance to the handicapped. The American Psychological Association is planning to expand its services to the handicapped at its meeting in Washington this fall.

One highlight of the AAAS meeting as it concerned the physically disabled was a symposium, "Science, Technology, and the Handicapped," which focused on technological innovations and research needs, as well as on the removal of physical, educational, and career barriers for the handicapped. Featured were two computers, one that reads to the blind, the other that helps teach the deaf to speak, and communication devices for the nonvocal. Special attention was given to the implications for action by professional societies in the removal of barriers to the physically disabled. Proceedings of the symposium will be available by the end of the summer from AAAS.

Also, as part of the Science Inter-

Fig. 1 (left). Martha Ross Redden (far right), director of the AAAS Project on the Handicapped in Science, discusses the program with several disabled scientists at the Boston meeting. Left to right, Frances Lowder, Phyllis Stearner, Cheryl Davis, and Robert Larsen.   Fig. 2 (right). Robert Haushalter of American University explains some of the features of Laboratory Science and Art for the Blind to an exhibit visitor at the AAAS meeting. [Photos by Steven Brody]

national exposition at the AAAS meeting, 14 booths demonstrated the work of rehabilitation research and training centers across the country; instructional methods for teaching science and art to blind students; the work of state

agencies and local organizations serving the needs of the deaf, blind, and physically disabled; and some of the technological developments to aid the disabled.

AAAS began to actively consider the needs of its physically disabled members over 2 years ago, at the urging of one of its members, a deaf biologist. During the past year an all-out effort has been launched to facilitate the full participation of handicapped scientists in the activities of the Association. The steps taken thus far are intended to be only the beginning of activities to remove the barriers to the handicapped for education and careers in science. AAAS also is encouraging its affiliates to become involved in programs toward this end.

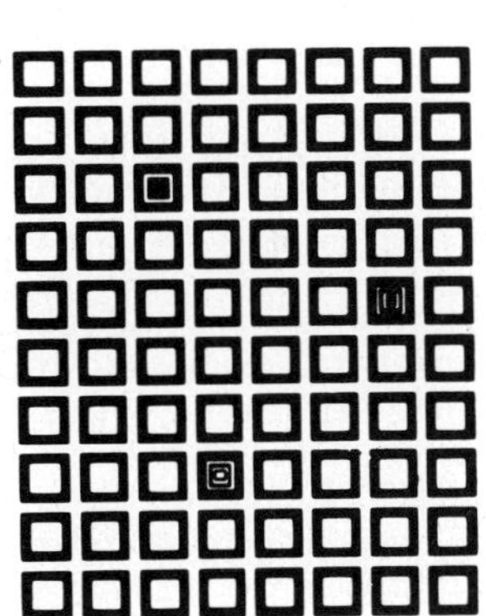

PSYCHOLOGY OF EXCEPTIONAL CHILDREN

Designed for the introductory courses of study in special education, this book provides an overview of the exceptional child. The social, emotional, linguistic and cognitive development of handicapped children are looked at, along with a special section dealing with support systems for the exceptional child, specifically family relationships.

Special Learning Corporation

42 Boston Post Rd. Guilford, Connecticut 06437 (203) 453-6525

Seaside Holidays for Severely Disabled

Leonard Tasker

Leonard Tasker was for 15 years editor of The Voice of the Disabled, *official publication of "The National Cripples' Journal Organisation" in Britain. He is now NCJO Holiday Secretary. He is also a founding member and Trustee of The Enterprise Club for Disabled People, a social club for disabled people in Coventry.*

The young woman lying in the bulky iron lung looked at me and said, "Len, this bungalow has become a second home to me."

The smile in Kathleen Crowhurst's eyes belied the fact that for the last 10 years she has been confined to this bed of iron, pumps pounding the air pressures to her body enabling helpless lungs to breathe. A nurse by her side brushed away a wisp of hair from her eyes, while above the noise of the pumps the singing of a kettle announced that all was ready for a pot of tea. The nurse prepared the pipe through which Kathleen would sip her tea while looking out the large windows that faced onto a carpet of sweet-smelling freshly mown grass. The sea was just beyond, and the clear sea air was already restoring color to her cheeks.

Kathleen Crowhurst's vacation represents the realization of a dream — a dream born many years before when I was given a similar holiday.

I had emerged into the outside world at 21 after 10 years of confinement in hospital wards with tubercular hip. I received a surprise letter from Leonard Inskip, then editor of a magazine called *The National Cripples Journal,* inviting me to spend two weeks, completely free of charge, at the seaside holiday home which he rented in Caister. I did not know Len Inskip personally at the time, and I suppose that he must have heard that I was unable to work and in poor circumstances. I accepted his invitation, and enjoyed a marvelous holiday. It was a fairly large house and, although it could not accommodate the more severely disabled, it was ideal for us walking disabled. This

became a holiday that I was never to forget.

Some years later I unexpectedly took over the editorship of *The National Cripples Journal* (later changing the name to *The Voice of the Disabled*). That first seaside holiday house had been closed due to World War II, but I determined to open another so that other disabled, even the more severely handicapped, could have the holiday experience that I had enjoyed. My wife Peggy and the board of the magazine agreed and supported my plan, and we soon designed and built our pioneering bungalow at Chapel-St.-Leonards on the east coast of England.

Specially Equipped

Simplicity of design was the keynote: doors wide enough to take the bulkiest equipment, an easily accessible pathway to the doors, no steps anywhere, and toilet facilities suitable for people in wheelchairs. For those in iron lungs and dependent on respiratory equipment, special electrical connections bypassing the normal meters were installed to ensure a constant electrical supply. Perhaps most important is an emergency generator which automatically takes over in case of an electrical break-down. This life-saving device, which has had to be used on several occasions, gives our friends who depend on respiratory equipment an extra feeling of safety and confidence.

There are four bedrooms in the bungalow, two single beds in each. In addition, there is a bed-settee and a space allocated for the iron lung.

Another important feature is the fact that when the disabled arrive with their party, the bungalow provides an intimate and comfortable atmosphere — the feeling that the bungalow really belongs to them. As Kathleen Crowhurst said, it becomes their "second home." Being self-catering, complete with cooker, refrigerator, every cooking utensil, cutlery, crockery, ample hot water and a color television, guests can really feel at home. They can go to bed when they like, get up when they wish and have their personal needs attended to in complete privacy without causing inconvenience or embarrassment to others. This is most important to a disabled person.

To ensure privacy, only one party at a time may rent the bungalow, even if there are only two or three in the party. Our fee for renting the bungalow is perhaps the lowest known for such a holiday house, and the disabled person can obtain financial help for his or her holiday from the local Social Service Department. In some cases, such as Kathleen Crowhurst's, we do not charge a fee. I remember my first holiday, and we are happy to be able in these special cases to provide the facilities free of charge. Although our income just about covers our expenses, we do receive donations, without which we could not carry on.

The Greatest Pioneer

When this bungalow was built some 12 years ago it was the only one of its kind in Britain. Other organizations have since imitated this pioneering venture. But perhaps the greatest pioneer of all has been Kathleen Crowhurst herself. She was prepared to travel the 100 miles from her hospital in London to the Lincolnshire coast, in her iron lung, to spend two weeks on holiday in unknown surroundings. The hospital's special ambulance transported her with all her bulky equipment, under constant supervision of her nurse and helpers. The police escorted her all the way to ensure that there were no traffic hold-ups and to assist if there was an equipment failure en route. Kathy placed her life in the hands of many unknown people, and her courage was to prove that this great holiday experience was possible.

Kathleen has returned to the bungalow for her two weeks' annual holiday during each of the last 10 years.

The demand for the bungalow from disabled people living in all parts of England became so great that we purchased a second, smaller bungalow on the same site eight years ago. There is a recreation club on the site which provides friendly social meetings with other holiday-makers. The sea is within a short walking distance, and a special path has been built to help wheelchairs get up a slope to the promenade.

There is no more room to build on this site, however, so any future expansion would involve construction of a specially designed center adequate to cater to any type of disability. At the moment this is just an idea, but then, we had no money when we started our present bungalow — I borrowed the money, launched an appeal, and was able to repay the loan in 18 months.

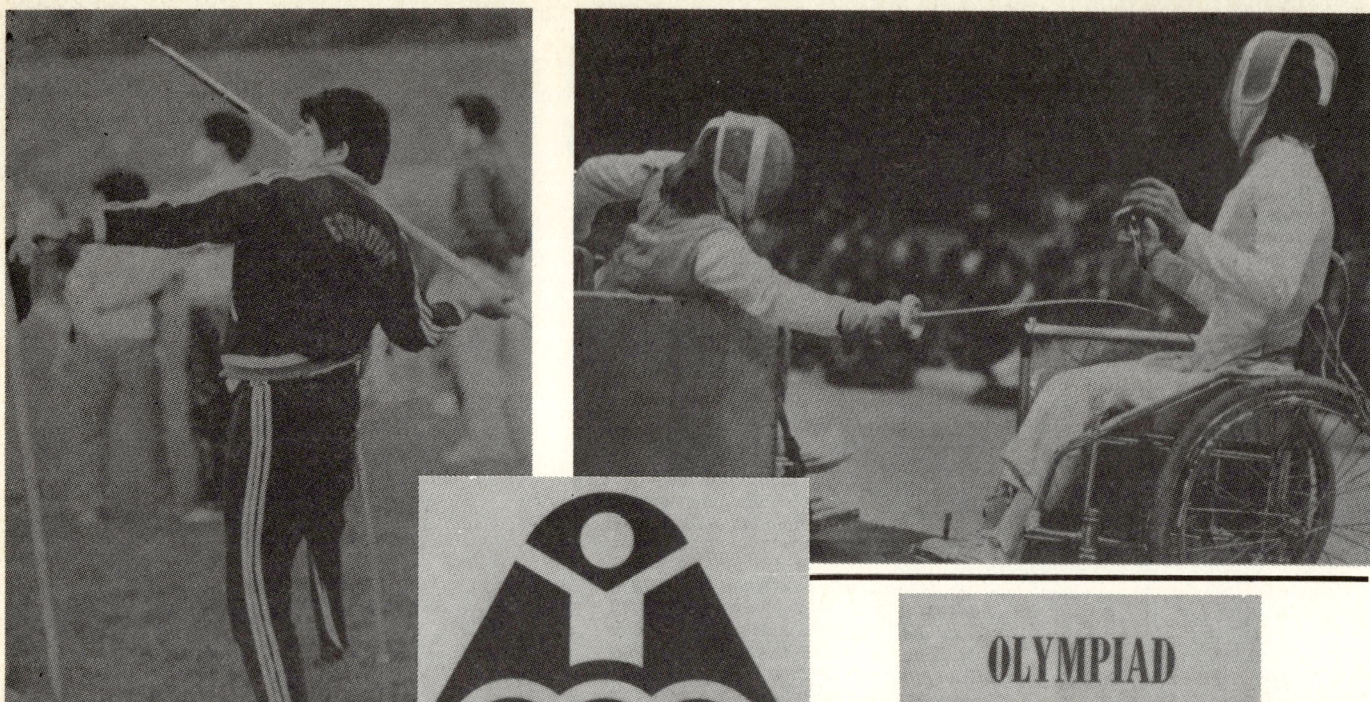

OLYMPIAD

Emerging Directions

A new day has dawned for the handicapped of America. Federal legislation and spending, public awareness, improved attitudes of society, all are factors alloting for this change. In addition, unprecedented medical and technological advances have vastly increased the potential of the physically handicapped person. The use of modern prosthetic devices have allowed the physically handicapped individual, who before might have been denied entrance into the mainstream of society, a new chance. Pacemakers placed in the brain of a child or adult affected by a neurological impairment, now aid the individual in approaching more closely than ever before, normal physiological and neurological functioning.

As these developments continue to emerge, and the physically handicapped progress into society's maintream, a new barrier free world must develop concurrently. The physically handicapped population for too long has been shelved away as worthless drains on society. A new awareness of their worthwhile talents and contributions has now appeared on the horizon and can serve as an example for all handicapped persons today.

TECHNICAL AIDS FOR DISABLED PERSONS

R & D and World Cooperation:

Situation Serious . . .

. . . But Not Hopeless

Karl Montan

Karl Montan, who has been actively involved with the problems of physical disability since 1939, has since 1968 been director of the Swedish Institute for the Handicapped, a national institution which deals mainly with technical aids and environmental facilities. The Swedish Institute also houses the ICTA Information Centre. Mr. Montan is also chairman of the Nordic Association of Rehabilitation and is a member of the Council of Rehabilitation International.

Nothing is of more obvious value than international cooperation in the promotion of assistance to the disabled, and yet nothing seems as difficult to achieve.

This is my conclusion from several years of struggle for such cooperation concerning technical aids and environmental facilities for the handicapped. Yet I have no doubt that in the present situation, with needs far outweighing resources, combined planning and systematic use of accumulated knowledge are essential and can be achieved.

Let us look for a moment at general economic conditions. Despite economic crises, our standard of living is continually rising. We are likely to meet both our real and artificial needs through an expanded system of mass production, the premise of which is simple: the greater the market, the cheaper the product. International marketing plays a major role in making the mass production system a reality.

But neither system nor premise are necessarily applicable to the disabled consumer. In order for the prices of technical aids for these consumers to be in line with prices for goods on the general market, there must be sufficient numbers of disabled consumers to assure efficient large-scale production. While some groups of handicapped consumers are fairly large (hearing impaired, wheelchair users), other groups are very small (the deaf-blind and others with multiple handicaps). The more handicapped a group is, the smaller it is, and it therefore costs much more to develop and supply technical aids to those who need them the most. The world is full of sophisticated prototypes of such devices, but comparatively few come on to the marketplace.

International cooperation is required if we are to identify the most essential needs of the handicapped, connect research and development, and standardize testing procedures among the different countries. But success in these goals may decrease only the costs of development of technical aids, and have no effect on the greater problem: the cost of production. To get a prototype on the market we very much depend on commercial firms' judgments of risk and profit. Of course, non-commercial interests are also involved in this process, and in some countries a variety of measures are taken to stimulate production of such aids through public or private economic support.

The Origins of ICTA

The list of international organizations that have become involved in the work of stimulating creation and improvement of technical aids for the disabled is a very long one. We shall discuss mainly the work of Rehabilitation International and its International Commission on Technical Aids, Housing and Transportation (ICTA), which I serve as Director.

The Fifth World Congress of Rehabilitation International met in Stockholm in 1951. At that Congress a technical committee was created to deal with technical aids for the disabled, with its major emphasis on prosthetics and orthotics (artificial replacement of missing body parts and the support and bracing of weak or ineffective joints and muscles). In 1964 this committee was divided into two new committees, one for prosthetics and orthotics, the other for technical aids. The technical aids committee was placed in Stockholm, and an information center was created for it in that city. This latter committee was ICTA, and since 1975 it has had the status of a standing commission within Rehabilitation International.

The prosthetics and orthotics committee, headquartered in Copenhagen, became an independent organization in 1970 and took on the name International Society for Prosthetics and Orthotics (ISPO).

Thus for more than a decade ICTA's work has been mainly with aids and facilities of a general type for motor disabled persons, while ISPO has concentrated on prostheses and orthoses. However, during the past few years ISPO has shown increasing interest in broadening its area of work. This has resulted in some organizing problems between the two groups, but positive negotiations to solve these problems have now begun.

As an example of the increasing cooperation between the two organizations, ICTA has been invited to take part in the program of the Second World Congress of ISPO, to be held in New York City from May 26 through June 2, 1977.

Three Areas of Work

To meet its goal of stimulating the development of better technical aids and environmental facilities for the handicapped, ICTA works in three different areas:

• Aids especially made for handicapped consumers, such as wheelchairs and environmental control systems.

• Items made for consumers in general but adaptable to meet the special needs of the disabled, such as tape recorders with special functions and automobiles adapted for hand controls.

• Items produced for the general consumer that could incorporate design features to make them more usable by disabled individuals. Included in this category would be the design of dwellings, handles and grips, and mass transportation facilities.

While these three areas of attention are all important, the last, which intends to create a society for all people, seems in the long run to be the most crucial.

Specification of the needs of handicapped consumers is a most complicated process. Interviews with such consumers and systematic observation of their problems in daily life appear to be the best means, but very few such investigations have been made — and these often lack necessary detail.

ICTA has done work in this area, as for example in its publication of need analyses concerning the dwelling requirements for different disability groups and the environmental requirements of the visually impaired.[1] But the classification of different disability consumer groups based on anthropometric studies is at present at only a very early stage of development; this is one reason why it is so difficult to quantify the various consumer groups within the handicapped population.

R & D Very Expensive

Most research and development work is very expensive. Such work in technical aids and environmental facilities for the handicapped is certainly no exception. The willingness to pay research and development costs is very low when the consumer group to be served is small. A solution — perhaps, is our special area of interest, the only solution — may be found in international cooperation.

For there to be such international cooperation, there must exist an ongoing exchange of information on planned, operative and terminated research and development projects. ICTA is attempting to create such an exchange through a continuous (though not yet quite systematic) registration of institutions involved in such work. These institutions are to be found largely in the highly industrialized areas of North America, Europe and Japan. Very little work of this kind is done in Africa and South America.

Karl Montan

ISPO is also attempting to specify the research and development interests and resources of its members. A notable attempt to create an inventory of planned and ongoing projects is being made by the Smithsonian Science Information Exchange, Inc. in Washington, D. C.[2] But up to this time the input of project information from the disability field into the Smithsonian data base seems rather poor.

In the Nordic countries an annual inventory of such projects is made; three have up to now been published. The first two, now out of print, were published by the Swedish Institute for the Handicapped. The current edition, *Registration of Nordic Projects Relating to Disability 1976,*[3] covers projects ongoing through the end of 1975 and lists 207 different undertakings (see box). It is published by the Nordic Committee on Disability, which has been assigned

5. EMERGING DIRECTIONS

responsibility for this annual inventory in the future. All this data has now been incorporated into the Smithsonian system.

ICTA recommends that other countries emulate this Nordic example so that a worldwide clearinghouse for such information can eventually be realized. There appears to be progress on this front, but it is slow.

Another facet of our work is the stimulation of national organizations to promote projects of international value. Examples include an ongoing study of air travel by disabled persons[4] sponsored by the Home and Society for the Disabled in Copenhagen and another by the Netherlands Society for Rehabilitation on architectural facilities.[5] Simple inventories of aids on the market are of value, such as *Electronic Environmental Control Systems for the Severely Physically Disabled*[6] done by the Department of Health and Social Security in London and ICTA's own *Aids for Children*.[7]

Speech Handicaps Study

The Swedish Institute for the Handicapped in collaboration with ICTA has initiated a project dealing with technical aids for the speech handicapped. Financial support is provided by the National Swedish Board for Technical Development. This project, scheduled to run for three years, was formed in 1975 by Swedish representatives from such disciplines as speech therapy, speech transmission, phoniatrics and neurological rehabilitation.

For this project information is required concerning national and international research and development, statistical data and needs analyses. Along with a study of the existing literature, a questionnaire was prepared and sent in late 1975 to 257 institutions around the world involved with problems of speech disability. Responses were received from 176 institutions (68 percent), and these were processed and distributed to the respondents together with a second questionnaire seeking details on projects described in the first responses. Final results of this survey process will probably be presented in a catalogue of projects which will have value for researchers in this field the world over. It is also hoped that international negotiations to establish systematic cooperation in this field of disability will take place in 1977.

Standardization and Testing

Both Rehabilitation International and ICTA are well aware of the value of standardization and testing of technical aids. The evaluation process can establish that an aid fulfills needs specifications (standards), which can then be transmitted to manufacturers. This adds reliability to the product and increases the security and comfort of the consumer. This process can also be a positive influence on production costs. There are already some national standards that have been developed for electrically powered wheelchairs and elevators,[8] and on the international level there are some standards for hearing aids (measurement methods, flexes and earmolds) through the International Electrotechnical Commission (IEC).[9]

International standardization is largely the province of the IEC and the International Organization for Standardization (ISO), which has several committees where the concerns of the disabled persons receive special attention. But while these are certainly interesting and important developments, disabled consumers should not expect that their situation will as a result improve overnight. The work of the ISO is proceeding slowly and requires great effort and resources.

In addition to the activities of the ISO and IEC, work is going on in some other places concerning testing procedures for technical aids and facilities for the handicapped. It remains a goal of ICTA to rationalize those achievements so that testing results from one institution can be used elsewhere.

Information Exchange

Information remains the universal ingredient at every stage of rehabilitation technology: research, development and production.

International congresses such as the quadrennial World Congresses of Rehabilitation International are important occasions both for the exchange of information and for discussions of how to routinize such communications in the future.

ICTA feels a responsibility to promote this process, and does so through printed publications, conferences and seminars. In addition to one or two comprehensive studies each year, ICTA annually publishes approximately ten looseleaf sheets, each describing a new technical aid in English, French, German and Spanish and including price and the name of the manufacturer as well as essential technical data. In addition, ICTA plans to publish a more general newsletter on a quarterly basis.[10]

Other publications devoted to the international exchange of information in the rehabilitation field include *Excerpta Medica*,[11] which abstracts most reports and articles printed on the subjects of rehabilitation and physical medicine *(Excerpta Medica* Section 19) and on biophysics, bioengineering and medical instrumentation (Section 27). While these surveys cover the world literature well, they do not appear until 12 to 18 months after initial publication of the articles. *The Journal of Medical Engineering and Technology*,[12] a British publication, gets this bibliographic information into print faster, but it is not as complete and lacks summaries of the articles' contents.

Diagnosis and Prognosis

Given the obvious value of the international cooperation described in this article, it becomes so much more mysterious that so few resources are available to promote this work.

The resources of ICTA — aside from the support furnished by various institutions in the form of projects — amount to about $70,000 annually. Our budget has grown very slowly over the past decade. Other international organizations, including the United Nations and its agencies, work in this field on yet a smaller scale. Attempts to garner support from international funding sources have up to now failed.

The situation is serious, but not hopeless. We see hope in the work now in progress, and in the cooperative spirit on the personal level among experts and institutions in the different countries.

REFERENCES

1. *Disability and Housing Needs* ($3.50) and *The Physical Environment and the Visually Impaired* ($3.00), both available from: ICTA Information Centre, Fack, S-161 25 Bromma 1, Sweden.

2. For further information write: Smithsonian Science Information Exchange, Inc., Room 300, 1730 M Street N.W., Washington, D. C. 20036.

3. *Registration of Nordic Projects Relating to Disability 1976* is available from: Nordic Committee on Disability, c/o Swedish Institute for the Handicapped, Fack, S-161 25 Bromma 1, Sweden.

4. *Airlines and Disabled Travellers*, to be available from the ICTA Information Centre in June, 1977.

5. *Architectural Facilities for the Disabled*, almost out of stock but still available on special request from the ICTA Information Centre.

6. *Electronic Environmental Control Systems for the Severely Physically Disabled* (1976), available on request from the ICTA Information Centre.

7. *Aids for Children* (1972), available for $2.00 from the ICTA Information Centre.

8. *Wheelchairs*, the Veterans Administration's standards and specifications for wheelchairs, available from: Veterans Administration Prosthetics Center, 252 Seventh Avenue, New York, N.Y. 10001. *H-Requirement Specification, Electrical Wheelchairs*, Swedish Institute for the Handicapped, Fack, S-161 25 Bromma 1, Sweden. The proposed international elevator standard, ISO/DIS 3751/1, is already accepted as the Swedish standard.

9. International Electrotechnical Commission, Working Group #6 "Hearing Aids," inside Technical Committee #29, "Electroacoustics."

10. Annual subscriptions for the loose technical aids information sheets (as well as for all other ICTA publications during the year) are available for $10.00 from the ICTA Information Centre. A set of previous publications 1964-1973 is available for $15.00.

11. For more information write: *Excerpta Medica*, Nassau Building, 228 Alexander Street, Princeton, N.J. 18540.

12. For information concerning *The Journal of Medical Engineering and Technology* (formerly *Biomedical Engineering*) write: United Trade Press, 42/43 Gerrard Street, London W1V 7LP, England.

A Page from the Nordic Register

Registration of Nordic Projects Relating to Disability 1976 is published by the Nordic Committee on the Problems of Disability, located at the Swedish Institute for the Handicapped in Bromma.

This publication contains descriptions of 207 projects being undertaken in Denmark, Sweden, Norway and Finland. The descriptions are furnished by the project researchers themselves. 177 are in English; translated titles are provided for the remainder. The projects in progress (as well as reports of projects newly begun and terminated) are as of January 1, 1976. The 207 projects have the following distribution:

Project Category	Number
Aurally handicapped, deaf	31
Visually handicapped, deaf-blind	28
Motor physically handicapped	59
Speech handicapped	6
Ostomy and incontinence	5
Mental retardation	20
Measurement methodology, technical and functional testing and adaptation of aids, need analyses	10
Housing and community planning, public transportation	18
Work environments and aids	4
Social, psychological and educational aspects	26

Title of project

Control of multifunctional hand prosthesis using pattern recognition technique

Ordering agent or institution (address and contact)

Professor Robert Magnusson, Dept. of Applied Electronics, Chalmers University of Technology, Fack, 402 20 Göteborg, Sweden; Professor Ingemar Petersén, Dept. of Clinical Neurophysiology, Sahlgren Hospital, 413 45 Göteborg, Sweden

Principal investigator (name, institution, address) and assistant(s)

Peter Herberts, M.D., Dept. of Orthopaedic Surgery I, Sahlgren Hospital, 413 45 Göteborg, Sweden;
Christian Almström, M.Sc., Dept. of Applied Electronics, Chalmers University of Technology, Fack, 402 20 Göteborg, Sweden

Funding agency/institution (name and address)

Swedish Board for Technical Development, Fack, 100 72 Stockholm, Sweden

Starting date	Estimated date of completion	Costs 1975/76	Estimated total costs
1974	1977	194.454	591.356

Summary of project (problem, method, aim)

The lack of control sites and the necessity of extensive training entail difficult problems in the control of multifunctional hand prostheses. A possible solution to these problems is to use the phantom limb perception. With a number of skin electrodes, myoelectric signals can be picked up when the amputee performs various, imagined phantom limb movements. The patterns formed by these signals can be interpreted by applying pattern recognition technique, which means that the imagined phantom limb movements can be identified.

Our group has developed a complete system, based on pattern recognition technique, for control of a prosthesis with three bi-directional movements. The signals are picked up with six electrodes, which are anatomically located over the stump muscles. The classification procedure is performed by an analog electronic network, individually adapted by computer analysis of the amputee's signal patterns.

A portable electronic network and electrodes for picking up myoelectric signals has been constructed and adapted to two amputees. Without any training they could control all prosthesis movements. The system is now functionally evaluated.

Keywords

Myoelectric control; pattern recognition; prosthesis control.

Date	Signature
16 February 1976	Christian Almström

APPLYING TECHNOLOGY
TO SPECIAL EDUCATION

VIVIAN HEDRICH

Mrs. Hedrich is Publications Specialist
for Seattle Public Schools.

Advanced scientific technology and a good deal of hope are being injected this year into a Seattle Public Schools Special Education program that appears to be breaking new ground in the teaching of severely handicapped children. At its core is a team composed of a neurophysiologist, an electrical engineer, an electronics technician, and skilled persons in many other fields, and backed by $55,000 in Federal funds provided under title VI-B of the Elementary and Secondary Education Act.

The intent is to demonstrate some of the practical applications of technology and research to the critical educational problems inherent in such grievous disabilities as cerebral palsy. The evidence so far suggests that such applications are practical indeed.

Five-year-old Lori attends Seattle's Lowell Elementary School. A pretty child with strawberry blond hair and a winsome smile, she daily faces difficulties of such magnitude as to challenge the most skilled and understanding of teachers.

Since birth, cerebral palsy has cheated Lori of much of what living is all about. Faulty sensory "input" makes it difficult for her to interpret events in the world around her, and poor muscular control severely restricts her movement and ability to respond appropriately to what she does perceive. Her academic world is Room 109 in Lowell's modern orthopedic wing, cheerfully carpeted and filled with colorful toys and special equipment.

One morning recently she had an opportunity to try on a new piece of wearing apparel—a lightweight plastic prototype model helmet being field-tested as a "stabilizer" to help children such as Lori control the position of their heads. The new device includes a gravity-sensitive "pickup" and small circular vibrators positioned near the ears. When the head

tilts beyond a certain point, the vibrator emits a clicking sound on the appropriate side. The frequency of the clicking corresponds to the degree of tilt and alerts the wearer to return his head to the "neutral" position.

A few minutes after the helmet was in place, observers began to see a marked change in Lori's ability to hold her head erect. The experience will be repeated daily, with the goal of building new habit patterns that eventually will enable Lori to maintain head balance without the assistance of any device.

Among the most interested of the onlookers that morning was Francis Spelman, senior engineer at the University of Washington's Regional Primate Center. He along with neurophysiologist Fredric Harris, the chief consultant for the project, and electronics specialist John Hymer have developed a new model of the "head stabilizer" and are continuing to refine the equipment for further tests this year.

Spelman brings a unique background to the project. In his capacity as head of the primate center's instrumentation development division, he has designed over the past decade a number of electronic instruments for biological research. His experience with cardiovascular control systems is invaluable background for the sensory motor control systems study under way at Lowell School.

"My work in radiotelemetry of physiological functions in free-moving monkeys should also apply when we extend this project to freely moving children," Spelman says. "Ideas from an automatic monkey-training apparatus will lend themselves to the design of an automatic response/reward device that will be used with the children in this project."

One of the bounciest members of the special education class at Lowell Elementary School is dark-eyed Paula, who arrived in Seattle recently from the Philippine Islands specifically to participate in this program. Of above-normal intelligence, Paula seems to be everywhere at once, despite a speech problem and a birth injury that left her right arm so severely disabled that a doctor had recommended

amputation. Her parents instead decided to see what the people at Lowell could do. Barbara Harris, school district supervisor of the physically handicapped and wife of the project director, says chances look good that the child will be able to achieve reasonably normal development.

In the coming weeks she will be fitted with a new artificial sensory device—developed in the laboratory by specialists to meet her special needs, as observed in the classroom and in therapy sessions—that will help her learn to move and control the damaged arm. Meanwhile, toward dealing with her speech problem, Paula will be taught to use a microphone connected to an oscilloscope. Thus combined, the instruments convert sound into electrical "potential variations" which are made visible as a pattern on a cathode-ray tube.

As the little girl pronounces a new word she will watch the small screen carefully, trying to make "her picture" match the correct image made by normal speech. It is hoped this visual feedback will help Paula compensate for her faulty auditory monitoring of sound.

Bringing neurophysiological concepts and theory together with electronics know-how to improve the perceptual skills and mobility of handicapped children is only one of the title VI project's objectives. Another is to provide valuable inservice training to Seattle professionals who work with the neurologically impaired. These include the physically handicapped, children with learning and language disabilities, and a selected group of preschool-age children with thus far uncategorized learning problems. A special program for the latter group has been established at Stevens School, to which children are referred by community agencies, private physicians, and parents who suspect their youngsters have special problems.

In this project new diagnostic and screening tests are being developed as specialists representing many medical and paramedical disciplines contribute their expertise in identifying each youngster's problems. As those who work closely with the handicapped have long observed,

such early identification is vital if successful remedies are to be found.

Charlene Davis, who teaches the ten children assigned to Room 109, explains why:

"All children learn by doing, beginning with such basic movements as sitting up, rolling over, crawling, and walking. Children with motor handicaps such as Lori's and to a lesser extent Paula's are necessarily much slower than normal children in engaging in this kind of exploration and manipulation. And yet it is through such activity that the child begins to comprehend distance, discover which lid fits on which pan, observe that a banana feels squishy, and learn that the right shoe is somehow different from the left. Denied this essential preliminary training, the handicapped child just cannot be ready to begin his formal education at the age of five."

Susan Boll, a physical therapist who works closely with Mrs. Davis, has high hopes that new technology and the people behind it will do much to compensate for the handicapped child's inherent learning disadvantages.

"Left alone, a motor-handicapped child will do nothing and learn nothing," Mrs. Boll says. "A person with training can provide constant assistance to correct the child's movements and help build more normal muscle tone, but so far this has only been possible on a one-to-one basis. There are literally hundreds of ways that technology could help reinforce our work, such as by providing means to monitor children's movements and reactions. With each new breakthrough many more new possibilities will open up."

No matter how dedicated and expert the classroom personnel may be, however, and irrespective of what developments may come from the laboratory, Mrs. Boll says that parents have an irreplaceable role to play in the handicapped child's education.

"We only see the child for a few hours a day," she points out. "Without cooperation at home our efforts cannot really succeed. If the parent works consistently with the child and continues to reinforce what he has learned during the day, we often see progress that is amazing. It boils down to parents needing to learn more about how to handle their own children, who require special help."

One of the consequences of failure to achieve this school-home carryover is what many educators often call "therapy behavior," in which the handicapped child drops the improved habit patterns he has laboriously developed the minute he leaves school. A poignant example occurred at Lowell recently.

"After many months of effort," Mrs. Boll recalls, "I was able to bring one of the cerebral palsy children up to a nearly normal walking gait. You can imagine how dejected I felt one afternoon when I happened to observe her leaving the building and saw her walk revert to the previous pattern almost as soon as she reached the sidewalk. Later when I asked her why this happened, she told me she felt more comfortable 'the old way.' From the child's point of view, what society calls normal is in fact abnormal. These children need to be conditioned to the correct ways of doing things 24 hours a day in order to accept them."

Toward this end parents of the approximately 200 children involved have been carefully briefed on what the project is seeking to accomplish and how, and they are invited to periodic meetings for discussion and demonstration of the materials and techniques in use. At a typical session they might be alerted to such matters as the staff's efforts to counter the behavioral and emotional problems that often develop in children whose physical condition prevents them from moving about at will.

"The emotional gains that customarily accompany the 'repair' of functional de-

5. EMERGING DIRECTIONS

fects have a significant effect on the learning process," Dr. Harris says. "The application of appropriate technology can help handicapped children escape chronic failure and begin to succeed in mastering their problems, and thus begin to build a new self-image."

As a consultant in such activities as these, Dr. Harris currently divides his time between the three project centers—Lowell, Stevens, and Surrey Downs Reading Laboratory located in suburban Bellevue—and the University of Washington Medical School. A "doer," he believes in trying the untried, whenever doing so appears theoretically sound.

"Over the years since I first offered a class for public school Special Education teachers in 1967, I have become more and more aware of the importance of moving promising theoretical concepts out into the classroom where they can be tried and the results reported back," he says. "At each of our project centers we have provided the opportunity for a high-intensity, one-to-one relationship between the child and the teacher or therapist. Throughout the year as refinement of diagnostic tests and remedial breakthroughs occur at any one of the centers, we will immediately disseminate the information to everyone involved."

It is most frequently the public school educator, Dr. Harris points out, who is in a position to bring a problem to the attention of the researcher and thus help to speed new developments. Nor should teachers be inhibited by the fact that some of the devices emerging from the laboratory are highly sophisticated and complex, for many others are relatively simple and inexpensive.

"For example," Dr. Harris says, "we use wooden boards on which letters of the alphabet are routed with a hand tool to help children remedy such problems as letter 'reversals.' This approach is based on research showing that under certain conditions, special information gained through the senses of touch and kinesthesia dominates that gained through sight."

Some dyslexic children may reverse letters or letter combinations, Dr. Harris says, because they have accidently learned an "abnormal pattern" of eye movement, such as tracing horizontal portions of letters from right to left rather than from left to right. In the classroom a dyslexic child is blindfolded and helped to trace letters properly, using the sense of touch for guidance and obtaining kinesthetic feedback. When the blindfold is removed the child's eyes tend to continue to follow his hand in correct sequence. Correcting the eye movement habit often seems to remedy the visual perceptual problem and help "build out" the reversal tendency.

Dr. Harris believes that one of the most readily identifiable gaps in special education efforts has been the lack of a unifying conceptual framework within which to view the problems of handicapped children. There is a great need, he feels, to "educate the educators" to understand how the brain functions in relationship to such aspects of the learning process as memory, attention, and motivation.

"Just as one needs to know about the container into which he is attempting to pack merchandise, teachers need to know something about the properties of the brain into which they are attempting to cram information," he says. "How can we get it in? How long will it stay there? In what condition will it be after various intervals of time? How can we get it out and in what forms? Every teacher should be concerned with these questions and be knowledgeable about answers that are being supplied by research."

Thus a key element in the project is in-service education for Seattle's special education teachers and for the many from outside the district who have requested to participate. Members of the staff share their experiences and observations primarily through lectures and demonstrations and make videotapes of these demonstrations available to nonparticipating local agencies.

"The many professions, interests, and backgrounds represented in this effort add up to a major resource," says Dr. Harris. "Together we hope to bring new scientific theory and instrumentation—represented at present by the balance control device, the limb position monitor, speech training apparatus, and equipment for automated visual discrimination presentation—in a way that will help to 'make it up' to children with serious physical and academic handicaps.

"We want our efforts to bring something really 'special' to special education."

THE REMARKABLE NEW PROSTHETICS

DEVICES MADE POSSIBLE BY ADVANCES IN MEDICINE AND ENGINEERING ARE ENABLING THOUSANDS OF LIMB-DEFICIENT YOUNGSTERS TO HOLD THEIR OWN

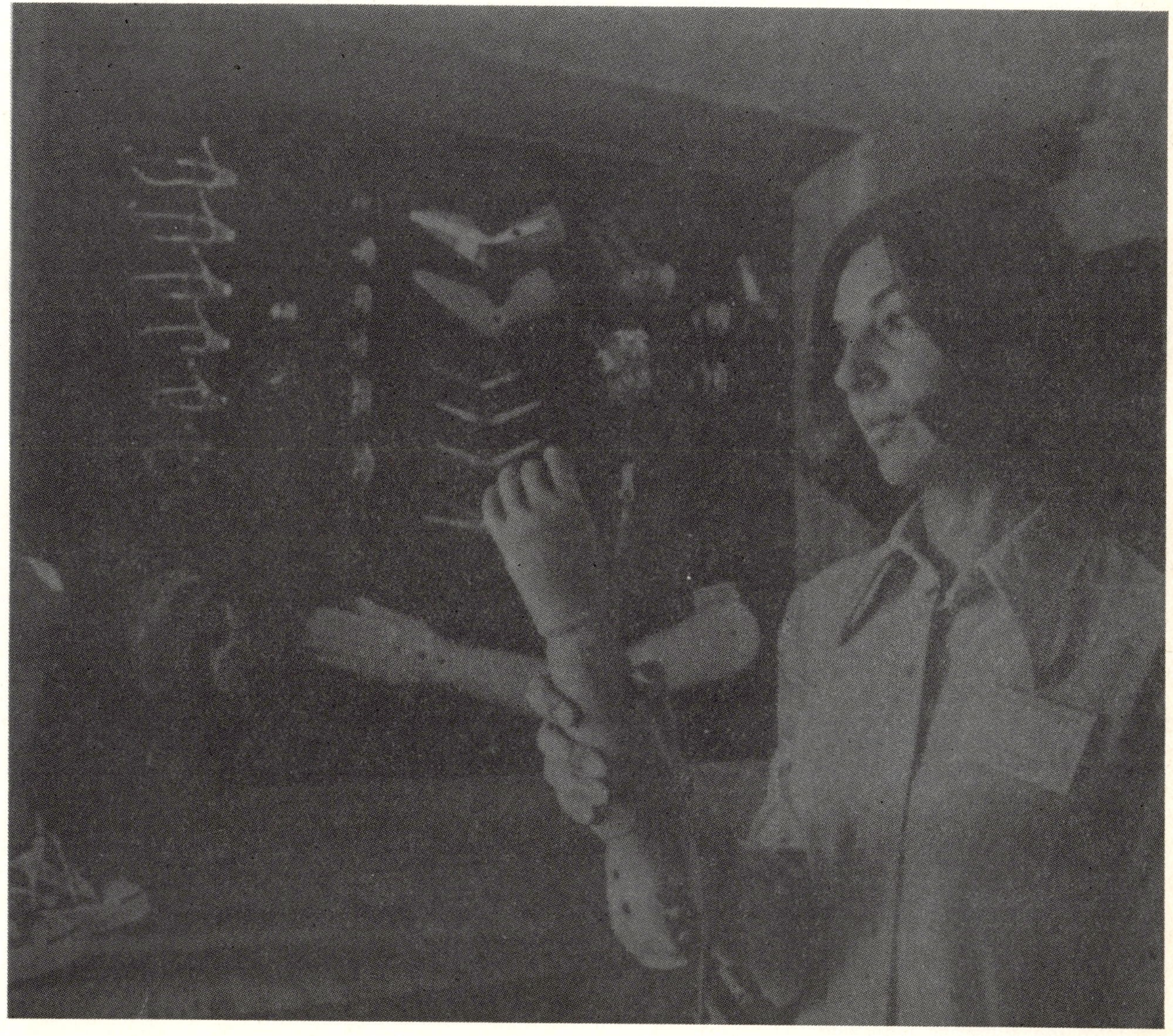

"The Remarkable New Prosthetics," *American Education*, Vol. 11 No. 1, January/February 1975. ©1975 United States Department of Health, Education and Welfare.

5. EMERGING DIRECTIONS

"When our baby was born malformed I cried my eyes out—for myself, for my husband, but most of all for our child. I felt I had failed. I didn't want to live." So spoke a new mother denied the happiness and excitement that normally accompanies the birth of a child. Only slightly less soul-wrenching are the hands, arms, feet, and legs children lose to disease or in accidents.

A generation ago chances are that youngsters with missing or defective limbs would have had to contend with clumsy crutches, a wooden leg, an empty sleeve, and little prospect for leading a reasonably normal life. Since then scientific medical-engineering skills have come onto the scene. Today materials and techniques developed since World War II are helping to heal the heartbreak and give an estimated 10,000 limb-deficient children in the United States alone (nobody is sure of the exact number) a chance to hold their own. Such benefits extend also to similarly handicapped youngsters in other parts of the world—including Canada, England, Scotland, Holland, Germany, and Denmark.

This new specialty, called children's prosthetics, provides the best possible artificial limbs that space-age medical and engineering experts can make. More importantly, it is giving the youngsters new courage, new skills, and new confidence. The Little Leaguer who lost a hand can still bat and play the outfield; the "outdoors type" with only one leg can learn to ski; and automobile crash victims as well as congenital limb-deficient teenagers can drive their own cars.

In the late 1940s, General Omar Bradley, then Director of the Veterans Administration, and Paul Magnuson, VA's Medical Director, became convinced that artificial limbs of new design and materials developed during and after World War II could be adapted to child amputee problems. A few years later, experimental clinics were established at the Michigan Crippled Children's Service in Grand Rapids, at the University of Illinois in Chicago, and at the University of California, Los Angeles. From that modest beginning has evolved a network of 66 child amputee clinics in the United States and Canada and 115 others serving both children and adults. They are supported by private, State, and Federal funds, the latter being made available through grants from the Maternal and Child Service, Health Services and Mental Health Administration of the Department of Health, Education, and Welfare.

Over the past two decades the clinics have developed some interesting statistics. Because of emphasis on early treatment, for example, 50 percent of the patients are under six years of age, and 25 percent under three years. Also, congenital limb deficiencies outnumber accident and disease amputations by a 3-2 ratio.

The UCLA Child Amputee Prosthetics Project, started in 1954 by Milo Brooks, is perhaps the largest and most active in the Nation, currently serving 580 patients. Built around a team concept, it utilizes the services of several disciplines, including medical social workers, pediatricians, orthopedic surgeons, prosthetists, and physical and occupational therapists—all under the direction of the project's medical director.

"Early intervention with counseling for the parents is essential for optimal therapy," says Yoshio Setoguchi, present medical director of the UCLA project. "At least one member of the team should see the child's parents within 72 hours after the birth of a limb-deficient child or traumatic injury that requires amputation."

Adds Dr. Brooks: "The extent of the deficiency makes little difference in the depth of loneliness and helplessness felt by the parents. At no other time are they so in need of expert advice and counsel."

To observe how each member of the project team functions, let's examine a fairly complex case, that of blond, blue-eyed Sally Smith, who was born with all four limbs malformed. Referred by the family doctor to the UCLA Child Amputee Prosthetics Project, the parents get to see each team member one at a time in his or her own office. Later the team meets together to chart Sally's treatment. Here are their individual responsibilities:

☐ The *medical social worker,* usually the initial contact between parents and team, meets with Sally's parents, encouraging them to express freely their grief and anxiety and whatever sense of guilt they might feel, and to face up to their problem realistically. The social worker outlines what is involved in a prosthetics program and attempts to answer some of the Smiths' questions: "Will she be able to do at least some of the things a normal child would?" "How much will the treatment cost?" "How can we, as parents, help in ways that are best?"

☐ Next, the *pediatrician,* a specialist in children's diseases and injuries, gives Sally a complete checkup to determine her general health as well as possible other medical problems. The pediatrician reinforces and expands on what the social worker has told the parents, calming their fears and letting them know that professional help is available. "Prosthetic devices, properly fitted, can assist boys and girls who have missing or deformed limbs to be almost as independent as other kids," he says. "They can go to school, engage in many sports, work at jobs, get married." The pediatrician assures Sally's parents that only in a few cases is limb deficiency hereditary.

☐ Next the Smiths see the *orthopedic surgeon,* who works closely with the medical director. The surgeon measures limb strength and determines whether surgery is required. In birth deformities, fingers may need separating; in accident cases a stump may need grafting over or a bony overgrowth removed. The surgeon is competent to field such questions as "Will a deficient limb grow as fast as a normal one?" "Should a badly deformed limb be surgically removed or not?"

☐ The *prosthetist* explains what kind of artificial limbs are needed. Sally required two above-elbow prostheses, a below-knee prosthesis on her left foot, and a partial shoe-filler on her right foot. Among the questions answered are: "Is it better to have metal hands or ones made of plastic?" "Can artificial limbs be used in water?" "Can a prosthesis do everything a normal limb can?" To the last question the prosthetist replies, "We haven't reached that point yet, but we can produce artificial limbs that can help a child to be independent and useful."

☐ *Physical and occupational therapists* evaluate the patients' strength, range of motion, and developmental achievements. After Sally is fitted with artificial limbs, these specialists take over to help train her and her parents in the use of her prostheses. As one of them says, "There is no right way of using a prosthesis—only a *best* way for the individual child." Consequently in showing parents how to create problem-solving situations, therapists place a taboo on the dictated instruction: "This is the way to button your coat." A much more productive approach is to ask the child, "How do *you* think it should be done?" Parents participate in the training routine not only so they may learn the proper way to use prothesis and encourage their child, but also to pass on the information to the teacher when the child attends school.

☐ The *medical director*—who may also be a pediatrician—is the crew chief, who, after conferring with other staff specialists in a group meeting, meets with the Smiths and outlines a program for Sally. (A child old enough to understand the problem is also included in the consultation.) When there is concurrence that a prosthesis would help a child's development, a prescription is written and fabrication started.

During the first year, the Smiths bring Sally to the UCLA Child Amputee Prosthetics Project Center every few months, and the staff assumes major responsibility for the youngster's care. But gradually such care is shifted to her local doctor, school, and community, her visits to

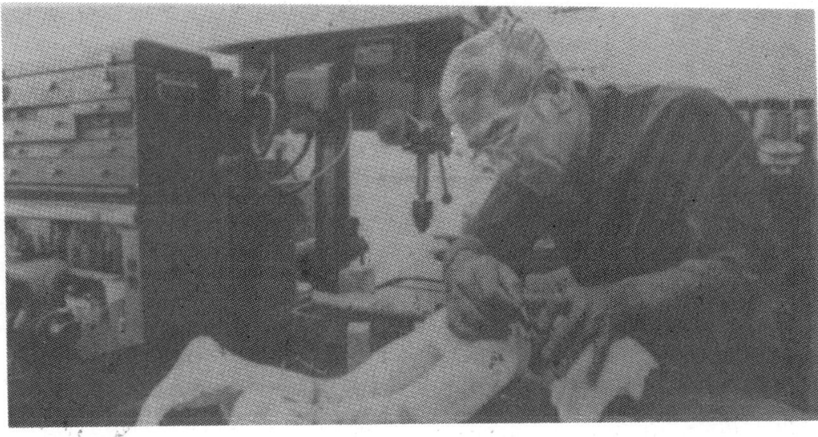

UCLA being cut to once a year for a checkup; she will continue these checkups until she is 21.

Today Sally is almost entirely independent. She keeps her own room in order, babysits for her two younger brothers, and is active in the Girl Scouts—participating in horseback riding and hiking. Last year, she finished a hike with a knotted shoelace holding her below-knee prosthesis in place after the support strap had broken.

At home Sally uses a swivel "spork" (a combination fork and spoon) while eating. Her mother helps her dress in the morning when she's pressed for time, but she can dress herself when not rushed. Her clothes have few buttons and no back zippers. Sally had a little problem when she began to use lipstick, because she uses her mouth for certain dressing tasks (buttoning, for example). The solution was simple: She puts on her lipstick last.

In school Sally uses no special equipment. She carries her books in a straw basket shaped like a briefcase with a large opening at the top, and takes notes with a pencil gripped by one of her hooks. She is an excellent student and hopes to become a biology teacher or a computer programer. Thus she is taking all the college preparatory courses—including laboratory sciences and mathematics.

"Most of the credit for Sally's excellent progress must go to her parents, who are understanding and who have supported her efforts to achieve independence," says Susan D. Clarke, occupational therapist assigned to her case. "She has never been treated as a special member of the family because of her limb deficiencies—only in the sense that every child is special in his or her own way."

Ideally, artificial limbs for children should be fitted as soon as possible. In cases of congenital deformities of the upper limbs, this may be when a baby can maintain good sitting balance—as early as eight to ten months. Lower limbs are fitted with prosthetic devices when a child starts pulling herself or himself up to a standing position by holding to a chair or low table—at around 12 to 14 months. The natural instinct to walk greatly assists in learning to use a prosthesis.

First prosthetic devices are "passive," used only for balancing and early acceptance. Later, "active" devices that can be manipulated by a shoulder harness or knee flexing are fitted to simulate the action of a real limb.

In their early years, prosthetics-equipped children learn to tie their shoelaces, brush their teeth, and drink from a cup almost as quickly as nonamputee youngsters. As they grow older, they play tennis, bowl, and participate in other sports; do chores around the house; use tools. One child learned to play the trumpet; another became a crack target range pistol shooter; a third took up scuba diving when equipped with special swim fins.

Formerly, artificial limbs for children were mostly scaled-down versions of adult prostheses. But today, engineered from thermal plastics, foam rubber, aluminum, chrome molysteel, and occasionally miniaturized electric components, they are lighter, more comfortable, and easier to keep clean and in working order.

Even more highly sophisticated devices are in the research and development stages. At UCLA, an electric-powered, four-wheeled, rubber-tired cart has been built by research prosthetist Carl Sumida that can be switch-operated by a multiple amputee using only a finger, a toe, or a chin. In Canada, prosthetic elbows and hands have been developed that contain motorized components activated by muscle contraction.

How much do artificial limbs cost? A simple arm fitted with a hook may run from $450 to $500, while a complex arm, shoulder or leg prosthesis may cost $1,000 or more. Of course children require new devices from time to time to fit their growing bodies. Hard-pressed families, however, can seek financial relief through agencies such as the Crippled Children's Service.

A critical period for limb-deficient children is when they start attending school. During the early years most of them have been somewhat sheltered, attended by kindness and understanding and assisted by family and clinical specialists, but in the classroom and on the playground they are on their own. Nor can they expect a sympathetic and generous spirit on the part of all their classmates—rude stares, cruel remarks, and sometimes downright hostility being more often than not the way it is. Most teachers, however, are helpful and understanding. A wise one will ask the amputee child to show the prosthesis to the class and explain how it works. Some youngsters even have names for their artificial limbs—"My Helper," "Old Reliable," or "Trusty Sidekick"—by which they introduce their mechanical parts to the class. Through such openness the natural curiosity of the class is satisfied and the amputee child loses that aura of being "different" that sets him or her apart and arouses suspicion and discomfort in classmates. In a word, a potential emotional confrontation is defused.

Concerned parents, teachers, and other advocates of the rights of handicapped children feel that—after long years of struggle—there is optimism about getting the Nation's public schools to assume the same responsibility for the physically handicapped as for normal youngsters. "The idea is to get the attitude toward educating the handicapped changed from charity to equal opportunity," says Edwin W. Martin, Jr., Acting Deputy Commissioner of the Office of Education's Bureau of Education for the Handicapped. To help bring this about, many handicapped children are being placed in classes with other students, a practice known as "mainstreaming." Advocates of mainstreaming contend that it is wrong to stigmatize handicapped children by isolating them and keeping them in separate schools or classrooms, and most of those who work with limb-deficient children agree.

No matter the emotional drain on parents, the financial cost, or the pedagogical debate over the best way to educate child amputees, the fact is that a long list of success stories can be cited by Dr. Brooks and Dr. Setoguchi to prove that giving crippled children a better chance in life is worthwhile.

Picked at random, here are three examples:

□ *Howard M.*—A black youngster with superior athletic ability was consumed with the idea of being a professional football player. But a water skiing accident made it necessary to amputate one leg and fit it with a prosthesis. That did not prove to be the end of his world. He switched his interest to law and has just passed the bar examination.

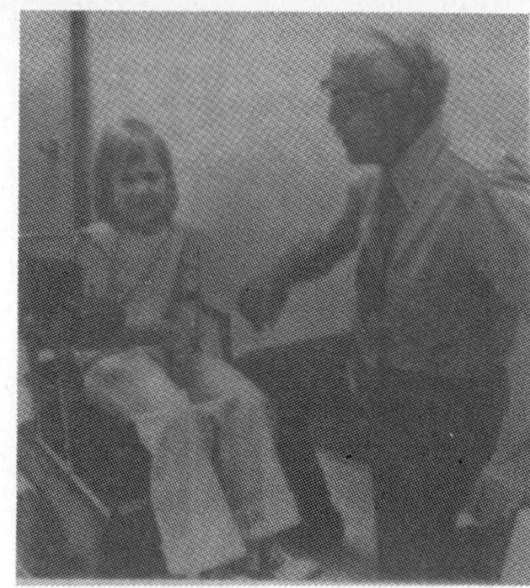

□ *Katherine J.*—A teenager had to give up her dream of becoming a concert pianist when she lost her hand to a bone disease. She decided to train as an occupational therapist and help others as she had been helped. She graduated from college, found a job, and is now successfully pursuing her career.

□ *David T.*—Up to the age of 18, David stubbornly rejected all prosthetic devices to assist his four congenitally malformed limbs. But he was a "car nut." Carl Sumida re-engineered the controls of an automobile on the joy-stick principle so that it could be operated by means of the feet and prehensile toes. When the car was completed, David proved he could drive it safely and was issued a California driver's license. "The car itself is *my* prosthetic device," he says proudly. Today he is a successful young executive in the import-export business.

UCLA's Child Amputee Prosthetics Project involves not only treatment and research, but a continuing educational program of workshops, seminars, and short courses for all the disciplines involved in helping limb-deficient children. A steady stream of reports flows from this center, and a comprehensive guide for parents is planned for publication in the near future.

"Put in perspective, what we've done with more than 800 child amputees at UCLA," says Dr. Setoguchi, "is to improve medical diagnosis, treatment, and education, to engineer new and better artificial limbs, to reassure grief-stricken parents and enlist their cooperation, and to send young patients out into the world with an excellent chance of making good in school, in their jobs, and in the daily routine of living."

Dr. Brooks, who still serves as a consultant, adds: "In the two decades I've been working with these youngsters, I've noticed something different about them—a special sparkle in their personality. Maybe it's what such children have, not what they haven't, that *really* counts."

Integrated Living for the Severely Disabled

by Sven-Olof Brattgard, M.D.

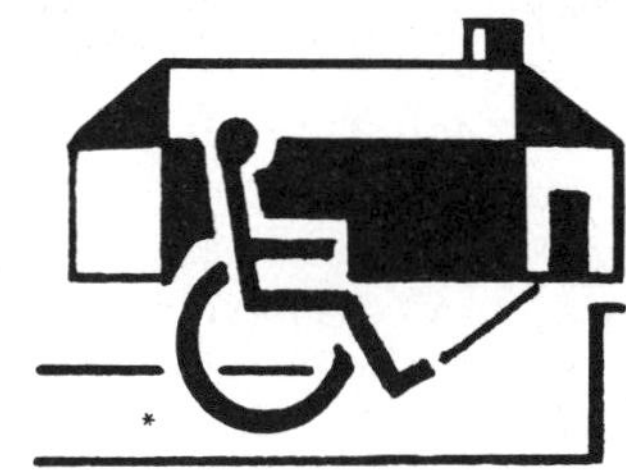

(Editor's note: The following article is reprinted from the July/August, 1974 issue of "Contact," the official magazine of the Central Council for the Disabled, London, England.)

One of the great pioneers of rehabilitation, Dr. Howard Rusk, once asserted that the successful rehabilitation of a disabled person is assured only when the following three questions can be answered in the affirmative:

Does the disabled person have somewhere to live, a home?

Does he have somebody who takes care of him, loves him?

Does he have something to do, a job?

To these three fundamental conditions a fourth may be added. If expressed as a question like the others, it might be this:

Can he have relaxation and fun with his friends in his leisure time?

I would like to use the aim of rehabilitation, as expressed here, as a basis for discussion about "Patterns of Residential Living." The aim of all projects on housing and activities can be expressed in three words: integration in society.

Integration in society cannot be accomplished by medical measures alone. It is important to give the disabled person all the medical aid necessary for him to improve his functional possibilities and counteract additional disabilities. This is not enough, however. Many people are isolated in society, individually or in groups, without being disabled. Disability increases the isolation and the problems are magnified. The chances of choosing one's own way of life and pursuing different activities are restricted. The possibilities of employment are reduced and financial circumstances straitened. New problems arise. The interest of relatives and friends is often concentrated on the disability. They forget that the disabled person still has abilities. Disability does not equal non-ability. Ways of life must be adjusted to the abilities — and the disabilities — when medical rehabilitation has achieved its utmost.

Integration in society is mostly a question of interaction between society and the disabled person. In all circumstances this will mean new attitudes. It will also mean that society must change its priorities and increase its welfare resources.

Before discussing the housing problems of the disabled, I must point out that certain factors of the present system of caring for the disabled counteract integration. One of them is the long periods spent in hospitals, rehabilitation clinics and special boarding-schools for the disabled. These institutions are often necessary for an effective medical treatment or a satisfactory training of the severely disabled. It is extremely important, however, that the organization of these institutions allows the disabled person to preserve his integrity and his will to be responsible for himself. They must awaken an interest in the outside world and the future and allow for a continuous planning of medical treatment and training. The organization of emergency nursing, on which rehabilitation clinics and other institutions for the disabled have been modelled, implies that the responsibility is handed over to specialists who make all decisions for the patient. Another factor counteracting integration is the tendency to regard a handicap as something peculiar. The disabled are defined by their disabilities, i.e. grouped according to medical diagnoses or functional disturbances. The disabled are individuals like all others with many interests, intellectual resources, financial circumstances and educational levels. When society makes plans for the disabled it ignores the fact that they are an average group—although with certain difficulties. A third factor counteracting integration is fear, for disability is something which all people are afraid of. To fear something is to flee from it: unpleasant things are to be avoided. The disabled are shunned. Many people are also afraid of hurting them. They do not know how to behave in their company, what to say to them, what to do. This is an added reason for not daring to associate with disabled people and as such it counteracts integration.

The essential problem of integration may serve as a basis for discussion. Much too wide-spread is the belief that life for the disabled in society is a question of architectural details, such as curb-stones, thresholds and the width of doors or, alternately, an access to trained assistants and financial resources. These matters are admittedly of importance, but still more significant is the fact that we are all determined to work together for the realisation of integration. This is a question of true intentions and effective measures, not only from the politicians responsible for the final decisions and from all of us who have disabled friends, but also from the disabled themselves. They cannot wait passively for society to solve their problems and bring about integration. They themselves must co-operate.

An important part of rehabilitation is to awaken and strengthen the desire of achieving a free and independent life in spite of all disabilities.

Life for the disabled must be such that we can answer "yes" to all the four introductory questions about housing, service, work, and leisure pastimes. In Sweden during the late sixties, the Fokus Society initiated a comprehensive series of experiments. The aim of the Society was to ascertain the possibilities for severely disabled people — youngsters especially — to achieve an independent life in the community; to live, work and associate with non-disabled people. Like all others, the disabled person must have a chance of choosing where he wants to live. In Sweden those with minor disabilities can have their ordinary flats adapted to their needs. Home helpers assist them for an hour or two each day. For other disabled people, these adapted flats, with only a limited service, would not be sufficient. It was especially out of consideration to these that the Fokus experiment was initiated. The flats provided by Fokus were primarily meant for severely disabled persons in need of night and day service. Most of the Fokus tenants are wheelchair-bound. 70% need help with dressing, going to the lavatory and so on. 30% have to be fed, 25% have to be turned over in bed during the night. Among the disabled tenants are those who cannot use their arms and legs and must manoeuvre their wheelchairs, open doors, and call for help with a suck-and-blow system like the Possum. Paralysis is not the only disability. Most of these people

are handicapped in other ways also, they have physical disabilities or mental disturbances. Many have a deficient education, others lack the necessary training for employment. Most of those who move into the Fokus flats came from long-term clinics, nursing homes or special boarding schools. Many came from the homes of their parents, where they had been cared for all their lives. This presentation of the Fokus tenants shows the degree of their disability — the Fokus Society has not avoided the severely disabled. On the contrary, they have concentrated their efforts on this category.

To start with there were doctors, superintendents of nursing-homes, parents and other people who quite understandably assumed a doubtful or negative attitude to the project. They feared that the disabled would be incapable of living in the outside world without constant supervision. They were fortunately proved wrong.

An account of the Fokus project can be concentrated to four fundamental factors: the flats and their designing, the service and its organization, transport system for the disabled and, finally, the aspects of organization and finance.

Design

The Fokus project is based on the principle that the disabled have the same right as all others to a home of their own. These homes should be integrated with homes for the non-disabled. The fact that the Fokus tenants need permanent access to service necessitates the concentration of a group of flats to one block or building, so that they can be easily reached by members of the service staff. After some experimenting we found that the best solution is 10-15 flats in each group. In a high building these can be situated near the elevators and with one or two flats on each floor. The rest of the flats on the floor are intended for non-disabled tenants. The flats are planned in such a way that they

are easily adaptable to persons with different kinds and degrees of disability. Carefully designed lavatories, kitchens and bedrooms are of special importance. The Fokus Society has produced new and flexible solutions to the problem of designing homes for the disabled.[1] Examples of these solutions are given in Figs. 1, 2 and 3.

Providing the flats with the necessary technical aids is important not only for the tenants themselves, but for making work easier for the staff. Some tenants require automatically opening doors. Signal systems, enabling the tenants to summon the staff and talk to them, are necessary. Safety devices, such as fire alarms, are also needed. Labour saving hoists are valuable aids. As well as the unit of approximately fifteen flats for the disabled in each building, there are certain rooms which are common to all. These common rooms are not intended only for the disabled, they are open to all tenants in the building. The service staff have an office and a lounge; in the latter the staff on duty also sleep at night. There are special bathrooms, with all kinds of technical aids, such as hydraulic hoists, hydraulic baths and so on. In each unit there is also a specially equipped laundry and a room equipped with apparatus for physical training. Usually there is also a hobby-room. There is a lounge common to all and in connection with this a small kitchen and dining-room for the disabled. Most prefer to have their meals in their own homes, however. The common rooms have proved to be very important. Fewer assistants are needed, service is facilitated and the disabled have a chance of mixing with other people.

Service

The disabled person living in a Fokus flat has access to as much service as he needs. In Sweden all urban and rural districts have communally employed home helpers who serve old, sick and disabled people. They are often housewives who, having undergone a certain training, are then on duty some 3-5 hours a day, attending one or several people who may need them. They are paid by the local authorities who in their turn charge a small fee for the assistance — if the person receiving help is able to pay for it. The disabled living in Fokus flats are also given this service 2-4 hours a day as a rule. The home helpers tidy the disabled tenants' rooms, wash their clothes and do their shopping. In some cases the disabled also receive help with getting dressed and going to the lavatory. As well as these home helpers, each Fokus unit of approximately 15 flats has a special staff working in shifts of eight hours. Day and night somebody is thus always on duty. The disabled can call for this service whenever he needs it; when he wants to get dressed, go to the lavatory, be turned over in bed, or fed, etc. This special personnel, which is on continuous day and night duty, is employed and paid by the Fokus Society.

The Fokus Society has attempted to find a joint answer to the problems of housing and service. Well planned and located living quarters means a reduced need for service. Badly designed flats must often be compensated for by increased service, which in the long run has proved to be an expensive solution.

The disabled Fokus tenant leases his flat on the same terms as all other Swedish tenants, which means that he cannot be evicted as long as he pays his rent. The flat is his. This means that the disabled tenant has the use of it also during those periods when he is in the hospital or a rehabilitation clinic.

The Fokus Society supplies no medical service. The disabled person in need of medical help must contact his own doctor or rehabilitation clinic. Like all other people he is responsible for his own health. Members of the service staff are naturally prepared to help him when he wishes to see a doctor or a dentist or go to a hospital. But the circumstances are not the same as in institutions,

where it is the duty of doctors and nurses to visit him regularly. The Fokus tenants are responsible for themselves. It is up to them to ask for medical care just as they do for other kinds of service. The disabled person receives no service if he does not ask for it. He knows how many hours of daily service he is entitled to and decides how they should be used. If his planning of this service is at fault, he himself will suffer for it.

To start with there are many disabled who find this responsibility difficult to cope with. They may have spent too much time in hospitals, boarding schools and nursing homes or they may have been spoilt by too much care from their parents. Unlike other people they have not been trained to take responsibility for themselves. They are accustomed to being cared for by others and are unfamiliar with the need to make their own decisions. To begin with this may seem difficult and cause discomfort, but in the long run it is the only way to a free and independent life. It is part of being re-socialized and may already have been an element of their rehabilitation. The difficulty of finding the right kind of relationship with the service personnel is reciprocal. On the staff side there may be wrong ambitions. It wants to organize everything for the disabled. It watches over him in the same way doctors and nurses in hospitals look after their patients. In hospitals and institutions, the personnel is responsible for the welfare of the patient. In the Fokus project, the disabled takes on the responsibility for himself, and the staff helps him only with things he cannot do himself. This kind of relationship requires a carefully trained and well-informed personnel.

Transportation

Functional living accommodation with service is necessary if the disabled person is to have any form of social life. To become a full member of society, he must also be offered opportunities of work and occupation and be al-

lowed to participate in training and different kinds of activities. He must have a chance of going to church or discotheques, of meeting his friends in bars, in their homes and in his own.

This kind of mobility presupposes a system of transport which functions for the disabled. Many get along quite successfully in taxis or their own cars. Many others do not, however. In Sweden during the last five years a special transport system for old and disabled people has been financed and tested by the local authorities. The idea is to have specially equipped buses with trained drivers who call for the disabled, help him down to the street in his electric wheelchair, lift him onto the bus and drive him to the required destination. The disabled persons in need of this aid must phone in advance for a bus when going to and from work, school, lectures, theatres and discotheques. They pay as much for the trip as they would have done on an ordinary bus. Thanks to this transport system the disabled are no longer confined to their homes. They have acquired a new freedom and mobility in society.

Homes with service and a good transport system have proved to be of conclusive importance to the disabled person's possibilities of a social life. For example: When the severely disabled moved into the Fokus flats, more than 90% of them were receiving invalid pensions — which meant that society and they themselves had judged them incapable of work. When two years of integrated life had passed 80% of the disabled were working. They had full-time or part-time jobs or were receiving a methodical training in ordinary schools. The success previously obtained through good care and traditional medical rehabilitation is now achieved when the disabled person is allowed to be— and feels himself to be—a useful member of society.

Even if the problem of transporting the disabled to and from his work has now been solved, many difficulties remain in ob-

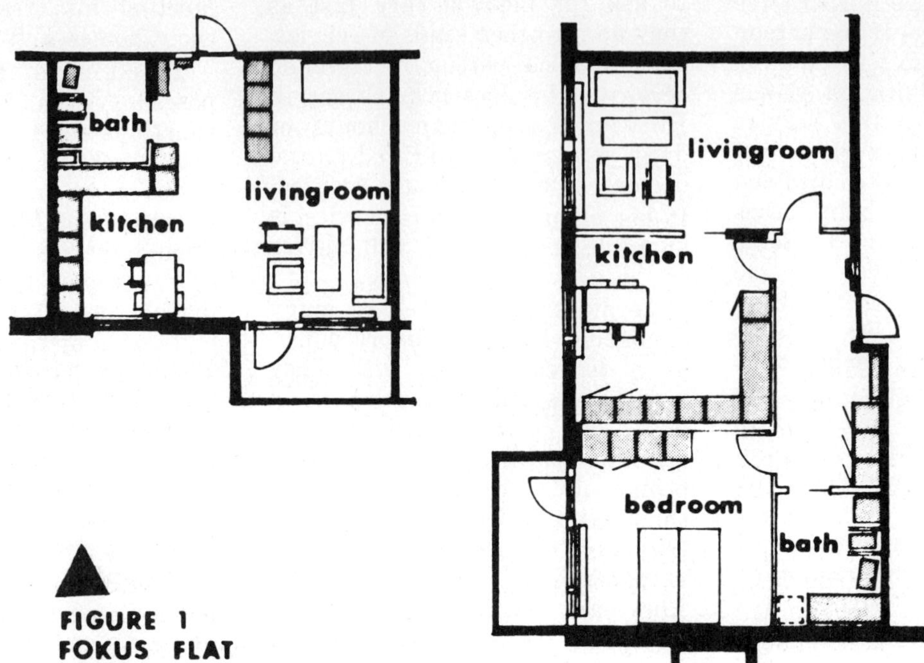

FIGURE 1
FOKUS FLAT
1 ROOM AND KITCHEN

FIGURE 2
FOKUS FLAT
2 ROOMS AND KITCHEN

FIGURE 3
FOKUS FLAT
3 ROOMS AND KITCHEN

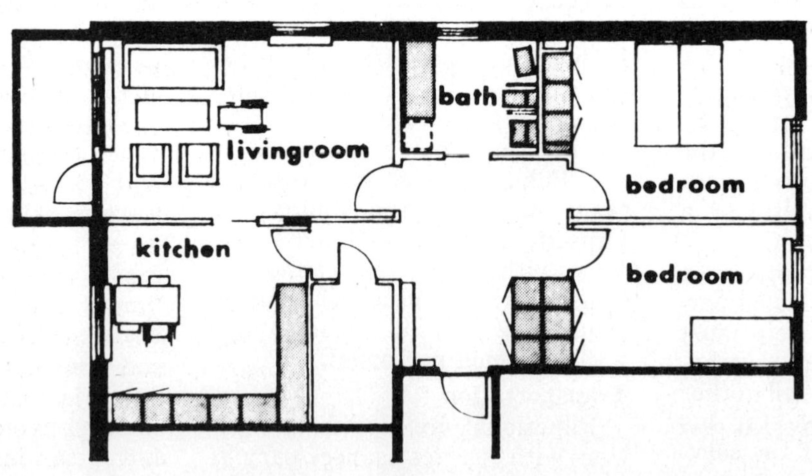

taining appropriate employment and work for the disabled. This is true also of leisure time activities. Not all communities are prepared to receive the severely disabled; few have planned for this. In addition to providing homes and organizing service and transport, we must consider employment and occupation. In certain cases we must resort to the alternative of sheltered workshops, although the isolated environment they have to offer is of very little help in the process of integration. Government owned organizations must be the first to employ the disabled. Instead of planning sheltered work-shops, the problem is to provide a working environment offering security for the disabled. The nature of the work as well as the working place must comply with their resources. In hospitals, government offices, universities, schools and many such places there is work in abundance which can be done by the disabled. It is only a question of keeping our eyes open for such positions.

When choosing a location for homes for the disabled we must be sure that there is ready access, not only to the right kind of work but also to cultural activities. In earlier days there was a tendency to build homes for the disabled in country surroundings. The idea is understandable, but the consequences were isolation.

The principle of the Fokus project is to locate the flats where there are abundant opportunities for work, occupation and schooling. Preferably they should be placed in the center of the town or city so that the disabled have an easy access to different activities. It is only through such arrangements that we can offer the conditions prerequisite for integration.

What has been said here about work and occupation applies in principle also to the leisure activities of the disabled. When we make plans for entertainments, tours, courses, etc., we must include the disabled, but not in such a way as to offer them charity. What we must give them is the opportunity of participating with others and being accepted by them, not because of their disability, but in spite of it. In this matter, unions for the disabled have the very important function of influencing society. The disabled are often isolated in such unions; these should instead be used as doors leading out into the greater unity of society.

Finances

An analysis of finances is important to the Fokus project. Financial systems in different countries are not easily comparable. Estimated costs expressed in plain figures imply little value. A comparison between the expenses for a Swedish Fokus flat with service and the corresponding cost of life in long-term clinics, nursing-homes or institutional schools may tell us much more.

The total expense for a Fokus flat — including rent and service — is approximately half of what the care of a disabled person would cost in a long-term clinic and two-thirds of that in a nursing-home.

Each time a disabled person moves from an institution to a Fokus flat he is saving money for society. The total cost of a Fokus flat with service is approximately $6,000 for each disabled person, regardless of who is responsible for the payment. In Sweden there is a federal grant for the adapting of flats for the disabled. This subvention is intended for the payment of additional costs incurred during the project and may amount to about $3,500. Similar federal grants are issued in other countries.

How much of this total cost does the disabled person pay? If he is living on an invalid pension and has no other income, his rent in Sweden will in most cases be subsidized, as will the cost for home service. If the disabled person has his own income, he is required to pay approximately 20% of this for rent and service. Most of the Fokus tenants are severely disabled however, and their incomes, if any, are very small. The main part of the expenses for rent and service is therefore paid by the authorities or by the Fokus Society. The invalid pension is used for food, clothing, mobility, entertainment, etc. The main principle of this financial system is that the costs incurred by the disabled person because of his disability should be compensated for by society. The invalid pension should be used for those general expenses which we must all pay, whether we are disabled or not.

This brief description of the Fokus project and the satisfactory results we have experienced in Sweden, may give rise to the question: "Does it answer the needs?" Clearly established is the fact that the Fokus project answers the great need of housing and service for the severely disabled. Most of them have previously been reduced to spending their whole lives in nursing-homes and hospitals. To many of us it may come as a surprise that the severely disabled have been able to live so freely and independently in the outside world. This kind of life demands much of the disabled person himself, however. Even if none of the 300 tenants has expressed any desire to return to his previous life in an institution, we must face the fact that there will always be disabled persons who lack the courage or ability necessary for independent life. Their disability is too pronounced. They are happier in a closed society where they can have greater security. This group has the same right to see its hopes realized and must therefore have institutions which answer its needs. And yet it is important for those who are responsible for future plans to remember that closed societies must never be the primary answer to the problem. We must endeavour to give as many people as possible an opportunity for integration in society. Only when the disabled are clearly unable to brave the outside world should we offer them the alternative of closed societies.

What are the advantages and

5. EMERGING DIRECTIONS

the disadvantages of the Fokus project? The advantages for the disabled person are most important. He is offered the possibility of a home of his own where he can shape the life he wants. For him or for her there are new possibilities of contact. One result of the Fokus project is that many of the disabled tenants have been able to marry or live together and have children. The disabled person chooses where he wants to live. He decides which service he wants and takes the consequences when his planning is wrong. His opportunities for employment and occupation are increased. His life acquires new excitement and variation — and admittedly more risk. And yet life itself is a risk, there is no total security for anyone. The advantages gained by the disabled person can be summed up shortly as the aim we started with: possibilities of integration, of becoming a full member of society.

For society the advantages are just as obvious. The Fokus project is clearly superior — at least from a Swedish point of view — to the alternatives of nursing-homes and other institutions. The disabled are not banished to an isolated group outside society, they become part of it. We must therefore ensure that society functions for them also. Gradually we learn to consider people with special difficulties. We see to it that curb-stones and stairs disappear. We design buses and other means of conveyance so that they are adapted to people in wheelchairs and to those who walk with difficulty. We realize that the disabled are a group of people who may have difficulties but who get along in life all the same. The fact that the service-units of approximately 15 flats are easily adapted to building operations and town-planning is another advantage for society. In nearly all modern building operations of any considerable size it would be possible to fit in one such unit. Thanks to its adaptability it can be planned just when it is needed. As a rule these

flats can also be constructed on the usual building loans and paid for in the usual way. Special subscriptions or government grants are not needed.

Are there then no disadvantages? The Fokus project naturally makes some considerable demands on the community as well as the disabled themselves. Many difficulties arise, especially to start with. During this period all concerned must cooperate to find the best solutions. This necessitates a survey of social resources and a readiness to co-operate. Social leaders, politicians and specialists—may find it hard to change their opinions from "institutional care" to an offer of "own homes with service." This may prove to be the worst difficulty. In order to surmount the obstacle we must listen to what the disabled themselves have to say. They alone really know what the problems are. This means an organization of reciprocal aid — as proved already by the Fokus Society — an interaction of the disabled on one side and the representatives of society and its specialists on the other.

Planning FOR the disabled is not enough, we must plan WITH their help.

Adaptability

Is the Fokus project applicable to conditions in other countries also? This question is justified. It may be of some interest to know how we have solved the problem of housing for the severely disabled in Sweden, but is of much greater interest if the solution is applicable to most countries. It is always difficult to transfer a scheme from the country it has been devised for to another country with another social system. The Fokus project has proved so flexible, however, that this is possible. In Germany and Holland Fokus units are already being built. England and Canada have also shown considerable interest. The technical plans of the flats must be adapted to the conditions of each country.

The standard of building is of less importance than designing

the flats in such a way that they can be adapted to the individual needs of each tenant. A survey of these varying needs has been made by the Department of Handicap Research at the University of Gothenburg and answers to them have been found.[2,3,4] The problems of service must be solved according to the resources of each country. In Sweden the local authorities hold themselves responsible for this expense. We have allowed youngsters doing their so called "civilian military service" to work as service assistants for the disabled, an experiment which has met with success. After a short period of training they assume their duties—usually for one year — and are paid by the government. The same scheme is to be tried in Germany. In other countries it might be suitable to engage voluntary workers.

In Sweden, the local authorities have taken on the transport service. In other countries this might be a task for Lions • Clubs or similar organizations. There are often several answers to a problem; the important thing is to choose one which has been arrived at by a common decision. It may prove a value in other countries—as we in Sweden have done — to form some kind of organization which takes on the main responsibility, at least during the period when the flats are being planned and constructed. In this committee, the authorities, unions for the disabled and the disabled themselves, should all be represented. An important thing to remember is that the committee must not only devote itself to a detailed planning of the flats and organization of the service. It must also exert an active influence on society and its individual members. All must be conscious of the fact that this is a matter concerning society. Politicians, civil servants and specialists of different kinds, must all be made to feel responsible for the outcome of the project. In Sweden, the Fokus project has proved to be of great importance for the integration of the severely disabled in society. It is one of several answers to a complicated and difficult problem. In other countries other solutions have been tried.[5] Het Dorp in Holland and Kollektivhus in Copenhagen are such examples. When we make our plans for the severely disabled we must follow up the results of experiments and learn from their success or failure. Above all, those who are responsible for the organization must not allow themselves to be disturbed by difficulties and avoid the problems confronting them. Proceeding experimentally, they must endeavour to overcome them. Life is an adventure. Only by daring the hazards can we experience the whole of it.

REFERENCES

1. *Principles of the Fokus Housing Units for the Severely Disabled.* Distribution: Stiftelsen Fokus, Vastra Hamngatan 24-26, S-411 17 Göteborg, Sweden. Price: Sw. Cr. 60:-.

2. *Normalbostaden och de rörelsehindrade.* (The Ordinary Flat Adapted for Disabled.) (In Swedish) 1970. Dept. of Handicap Research, Ovre Husargatan 36, S-413 14 Göteborg, Sweden. Price: Sw. Cr. 15:-.

3. *Accessible Towns—Workable Homes.* National Swedish Building Research D9: 1972. Distribution: Svensk Byggtjänst, Box 1403, S-111 84 Stockholm, Sweden. Price: Sw. Cr. 13:-.

4. *Normalkoket öch de rörelsehindrade.* (The Kitchen and the Disabled.) (In Swedish.) 1973. Dept. of Handicap Research, Ovre Husargatan 36, S-413 14 Göteborg, Sweden. Stencil 25: Price Sw. Cr. 30:-. Stencil 28: Price Sw. Cr. 25:-.

5. *Personal Relationships, the Handicapped and the Community, 1972.* Editor: Derek Lancaster - Gaye. Routledge & Kegan Paul, London and Boston.

Study Compares Transport for Disabled In Canada, Sweden and United Kingdom

by Sally D. Liff

Sally D. Liff is Senior Associate Planner with Alan M. Voorhees & Associates, Inc. in McLean, Virginia. She has participated in numerous transit planning studies for American communities, focusing particularly on needs of the transportation disadvantaged. This article is adapted from a study Ms. Liff prepared for the National Conference for the Transportation Disadvantaged, Washington, D.C., December 4, 1975.

Heightened social awareness in the United States concerning the mobility needs of those unable to utilize a private automobile or public transportation due to either physical or financial constraints has led to numerous programs to assist the transportation disadvantaged. These have been well documented elsewhere.[1]

This study focuses on the experiences of three other countries —Canada, Sweden and the United Kingdom — in assisting the transportation disadvantaged in public transport. Their experience may well be applicable to the United States.

CANADA

A recent extensive study surveyed the existing use of public transportation in Toronto by the physically handicapped and prepared an evaluation of alternatives to better serve that portion of the population.[2] It was estimated that approximately 72,000 physically disabled people can use Toronto public transport with little or no difficulty, while an additional 75,000 would have some problem using the existing system. Several alternative demonstration projects for improving the existing system were proposed:

(1) Coordinate public and private services and provide financial assistance to the disabled who cannot use public transit to offset taxi and special van fares.

(2) Establish a public special transit service for: work trips only; all-purpose trips restricted to those who require a special vehicle; or all-purpose trips for all physically handicapped persons not capable of using the public transport system.

(3) Improve the existing public transit system through: limited, low-cost modifications such as better information programs and designated seats for the handicapped; or capital-intensive improvements such as lower bus steps and increased use of escalators at subway stations.

Each of these options was in-

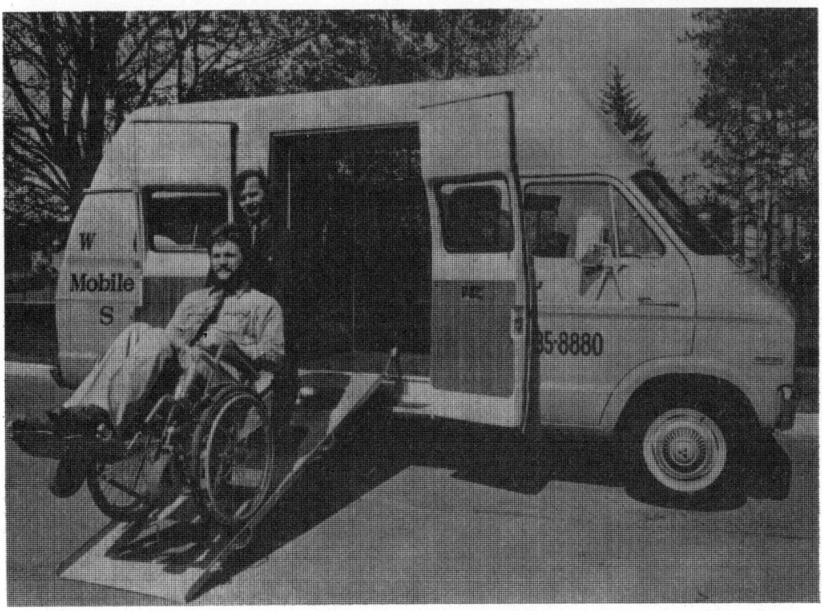

One of three vans used in the Wheel-Trans program of the Toronto Transit Commission to provide transportation for the disabled.

vestigated and the special transit services emerged as the most effective.

As a result, a pilot program was initiated by the Toronto Transit Commission. Called "Wheel-Trans", the two-year demonstration project is funded primarily by the Province of Ontario. The first passengers were carried in February, 1975.

Three small vans with wheelchair lifts are in service to provide transportation for work trips. Approximately 50 persons are using the service on a subscription basis. They pay a 33-cent fare for each trip, which is the same as the regular transit fare. This represents about two percent of the cost of the program.

In October, 1975 the Wheel-Trans Project Evaluation Committee issued an interim report on the first six months of opera-

TABLE 1
SPECIAL TRANSPORTATION SYSTEM IN GOTHENBURG, SWEDEN 1967–1973

| Year | Total Number of Persons | Number of Special Buses | Total Number of Trips | | Number of Trips per Person | Total Cost (000's of Krona) | Cost per Trip (Krona) |
			Taxis	Special Buses			
1967	525	18	65,600	27,000	176	—	—
1968	1,456	22	186,000	71,600	177	4,687	18
1969	2,246	30	237,200	87,800	145	6,526	20
1970	3,265	35	348,800	98,700	137	8,334	19
1971	5,597	37	482,200	102,700	105	10,759	18
1972	7,794	39	631,600	107,800	95	13,620	19
1973	9,359	38	705,000	93,600	85	15,614	20

Source: Sven-Olof Brattgard and Carl-Eric Sandstrom. "Special Public Transportation in Sweden," Rehabilitation International Congress, Lisbon. 1974.

tion. Passengers were in general completely satisfied with the service, although non-flexible scheduling of work-to-home trips was mentioned as a drawback. Rising costs have recently forced a renegotiation of the contract with the private company providing the service; the daily cost of the Wheel-Trans project has risen from $574 under the old contract to $921.

Similar special transport service is provided by private agencies in several other Canadian cities.

SWEDEN

In Sweden the disadvantaged transport program is widespread throughout the country and reflects the strong concern of Sweden's citizens for making the living environment more harmonious. Swedish law requires that social service agencies for the handicapped also be responsible for their transportation. This includes mobility for access to social services as well as for other needs. The special system is called *Fardtjanst* and has been in effect for about 10 years.[3]

Throughout Sweden the special buses serve about 20 percent of the registered users; the remaining 80 percent use taxis on a regular basis. The user obtains a license from the municipality, shows it to the taxi driver, and signs a receipt for the journey.

The receipt is then submitted to the municipality for payment.

An outstanding example of the ongoing special bus program is in Gothenburg, where it has been in effect for about eight years. Under this program, 40 specialized 12-passenger vehicles serve about 2.5 percent of the population on a regular basis. Registrants are qualified by physical limitations, including age, with no income or auto ownership requirements. The average usage is 1.8 rides per week per user.

The service is effectively a subsidized subscription service to all qualified registrants on the following basis:

Quota — for personal use, up to 12 trips per week. Leisure trips are limited to four per month.

TABLE 2
AGE CATEGORIES OF USERS OF SPECIAL SERVICES GOTHENBURG, SWEDEN

Age	Percent
67 or older	75
17-66	22
16 or younger	3
Total	100

Source: Sven-Olof Brattgard and Carl-Eric Sandstrom. "Special Public Transportation in Sweden," Rehabilitation International Congress, Lisbon. 1974

Non-quota — for employment, education, medical care. No limitation on trips.

Agency arrangement — no limitation on usage.

Service is scheduled at least a day in advance, and the routes have been fairly stable over time. The driver and assistant are responsible for helping passengers from door-to-door, even up and down stairs. The vehicles are equipped with movable stairs and ramps or hoists and safety belts for wheelchairs. Similar *Fardtjanst* services are operated in other cities.

Table I illustrates the Gothenburg experience 1967-1973. The number of trips has increased substantially since the inception of the service as more persons have become eligible; however, the number of trips per person has decreased as more elderly persons, who customarily make fewer trips, have participated.

In Gothenburg, users pay 1.25 Swedish krona, which is equivalent to the transit fare. The average cost, however, is 20 Swedish krona, with the difference being subsidized by the city. The average trip by taxi costs 13.50 Swedish krona, while the special bus trips average 34.75 Swedish krona. The special buses are used more intensively for medical trips, while taxis supply a higher proportion of trips for school and

5. EMERGING DIRECTIONS

personal activities.

On the Stockholm subway system, platforms can be reached from street level in 29 of 74 stations, with another 13 stations scheduled to be rebuilt this year. All new stations will be accessible to wheelchairs. In addition, each subway car has four elevated seats with grip bars. All new cars will have slightly elevated seats, with eight being extra high; all seats will have grip bars.[4]

The Swedish experience is unique in degree, but is adaptable to other countries having a high level of social service and willing to subsidize the cost of providing total mobility to disabled persons.

UNITED KINGDOM

An extensive study on physical design for public transport vehicles has been completed for the Transport and Road Research Laboratory.[5] The study, conducted by British Leyland, was directed at "Factors Affecting Use of Buses by Both Elderly and Ambulant Disabled Persons." Through a series of tests of some 200 elderly and disabled to determine the optimum dimensions of entrance steps, seats, and other aids, certain modifications have been made in new bus design. For example, the former standard 17-inch step has been lowered to 12 inches on the new vehicles.

In Britain, as in Sweden, the high level of social service is associated with transport for users of the service. For example, users can have access to day centers, clinics, special schools, outpatient clinics, hospitals, and special outings for the elderly. Several private driver services are provided in rural areas.

British Rail now has a removable seat on certain trains where a wheelchair can be locked into place. While this space is located in the first-class section, it can be used by a passenger traveling at the lower second-class fare.

Special fare schemes exist in London for the elderly (pensioners) and registered blind and handicapped persons. They may obtain a bus pass which entitles them to travel free between 9:30 a.m. and 4:00 p.m. and after 7:00 p.m. Monday through Friday and all day on weekends on all central bus routes. Children under 16 may travel at 4 p. flat fare anywhere on the system. In other areas passes are available allowing off-peak travel at reduced rates or travel for a low flat fare. In Kent, for example, the fare is reduced by 2 p. British Rail offers a "Senior Citizen Railcard" for £6 which enables the holder to travel anywhere on the system for

British Rail provides space on certain trains for wheelchairs, to be locked into place.

half-fare for one year. Another card, permitting half-fare travel only during off-peak hours is available for £3.

* * *

In certain areas of the world, particularly much of Africa, Asia, and Latin America, many people are so destitute that they cannot even afford the relatively low public transit fare. Social services and concerns for handicapped and/or elderly persons are minimal, and many such persons are forced onto the streets, often as beggars. In many cases, wages are so low that transit fares may take one-third to one half of the daily earnings, and the governments offer no subsidy.

On the other hand, there is greater opportunity in these areas for people to have access to public transportation due to the intensive coverage and low operating headways of bus service. Needs for medical care and personal services are handled primarily on an emergency basis, with religious groups frequently providing shelter and services.

The degree of implementation of special services for the transportation disadvantaged throughout the world appears to be correlated with the degree of social consciousness and economic development. The specific research cited from Canada, Sweden and England should aid future programs, not only in those countries but others as well. As new systems are planned, it is assumed that good practice will include barrier-free design for accessibility. The United Nations has developed a checklist[6] for such planning:

Have the needs of disabled passengers, both ambulant and wheelchair users, been considered in the design of terminal buildings and railway stations? Specific areas of attention: parking and setting down points, minimal pedestrian distances, through route signposting, vertical circulation, accessible toilet facilities, telephones and cafeterias.

BUS SERVICES

Have the needs of wheelchair users been considered in situations where railways have closed and buses have become the only means of transport? Are town center bus stops sited next to access points convenient to pedestrian circulation and to vertical access points? Have adequate shelters and some seating been provided at bus stops most likely to be used by disabled people? Are bus stations accessible to ambulant disabled people?

FUTURE TRANSPORTATION FORMS

Do new forms of public transport provide good access and level loading for disabled persons, and if so are their setting down points and terminal buildings accessible? Where public transport is unsuitable for disabled people is there a convenient alternative available to them?

With these guidelines it should be possible to provide better access for the transportation disadvantaged in the planning and implementation of transport systems.

REFERENCES

1. William G. Bell and William T. Olsen (eds.), TOWARD A UNIFICATION OF NATIONAL AND STATE POLICY ON THE TRANSPORTATION DISADVANTAGED. 3 vols. Proceedings of Fourth Annual Conference on the Transportation Disadvantaged, St. Petersburg, Florida, September, 1974. Tallahassee: Florida State University, 1975.
John Crain, "The Role of Para-Transit in Serving the Needs of Special Groups," Resource Paper, for Transportation Research Board Para-Transit Workshop, November, 1975.

2. "Transportation for the Disabled," Report No. 33., Metropolitan Toronto Transportation Plan Review, for Municipality of Metropolitan Toronto, Toronto Transit Commissioner, Ministry of Transportation and Communication, Ontario, Kates, Peat, Marwich & Co., February 1974.

3. Sven Olof Brattgard and Carl-Eric Sandstrom, "Special Public Transportation in Sweden," Lisbon, Rehabilitation International Congress, 1974. The information in this section is derived from this source.

4. "Mobility for Spinal Cord Impaired People," Workshop Report, February 22-24, 1974, held at Rancho Los Amigos Hospital, Downey, California, National Academy of Sciences, 1975.

5. British Leyland, U.K. Ltd. (Travel and Bus Division). "An Investigation of Factors Affecting the Use of Buses by Both Elderly and Ambulant Disabled Persons," for Transport and Road Research Laboratory, Department of the Environment. No date.

6. "Barrier-Free Design," report of the United Nations Expert Group Meeting held June 3-8, 1974, at U.N. Secretariat, New York, *International Rehabilitation Review*, June 1975.

Profile: Creator of Electronic Aids Both Great and Small

A person deprived of hand and foot movement can't turn on a television set, answer the door or dial a telephone.

But such a person can do all these things — and many more — if he or she is furnished with an "environmental control system," a sophisticated piece of electronic gadgetry that is able to translate a slight movement of the chin or even a breath into any of these actions.

Amazingly, almost every severely disabled person in Great Britain who needs such a device has one. This is in large part because these expensive systems are paid for by the National Health Service. But credit also must be given to Roger M. Jefcoate, a young British electronics expert who has chosen to make a career out of devising such aids for his country's disabled and elderly.

Mr. Jefcoate, 35, recently visited the United States to talk with American rehabilitation specialists about his work. He found time in his busy schedule to chat with *Rehabilitation/ WORLD* about the history of environmental control system development in Britain as well as about his experiences as perhaps the world's only independent consultant on technical aids for the disabled and elderly.

Staring at the Ceiling

Mr. Jefcoate was one of a trio that developed the POSM (Patient-Operated Selecto-Mechanism) System in the early 1960's at the National Spinal Injuries Center, Stoke Mandeville Hospital.

"We saw these spinal-injured people, many of them highly intelligent and with very active personalities, spending two or three months stretched out in traction, staring at the ceiling, doing absolutely nothing. It was a terrible time for them, desperately frustrating. And then they were sent home to just look at the scenery.

"We thought this was absolutely crazy. We realized that if we could find some sort of electronic device that would respond to their limited

Roger Jefcoate with two simple aids he developed for the elderly and disabled: on the left, a unit which automatically turns on an electric light after dark; on the right, a device which delivers 10 minutes of electricity from a central main to an appliance such as a cooker before turning off automatically.

residual control — maybe a microswitch, maybe even an air type of switch — which in its turn could operate a simple control system, at least we could enable them to switch on the light, the television, the heater. Using perfectly standard telephone switchboard equipment.

"And that was how the first POSM started."

Pronounced "possum" (Latin for "I can"), POSM operates on the basic principle of a light moving at a steady rate across labeled squares on a control panel. Each square has an assigned function, such as "front door intercom" or "change television station." The user, by depressing a switch with chin or foot or by sucking on a tube, can stop the light on the appropriate square. The function is then performed electronically.

The most elaborate POSM-type units developed to date have 36 squares on their indicator panels.

Cost-Effective Argument

In 1966 the National Health Service agreed to supply basic POSM units to all the severely disabled in Britain who could benefit from the use of one. The cost was high: at least $1,500 each.

"We didn't use the argument with

"Profile: Creator of Electronic Aids Both Great and Small," *Rehabilitation World*, Vol. 3, No. 1, Spring (April) 1977. ©1977 The Rehabilitation International U.S.A.

out these, he feels that the disabled person might not be able to maximize use of the system.

Some 850 environmental control systems for severely disabled persons have now been installed in Great Britain. If a unit malfunctions, it will be fixed within 48 hours. Coupled with this service commitment by the various manufacturers is a record of high technical reliability which Mr. Jefcoate credits in part to the built-in method of installation. "There's very little playing with switches or tugging at wires," he noted.

Comparing U.S. to U.K.

Mr. Jefcoate remarked that many of the components used in making these advanced electronic devices for the disabled have to be imported from the United States or Japan. The decline in value of the British pound has created some problems for manufacturers in England.

"But one skill that I would, say we have got in Britain," he added, "is that while you have the innovative technology — I've seen some brilliant devices here — we do seem to have the ability to get the stuff made and out to the handicapped people who need them."

Why the difference? "I've no idea why that should be," he mused. "Maybe it has something to do with the size of your country."

He also thinks it curious that the Japanese, despite their highly advanced electronics industry, still tend to buy equipment for their disabled from other countries.

"When we first developed the POSM at Stoke Mandeville Hospital, we were frightened to death when we had all these droves of Japanese doctors coming along with their cameras, clicking their Nikons and their Minoltas, and we thought, 'for God's sake, within two years they'll be sending them back here in a matchbox for about two dollars!'

"But no, it didn't happen, and I've never really understood why."

Independent Consultant

In 1972 Mr. Jefcoate resigned his position as deputy director of the POSM research project and launched a new career as a freelance consultant and lecturer on technical aids for the disabled. Dr. Howard Rusk of the Institute for Rehabilitation Medicine in New York has termed him the

Mr. Jefcoate talks with a British housewife who is unable to speak and has residual control only in her knees, the result of a motor neurone disease. She uses a remote typewriter as a speech substitute.

only such independent consultant in the world.

"It's been a precarious situation financially," says Mr. Jefcoate. "But it's worth it, because I can do what I want, and there are a lot of things that need doing." He noted that with the wide variety of aids now on the market he is free to recommend the ones most appropriate for an individual without feeling any commercial pressures.

In addition to consulting and lecturing, he has been very busy over the past few years with a number of special projects.

One such project is the Aidis Trust, which Mr. Jefcoate founded to supply much-needed technical aids to the disabled and elderly quickly, without going through the necessarily time-consuming process of securing local or central government approval and funding. "If you're dying of multiple sclerosis, you need the stuff quickly. And if you're elderly and simply need a door intercom, it's not worth all the red tape."

A second project that Mr. Jefcoate has pioneered is a mobile laboratory, funded with $50,000 to employ a technician to travel around Britain in a van for three years to test and fit the residual control of the disabled and elderly to appropriate technical aids.

Mr. Jefcoate is also the chairman of ACTIVE, an organization which he created to devise toys, games and leisure activities for disabled children and the mentally handicapped. Now almost three years old, ACTIVE consists of a group of interested technicians, therapists and parents who either devise toys or simple methods of modifying commercially available toys so that they are usable by disabled children.

"If you can catch disabled and/or mentally retarded children young enough with toys that they can operate themselves and that give them color, movement and sound, they'll be stimulated mentally and physically. But the average toy at Woolworth's has a tiny little switch that was designed for the ordinary non-handicapped child.

"In Britain the Toy Libraries Association sponsors hundreds of the government that the POSM would make the disabled person more independent, that it would improve his or her social situation," Mr. Jefcoate recalled. "No, we argued that it would save money in the long run, that the cost of a POSM was equivalent to only a dozen weeks' hospital stay and that provision of a system would mean that the disabled person could go home much sooner and would require less help in the future."

The government was convinced, and to date hundreds of people have been kept out of expensive hospitals because they have been given these units.

The severely disabled person in Britain can choose one of three environmental control systems, although according to Mr. Jefcoate the decision in each case is actually made by a consultant neurologist or rehabilitation specialist. The choice is usually self-evident, he added, because the three systems have different capabilities and the degree of disability dictates the system chosen:

- *System 7:* only three or four options, and no telephone device. Similar to the American Prentke-Romich ECU model's simplest version.
- *Maling Unit:* allows dialing on the telephone, more options. Marketed by Reginald Maling, one of the original POSM inventors.
- *POSM:* a wide range of options including television, several intercoms, even automatic dialing of often-used telephone numbers.

Installed First Systems

Mr. Jefcoate remembers with obvious delight his experiences as the actual installer of the first 250 POSM systems in Great Britain.

"After the Health Service agreed to supply units to the disabled, I thought I'd be installing perhaps the first score or so. I never dreamed I'd end up installing so many. The reason I did is because I was enjoying myself so much.

"You don't just wander into someone's home and stick the thing on a table and plug it in. You make two visits. The first is a careful planning visit: you see the house and show the available equipment to the individual. There's a wide range of choice; the unit is in effect custom-tailored to the individual's needs and desires. Then we'd return to build the unit into the room. We hide the wires so nothing is visible but the control panel.

"Now while the unit is being installed — and it could take three or four hours — the disabled person is able to practice on it with the specialist there. There's a high degree of involvement. I really enjoyed myself when I was lifting a floorboard here and there was a disabled person in bed watching it all. It was a red-letter day for them, with a team of workers — perhaps a local telephone engineer, electrician, carpenter and myself — working all around them. We'd all have a smashing day, and by the time we left the disabled person would really understand what the unit could do."

Mr. Jefcoate remarked on the lack of such specialist involvement during installation of environmental control devices in the United States. "It seems to me that what happens here is that the stuff is ordered from a manufacturer and sent through the post. A local electrician installs it as best he can, but without the knowledge and sense of involvement that a specialist could bring." And with toy libraries throughout the country which stock toys for loan to handicapped and retarded children. A parent or therapist involved with such a local toy library might write us and say, 'Look, we've got an athetoid kid who can only reach out and bang a large switch. Got any suggestions?'

And we say, 'Well, in our experience there's a roller coaster toy that you can buy for $10, and with this simple modification it would do the job. Here are the plans.'"

Mr. Jefcoate also points out that these disabled children often will eventually have to learn to use sophisticated electronic devices such as typewriters or POSM units. The experience of using toys adapted with special levers will prepare them for this higher technology.

"I'm also certain that if you catch these kids young enough you will reduce handicap, perhaps quite significantly, so that in the longer term many of them might never need these expensive technical devices."

Trend Toward Simplicity

"There is very much now an emphasis — in Britain as much as anywhere else, I suspect — on much simpler equipment. You see, we've done our thing with the sophisticated technology. We've shown what can be done; we've got an array of stuff which can cover a broad range of disabilities at the severe end. But what about our increasing numbers of elderly people? What about the person who wants a simple intercom link with the front door? Or maybe to communicate from room to room?"

One of the first things that Mr. Jefcoate did after leaving POSM in 1972 was to design a range of simple devices, "easy to understand, inexpensive, and plug-inable even by a person with no technical knowledge whatever." These devices are assembled from components by disabled workers.

Roger Jefcoate is very interested in what's happening in the rehabilitation field in the United States, and hopes to visit North America again in 1977.

Delbert Gets A Brain Pacemaker-- And A Dream Is Coming True

An eight-year-old cerebral palsy victim who could barely crawl at seven is now learning to walk.

By Roger Simon

For eight days they did not name the baby. There seemed to be no need. Born three months prematurely on June 1, 1967, the infant weighed only 25¼ ounces, and for precious moments after his birth, he did not breathe.

His parents, John and Virginia Searles, were not allowed to see him. They would not know it for some time, but like many children who have breathing difficulties at birth, their baby would suffer from spastic cerebral palsy. And later he would develop epilepsy. It seemed a hopeless case the day they finally named him Delbert Samuel Searles.

On May 19, 1975, Delbert once more entered a hospital. Because of his crippling disease, his left arm was permanently twisted and bent, his legs involuntarily twisted in pretzel fashion. At seven years of age, he could barely crawl.

But at the end of this hospital stay his heartsick parents were able to rejoice. A small device was placed on Delbert's brain, and when electrical currents ran through that device, Delbert's dream and the dream of his family came true: Nearly a month after surgery, Delbert Searles, the boy who almost didn't make it, the boy who was almost placed in an institution for the rest of his life, the boy who almost had no name, did what seemed medically impossible only a few years ago. Delbert Searles walked.

His success was a very near thing though—a near thing that never would

have happened without the extraordinary determination of a tough family that refused to accept defeat. Nor would Delbert be learning to walk today if it hadn't been for the skilled efforts of a 34-year-old Chicago neurosurgeon, Richard D. Penn, M.D., who, even now, shuns the publicity that Delbert's operation has brought him.

It was on April 21, 1975 that Virginia Searles sat in her kitchen and drank her coffee over the morning newspaper. The family lives in Chicago's famed "back-of-the-yards" neighborhood, a tough, inner-city section originally inhabited by Poles and other Eastern European immigrants and now peopled by an ethnically diverse mixture. The Chicago Stockyards, which gave the area its name, have been torn down and the smells of the slaughterhouse no longer pervade, but it is still a blue-collar neighborhood. The streets are lined with small bungalows and neat lawns, and sitting on one's front stoop is the major form of community recreation.

Four of Mrs. Searles's five children were in school that morning and Delbert played on the floor, dragging himself along with his "good" right arm. Idly flipping open the morning tabloid, *The Chicago Sun-Times*, Mrs. Searles stopped on page three as an almost electric shock ran up her spine.

There was a picture of a young boy, just like Delbert, under the headline:

"Palsy victim, 7, youngest to receive brain pacemaker." The story told of how Jeffrey Panotti, a Florida youngster who suffered from spastic cerebral palsy, had had a "pacemaker" implanted in his skull. The article went on to say that the revolutionary device was to send electrical instructions that would allow the boy's muscles to relax and be released from their crippling grip.

But the sentence that caught Mrs. Searles's eye was the one that read: "With the aid of crutches, Jeffrey left Children's Variety Hospital last weekend."

Mrs. Searles had known tragedy in her life. In addition to Delbert, her 10-year-old daughter, Virginia Lee, had developed a viral infection some years ago and for a period of months was in and out of an iron lung. And when Jana Lee was born nine years ago, doctors had said she would be retarded. Then, four years ago, Mrs. Searles lost the sight in her left eye.

But Virginia Searles also knew, when she put down the paper that April morning, that if a boy in Florida with cerebral palsy could walk, then her Delbert could and would walk, too.

A few months later, after Delbert's operation, Mrs. Searles and her husband sat in the living room of their very modest home, and talked with me about those fateful days and months.

Mrs. Searles's angry-red hair is set off

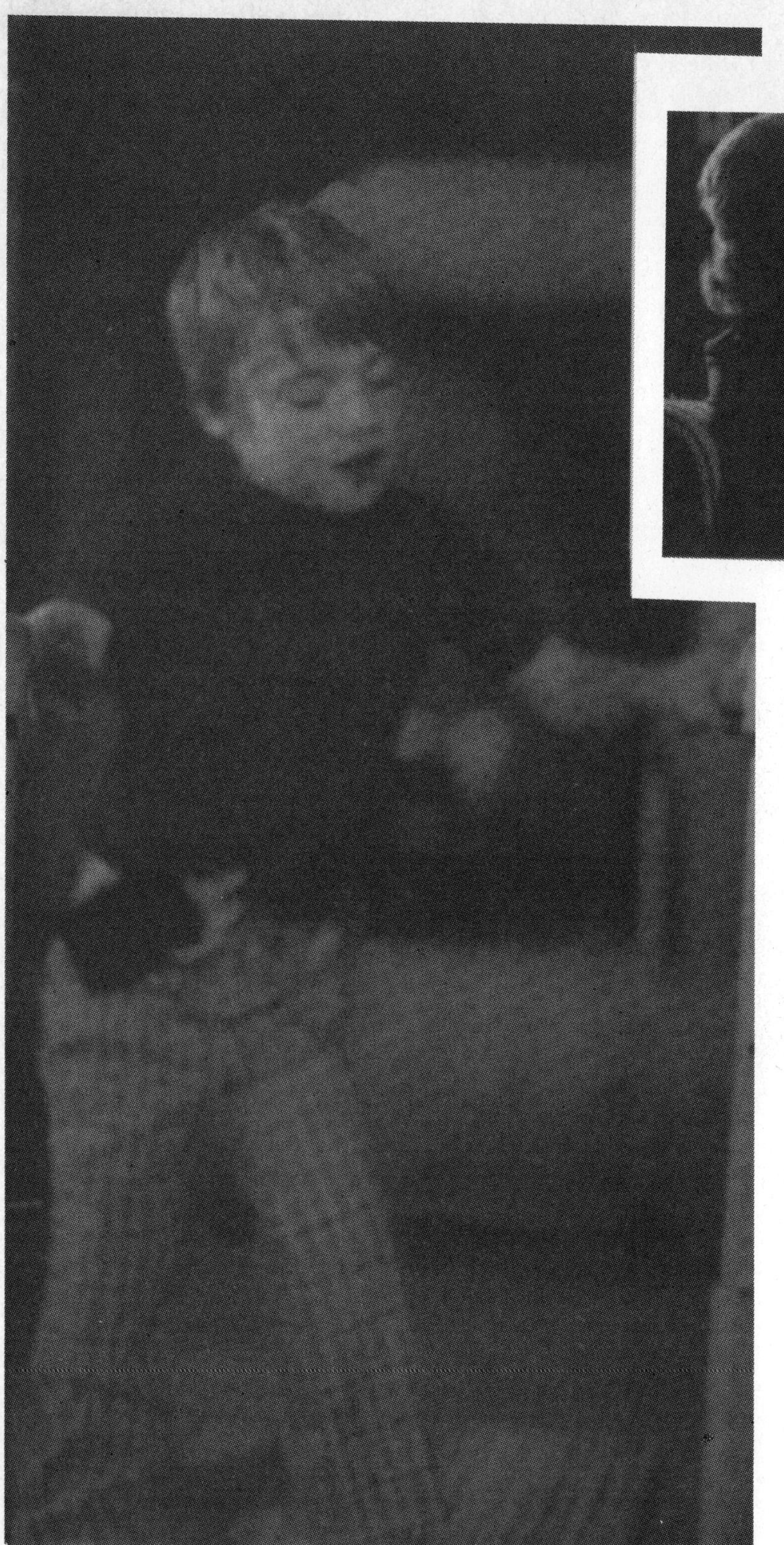

The Searles family had faith that young Delbert (left) would one day walk—despite the fact that in his first seven years of life he had never been able to take even a single step on his own. When his parents, John and Virginia (above), heard of a revolutionary operation that could help bring a normal life to their youngest child, a victim of cerebral palsy, their minds were made up: They would give it a try.

by her small frame and alabaster complexion. She has the temperament of a strong-willed and determined Irish woman. Mr. Searles, a solid, square-jawed man who takes home $156 a week as an electric truck operator at a nearby factory, sits on the couch in his T-shirt and slacks. A U.S. Navy tatoo on one arm speaks quietly of his past.

"I went straight to the phone after reading that article," Mrs. Searles began. "I called the University of Illinois Hospital because I figured if anyone in Chicago could do this operation, it would be them. They told me to call Dr. Richard Penn, a neurosurgeon at Rush-Presbyterian-St. Luke's Hospital, on Chicago's near West side. He listened to me and we set up an appointment. This was Monday and he made the appointment for Friday. I was amazed he would see us so soon."

In those five days the Searleses had a lot of past history to think about. Neither they nor Delbert were strangers to doctors. Mr. Searles remembers an encounter with his son's first physician.

It was the day of Delbert's birth. John Searles was worried—about his wife and the four other children at home. Jana and Virginia had both been premature and delivered by cesarean section, and Delbert was to be born the same way.

"I was waiting outside the delivery room when the doctor came out to me and said, 'Who do you want to save, your wife or your child?' I looked at him and shouted, 'My wife, my wife; I don't even know the baby!' And later I went in to see Virginia. I told her I was praying."

His wife recalled with a laugh, "That's what worried me. He hadn't been in a church for years!"

The Searleses laugh a lot now, but then it didn't seem they would ever be joyful again. They weren't allowed to see Delbert for 10 days after his birth and he remained in the hospital for four months. Once home, Delbert developed pneumonia, which was soon cured, but then at seven months his parents began to notice that the baby would often cock his head backwards at an odd angle.

"We didn't worry so much at first," Searles said. "Jana Lee had serious troubles as an infant. They said she was retarded and she would never crawl. Well she's perfect now; she's in the fifth grade and she's only nine!"

The Searles family has always been close-knit, perhaps because of the almost constant health crises they have faced.

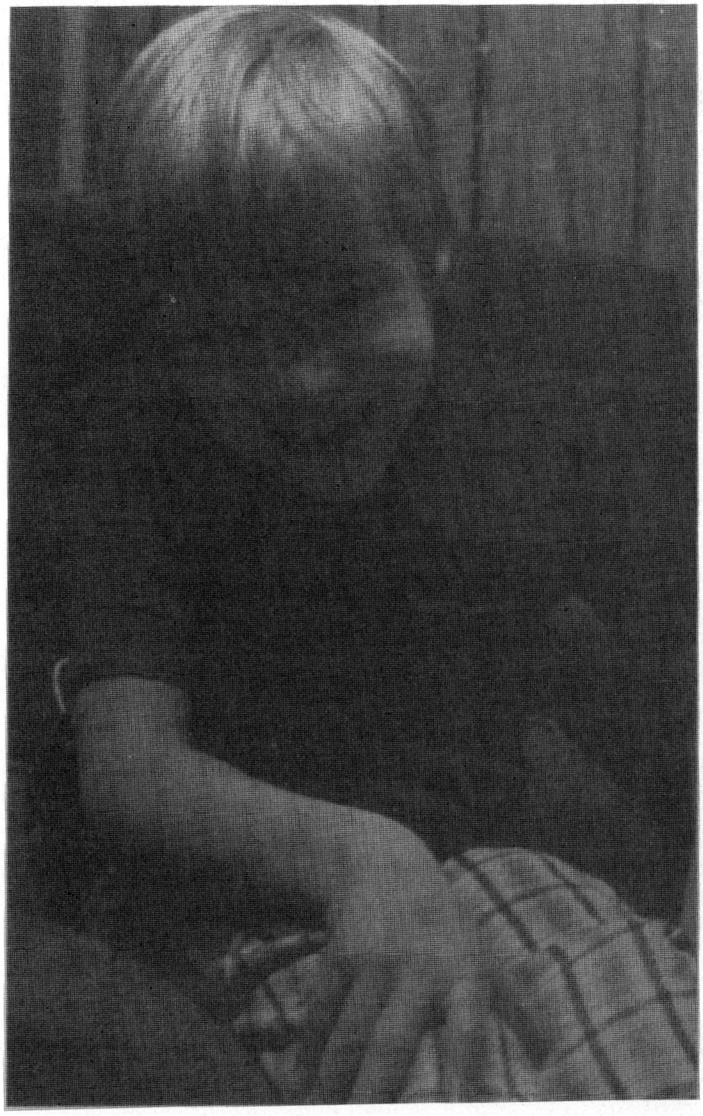

Before a brain pacemaker was implanted in the skull of Delbert Samuel Searles (above), the boy had virtually no control over his left arm or his legs. His only means of movement was to drag himself across the floor.

They all felt the pain when the signs in Delbert became unmistakable.

"We noticed his left hand," Mrs. Searles explained. "Something was wrong . . . and then his whole left side."

When the diagnosis of cerebral palsy was finally made, Mrs. Searles received the news in a telephone call. "I just dropped the phone and started screaming," she recalled. "I went into hysterics. I knew cerebral palsy had something to do with the brain. That's all I knew. That was enough."

In a certain sense, cerebral palsy is a case of the body making war on itself. The human brain is always active, receiving information from the various sense organs and nerves and passing along instructions produced by the brain cells or neurons. The instructions, in the form of electrochemical messages, are transferred by the neurons along networks to the various parts of the body, including the muscles.

But with cerebral palsy, the brain sends out "false" messages or forgets to turn off a message. In Delbert's case, the brain messages sent to the left side of his body, causing his muscles to contract, had not been "turned-off," and the result was their constantly rigid state.

The boy's condition was indeed tragic for the family, but as Mr. Searles explained, "You got to accept it. So you accept it. You take it. You see what to do. Then you do it. That's all."

From ages one to three Delbert could rock his body back and forth but he had no control over his head movements. He had voluntary control only over his right hand, and at three his mental age was that of a one-year-old. Delbert began to talk during those years but his speech was slurred.

The Searleses reacted to Delbert as any family might have. "He led a king's life," his mother said. "He was pampered. He wasn't allowed on the floor. We treated him like a little doll. When he was three, he was still in a high chair. Everything was done for him. Boy, was that a mistake."

In fact, it could have been a bigger mistake than the family knew. The brain implant or pacemaker that was recently placed in Delbert's skull sends out messages to his muscles. But if his muscles were no good, if they had atrophied from disuse, then the implant too would have been useless. Had Delbert continued his life as "a little doll," he might never have been able to walk.

But when he was three, Delbert's life turned around. He was sitting in his high chair waiting, as usual, to be fed by his mother. She had always placed two spoons in front of Delbert—one she used to feed him and the other she hoped he would use himself, though in three years he never had.

But on that day, in the middle of Delbert's feeding, the phone rang and Mrs. Searles got up to answer it. "While I was on the phone Delbert kept yelling that he was hungry," she said, "I kept telling him to wait a minute. I was on the phone about 10 minutes and when I turned around Delbert had the spoon in his hand and he was feeding himself."

For Delbert and the rest of the family it was a staggering breakthrough. "That was it," Mrs. Searles explained. "From that day on Delbert led a regular life. It was rough and tumble. He played with the rest of the kids, and we made him do what he could."

"We stopped this handicapped business at age three," Mr. Searles stated flatly.

At age four Delbert regained some head control. His brothers and sisters took him around the neighborhood until he knew everyone's name. He developed good control of his right side and he would use his nearly useless left hand to grasp at the floor, then grab with his right hand and drag himself along, his legs crossed scissors-style. That was his only means of locomotion, and though it was painful—almost pathetic—for others to watch, his family encouraged him.

But Delbert's life was never to be easy. When he was five years old, he had his first epileptic seizure. He began having major motor seizures about every six months after that. On October 17, 1974, on a trip to his grandmother's funeral, Delbert had a seizure. An ambulance was summoned, and on the way to the hospital, the boy's heart stopped temporarily. Since the onset of his attacks, Delbert had taken anticonvulsants, but the seizures increased in severity and after each attack he experienced respiratory failure and would have to spend a day or two in intensive care.

At about the same time, Mrs. Searles lost the sight in her left eye. The burdens on the family were so great that, not surprisingly, the Searleses were advised to put Delbert in an institution for the rest of his life.

But such a choice was simply out of the question. "We're a family," Mr. Searles explained, as if the answer were obvious. "And families stick together."

With the family's support and encouragement, Delbert slowly progressed. His mental ability increased, and by the time he was seven, his mental age was evaluated to be about six. It was when he was seven that Delbert also had his first meeting with Dr. Richard Penn.

The physician looks younger than his 34 years. His slightly unruly black hair falls forward in a wave across his forehead, over his gold-framed glasses. He is usually seen with his tie tucked in between the second and third buttons of his button-down-collar blue shirts.

To Dr. Penn, Delbert looked like a good candidate for the implant operation. The surgeon had performed one such operation already, on an 18-year-old epileptic who had been on toxic doses of anticonvulsant drugs. The operation was a success, and although the patient was not seizure-free, his epilepsy was greatly controlled.

When Dr. Penn examined Delbert, he told the Searleses that an implant would control Delbert's cerebral palsy but was not needed for his epilepsy, which could be controlled by medication. He also told them of the high risks involved.

"Delbert had all this spasticity (overactive reflexiveness) and rigidity (high resistance to movement)," the physician explains. "He was just mildly retarded and yet he was so seriously incapacitated that the procedure of this magnitude seemed warranted.

"Had Delbert been more ambulatory I might not have done it," he says.

The operation which Delbert was to undergo was the latest in a developing field of study called neuro-control. "That phrase is good because we want to control certain things," Dr. Penn explains. "But it is bad because it can imply that we can control the nervous system. We don't have as much control of things by putting electrodes in the head as the lay press would like to believe."

Research into neuro-control began as far back as the 1890s when a British physiologist found that if animals were decerebrated (the main part of the brain, the cerebrum, was removed) the muscles in the animals went rigid. But when the cerebellum (still intact) was activated electrically, the rigidity would ease.

Based on this knowledge, Irving Spencer Cooper, M.D., a neurosurgeon at St. Barnabas Hospital for Chronic Disease in New York City, developed the first "brain pacemaker" in late 1972. The pacemaker, when placed on the surface of the cerebellum, blocks the incorrect messages being sent to the muscles and allows those muscles to relax.

The Chicago neurosurgeon visited Dr. Cooper before doing his own brain pacemaker implants. Like many physicians, he is guarded about Cooper's results. "He has reduced seizures (of epileptics) significantly in a number of patients," Dr. Penn says. "I've seen his successes and also his failures."

The Searleses heard from Dr. Penn about the risks involved. "Oh, yes, he laid the list on me," Mrs. Searles said. "He talked about arterial ruptures in the brain, the chance of rejection and infection. He said it was a high-risk operation. He asked how we would feel if we spent all that money for something that might not work. He also said not to expect any changes for a year."

The implant device alone is not cheap —about $2,000. The Searleses were then faced with the choice of whether or not to proceed. Delbert's mental ability was developing and his family was told that with physical therapy he might be able to lead a near normal life, handicapped only slightly on his left side.

"We had all this on our minds," John Searles said quietly as he remembered those days of decision. "Delbert wasn't scared of anything. Not water, not height, not anything. We saw him try so hard. It looked so hard for him. The strain, you could see the strain. Just to stand. Just standing there rigid and spastic."

The family called a meeting. "It was in the kitchen," Mrs. Searles said. "This is an Irish family and the kitchen is where all the big decisions are made." Around the table sat John and Virginia; John Jr., 16; Julia Kay, 13; Virginia Lee; and Jana Lee.

All the risks were explained to the children, but the father carried the day in his final argument. "Sure, Delbert has come a long way," he said. "But do we want to see him still crawling on the floor when he's 12 or 16?"

The family voted for the operation—to take place near Delbert's eighth birthday.

Delbert entered the hospital on May 19, 1975 and his surgery was scheduled for May 23. In the hospital, Mrs. Searles told Delbert about the operation. "I sat down with him and asked him if he wanted to walk. He said, 'I wanna walk.' He'd been saying that for two or three years. I told him they would have to make cuts—that's what I called them, cuts—and Delbert knew why he was t ere. I said that afterwards he'd have a little box and a wire and his head would be sore."

At 8 A.M. on May 23, the operation began. Dr. Penn cut two holes, or windows, about 1 inch by 3 inches (2 centimeters by 3 centimeters) in the back of Delbert's skull just above the neck. He cut through the dura (the tough, fibrous layer covering the brain) and placed two sets of electrodes on the right and left side of the anterior (upper) surface of the cerebellum.

Each electrode grouping contains a number of small electrodes made out of platinum and coated with silicone. Penn implanted the electrodes and then ran the wires leading from them under Delbert's skin, over his left shoulder and to the left part of his chest. The wires ended in an antenna that was just under his skin. This was the part of the pacemaker system that was invisible. The visible part began in a little box, about the size of a pack of cigarettes, that Delbert would carry in his pocket. In the box was a

nine-volt battery—just like the kind in a transistor radio—that would supply the power. The electrical power from the battery is converted in the box to AM radio waves and carried by a wire that is taped on the outside of Delbert's skin.

The box, or activator, initiates the radio impulse that is then picked up by the antenna, transmitted to Delbert's brain, and there converted back to an electrical impulse.

This system was chosen so that no puncture that could lead to an infection was made in Delbert's skin. The activator can send out impulses of various strengths (from 7 to 14 volts) and for various periods of time.

"The question was this," Penn explains. "Would reducing rigidity in Delbert's muscles allow him to move? The brain was sending out incorrect signals to Delbert's muscles. The activator blocks the path of those signals through the spinal cord and allows the muscles to relax. We have a clinical result, but we don't know why. We don't know if we are causing a lack of function in the cerebellum or whether the stimulator is activating a neuro-circuit."

The day of the operation Mrs. Searles had told her husband to go to work as usual, but by 9 A.M. she called him in tears and asked him to get down to the hospital and sit with her.

"All I could think about was the last thing Delbert had said to me," Mrs. Searles said. "Delbert looked up at me and said, 'You aren't going to leave me, are you mommy?'"

Twice during the operation, Dr. Penn called down to the Searleses to say things were going well. At 4:30 P.M. the elevator doors opened to the visiting room and the physician stepped out saying, "Everything went beautifully." Four hours later, Delbert was awake and his parents saw him. (Although much brain surgery can be done with the patient awake— since the brain, alone among the organs, feels no pain—implants are done under a general anesthetic.)

Four days later, Delbert's electrodes were activated. Originally, the activator was cycled for seven minutes on and seven minutes off, but now it is merely turned on when Delbert wakes up in the morning and turned off when he goes to sleep. That first day, according to Dr. Penn, "not much happened" when the activator was turned on. He had warned the Searleses not to start looking for results immediately. But on the sixth day,

Delbert was able to relax his left arm.

On June 3, the doctor gave a lecture about the operation to a group of medical students. Delbert, dressed in a blue bathrobe and blue slippers, was wheeled in. He looked shyly at the students from out of his round, almost angelic face. With his mother standing at his side, Delbert sucked his thumb. His left arm was bent into his body and his legs were scissored.

Dr. Penn reached over and, with a pocket screwdriver, turned on the activator. Almost immediately, Delbert's left arm relaxed, dropping slowly away from his body into a normal position. His legs uncrossed and without even thinking about it, Delbert began playing with his mother's purse with his left hand—the hand he had never used.

The medical students, usually blasé about the wonders of modern science, reacted with pleased outcries. "Oh, my God, look," one shouted as Delbert started uncrossing his legs. Delbert grabbed for his storybook and started leafing through the pages, using his left arm— what he used to call his "dumb" arm—as if it were the easiest thing in the world.

On June 27, Delbert went home and, after a week, took the first steps of his life, between two parallel metal bars. The family is adjusting casually to Delbert's new life. As I talked with the parents, the other children rushed in and out of the house, wrestling with Delbert or yelling at him. "Hey, fatso!" John Jr. called as he almost ran him over on his bike, "Get out of the way!"

Very little is still known about the whole branch of medicine that surrounds Delbert's success. Dr. Penn, who has performed two further implants—both for epileptics—continues to play down his achievements.

"Delbert is able to walk now with the aid of parallel bars and is learning exercises designed to lead him to walking with a minimum of supports," Penn explains. "His rigidity and spasticity are reduced and his mother says his speech is better. His wound is well healed and there are no signs of damage. He is progressing at a rapid rate and I am pleased. There have been no epileptic seizures since the implant.

"All this is very hopeful," Dr. Penn adds. "But we have to gain a lot more knowledge and understanding in the general field."

At Rush-Presbyterian-St. Luke's Hospital, a full-time research project on the possible uses of brain implants has been

5. EMERGING DIRECTIONS

started. But the medical community has by no means completely accepted the devices. A special report of the National Institute of Neurological Diseases and Stroke states that the implant surgery "has raised more questions than it has answered." The report cautions that it is too soon to know, but the implanted electrodes and the constant stimulation of the brain could have harmful and permanent effects.

As far as the Searleses are concerned, however, Delbert's new life has been nothing short of a miracle. The phrase "with the help of God and Dr. Penn" is heard often in their conversation. Recently Delbert had an operation in which the tendons in his hips were cut to take pressure off the joints in his legs. Even with casts on both legs, he is showing progress.

All is not absolutely smooth—implant patients faced with new physical freedoms often have emotional adjustments to make, and Delbert is no exception. Sometimes he rebels against his mother's orders to exercise. But when, on the advice of the doctors, Mrs. Searles leaves Delbert alone, he resumes the exercises.

The cost of the operation has also hit the Searleses hard. Of the initial hospital bill for $9,100, they have had to pay about $1,000. Insurance covered the rest. Batteries for Delbert's activator, at $1 a day, are another costly drain on the family income. A fund set up for Delbert at Drovers National Bank of Chicago has drawn $1,800 from contributors, but the Searleses are also searching for a battery company to donate a supply.

But the problems are minor compared to what the operation has done for Delbert. While his parents talked about his operation, Delbert crawled off his mother's lap and started moving around the house as the rest of the Searles children banged in and out of the front door.

After a few minutes of conversation, Mrs. Searles looked up and asked, "Where's Delbert?"

And everyone turned to see Delbert Samuel Searles making his way through the front door to join his brothers and sisters playing outside.

INDEX

STAFF

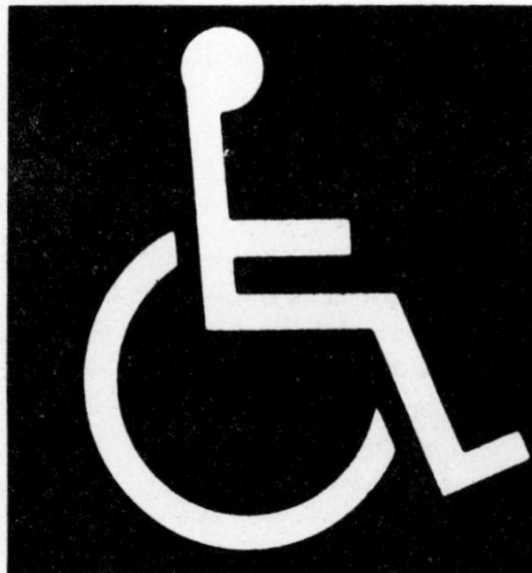

Publisher	John Quirk
Editor	Roberta Garland
Editorial Ass't.	Carol Carr
Permissions Editor	Audrey Weber
Director of Production	Richard Pawlikowski
Director of Design	Donald Burns
Customer Service	Cindy Finocchio
Sales Service	Dianne Hubbard
Administration	Linda Calano
Index	Mary Russell
Cover Design	Donald Burns
Cover Photo	Richard Pawlikowski

Appendix: Agencies and Services for Exceptional Children

Alexander Graham Bell Association for the Deaf,
Inc.
Volta Bureau for the Deaf
3417 Volta Place, NW
Washington, D.C. 20007

American Academy of Pediatrics
1801 Hinman Avenue
Evanston, Illinois 60204

American Association for Gifted Children
15 Gramercy Park
New York, N.Y. 10003

American Association on Mental Deficiency
5201 Connecticut Avenue, NW
Washington, D.C. 20015

American Association of Psychiatric Clinics for
Children
250 West 57th Street
New York, N.Y.

American Bar Association
Commission on the Mentally Disabled
1800 M Street, NW
Washington, D.C. 20036

American Foundation for the Blind
15 W. 16th Street
New York, N.Y. 10011

American Medical Association
535 N. Dearborn Street
Chicago, Illinois 60610

American Speech and Hearing Association
9030 Old Georgetown Road
Washington, D.C. 20014

Association for the Aid of Crippled Children
345 E. 46th Street
New York, N.Y. 10017

Association for Children with Learning Disabilities
2200 Brownsville Road
Pittsburgh, Pennsylvania 15210

Association for Education of the Visually
Handicapped
1604 Spruce Street
Philadelphia, Pennsylvania 19103

Association for the Help of Retarded Children
200 Park Avenue, South
New York, N.Y.

Association for the Visually Handicapped
1839 Frankfort Avenue
Louisville, Kentucky 40206

Center on Human Policy
Division of Special Education and Rehabilitation
Syracuse University
Syracuse, New York 13210

Child Fund
275 Windsor Street
Hartford, Connecticut 06120

Children's Defense Fund
1520 New Hampshire Avenue NW
Washington, D.C. 20036

Closer Look
National Information Center for the Handicapped
1201 Sixteenth Street NW
Washington, D.C. 20036

Clifford W. Beers Guidance Clinic
432 Temple Street
New Haven, Connecticut 06510

Child Study Center
Yale University
333 Cedar Street
New Haven, Connecticut 06520

Child Welfare League of America, Inc.
44 East 23rd Street
New York, N.Y. 10010

Children's Bureau
United States Department of Health, Education
and Welfare
Washington, D.C.

Council for Exceptional Children
1411 Jefferson Davis Highway
Arlington, Virginia 22202

Epilepsy Foundation of America
1828 ''L'' Street NW
Washington, D.C. 20036

Gifted Child Society, Inc.
59 Glen Gray Road
Oakland, New Jersey 07436

Institute for the Study of Mental Retardation
and Related Disabilities
130 South First
University of Michigan
Ann Arbor, Michigan 48108

International Association for the Scientific Study
of Mental Deficiency
Ellen Horn, AAMD
5201 Connecticut Avenue NW
Washington, D.C. 20015

International League of Societies for the Mentally
Handicapped
Rue Forestiere 12
Brussels, Belgium

Joseph P. Kennedy, Jr. Foundation
1701 K Street NW
Washington, D.C. 20006

League for Emotially Disturbed Children
171 Madison Avenue
New York, N.Y.

Muscular Dystrophy Associations of America
1790 Broadway
New York, N.Y. 10019

National Aid to the Visually Handicapped
3201 Balboa Street
San Francisco, California 94121

National Association of Coordinators of State
Programs for the Mentally Retarded
2001 Jefferson Davis Highway
Arlington, Virginai 22202

National Association of Hearing and Speech
Agencies
919 18th Street NW
Washington, D.C. 20006

National Association for Creative Children and
Adults
8080 Springvalley Drive
Cincinnati, Ohio 45236
(Mrs. Ann F. Isaacs, Executive Director)

National Association for Retarded Children
420 Lexington Avenue
New York, N.Y.

National Association for Retarded Citizens
2709 Avenue E East
Arlington, Texas 76010

National Children's Rehabilitation Center
P.O. Box 1260
Leesburg, Virginia

National Association for the Visually Handicapped
3201 Balboa Street
San Francisco, California 94121

National Association of the Deaf
814 Thayer Avenue
Silver Spring, Maryland 20910

National Cystic Fibrosis Foundation
3379 Peachtree Road NE
Atlanta, Georgia 30326

National Easter Seal Society for Crippled Children
and Adults
2023 W. Ogden Avenue
Chicago, Illinois 60612

National Federation of the Blind
218 Randolph Hotel
Des Moines, Iowa 50309

National Paraplegia Foundation
333 N. Michigan Avenue
Chicago, Illinois 60601

National Society for Autistic Children
621 Central Avenue
Albany, N.Y. 12206

National Society for Prevention of Blindness, Inc.
79 Madison Avenue
New York, N.Y. 10016

Orton Society, Inc.
8415 Bellona Lane
Baltimore, Maryland 21204

President's Committee on Mental Retardation
Regional Office Building #3
7th and D Streets SW
Room 2614
Washington, D.C. 20201

United Cerebral Palsy Associations
66 E 34th Street
New York, N.Y. 10016

TOPIC MATRIX

Readings in Physically Handicapped Education provides the college student in special education an overview of the nature, needs and educational techniques in teaching the physically handicapped.

COURSE OUTLINE:

Teaching the Physically Handicapped	Readings in Physically Handicapped Education	Related Special Learning Corporation Readers
I. Characteristics and needs of physically handicapped children	I. Physical Handicaps: An Overview	I. Readings in Special Education
II. Etiology of physical handicaps	II. Causes and Prevention	II. Readings in Mainstreaming
III. Methods and materials for teaching the physically handicapped	III. Educational and Occupational Services	III. Readings in Diagnosis and Placement
IV. Emotional and social problems of the physically handicapped	IV. Barrier-free Design: a New Direction	IV. Readings in Psychology of Exceptional Children

SPECIAL LEARNING CORPORATION

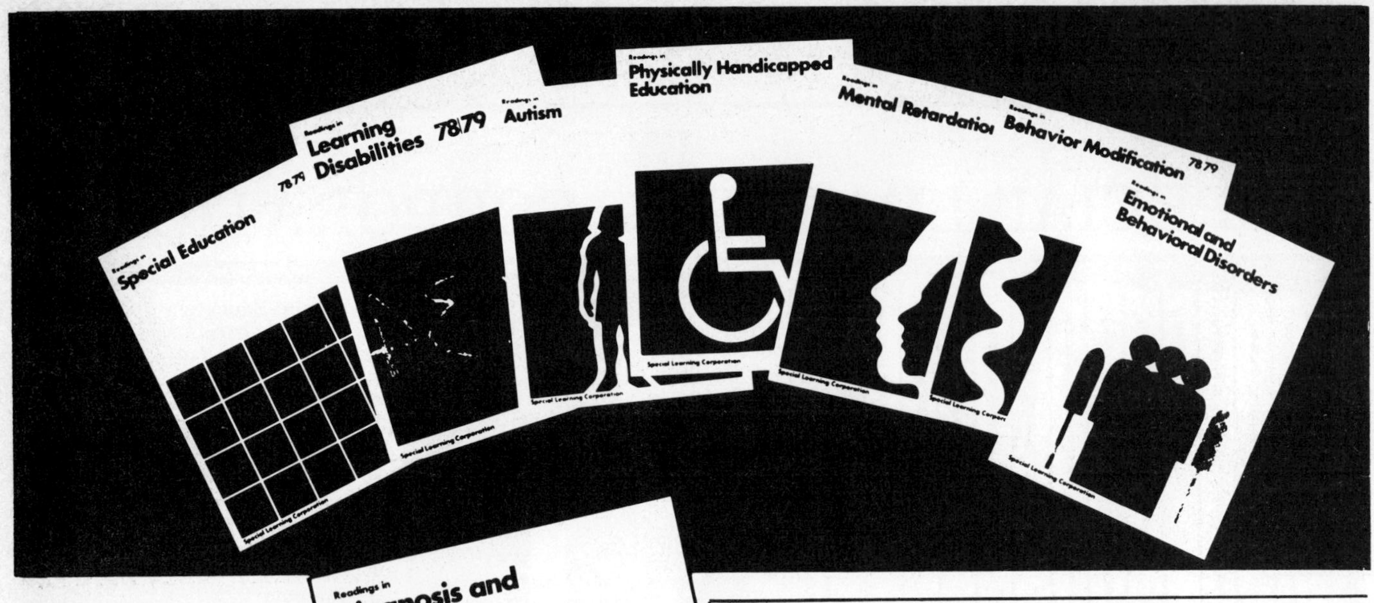

NOW AVAILABLE

INTRODUCING:

Special Learning Corporation's
First Annualized Series in

SPECIAL EDUCATION

Designed for special education teachers and other professionals.

Focus (special feature)

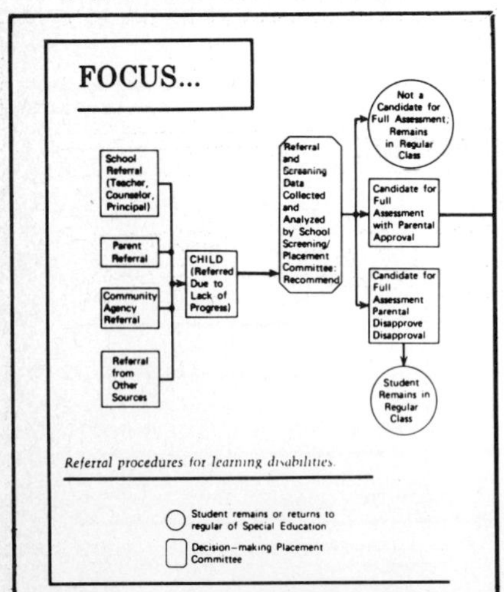

Each reader contains a special in-depth look at a particular aspect of special education.

Table of Contents

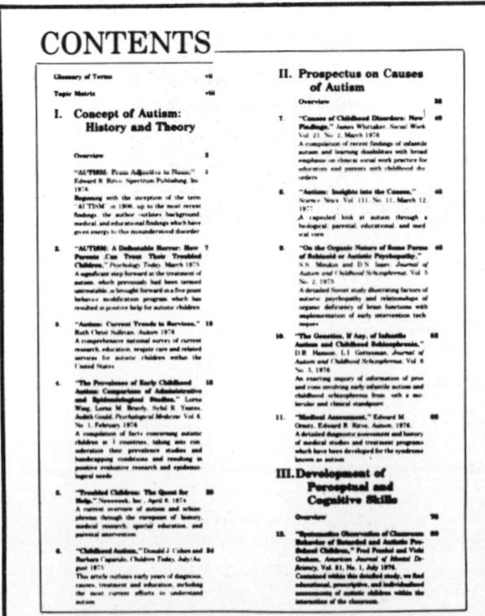

An abstracted table of contents begins each reader, containing a brief description of each article.

Appendix

The Special Education Reader features a listing of all professional agencies and organizations dealing with exceptional children.

42 Boston Post Rd. Guilford, Connecticut 06437   (203) 453-6525

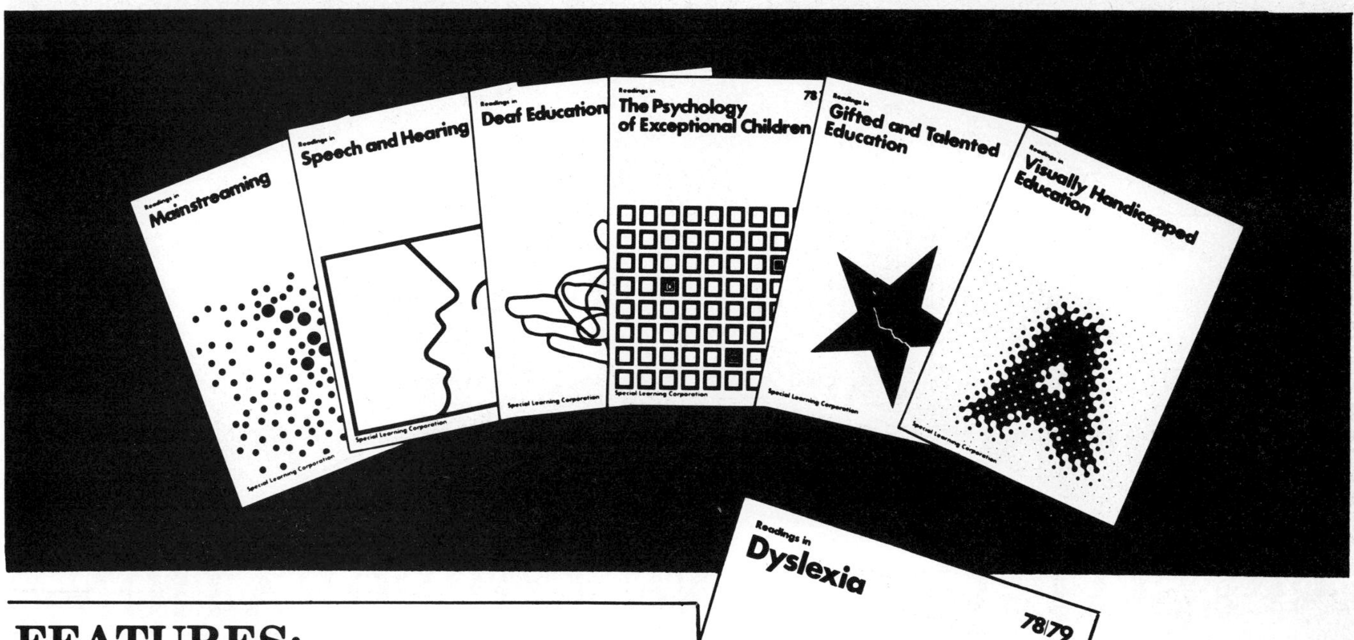

FEATURES:

- 224-320 pages
- course overviews
- topic-course-matrix
- glossary of terms
- 2-page special feature
- heavily illustrated
- abstracted table of contents
- appendix of organizations for the handicapped

NOW AVAILABLE

Glossary of Terms

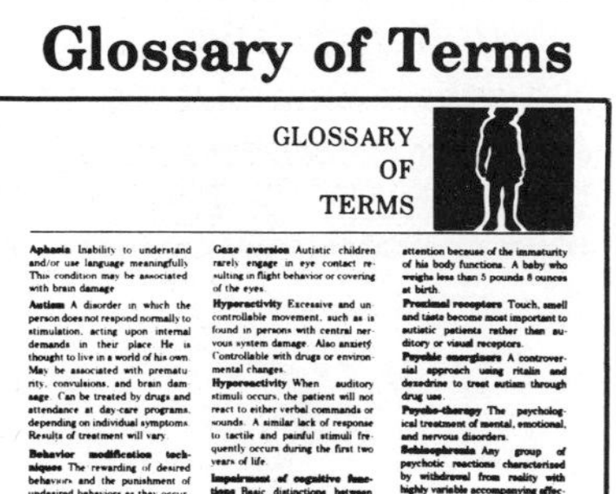

Included in each reader is a comprehensive glossary with brief definitions of pertinent terms.

Index

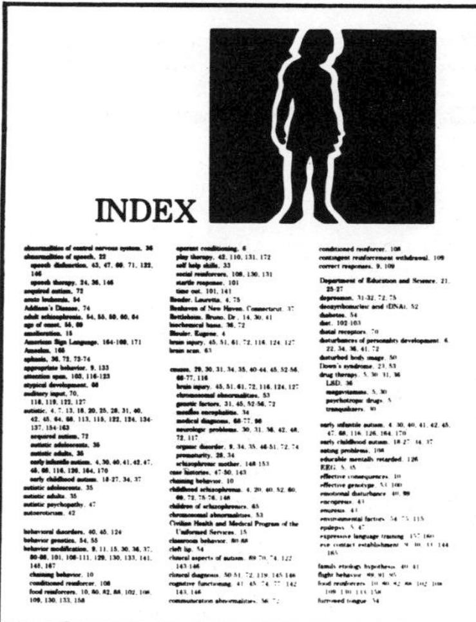

Each reader contains a complete index for easy reference.

Topic Matrix

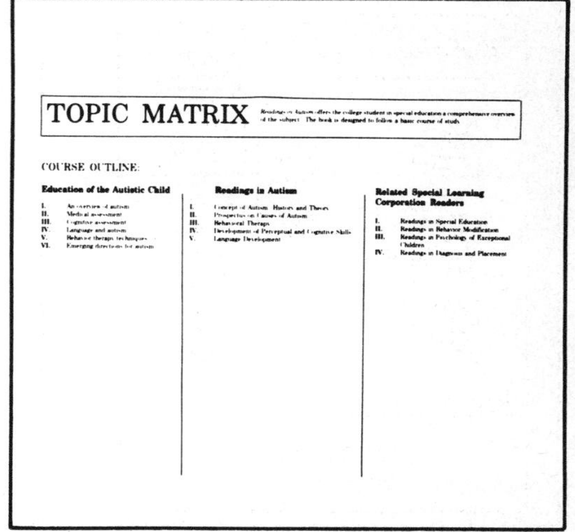

A topic matrix illustrating the correlation of each reader to specific course studies and other related readings is included.

The Special Learning Corporation has developed a series of readers designed for the college student in preparation for teaching exceptional children. Each reader in this high quality series closely follows a college course of study in the special education field. Sending for our free college catalog will provide you with a complete listing of this series, along with a selection of instructional materials and media appropriate for use in special education.

For further information please contact:

College Catalog Division
Special Learning Corporation

SPECIAL LEARNING CORPORATION

42 Boston Post Rd. Guilford, Conn. 06437

1979 Catalog
SPECIAL LEARNING CORPORATION

Programs in Special Education

Table of Contents

Basic Skills

- special education ● learning disabilities ● mental retardation
- autism ● behavior modification ● mainstreaming ● gifted and talented
- physically handicapped ● deaf education ● speech and hearing
- emotional and behavioral disorders ● visually handicapped
- diagnosis and placement ● psychology of exceptional children

Special Learning Corporation
42 Boston Post Rd. Guilford, Connecticut 06437 (203) 453-6212

COMMENTS PLEASE:

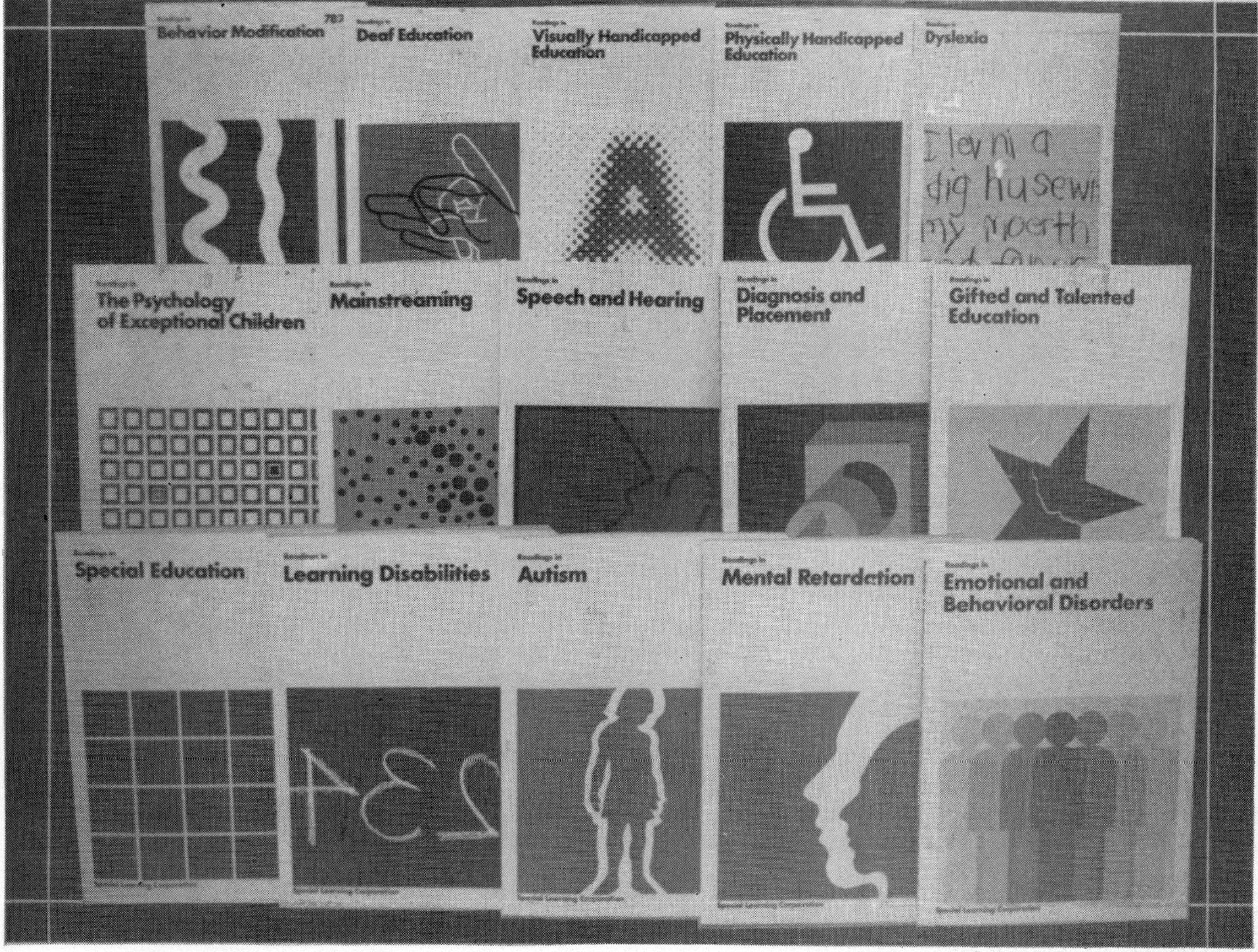

SPECIAL LEARNING CORPORATION

COMMENTS PLEASE:

Does this book fit your course of study?

Why? (Why not?)

Is this book useable for other courses of study? Please list.

What other areas would you like us to publish in using this format?

What type of exceptional child are you interested in learning more about?

Would you use this as a basic text?

How many students are enrolled in these course areas?

______Special Education ______ Mental Retardation ______Psychology ______ Emotional Disorders
______ Exceptional Children ______Learning Disabilities   Other ______________

Do you want to be sent a copy of our elementary student materials catalog?

Do you want a copy of our college catalog?

Would you like a copy of our next edition? ☐ yes ☐ no

<table>
<tr><td>

Are you a ☐ student or an ☐ instructor?

Your name __________________________ school __________________

Term used __________________________ Date __________________

address ____

city ________________________ state ________________ zip ____

telephone number __________________________________

</td></tr>
</table>

P/H